A Chinese Odyssey

Also by Anne F. Thurston

ENEMIES OF THE PEOPLE

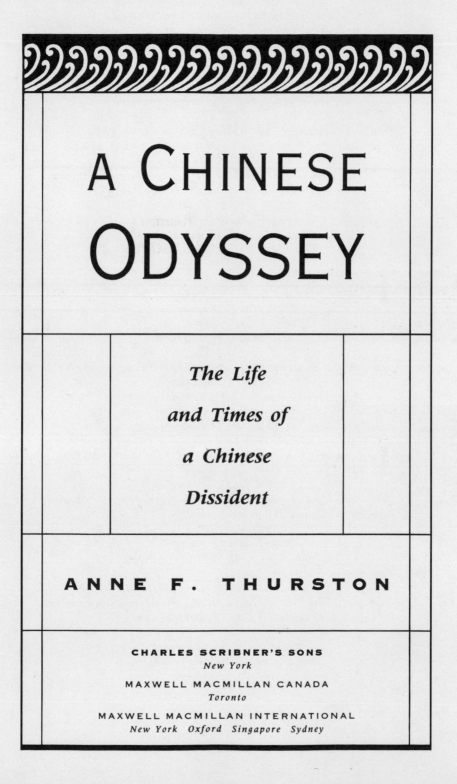

A CHINESE ODYSSEY

The Life

and Times of

a Chinese

Dissident

ANNE F. THURSTON

CHARLES SCRIBNER'S SONS
New York

MAXWELL MACMILLAN CANADA
Toronto

MAXWELL MACMILLAN INTERNATIONAL
New York Oxford Singapore Sydney

Charles Scribner's Sons
Macmillan Publishing Company
866 Third Avenue
New York, NY 10022

Maxwell Macmillan Canada, Inc.
1200 Eglinton Avenue East
Suite 200
Don Mills, Ontario M3C 3N1

Macmillan Publishing Company is part of the Maxwell Communication
Group of Companies.

Library of Congress Cataloging-in-Publication Data
Thurston, Anne F.
A Chinese odyssey / Anne F. Thurston.
p. cm.
Includes index.
ISBN 0-684-19219-5
1. Ni, Yuxian. 2. Dissenters—China—Biography. 3. China—
Politics and government—1949–   I. Title.
DS778.N53T48 1991
951.05'092—dc20
[B]   91-23216   CIP

To everyone

who has ever struggled

to bring democracy to China;

in memory of those

who died in the effort;

with respect for those

imprisoned for trying.

ACKNOWLEDGMENTS

My deepest debt of gratitude is to Ni Yuxian himself, who shared his story with me for hundreds of hours, and to his family members in Shanghai who were unfailingly generous with their time and overflowing in their hospitality, even when the political climate rendered hospitality to a foreigner difficult and even dangerous. Special thanks go, too, to his wife Zhao Yuefang, and to his friends who met with me, even when, as the Chinese say, it was very "inconvenient." I appreciate the time that Liu Binyan and Zhu Hong spent with me as well.

Andrew Nathan of Columbia University both introduced me to Ni, encouraged me to write about him, wrote letters of recommendation on my behalf, allowed me to share my dilemmas with him, and has read and commented on the text. I have greatly benefitted from his advice and deeply appreciate his help.

The National Endowment for the Humanities funded this research, as they did my earlier work on the cultural revolution. Without the Endowment's generosity this book would have been impossible, and I am most grateful for the confidence they have shown.

At Scribner, I would like to thank both Robert Stewart and Susanne Kirk, who took an early and active interest in the book and brought me into the Scribner fold. Erika Goldman has served as my editor there, reading and commenting on the manuscript at every step of the way, prodding me here and pushing me there, and offering praise to keep me going. I have greatly profited from our many discussions and genuinely enjoyed working together as the book evolved. A very special thanks to her.

There are friends I would like to thank, too—Weaver Gaines, for the support he offered and the advice he gave knowing I would not always follow; Burton Pasternak, for his wealth of perspective and advice; Daniel Southerland, for our many discussions about China and democracy and dissent; and Hsu Yamin, for providing his invaluable perspectives on China and offering me the Chinese interpretation of behavior and attitudes that this foreigner often found perplexing.

Finally, I would like to thank Mildred Marmur, not just for her contributions as an agent and for bringing me and Scribner's together, but for having taken me in at the beginning, for her constant prodding and encouragment and unfailing good humor, and for becoming in the course a very good friend.

So much of this book has come from Ni Yuxian himself that I cannot claim complete responsibility for its contents. Ni Yuxian aside, however, let others be absolved of my errors and accept my heartfelt thanks.

A.F.T., *May 1991*

PREFACE

Ni loitered, waiting for the guards to relax their vigilance. Two elevators reached the ground floor at the same time, and there was a flurry of activity as people began pouring out. He stepped into the elevator and pressed the button for the eleventh floor, the consular offices of the United States.

Two soldiers from the Chinese People's Liberation Army were waiting as he got off. "What do you want?" one of them asked gruffly.

"I want to see the consul," he replied.

"Let's see your passport," the soldier commanded. He handed the soldier his passport.

"Do you have an appointment?"

"No, but I know him. He'll want to see me," he lied.

The soldier took his passport and disappeared into another office, returning moments later accompanied by a Chinese secretary.

"You want to see the consul?" the woman inquired.

"Yes, we're friends. He doesn't know I'm coming today, but when he knows I'm here, if he's not too busy, I know he'll want to see me." He handed her his work card. "Ni Yuxian," read the name. The Shanghai Maritime Academy was listed as his work unit. The photograph showed a picture of a handsome man of about forty, with a round, healthy face, dressed in a Western-style jacket and tie. It had been taken some five years before.

The woman took the card.

Moments later, Ni was escorted into the office of an American official.

"Can I talk to you privately?" Ni asked.

The American official escorted Ni to another room and closed the door. The two were alone. Ni's life depended on their conversation.

"You don't really know me," Ni began. "I just want a chance to tell you my story."

"But I do know you," John Lundeen responded in perfectly fluent Chinese. "I recognized your photograph. I know your story. I've been reading the Hong Kong newspapers. What can I do to help?"

John Lundeen was head of the cultural section of the American consulate in Guangzhou. It was his job to know stories like Ni's.

Ni Yuxian had been catapulted to fame—or infamy, depending on one's perspective—when he became one of the two heroes in a story written by Liu Binyan, China's leading, most courageous, most widely admired muckraker, a journalist with the *People's Daily*—the nationally circulated daily newspaper of the Chinese Communist Party.

"A Second Kind of Loyalty" was the story of two Chinese men, Chen Shizhong and Ni Yuxian, who had persisted all their lives in putting principle before politics and who, as a result, had suffered grievously. As the official policies of the Chinese Communist Party had wavered first in one direction and then in the other, as political campaign had followed political campaign, and each had claimed its tens and hundreds of thousands of victims, as ill-advised policies like the Great Leap Forward of the late 1950s had plunged the country into economic depression and widespread famine, not only had these two men refused to bend but they had spoken out against those ill-conceived policies, the cult of personality of party leader Mao Zedong, party privilege, and the abuse of power. Chen Shizhong, the older of the two heroes of Liu's story, had written letters to the Communist Party Central Committee, party chairman Mao Zedong, and the Soviet Union's Nikita Khrushchev criticizing the leftist policies of the Chinese Communist Party, urging reconciliation between China and its one-time big brother the Soviet Union, and lambasting the cult of personality that surrounded Mao. In 1962 he was sentenced to eight years in prison. When his prison term was up, he was sent to spend another six years at labor reform.

In 1962 Ni Yuxian, too, had written a letter to Chairman Mao criticizing the leftist policies of the Great Leap Forward and informing the party chairman of the millions of people who were starving to death in the Chinese countryside. He was dismissed from the military. When the Cultural Revolution began in 1966 and students were called upon to criticize "party persons in authority taking the capitalist road," Ni Yuxian had witnessed what Liu Binyan described as "despicable acts of armed struggle, murder, and cruel torture," and spoken out in criticism against party officials in his own university, the leftist leadership of Shanghai, and the radical central leadership of the Cultural Revolution. He had been incarcerated, then expelled from the Shanghai Maritime Academy where he had been a student.

It would not be long before Ni Yuxian was again in trouble with the authorities. In early April 1976, millions of Beijing citizens, laden with funeral wreaths and reciting poetry, converged peacefully on Tiananmen Square to commemorate the death of Premier Zhou Enlai and to protest the radical policies of Mao and those closest to him. When the authorities removed the wreaths, the demonstrators turned angry, and the militia used violence to quell the crowd. Scores were arrested. An unknown number died. The event and the participants were labeled "counterrevolutionary."

As the first anniversary of the Tiananmen incident approached, Ni Yuxian pasted a huge poem, thirty feet long and ten feet high, on the wall of one of Shanghai's busiest hotels. Lashing out in anger against the Chinese leadership, the poem demanded redress of the Tiananmen incident. Ni was caught, and spent the next two years on death row, waiting for his execution.

Even after Ni was released from jail and officially exonerated, party officials at the Martime Academy continued to persecute him.

They persecuted him even more when Liu Binyan wrote a story exposing the Maritime Academy's treatment of Ni. The party leadership at the Maritime Academy did not want the article published and mobilized all its forces to prevent it from appearing. Indeed, the article never was printed in the *People's Daily*, appearing instead in the March 1985 inaugural issue of *Kaituo* magazine and reprinted in numerous (eleven, to be exact) smaller regional magazines and newspapers throughout the country. Shanxi Province alone sold a million copies of the piece. Among the Chinese reading public, Ni Yuxian's name became a household word.

Liu Binyan, too, was persecuted for having written the article. Facing the barrage of official criticism, Liu, in July, took a vow of silence, withdrawing from the world of letters, while a special investigative team was formed to reinvestigate the case of Ni Yuxian. Ni feared the committee would send him to jail again. He had to escape. That is the story he wanted to tell John Lundeen. It is the story John Lundeen had already read in the Hong Kong press.

There was little John Lundeen could do for Ni Yuxian in Guangzhou. Ni's household registration was in Shanghai, and only the Shanghai consulate could grant him a visa. Lundeen wrote a letter to Lloyd Neighbors, his colleague in the cultural section of the Shanghai consulate and gave both the letter and one of Neighbors' name cards to Ni. He phoned Neighbors to warn him of what was coming.

Ni returned immediately to Shanghai. He was refused entrance to the consulate.

He called Lloyd Neighbors from a nearby phone. Neighbors was prepared for the call.

"Where are you now?" the American official asked.

"At a public phone just a few blocks from the consulate," Ni responded.

"I'll come out to meet you," Neighbors assured the nervous Ni. "Wait for me just across the street from the consulate."

"How will I recognize you?" Ni wanted to know.

"I'm wearing a red sweater," the official said.

"I'll be carrying a newspaper and a briefcase, and I'm wearing gray," Ni explained.

"I'll recognize you," Neighbors responded. "I have seen your photograph."

From his position across the street, Ni Yuxian saw a man in a red sweater walk across the courtyard in front of the small make-shift building that houses the offices of the cultural affairs section of the American consulate in Shanghai. He watched the man come through the gate and wend his way past the crowd of young people waiting for admittance to the visa section. Then he crossed the street. Lloyd Neighbors greeted him, escorting Ni back through the crowd and past the Chinese soldiers, through the gate and onto the consulate grounds. They talked outside, away from the listening devices that American officials assumed to be ubiquitous.

"I will do my very best," Neighbors assured him. "I can't promise anything, but I will bring your case up with the chief of mission and with the head of the visa section. They will write you as soon as the decision is made. It's best now that you just go home and wait."

Ni spent a nervous ten days waiting. He called Lloyd Neighbors again. "Be patient," Neighbors admonished. "The letter will be coming soon."

On January 15, 1986, Ni Yuxian received a letter requesting him to visit the American consulate. He went the next day. The letter was his pass through the guards.

"I must ask you whether you intend to return to China," the consular official explained.

"If China becomes more democratic," Ni responded, "I will return. I believe that in the years to come, China's reforms will continue and the country will become more democratic. So I will return."

The American official smiled. Ni Yuxian's visa was granted.

Two days later, he was in New York.

• • •

I had not wanted to meet Ni Yuxian—certainly not to write about him. When Andrew Nathan of Columbia University called to suggest that Ni Yuxian had a story to tell and that I might be the person to relate it, I already had other plans. My book about the victims of China's Cultural Revolution, *Enemies of the People*, was about to be published. The main lesson I had learned from that book was the extent to which the Maoist political system had corrupted not only the perpetrators of totalitarianism but its victims as well, how political repression serves to undermine the moral fabric of society, how the struggle for survival in situations of political extremity takes precedence over other values of human living together, how badly otherwise ordinary people behave in situations of adversity. But what had fascinated me most was not how human values are corrupted by prolonged political repression but rather those rare cases where individuals manage to stay good, their fundamental values intact; how in societies that have become morally bankrupt, pockets of good remain.

"Won't you at least meet him?" Andrew Nathan had prodded. I agreed.

For six hours that first night, Ni Yuxian fascinated me with his story. I saw in him a radical political reformer—a dissident—who had risked his life in the quest of democracy, who had been incarcerated and subjected to torture and who had refused to succumb. He was a representative not only of the good but of the political good. He seemed both a hero and a saint.

I had long been enamored with political heroes. My father was an army officer, a graduate of West Point, and I had perceived him from my earliest childhood as a man whose job it was to risk his life, to die if necessary, for the democracy and freedom of others. The pursuit of the political good, I thought, was what life was all about. I no longer wanted to write about evil, but about good. I determined to write Ni's story.

There was no doubt in my mind that the Chinese political system, even in its more liberal, post-Maoist form, was repressive, that the fundamental human rights that we in the West take for granted were aggressively denied. The nature of the political system cried out for dissent.

It is true that there is in China a persistent strain of suppressed democratic longing, that Chinese intellectuals have sporadically spoken out in favor of democracy, most recently in the spring of 1989. When they have, we Americans have been confirmed in our belief that democracy and fundamental human rights—life, liberty, and the pursuit of happiness—are the natural human inclination, and it is dictatorship that is deviant.

But the fact is that Chinese have not often spoken out, and not usually in great numbers, and not for very long. The political system has a remarkable capacity for control. The price of dissent—ostracism, jail, labor reform, even execution—is simply too high. Those who have dared to speak out have been killed or rendered mute.

And democracy is not a part of the Chinese tradition. The state has always governed dictatorially, even if benignly so, and hence there is a legitimacy to dictatorship and a willingness to comply that are anathema to the Western mind.

That ingrained subservience, Chinese will point out, begins in childhood. Children in the West are taught independence at an early age—to walk, to play, to ride bicycles, to fall and pick themselves up to try again, while Chinese children are taught dependence, encouraged to believe that they cannot exist without an adult—held rather than encouraged to explore. When a Chinese child cries, an adult immediately comforts him. As soon as a Chinese child is able to understand, he is taught to submit. If he does not obey, he is roundly scolded and accused of being "bad." Obedience continues into adulthood, the son obedient to his father until the father's death, the wife subservient to her husband, and every individual dependent upon and subordinate to the dictates of the state in the guise, under the communist system, of his particular work unit. The pattern of subservience is duplicated even within the political elite. Even Jiang Zemin, the chairman of the Communist Party, has to obey the preeminent elder, Deng Xiaoping.

Those rare Chinese who refuse to be subservient, who stand up and speak out against injustice, in favor of democracy and human rights, thus fall outside the norm. Ni Yuxian, I thought, was a man who had transcended his own cultural roots, his own parochial values, to stand as a courageous spokesman for the democratic longings not only of China but of all mankind. I wanted to know what made this man so special.

I have listened for hundreds of hours to Ni recount his life, and much of the substance of the story presented here comes from Ni Yuxian himself. But I needed to know Ni Yuxian not only as he presented himself to me but to delve into his past as well, tracing his roots and his early childhood to learn where his differences began. In the four years that have passed since I first met him, half my time has been spent in China, a considerable part of it in Pudong, on the eastern banks of the Huangpu River just across from the city of Shanghai, where Ni was born and raised.

My search for Ni's roots began in Three Forest Village, where his mother, Xu Fengzhen, had grown up, the place she left by sedan chair during the Chinese new year in February 1938 to marry Ni Jizhong. Xu Fengzhen's brother, Xu Jinjiang, still lives in the village with his aged wife, all gnarled and blind, and countless members of the extended family. My visit was treated as a great event, for I was the only foreigner, or so some calculated, to have spent any time in the village since the Japanese invasion of some fifty years before. People turned out to hold my hands and touch my hair, to marvel at my gold hoop earrings, and to smile, giggle, gawk, and nod.

The village has changed since the Japanese invasion and Xu Fengzhen's departure. The multitude of tiny shops that once lined the streets disappeared with the inauguration of socialism and have only recently, under Deng Xiaoping's official encouragement, revived. It is difficult to believe that anyone had ever been as wealthy as Xu Fengzhen's father was reputed to have been, social-ism having not only narrowed the gap between rich and poor but reduced everyone to the lower end of the economic scale. But much of the old flavor remains—the long, straight row of two-story bungalows lining the narrow street, the canals that hug the houses from the rear, the stone bridges and the verdant fields still dotted with the bunkers constructed during the Japanese invasion.

Cao Family Village, where Yuxian's grandfather Guansheng, his father Jizhong, Yuxian himself, and most of his siblings were born, no longer exists. It was torn down in 1958 to make room for the expansion of the steel factory when Guansheng was finally forced to move. The village that was once adjacent to Cao Family Village survives within the confines of the sprawling, gigantic steel complex, and it is ugly, poor, and polluted, devoid of the rural charm that ordinarily characterizes villages in that rich, rice-growing area.

The market town of Zhoudiadu, where as a child Ni had witnessed the Communists executing their enemies, continues to thrive. Part of Ni Jizhong's medical clinic is still there while another has been torn down to build a new, more modern hospital.

Yuxian's middle school is being upgraded to a teacher-training institute, and sterile new buildings are beginning to dot the grounds. But the lovely old one-story whitewashed traditional Chinese-style classrooms remain intact, and the magnificent garden is lovingly maintained. The old bunker where Yuxian and his friends once wrapped themselves in curtains to chant the Buddhist prayer, convincing their fellows that the school was haunted by ghosts, still solemnly stands. Pockfaced Huang is gone now, but others of Yuxian's teachers are there. Some, having taught his children, too, remember Ni, and are curious to know how he has fared in the United States, where the moon, they know, is brighter and life is inevitably good.

The water buffalo have disappeared from the fields along the banks of the Huangpu River where Yuxian once dreamed his dreams of escape to faraway places, and the land is no longer planted with rice. A water purification plant has been built nearby, and the junks are motorized now, noisy and devoid of sails. But if at dusk on a warm spring or summer day you wend your way by bicycle through the paths that bind the fields until you come to the river's edge, then sit and look and listen to the sounds of the distant harbor, you can still understand why Yuxian the child came here so often to dream.

Zhao Yuefang's family home, built sometime in the last century and passed down from generation to generation since, surrounded once by paddy fields and vegetable crops, stands now amid a small cluster of similar houses dwarfed by a huge high-rise housing project of the type now springing up all over Pudong. The area has been slated for major development, and foreign investment is being aggressively courted. The family, reluctantly, soon will move into one of the new buildings. They miss Zhao Yuefang terribly and worry about the daughter who so seldom writes.

Yuxian is remembered in the factories on Yanggao Road where he once worked. The woman who showed me around the electronics parts factory where he was sent after being dismissed from the army once had a crush on him, and she retains it still. Her eyes glowed as she recounted Ni's struggle to pass the university entrance exams and the encouragement she had enthusiastically given. The tour she gave of the storage room where he had worked and studied for nearly a year had the aura of a visit to a shrine.

Through all the years of my visits, I had saved my trip to the Shanghai Maritime Academy for last, knowing that entry would likely be denied. When I finally did try, the gatekeeper would not let me onto the grounds. The university's traditional hostility to outsiders had been bolstered by the approach of the first anniversary of the Beijing massacre of 1989. Increased security precautions were in effect on campuses throughout the country.

• • •

More important than visiting the places of Ni Yuxian's youth was the opportunity to meet with so many of the people who were important to him, to listen to their memories, too. Much of my time was spent in Ni's own home, among his many relatives, partaking of the family lore.

When Yuxian's father, Jizhong, developed cancer in 1988 and was confined to his magnificent Qing-dynasty, carved wooden bed, the extended family coming and going in constant vigil, I sat by his side, holding his hand and listening as he summoned his strength to look back over his life. Xu Fengzhen was there too, prodding his memory and supplementing the details.

When Jizhong died, I represented Yuxian at the first month's commemoration, accompanying Xu Fengzhen to the crematorium where her husband's ashes were kept, clothed in a bright red cotton bag and housed in a small wooden box with his picture on the front, occupying one small place among thousands of boxes in a room lined with shelves. The dictates of filial piety require a son to return home at the time of his father's death, but Yuxian's status as a political refugee prohibited his going back. I brought a bouquet of flowers, white for the color of mourning, with one red rose interspersed, symbolizing joy and life, in anticipation of the coming birth of Yuxian's brother's child. The mourners around us were dressed head to toe in the traditional white-colored sackcloth, and I held Xu Fengzhen as she took the small red bag of Jizhong's ashes and began to wail, mourning her husband in much the same manner they must have mourned Guansheng when he died some thirty years before.

Two years later, on my last visit to Yangsi Village, I myself slept on the Qing dynasty bed, together with Xu Fengzhen, Chinese style, my feet facing the direction of her head, the bed so huge we hardly knew the other was there. The description of the family myths and much of the early story recorded here comes from the time I spent with Ni Yuxian's family.

Ni Yuxian's wife, Zhao Yuefang, has also been an invaluable witness, testimony both to the price his family has been forced to pay for his continuing obsession with politics and to the nearly irresolvable contradictions, even for individuals who would be saints, between private obligations to family and the public demands of politics. Ni Yuxian's pursuit of democratic ideals, and the suffering he personally has been willing to endure to bring his country a little closer to them, have forced sacrifices upon his wife and children that they would have preferred to avoid. Zhao Yuefang singlehandedly has not only provided for her family's material well-being but has served as father and mother both to her children. Her life has been more vexingly difficult by far than the ordinarily difficult life of other Chinese women whose husbands have been rendered victims. Ni Yuxian's political vocation has been a luxury Zhao Yuefang could ill afford, and her personal tragedy is all the more poignant because Ni's political heroics have not been matched by personal loyalty to his wife. Ni Yuxian's request for political asylum was granted in April 1987, and a year later Zhao Yuefang and the two children were able to join him. In the freer, more open atmosphere of the United States, the already troubled marriage deteriorated still further. The two live separately now. Zhao Yuefang is embittered. Her life is more difficult here. The moon, she has discovered, is not really rounder in the United States. She is saving her money for a return to China. Her ability to carry on in the face of unrelenting pressure and loss of face is evidence of no small measure of courage.

Kajia, who spent six months in jail for aiding Ni in hanging his big character poster, who had loved him and expected him to divorce his wife to marry her, was a more reluctant witness. Her relationship with Ni had been filled with pain, and she stood to suffer further still should her whole story be told. For months after Ni's departure she waited for news that he was working to get her to the United States. In his moves between New York and Los Angeles, the letter she had written never reached him, and the two lost contact. She cried as she untied the ribbon that held the bundle of his earlier letters to read out loud to me from his poems. "Little sister," Ni had written, "how you have suffered on my behalf." She loves him still but wonders what manner of man he really is. Her final judgment, she says, will depend on whether he really does work to get her to the States. He owes her a debt that has yet to be repaid.

And Ni's political allies, his co-conspirators? I met them, too—often furtively, because the police never did learn of their connections to Ni. Ni remains, to most of them, a hero, more glorious still for his departure to the United States. We talked of politics, of the dissatisfactions of the Shanghai workers and their underlying democratic proclivities—and of the possibility of major political unrest. After the workers took to the streets in the spring of 1989, Ni's allies could no longer risk seeing me. They had all been deeply involved. Their names have been changed here to protect them.

• • •

Who is this Ni Yuxian? In many ways I know him better than I have ever known anyone, for never have I delved so deeply into another person's roots or known so many details of another person's life.

Ni Yuxian presented himself to me as committed to democratic principles and to fundamental conceptions of freedom and equality, a ceaseless fighter for the cause of justice and truth, supremely self-confident and courageous. But this is only part of his personal picture.

Sociologists would probably view him as deviant, for in the context of his own culture, with its history of authoritarian rule and its political culture of passivity and unquestioning obedience, Ni is a marginal man, a textbook case of the failure of the process of socialization. But to be a deviant in socialist China, to be committed to the transformation of such a society, is hardly a criticism of the man. In times of change it is often the individual who stands at the edge of society, unbalanced, who takes the risks and assumes the leadership that propels society forward.

Psychologists might see him as a man obsessed, a narcissist, locked still in an infantile perception of himself as imbued with special powers, invulnerable, better than all the rest. They would not be surprised to learn that he has often failed in his basic obligations to those closest to him, disappointing, sometimes bitterly so, his wife and his family, his teachers, his loves, and his friends. Lofty political ideals do not often correlate with personal sainthood.

Chinese who have grown up outside the mainland, free from the socialization of the Communist Party and convinced that the party has destroyed the best of traditional Chinese values, would see Ni as a product of communist culture. Ni's callous use of people, his disregard for procedure and process, and the cavalier manner in which he handled finances, are not unique to him but emblematic unfortunately of too many of China's current dissidents. The closer one gets to the heroes of Tiananmen Square, the more imperfect they seem.

Chinese who have grown up under the communist government see much in Ni's character they argue is distinctively Shanghaiese. He is, they say, *xiao congming*—"little smart"—a little too shrewd. Faced with danger, a *xiao congming* will sacrifice principle to protect himself. And Ni Yuxian is, after all, a cat with nine lives, constantly courting danger but always landing on his feet.

And there is a certain kind of Shanghaiese called a *xiaochilao*— a charming chap on the surface but one who revels in the unexpected, who deliberately works to create *luan*—disorder—wherever he goes. Ni Yuxian is like that, too.

Why write about this all too human hero with feet that seem made of clay? Because the story of his life parallels the history of China under Communist Party rule and provides for the foreign reader, as no other story I know, a richness of flavor and detail, a sense of the unrelenting pinpricks of daily life in a communist dictatorship. Ni's life helps us understand both the myriad petty injustices that ought to propel vast numbers of his countrymen to dissent and the equally petty panoply of workaday weapons the party employs to prevent dissent from ever finding expression. In Ni's life, too, we see again the propensity of the system to pull everyone, even its victims, into its web of corruption and everyday deceit. We see the difficulties of remaining honest and good in a system that demands subterfuge merely to survive.

Ni's story is important, too, for the lessons it teaches about the nature, limitations, and complexity of the political hero. Americans of many political hues have often made heroes of Chinese—Chiang Kai-shek and Mao Zedong, Zhou Enlai and Deng Xiaoping among them—and just as often our Chinese heroes have disappointed us. Most recently we have courted, and some have been disappointed by, the young heroes of Tiananmen Square, the student leaders of the 1989 democracy movement so bloodily crushed by the government. In awe of the dangers the hero so daringly courts and the sacrifices he is willing to endure, we easily miss the complexity of his motives and assume that the values he publicly espouses—democracy, freedom, human rights—are our values, too, that human aspirations are everywhere the same, and that the words to describe those aspirations are universally understood. China's struggle for democracy is still in its formative stage, and our disappointments can be tempered by a better understanding of the cultural filter through which we view the Chinese and through which the Chinese in turn view us—and our ideals.

But finally it must be said that for all his tragic flaws, Ni Yuxian stood for years in the vanguard, isolated and often alone, daring to shout in outrage while others still silently followed. To stand up repeatedly to shout that the emperor has no clothes in a society where the emperor really is naked and such observations are routinely punished by imprisonment, labor reform, and death requires remarkable strength of character. When, on death row, he demands to know the nature of his crime after being tortured for merely insisting on his own integrity, when he insists after his return to the Shanghai Maritime Academy that he is human and must be treated as a man, he is crying out not only for himself but for all Chinese and all individuals everywhere who have been denied their basic human rights. The day, we hope, will come when Ni's voice will be joined by others to become a chorus and Ni himself will be lost in the crowd, when the demand for democracy is no longer deviant, and the movement for human dignity and individual rights has grown so large the government has lost all power to resist.

A Chinese Odyssey

CHAPTER

1

Fifty years later, on a hot and sultry summer night, it would still be remembered as the finest wedding the county had ever seen.

Xu Fengzhen had had many suitors, on that they were all agreed. But had there been twelve—or fifteen? The women—sitting there on low small stools, legs spread wide, fanning their private parts—could not remember exactly. The story had mellowed with age. Its purpose had never been precise fact or historical accuracy but rather to demonstrate what a fine catch Xu Fengzhen had made and how perfidiously she had been deceived. It was part of the family myth.

By 1938 Xu Fengzhen's carpenter father was not as wealthy as before the Japanese invaders had burned his warehouse to the ground. But he was still one of the richest men in the village and respected far and wide for the furniture he made. On those grounds alone, Fengzhen made a desirable wife. But the young woman was also pretty and smart, a little wisp of a thing, with high cheekbones, white teeth, huge brown eyes, and the double eyelids that were more western than Chinese and hence considered a mark of beauty. In a village where most people had never ventured further than the city of Shanghai, just west across the Huangpu River, and then only several times in a life, Xu Fengzhen had already been all the way to Nanjing, more than 125 miles up the Yangtze. She was modern, a woman of the world, and she deserved a husband similarly out of the ordinary. It was only fitting that she should marry an intellectual.

As Xu Fengzhen's father interviewed the suitors one by one, the young doctor, Ni Jizhong, stood out above all the rest. The man was quiet and self-effacing, solid and honest, but his devotion to his profession lent him a powerful, haunting intensity. Jizhong had been only thirteen years old when he determined to become a doctor. His mother had died that year as Jizhong stood helplessly by, watching her slowly and painfully succumb.

"I could not cure my mother," he remembered, "but I wanted to learn to cure other people." While his friends played, Jizhong remained indoors poring over the medical books that remained to the end his most precious possession.

Today, the same disease that had killed his mother was eating away at him. Lying emaciated and weak on the magnificently carved Qing dynasty bed that had been in his wife's family for generations and was the last piece of elegance to survive the decades of turmoil, Ni Jizhong agreed to look back over his life and share it with me, to relive for the last time the stories that had long been part of the family lore. Surrounded by an extended family that spanned three generations and reached to several branches, Jizhong was taking final stock, "waiting" he said, "for death." In little more than a month, he would be gone.

There was not much in the balance sheet to console him, crowded as it was with war and government upheavals, with fortunes made and squandered, with private, family tragedy, with the succession of political campaigns that had rendered him and his family victims. His marriage to Xu Fengzhen was one of the few constants that fell on the positive side of the ledger.

Ni Jizhong had been unemployed when he presented himself to Xu Fengzhen's father. In the abyss of the depression the Japanese invasion had brought, no one could afford to consult a twenty-year-old untested doctor of traditional Chinese medicine. But the professional matchmaker who was arranging the interviews had assured Mr. Xu that the young man came from a good family of substantial means. As assurance, she had even shown Mr. Xu a picture of the elegant two-storied, whitewashed, Ni family house where Xu Fengzhen would live when the young couple married. Fortune-tellers were consulted. The couple was betrothed. The wedding was set for late February, just after the Chinese lunar new year. The matchmaker made plans for the event.

When the morning came, young Dr. Ni set out by simple but elegant sedan chair, together with the matchmaker and a small coterie of close friends, to the home of his fianceé. It was only three and a half miles from his father's home to that of his bride, but in a countryside where roads were rare and distances were traversed by footpaths, three and a half miles was a very long way—at least a three-hour walk. At Xu Fengzhen's home, ten tables of eight people each feasted raucously with the young bride-groom on an eighteen-course meal and endless bottles of wine and toasts. Xu Fengzhen, dressed in bridal red, waited quietly upstairs with Ni Jizhong's sister and an old lady come to instruct on the rites and ways of marriage.

Xu Fengzhen had never set eyes on the man she was about to marry. On the several occasions he had come to negotiate their alliance, it never even occurred to her to peek. All village marriages were arranged. That was the way things were, and she had never imagined that things might ever be different. "I was a little bit scared," she recalls, "but not very. Everyone had to do it. I just thought 'so now I am leaving my own house and going to one I have never seen before.' But I knew I was marrying a good man."

It was late morning when the firecrackers began noisily fright-ening away evil spirits still lurking on the path the bridal procession would take. Evil spirits had always been a problem in the villages around those parts. The countryside was dotted with the burial mounds of the dead, and everyone knew that the ghosts came out at night. They could trick even the most experienced elder with the games they played, suddenly putting up walls across a path, forcing the perambulator to turn in search of another route home. Everyone knew someone who had been kept out all night, lost and in terror, as the ghost walls popped up at every bend in the road. It was best, in such situations, to wait calmly until morning when the ghosts returned to their graves. Most people knew better than to venture out after dark.

Ghosts were less likely to emerge during the day, but they would be tempted by the occasion of a wedding. No one would want to take a risk. The way had to be made clear for the procession.

And what a splendid procession it was! The red and black and gold sedan chair that carried the bride, with its stained-glass win-dows as magnificent as any cathedral's, was as big as the bed on which Dr. Ni lay dying, and as heavy and elaborately carved, with dragons, phoenixes, peacocks, and tigers, intricately detailed scenes from Chinese folklore, and lifelike images of the Eight Immortals. It took eight strong and sturdy peasant men, already drunk and rowdy with wine, to carry the bridal chair. So great was the dis-tance that the carriers worked in shifts, an additional and equally drunken relief team taking turns jostling and bouncing and teasing the bride—endeavoring to embarrass her with their bawdy jokes and threatening always to drop the sedan chair and thereby plunge her into inextricable humiliation. In front of the sedan chair marched the musicians, a cacophony of gongs, horns, and ear-splitting cymbals inviting the villagers to come and gawk and be impressed by the spectacle. Indeed, it was the necessity of giving public face to the families involved that dictated such an elaborate and expensive rite.

The Three Forest Village from which the procession began was actually more a small town than a village—one long, straight, and very narrow cobblestone road lined on both sides by two-story, whitewashed buildings with gray tile roofs, each building connected to the next without interruption. The multipurpose buildings served as living quarters, shops, and tiny factories alike, each little shop, open to the front, specializing in the sale of one or another daily necessity. One shop might sell rice and another vinegar and soy sauce. One might specialize in the sale of kitchen utensils and another still would sell coal. One might lend comic books and another peddle cloth or yarn; a tailor might make clothes in one and young girls might embroider in another. There was a coffinmaker, of course, and an apothecary of herbal medicine, a barber and butcher and a renter of rickshaws, too. The texture of life in Three Forest Village was rich.

The rear of the bungalows sat just at the edge of a canal that was linked in an infinite crisscross with other canals and finally to the Huangpu River. The canals served as a a means of transportation and a source of irrigation. They provided the town with fish and with drinking water, each bungalow having a small balcony in the back from which a wooden bucket attached to a rope could be lowered into the canal and then raised again. The canal was the gathering place where women washed their laundry while gossiping with neighbors and the pool where young village boys skinny-dipped and learned to swim.

At periodic intervals the canals were linked to land by stone bridges, ordinarily built by or inscribed in memory of one of the more illustrious citizens of the area—or for a chaste widow who never remarried. On the other side of the bridges lay the village land—rich, fertile, and productive, spotted now not only with the burial mounds of the dead but with low, round brick bunkers constructed by both the Japanese invaders and Chinese defenders alike. The fields were planted with a myriad of crops, but rice paddy predominated. The city of Shanghai teemed to overflowing with people and hence was rich in the human waste that was daily transported by cart across the river to the Huangpu district of which Three Forest Village was a part. From the city core, the farmers' fields rippled out in concentric semicircles of ever descending hues of green. The deepest, lushest hue encircled the city, because those crops were most generously fertilized by the city's waste. By late summer the fields would be so verdant and emerald green they would look as though painted in watercolor. Even in February the fields were green with crops.

Often in the late summer, just as the crops were approaching their height, the nearby Yangtze and the Huangpu, and hence the canals connected to them, would flood. Families would wake up in the morning to find their homes awash, shoes and wooden chamberpots, chairs, stools, and tables floating freely through the rising waters. The children greeted the floods with joy, gathering on beds which their minds transformed into the junks that plied the waterways, gleefully imagining themselves captain of their ships.

As the children played, the adults turned stoically first to the task of reinforcing the walls of their homes with bamboo poles and then to joining other villagers in carrying mud to reinforce the dikes.

The village united at such times in turning to the local god whose job it was to assist them in matters of weather and harvest. For generations longer than any one could remember, the local god, whom they addressed as lord, in the same manner ancient officials had been addressed, had lived year-round in the village temple. Dressed in the colorful silks of traditional Chinese official-dom, red and green tassels hanging like Christmas ornaments from his hat, his image was brought out on parade only on special occasions. At time of flood or drought, he would be carried through the streets on a big open sedan chair, his way paved by flutes and cymbals and scruffy dark-coated Taoist monks, topknots piled high atop their heads, white spats covering their ankles, chanting the scriptures and dancing. At the very head of the procession, one of the village youths—a different one every year, for it was a competitive honor that had to be shared—cleared the way by beating a huge brass gong that was attached to his arm by a large iron hook, and sometimes by two or three. The hooks actually penetrated the flesh, dripping blood along the path.

At the climax of the ceremony, paper effigies of human forms, symbolizing evil ghosts, would be burned with great ceremony. Responsibility for everything bad that happened to the village inevitably rested with the ghosts.

The ghosts thus placated and the city god honored, the villagers would take part in a huge feast—the whole event costing an inordinate amount of money but fashioning the village, for all its divisions, into a community against adversity and ensuring that the harvest, if not bountiful, would carry them through another year.

There was no electricity in Xu Fengzhen's town, and no telephones either, but distances were nonetheless measured in the modern way, in terms of the length between telephone poles. Xu Fengzhen's wedding procession was the distance between three telephone poles long, which was considered very long indeed. In addition to the musicians and the sedan chair and the wedding party that was traveling the distance on foot, the procession included the bride's dowry and contributions of food and wine for the festivities that would take place at the groom's. The smaller parcels had been carefully and artfully stacked on numerous large red rectangular trays, carved and decorated in much the same manner as the sedan chair, suspended from carrying poles, and transported by another contingent of now drunk and rowdy youth hired for the occasion. There were red-covered quilts and trunks filled with silks and bedding. There were high-heeled shoes and several fur coats with muffs. There was a huge white goose and a big fish which served as symbols of plenty. There were whole hams and swinging trays laden with wine. The elegant cabinets and bookshelves and clothes chests built by her father's own hands were transported by cart. Truly the county had never seen such a display. The families of the betrothed gained face.

Hours of jostling later, as Xu Fengzhen stepped delicately from the sedan chair to the sound of music and singing and merriment all around, the red gauze veil still hiding her face, the young bride could not resist a peek. With a shock she realized that the house to which she was being escorted and the one she had been shown in the photograph were not the same. The house in front of her, with its main central room for receiving guests, flanked on each side by several smaller rooms, was large to be sure and might once have befit a family of means. But the place must have been over a century old and was dilapidated almost to the point of collapse. It was crowded too, already serving as home to several families. Ni Jizhong's father, Ni Guansheng, lived there in the east wing with his new wife, Jizhong's stepmother. Ni Guansheng's younger brother and his wife, and their two married sons and families lived in the several rooms in the west. Jizhong and his new bride would be assigned a single small room in the eastern wing, sharing a stove with the new bridegroom's father.

Great effort had been made to hide from the new bride the fact that this was a poor man's home. There were twenty banquet tables laden with food, and both the quality of the meal and the oil lanterns that lit the extravagant feast were worthy of a family of substantial means. Among the many guests her new father-in-law had invited were some of Shanghai's most illustrious personages, including the boss of one of the leading underworld gangs. But even the mosquito nets, Xu Fengzhen could not help but notice, were full of holes. And from beneath her veil as she watched those around her grow ever more raucous and drunk, she could see that her new husband was a cripple. He walked with a decided limp.

The matchmaker had lied. Xu Fengzhen's family had been badly deceived. She was marrying neither the family nor the man that had been promised. "This will never do," Xu Fengzhen repeated over and over to herself as the evening proceeded, even as she and the bridegroom went through the elaborate ritual of kowtowing thirty-six times, nose to the ground, before the Ni family ancestral tablets.

By then it was too late. Until the moment the wedding procession had left her family gate, revelation of such treachery could have annulled the marriage. But once she had crossed the threshold into her husband's home, Xu Fengzhen and Ni Jizhong were inextricably wed.

•　•　•

Ni Jizhong's father, Ni Guansheng, could not truly be accused of deceit in the matter. The matchmaker, after all, was the one who had so egregiously misrepresented the family circumstances. But everyone knew that it had been Guansheng who brought his family to the brink of collapse.

Ni Guansheng was a lusty hulk of a man, of peasant stock and smart as a whip. As a child, his family had been so grindingly poor that mere survival was a constant struggle. But impoverished and difficult though his childhood had been, he grew up with a love of life that led him early to squeeze everything that could be squeezed from whatever circumstance he faced. Ni Guansheng never went to school. He was illiterate. In all his life he never learned to read or write a single Chinese character. He could not even sign his name.

Guansheng's education was the Huangpu River. When still a mere child, his father sent him to work as an oarsman on one of the sailing junks that transported food and vegetables up and down the waterway. Decades later, Guansheng still delighted in startling an audience by suddenly leaping on a table, throwing back his head, thrusting forth his body and bursting into the bawdy songs of the Huangpu River boatmen, one minute imitating the rhythm of the oarsmen rowing and the next singing of the joys of taking a woman and lustily rubbing his chest in praise of the female anatomy. His wife would curse him, as the audience roared in embarrassment and fun. They had never seen anyone so happy. "He's crazy," they all said.

Guansheng was a born storyteller, too, and as the Qing dynasty tottered and finally fell in 1911, as the new republic fell apart and the warlords grew fat and corrupt, as foreign-dominated Shanghai festered with poverty and ill-gotten gain, the Huangpu River was an endless source of lore.

Eventually, the Huangpu made him rich. First he was promoted from oarsman to cook and later the owner of the boat loaned him enough money to invest in a boat of his own—a big boat with several sails and a crew of ten. A few more years passed, and he bought a second boat and then became part owner in a third. With the money he made from his boats, he also invested in land, as Chinese in search of respectability always have, and after a few years he became a major landowner in Cao Family Village.

It was when he became rich that people began saying that if only Ni Guansheng had been educated he could really have made something of himself. Even so, he was a man of no small reputation in the village. When the Nationalists established control in 1928, he became one of the village leaders. The Nationalists organized the villages from the bottom up, in pyramid fashion, into what they called the *baojia* system. At the lowest level, one male head of household became responsible for overseeing ten village families, known as a *jia*. At the next highest level, known as the *bao*, another leader was in charge of ten *jia*—one hundred families.

Ni Guansheng became the head of a *jia*, in charge of ten other village families. Everyone knew Guansheng and respected him, too.

But just as Ni Guansheng's fame and fortune reached their zenith, fate and his own character began to contrive against him. His fortune began an inexorable decline.

Part of the blame rested with Cao Xinfa.

Shanghai in the early 1930s was in an advanced state of moral decay, the contrast between rich and poor, good and evil, glaring. At the top of the heap, wealthiest by far, were the the foreigners, representatives in one way or another of the colonial powers, safely ensconced in placid settlements managed and governed by foreign rule and served by upper class Chinese, the compradors, who had grown rich by serving as agents for businessmen from the West. At the bottom, as Harold Isaacs described them, were the "great mass of helot-like poor that kept flocking in from the ravaged and impoverished countryside, providing an endless supply of the laborers, human beasts of burden, beggars, prostitutes, criminals, and ultimately helpless people who left some 50,000 dead babies on the streets of the city each year—there was a philanthropic organization whose sole activity consisted of picking up and disposing of these tiny corpses."

The Huangpu River, which fronted the Bund—the staid and massive foreign commercial section of Shanghai—linked the city east to the Pacific and west to the country's interior. The river seethed with intrigue and illegality. Some of the leaders of Shanghai's biggest and richest gangs, like Yu Heqing, whom Ni Guansheng called friend, had begun their careers on the boats. Their wealth had not always been legally obtained. Ni Guansheng's fellow villager Cao Xinfa was one of those men who got rich on the Huangpu by scandalously illegal means.

One day, a briefcase-carrying foreigner of unknown background and unspecified country had asked Cao Xinfa to take him to Wusongkou, where the Huangpu and the Yangtze rivers meet and flow together to the sea. Cao Xinfa suspected that the foreigner's briefcase was full of money. As the river widened and the boat approached the mouth where the brown of the river suddenly merges with the blue of the ocean, Cao Xinfa grabbed the briefcase and threw the man overboard. The foreigner grabbed on to the side of the boat. Cao took a hatchet and chopped off his hands. The foreigner drowned.

Cao Xinfa instantly became rich. The briefcase had been full of American dollars.

Cao Xinfa tried to destroy Ni Guansheng, too. Not content with his ill-gotten wealth, Cao Xinfa said that Ni Guansheng's land really belonged to him. When Ni Guansheng produced the legal document certifying the land as his own, Cao Xinfa insisted, so Ni Guansheng took him to court. The very name "Cao" in Cao Family Village testified to the fact that the village was dominated by members of the Cao family clan. People with the surname of Ni had moved in generations earlier from a place long forgotten. They had no ties to any other part of the country, but still they were regarded as outsiders. Of course the Cao family villagers all testified that the land belonged to one of their own. Besides, Cao Xinfa's payment was bigger. Legal decisions in those days depended largely on the size of the bribe. Cao Xinfa won the case. Ni Guansheng lost his land.

Some part of the blame for Ni Guansheng's decline rests with the Japanese. In August of 1937, when Guansheng heard that the Japanese invaders would soon be sailing up the Huangpu River and that henceforth all Chinese junks would be working under Japanese command, he joined with other patriotic boatmen in a dramatic act of defiance. They lined their boats, row after row, in barricades across the Huangpu River, drilled holes in the bottoms and sank them, thereby simultaneously hindering passage of the Japanese ships and ensuring that Chinese boats would not be forced to serve an enemy master. Later Ni Guansheng would resurrect his boats from the bottom of the Huangpu, but only after substantial losses.

In truth, however, it was gambling that made Guansheng poor. The gambling started not long after his first wife—Ni Jizhong's mother—died. The first time Ni Guansheng gambled, he won. Then he began to gamble the way alcoholics drink—obsessively, uncontrollably, and burdened afterward by guilt. When he gambled and won, he was on top of the world, ecstatic, swept away by his own generosity. He could not lavish enough on his family. Several times he even hired a taxi to take him and his family, dressed in their country finest, to Shanghai. They drove around the city like kings, staring open-mouthed at buildings more modern and higher than anything they could have imagined, dazzled by the brilliant neon lights. Afterward, they went to the Park Hotel and used knives and forks to eat Western-style food. To his dying day, Ni Guansheng was the only man in Cao Family Village to have ridden in a car, used a knife and fork, and eaten foreign food. The experience added to his public stature even as his financial fortune declined.

When Ni Guansheng lost, he lost big and he lost mean, returning to his family in the small hours of the morning wearing only his underwear, having gambled everything else away. At those times, he would curse his fate and his fellow gamblers. He would lash out in anger against his family. Then, when the anger subsided, he would be temporarily overcome by guilt, vowing never to gamble again.

Always, he gambled again.

Three nights before his eldest son's wedding, Ni Guansheng had gambled away his last remaining boat, the end of the family fortune. Ni Jizhong came home that night to find his father sobbing. "You are my eldest son," Guansheng cried when he saw his son. "I had saved all that money for your wedding. Now I have lost it all.

"I am going to kill myself," Guansheng concluded, heading with great drama for the door. "I will drown myself in the river." It was one of the peculiarities of the Huangpu River boatmen that they spent all their lives on the water and never learned to swim.

Ni Jizhong dissuaded his father. Guansheng lived another twenty years. But the son had no choice. Face had to be preserved at all costs. Not only must the wedding take place but it must be held with all the pomp and ceremony and extravagance that had been planned. Ni Jizhong would have to borrow the money.

In the three days remaining, Jizhong went by foot to every friend he knew, borrowing a little money from this one, a little more from that, until, exhausted, his feet so blistered he could only limp, he had put together enough to pay for the elaborate feast that half a century later would still be remembered as the finest wedding the county had ever seen. Eleven years and several children later, when the Communists took over the village, Jizhong would still be paying off the debt.

• • •

Ni Jizhong and Xu Fengzhen were not expected to fall in love. Village couples rarely did. With so much of living mobilized in pursuit of mere subsistence, love was a luxury so distant that its possibility entered consciousness only rarely and then only to the young and for fleeting moments.

Marriage was a contract, not between individuals but between two families, and its purpose was to secure the male family line and assure the patriarch of a satisfactorily comfortable old age. A woman upon marriage moved inevitably into the home of her husband's parents, where she was valued largely for the male off-spring she produced and for the household labor she performed. Always an outsider, she came under the immediate and often callous supervision of her mother-in-law, just as her husband remained subject to the authority of his father. The highest to which most women aspired was a son, which not only enhanced her value to the family but ensured her a daughter-in-law in her twilight years. Such was the nature of the Chinese family that with the transformation from daughter-in-law to mother-in-law, most women brought to their heightened role not the empathy of shared feminine oppression but the same insufferability to which they had earlier been subjected. In the tension-ridden atmosphere of the traditional Chinese village family, the conditions of love did not ordinarily pertain.

But Ni Jizhong and Xu Fengzhen, against all odds, discovered in each other something they came to recognize as love. The matchmaker had not been entirely amiss.

Ni Jizhong's dreams of curing sickness had been shattered by war and by his increasingly ne'er-do-well father. After his son's marriage, Ni Guansheng continued gambling, bringing ever greater shame and ruin to his family. Within the year, he had gambled away his son's small but cherished pharmacy and squandered most of Xu Fengzhen's magnificent dowry. When Xu Fengzhen cursed him and locked her room against further intrusion, an enraged Guansheng came with a hatchet and hacked a hole through the door. Humiliated, Ni Jizhong was forced to turn to Xu Fengzhen's family for help. Her family, shamed that their daughter should be plunged so unexpectedly and undecorously into poverty, loaned their still unemployed son-in-law some money to open a small rice shop. Ni Guansheng gambled that shop away, too. Ni Jizhong grew to hate his father.

Ni Jizhong became an itinerant salesman. He was temperamentally unsuited to salesmanship and woefully unsuccessful at his work but constantly on the move peddling his goods, the father found it more difficult to gamble his son's wares away.

As Ni Jizhong and his father grew more and more estranged, he turned to his pretty young wife for solace and support, and the bonds between the couple slowly grew. The children began coming, first a girl in 1940 and then another daughter, Kunkun, born in the year of the ram. Ni Jizhong was born in the year of the ram, too, which made him twenty-four in 1943.

Pregnant for the third time, Xu Fengzhen knew while the baby was still in the womb that the child she was carrying was no ordinary creature. One day as she knelt washing clothes by the side of the swiftly flowing, deep canal, she accidentally slipped and fell in. She could not swim, and would surely have drowned but for the fact that landlord Yang's son had unexpectedly returned home that day and heard her frantic cries. To have been saved by a member of so illustrious a family as landlord Yang was an omen that the future of the child in her womb would be similarly bright. That she had been rescued at all was a tribute to the tenacity and will to live of the child within her. "Surely," she thought, "heaven is sending me a son."

Xu Fengzhen was less certain about her own future on earth, and Ni Jizhong insisted after she nearly lost her life that a photographer be hired to take her picture and that her name be inscribed on the back. Jizhong's mother had died without a scrap of photographic evidence, and to his dying day her son never knew his mother's name. The photograph taken of Xu Fengzhen while her baby was still in the womb was the first in her life. It shows a bright-eyed and pretty, demure and somewhat shy, village girl, bangs ending just above her eyebrows, teeth somewhat protruding, single long plait brought forward to fall along her chest.

Heaven did send Xu Fengzhen a son.

When Xu Fengzhen's first male offspring entered the world that December night in 1945, Ni Jizhong was off somewhere in Xian county peddling cloth. Guansheng, naturally, was at the gambling table. There was not a single grain of rice in Xu Fengzhen's house. Only Ah Mei Popo—midwife, friend, and neighbor who was even poorer than the woman she served—was there to see Xu Fengzhen through the ordeal. After assisting Xu Fengzhen in the delivery of her child, Ah Mei Popo put the other two girl children in a basket, one at each end of a carrying pole, and set out on the three-hour trek for Xu Fengzhen's parents. There at least the children could eat and she could borrow enough rice to give Xu Fengzhen something to fill her stomach. "What a terrible loss of face," Ah Mei Popo thought, "for a woman to have to rely on her own family at the time of the birth of a son."

Ni Guansheng was still at the gambling table when his younger brother came to deliver the news. "Guansheng," his brother announced, "you have a grandson."

Ni Guansheng's life was irrevocably changed. From the moment he heard the news, his grandson became the most precious treasure in the old man's life. That the child was a boy and Guansheng's first grandson was sufficient cause for joy. But the little boy was born to Guansheng's oldest son and Guansheng himself was also the oldest son. This grandson was special indeed. Standing up from the gambling table, Guansheng announced in a booming voice, "From this day forth, I will never gamble again."

And from that day forth, Ni Guansheng never did gamble again. Instead, he opened a small shop along the banks of his Huangpu River, just at the edge of Cao Family Village, and while he never became rich, he regained a measure of stability and respectability. In time, Ni Jizhong stopped hating his father and began to forgive. Later, when the Communists came in, the whole family actually came to thank Guansheng for the destitution he had earlier wrought. When the Communists executed villagers because they were as wealthy as Guansheng had been at his height, the recently impoverished Nis were spared.

They named the little child Yuxian because his father had been in Xian county at the time of his birth, and because all the Ni children of that generation were called Yu. At home, they called him Yuyu. But Yuxian also means "one who brings forth virtue," and ignominious though his entry into the world had been, impoverished though his family would remain for years, neither Guansheng nor any other member of the family ever doubted that the infant male was destined for greatness. Surely one day Yuxian would manage to bring virtue into their corrupt and tumultuous world.

Guansheng's life became devoted to the protection of this tiny treasure. Was it something in the way the genes had been transmitted, leaping from grandfather to grandson without particular regard to the man who had actually sired him? Or was it simply because their relationship was so close? No other individual so greatly influenced the young child's life. In character, Guansheng and his grandson were remarkably alike, gripped by the same exuberant curiosity and ebullient love of life and burdened by the same tragic flaws. In the village, the child would always be known not as Yuxian or as Yuyu but as Guansheng's grandson.

Life in Cao Family Village was precarious. The Japanese invaders had left just months before Yuxian was born, and the country was poised for civil war between the Nationalists and the Communists. Enemies were everywhere. A one-time gambler like Guansheng, especially, had enemies who might want to do the young boy harm. Yuyu was still a babe in arms when Guansheng carried him to the piece of land he continued to claim as his own to repeat the story of Cao Xinfa's murderously acquired wealth and the treachery through which Guansheng was cheated out of his land, warning the little grandson against such a dangerous man.

Ah Xing was another enemy against whom Guansheng's grandson was warned.

Before the Communists came, Ah Xing had worked for the local village self-protection corps. One day, when a beggar from some distant place came to the village in search of food, Ah Xing had locked the beggar up and accused him of being a Communist. The next day, Ah Xing took a yard-long sword with a bright red tassel and sharpened it razor sharp. He fed the Communist beggar a delicious last meal, then led him to the bank of the Huangpu River, just next to burial ground. "Don't hate me," Ah Xing had said to the Communist beggar. "It is not me killing you. I am only following the orders of my superiors. Next year, this day will be your anniversary."

So saying, Ah Xing quickly brought out his sword and sliced off the Communist's head.

But the beggar was not a Communist. Ah Xing had never killed a man before. "I just wanted to taste the flavor of killing," he would explain to others later.

Since Ah Xing was from the Cao family clan, no one in the village reported him. But outsiders like the Nis were always wary of this man who liked the flavor of killing.

• • •

When Ni Yuxian was a full year old, his family followed local custom by inviting a fortune-teller to their home to calculate their young son's fate. They already knew that Yuyu's destiny was great. His will to life when his mother fell in the canal and his position as firstborn male to firstborn male of firstborn male were sufficient indications. A fortune-teller was needed only to provide the details.

• • •

The family believed in fortune-tellers not only because everyone believed in fortune-tellers but because they had good reason to believe.

Only a few years earlier, after the Japanese had come, Ni Jizhong had suddenly been snatched away by the invaders and put in a concentration camp. He nearly lost his life. The Japanese turned their dogs on him and he was nearly eaten alive. He had known not to try to escape from the dogs. Others who had run to the electric fence that surrounded the camp had died of the shock.

When her husband disappeared, Xu Fengzhen had become sick and sleepless with worry. She went every day to the camp. Trying to catch a glimpse of her husband, she could never be sure he was there or even still alive. She tried negotiating with the guards for his release or at least for some news of his condition. Finally, she approached some collaborators—Chinese who were openly cooperating with the Japanese invaders. For five hundred yuan, an enormous sum in those days, they would see what they could do.

She sold her jewelry and what little remained from her dowry and still she had to borrow. She waited. There was no word.

In desperation, she took her last bit of money and set out on a journey she rarely made, one that took several hours each way, ferrying across the Huangpu River to Shanghai. She went to the best, the wisest, and the most reliable fortune-teller she knew, a wizened old man in long traditional garb, explaining her plight. "My husband has been captured by the Japanese," she lamented. "I don't know how he is or even whether he is alive, let alone if he will ever be allowed to come home. Please tell me what will happen."

The old man brought down a wooden bird cage. Pulling off the dark blue cloth cover, he released a tiny yellow bird. He placed the bird before a long, narrow box that was full of cards. On each card was written a single Chinese character. The yellow bird hopped here and darted there and then picked out two cards with his beak, depositing them in the hand of his master.

The old man studied the cards. "Ah," he said thoughtfully, finally looking up. "Your husband is a very lucky man. He is alive. You will see him soon. Very soon."

"How do you know?" Xu Fengzhen asked.

The old man showed her the two cards. "Look, here is the character *jian*," he said, pointing to the ideograph that means "to see." "This means that you will see your husband again. And look at this character, *ti*," the character that means "to lift." "The left side of the character is composed of the symbol for hand, which means that someone has given your husband a helping hand to lift him out of the concentration camp. And look here, at the lower right part of the character. It is the symbol for 'go.' Your husband has already left the camp. And look here, at the upper right portion. It is the symbol for today. A helping hand has lifted your husband out of the concentration camp and you will see him again today."

Ni Jizhong was already at home when Xu Fengzhen returned several hours later. "I knew you would be back," she greeted her husband.

• • •

The fortune-teller sent to determine Yuxian's fate used two methods. He studied the size and shape of the little boy's face and head, and he calculated the eight characters that coincided with the precise time of the child's birth.

The art of judging a man by the shape of his face and his head has a long tradition in China. There are four different basic facial types. The rectangular face, symbolizing nobility and wealth, was the most cherished, typically associated with officials. Next in order of preference was the round, full face. The third type, broad at the top and narrow at the bottom was less than desirable, and an elongated, narrow face was the most inauspicious of all. Officials in traditional times were experts at judging men by the shape and size of their heads. Zhuge Liang, the immortal hero of the *Romance of the Three Kingdoms*, had known from the bone at the back of Wei Yan's head that Wei would rebel against him when Zhuge Liang died. Liang Qichao, the great turn-of-the-century reformer who had tried to modernize China within the dynastic system, had known that of his two most famous followers, Kang Youwei and Tan Sitong, Tan Sitong would be the one whose life would be lost at an early age. He could tell from Tan Sitong's head. In 1898 it was thirty-three-year-old Tan Sitong and not Kang Youwei who was beheaded when the Empress Dowager Ci Xi brought a violent halt to the scholars' efforts at reform. It was said that even Chiang Kai-shek chose his underlings as much on the basis of their facial characteristics as on their education and accomplishments.

Ni Yuxian's face was big and square and full, and his nose was straight. Like his mother, he had the double eyelids more common to the Westerner, and his eyes were big and round, lively and bright. The head, the fortune-teller concluded, was the head of a hero.

The fortune-teller's examination of the eight characters naturally confirmed that the child was extraordinarily smart and that he would accomplish great deeds before his death. Those deeds, surely, would fall into one of two realms. Either Ni Yuxian would become a military hero or he would make great contributions in political service—precisely which was still too early to tell.

There were portents as well. "Ni Yuxian will face two major and dangerous turning points in his life," the fortune-teller continued, "one at the age of thirty-three, the other at sixty-six. If he can pass the first juncture—and it will be a dangerous one indeed—he will live to accomplish great deeds."

Xu Fengzhen took the red piece of paper on which the fortune had been written in big black characters, locked it in an elegant, copper-studded red lacquer box, and put it in a special drawer. She would refer to it often in the years to come.

She turned to it frequently for solace and hope when Yuxian was in his thirty-third year. Ni Yuxian spent that year on death row, facing the first major turning point against which the fortune-teller had warned. Tan Sitong had been Yuxian's greatest hero and he feared that he might share his fate. But his fellow inmates who had never heard the young man's fortune also read Ni Yuxian's destiny from the shape of his head. "Your head is not the head of a man destined to be executed so young," they reassured him one after the other.

"But look at the head of Gao Fei," they would joke. "His face doesn't have three ounces of flesh. His cheeks are sunken. He has a puckered mouth and monkey cheeks and the back of his head looks like it's been bashed in. That's the head of a man whose fate is bad."

Gao Fei was taken from the cell one night and shot.

• • •

With so many omens portending his greatness, a measure of respect began entering into Xu Fengzhen's attitude toward her tiny son. Xu Fengzhen would give birth to nine children in her lifetime, but she had no sense that children ought to be equally treated and equally loved. Ni Yuxian was different from all the others. Even his siblings agree. "Our fate is just ordinary," avows one brother, representing them all. "Yuxian's is special."

The strength of Yuxian's fate seemed to have been sucked from that of his siblings, as though the total quantity of endowments granted to any generation is constant, and those destined for greatness must borrow their strength from others less fortunately endowed. A child whose fate is particularly strong is often thus a danger to other, more ordinary, siblings.

Before he had reached his second year, two of Yuxian's sisters had died on his behalf.

From the moment of little Kunkun's birth, some eighteen months before Yuyu entered the world, everyone knew that the little girl's childhood would be dangerous. She and her father were both born in the year of the ram, and when parent and child are both born in the year of the ram, special protection must be given to the child. Rams have horns and are often unaware of their own strength. Even without intention, the adult ram can do great harm to its tiny offspring. Years later, when little Yuxiu was born in the year of the ox, the family would know enough to send her away to be raised by Xu Fengzhen's older sister. With Kunkun, though, Ni Jizhong hoped that it would be sufficient just to be especially careful.

But when Yuyu arrived, they knew that the strength of his fate would cast an additional negative influence on Kunkun.

Everyone knew, too, that one day Xu Fengzhen's hungry ghost of a brother, Xu Ahe, might try to return. Maybe he would want revenge. Maybe he would simply want a companion. Years earlier, when his father had forced him to marry a village girl he did not want, Ahe and his father had quarreled. Ahe had run away from home, leaving his bewildered young wife behind, and never returned.

Later, the family learned that the youth had joined the army to fight the Japanese. They heard that he had been captured and died. Because he had died away from home and the family never saw the body, he could not be properly buried or mourned and hence had become a hungry ghost. It was only to be expected that one day he would return to earth.

A few months after the fortune-teller had come, and while Ni Jizhong was away on one of his periodic peddling trips, little Kunkun suddenly became frighteningly ill. That night, alone with the two children, Xu Fengzhen lay on the bed with Kunkun behind her and Yuyu nursing at her breast. Kunkun was feverish and cranky, crying and scratching at her mother's back. "Mama," the little girl begged, "'I'm afraid." But Xu Fengzhen continued nursing her infant son.

Suddenly, there was a loud sound of thunder and the whooshing of wind. The door opened and Xu Fengzhen saw her younger brother, his body covered in blood, his hands and feet manacled in heavy, clanking chains, accompanied by officials of yore. Xu Fengzhen knew her brother had come to seize a companion. She hugged Yuyu tightly to her breast to protect him from the hungry ghost.

Just as suddenly as Xu Fengzhen's brother appeared, he evaporated. The darkened room, lit only by a small oil lamp, was still.

When Xu Fengzhen turned to Kunkun, the little girl was dead.

• • •

"Kunkun died of scarlet fever," Ni Jizhong argued when he returned. "With the proper medicine, she could have been saved."

Xu Fengzhen did not dispute her husband, but she knew too that Kunkun had died because her hungry ghost brother was lonely and needed a partner in the netherworld. He would have preferred to take Yuyu, of course, because Yuyu was male and his destiny was great. But little Kunkun had sacrificed herself on Yuyu's behalf. Everyone in the family agreed that even as a tiny child, Kunkun was very smart and really understood the ways of the world. Even as Dr. Ni lay dying and the family was gathered round, they all still agreed that Kunkun had sacrificed her life for her brother. Her sacrifice only strengthened the belief that Yuxian's destiny was great.

• • •

So did the death of Ni Yuxian's younger sister.

• • •

Yuxian's baby sister was born when he was eighteen months old and died before she had been in the world a month. The rate of infant mortality was high in those days, and most families accepted the fact that one or more of their children would die before reaching adulthood. That was one of the reasons they had so many. Families even waited until a baby had lived a month before celebrating its birth. That was how long it usually took for the infections transmitted by unsanitary delivery techniques to claim an infant life.

That everyone agreed that Yuyu's baby sister had died of disease did not reduce the significance of her death for the future of Ni Yuxian. She, too, had died that he might live and accomplish mighty deeds. The destiny that everyone already knew to be great became weightier still.

Thus, from the time he was able to know anything at all, Ni Yuxian knew that he was no ordinary male. Everything about his childhood conspired to convince him that he was exceptional, endowed with powers beyond the ordinary and destined for greatness. He grew into his lofty role with apparent ease. His confidence in his ability, in his intelligence, his looks, and his charm, his belief in his destiny, began at his mother's breast and only blossomed as he grew. "I always thought that I could do anything," he recalls, "if only I wanted it badly enough."

The same sense of destiny that fed his growing ego would also profoundly influence his attitude toward the opposite sex. That females sacrificed themselves for his own growth was to become not merely a fact from his childhood but also the expectation of his adulthood, and the demands he made on the women closest to him would be high. He expected from them the same loyalty his little sisters had given, believing that they would be willing to sacrifice their lives on his behalf should he or the situation require.

• • •

While his hair was still tied in the traditional pigtail and before he was old enough to wear clothes, while his fat, rounded tummy still protruded from beneath the square silver choker around his neck, Yuxian learned both how to charm and how to use that charm to his own advantage. From the time he could walk, he could also sing, and often of an early evening he would set out from Guansheng's home, his older sister trailing shyly behind, to serenade his fellow villagers as they prepared their evening meals. The serenades were rewarded often with dinner, a welcome economy to the poor but growing family. Yuyu's repertoire of folk songs grew, together with his confidence and charm. Often he sang for his supper. Everyone in the village came to know him.

Knowing that he would not die until he had become a hero, the little boy deliberately courted danger, daring to do what other little children would not. He insisted on learning to ride a bicycle long before other boys his age, and soon thrilled at the speed he could attain by grabbing on to the rare tractor that occasionally passed along the public road. When he fell into the canal before he had learned to swim and was fished out by nearby adults, the lesson he learned was not fear of danger but his own invulnerability. Knowing he was invulnerable, Yuxian saw himself a hero. He came to revel in danger, developing a flair for the dramatic. "I knew that however dangerous the situation, I would always be saved," he says. "Some one or some thing would always save me."

• • •

There were those among Ni Yuxian's relatives who recognized that the lusty, carefree, devil-may-care ebullience the young boy both inherited from his grandfather and learned anew in his arms every day would somehow have to be restrained. Entrance into Chinese society would necessitate playing by its rules. To Yuxian's Grandmother Xu, Xu Fengzhen's mother, fell the task of instruction in matters of morality. From her Yuyu learned right from wrong and the moral underpinnings of society.

Grandmother Xu's view of the universe was typical of rural folk. The universe, she taught, was divided into three closely connected and interrelated spheres. In heaven were the gods, on earth were men, and in the netherworld were ghosts. Each sphere was governed by a supreme leader who on earth, by whatever other name (president, or party chairman, for instance) some might wish to label him, was the emperor. In recent years, she had heard that people were calling the emperor "president" and later he would be known as the party chairman, but to her those leaders were still the emperor. Because the emperor had originally been a dragon who lived in the stars, the choice of the earthly ruler remained not with men but with heaven, although in times of turmoil heaven's mandate was often unclear, and there were sometimes pretenders to the throne.

Yuan Shikai was one such pretender to the throne. Yuxian would be in middle school before he learned that Yuan Shikai, who had tried but failed to declare himself emperor in 1915 was Chinese and not foreign, a ranking military commander who had taken over as head of the new republic shortly after the collapse of the Qing dynasty in 1911. From Grandmother Xu he learned that Yuan Shikai was not only a pretender to the throne but a big-nosed, blue-eyed foreigner as well. When Yuan Shikai had attempted physically to assume the wooden dragon throne, she explained, the carved dragons that served as arms to the throne suddenly came alive, wrapping themselves around the would-be usurper and crushing him to death.

Historians have failed to record the incident of the dragons coming to life, preferring instead to attribute Yuan's death to natural causes. Some, though, say he died of a broken heart after failing in his bid to become emperor.

Chiang Kai-shek, according to Grandmother Xu, was probably another such pretender, as witnessed largely by the fact that his bid to power ultimately failed. On the question of Mao Zedong, there was still some confusion. He was more likely the real emperor, as evidenced not only by his defeat of Chiang Kai-shek but also by the fact that his face was that of an emperor—southern by birth, Mao had a northerner's face, just as the emperor invariably sat with his back to the north, facing south, and there was a large mole in the middle of the chin. The mole was decisive. It put heaven and earth in balance.

Grandmother Xu's morality was based on a system of retribution, if not in this life then in the hereafter. Good eventually would be rewarded with good. Evil would be repaid with evil.

After people die, Yuyu learned, they become ghosts and return to the netherworld for judgment. "If you are bad on earth," Grandmother Xu explained, "then in the netherworld maybe you will be thrown into a fire, or put in hot oil and fried, and next time you come back you will be a pig or a horse or an ox."

During heavy rainstorms, when it began to thunder, Grandmother Xu would explain that the dragon in heaven was angry, beating someone who had done wrong on earth. She and little Yuxian would kneel down together to beg for god's forgiveness. Later, she would often join other village women at the local temple to burn incense to placate the angry gods. Or she would stop in the Christian church to light a candle. She saw no great distinction, or at least no particular contradiction, between burning incense or lighting a candle. God was still in heaven and an angry god was an angry god. The attraction of Christianity was in the beauty of its songs, accompanied always by a magnificent organ, and the fact that at times of natural disaster, the Christians distributed food and clothing for free. Grandmother Xu's religious exclusivity began only after the Communists insisted that Christianity was both foreign and imperialist, after which she was given to excesses of Buddhism.

Grandmother Xu's cardinal moral rule was that rice must never be wasted, not even a single grain. On this point she was not only teacher but taskmaster, interrogating her grandson frequently about his relationship with food. "Did you waste any grain today?" she would ask. "Did you leave the table before you finished eating? If you do not eat everything at the table then when you die you will become a ghost." Admonitions against beating and other forms of violence were secondary to issues of food.

Both her Buddhism and her Christianity counseled Grandmother Xu in the importance of performing good works. "If you are good," she preached, "then after you die and come back to earth you can become a human being again. Maybe you could even grow up in a really good family."

"If you are really good," Grandmother Xu taught, "then maybe when you die you will become a star." Not only were emperors descended from the stars but so were all the best people on earth— the great scholars and ministers and military heroes. To become a star necessitated being a vegetarian on earth and performing an overwhelming number of good deeds. Short of securing one's place as a star, the performance of good deeds on earth would surely bring benefit to one's descendants.

Grandmother Xu never exactly said she wanted to become a star, but she was preoccupied with doing good deeds. Yuxian's propensity to do good works was no doubt instilled through her. From the time Yuxian could walk, the family remembers him sharing his rice with the sundry beggars who came to their door. Once when a woman from one of the boats along the canal came begging, the whole family teased him, agreeing that he was adopted and the beggar woman was his real mother. He ran to the poor woman, offering her a bowl of rice and crying because his mother had no food to eat. He was confused when the woman left on the boat without him.

• • •

From his early courtships with danger and from the uproariously serious swashbuckling battles the village children frequently staged, his family naturally assumed that Yuxian's future path to glory rested with the military. War permeated the young boy's life. Not only was he raised on the traditional folk stories of rebellion and war—*Water Margin* and the *Romance of the Three Kingdoms*—but China had just driven out the Japanese invaders and was again at war with itself.

The children's games more often imitated folklore than life. During the elaborate preparations for battle, childhood's imagination temporarily transformed the canal that ran behind the Ni family home into the Yangtze Jiang, the grandest river of them all. In the frequent and clandestine planning sessions held to plot strategy, Yuxian remembers that he always naturally emerged as the leader. His rank in battle was never lower than general, a title instantly recognized by all combatants from the paper insignia glued to his back and from his father's surreptitiously borrowed galoshes which hindered mobility but were a necessary a part of any young village general's attire.

Their battles rivaled in strategic significance and daring the battles between Cao Cao and Zhuge Liang handed down through history by the legendary *Romance of the Three Kingdoms,* and the bravery in battle of young General Ni was legion, too—or so he remembers today. When the hostile forces lined up on either side of their Yangtze River, hollow bamboo poles serving as their cannon and hardened, unripe berries or tightly wadded paper their ammunition, no one was a more enthusiastic combatant than Yuxian. Filled with hardened berries that were replenished frequently from the soldiers' pockets, the cannon reached all the way across the river, fired by rapidly jamming another, slimmer pole through the barrel. They fought with bamboo bows and arrows, too.

But the slingshot was the mightiest weapon of them all. Globs of dirt mixed with water, dried, and baked over fire, delivered a ferocious blow when shot from one of their slingshots. Yuxian's bravery was recognized when he never cried after being knocked on the head with hardened mudcakes.

Sometime after Yuxian was six years old, the repertoire of village war games expanded. The idea began after the children were taken on an exciting excursion by wooden ferry across the Huangpu River to see a movie in the city of Shanghai. Made in North Korea about the Korean War that had broken out in June 1950, and entitled *Korean Children's Guerrilla Squad,* it was the first movie Yuxian had ever seen.

The movie was terrifying. The children had already been taught something of American treachery in China and of the country's collusion with Chiang Kai-shek. They had been told that China was swarming with American spies and that the United States was engaged in germ warfare with China and that it had dropped many bombs filled with rats that in turn had been infected with lethal and contagious diseases designed to destroy the Chinese race. They knew the candy that Americans were dropping like bombs was really poison and that the toys and pens scattered by the United States might explode if a child picked them up. Honesty everywhere blossomed as young children knew to report any stray object to the local police station.

The children were still not prepared for what they saw on the screen. They screamed in terror when they saw pictures of the American soldiers tying cute little North Korean kids together, stringing them up, beating them, and finally stabbing them to death with bayonets. Some shots even showed the soldiers pouring gasoline over the little children and burning them to death.

For days thereafter, Yuxian could not sleep. He kept thinking of the lovable Korean children and how brutally the American soldiers had killed them.

The idea for adding the Korean War to the repertoire of childhood battles was given additional impetus by the parades that were staged with predictable regularity during Yuxian's early childhood—on May 1 for Worker's Day, on July 1 for the Communist Party's birthday, on October 1 to celebrate the founding of "new China," and on October 17 to celebrate the Russian Revolution. Everyone would participate, adults and children alike, and the content was predictable too. Huge posters of Party Chairman Mao Zedong and Marshal Zhu De, preeminent leader of the People's Liberation Army, dominated the first few rows. Then came hundreds of red flags with slogans like "Long Live the Chinese Communist Party," "Long Live Mao Zedong," or "Long Live Zhu De." The most important slogan, though, was "Down with American Imperialism," and the best part of the parade was all the people who got to dress up like Uncle Sam. The Uncle Sams would smear white paste over their faces, stick pieces of paper over their noses to make them big (were not Westerners known collectively as "big noses"?), and add a false beard to their chins. They would wear a tall hat and a cape and carry a wooden gun.

Uncle Sam would be accompanied by a group of dejected American soldiers dressed in ragged clothes, since, after all, American imperialism was in the final throes of death, on the verge of defeat by the courageous Chinese volunteers. Surrounding Uncle Sam and the dejected American soldiers would be scores of Chinese volunteers expressing righteous indignation against the American imperialists. The task of Uncle Sam and the American soldiers for the duration of the parade was to fall helpless on the ground in face of righteous Chinese indignation, get up, and fall again, repeatedly getting up and falling while simultaneously moving forward with the slowly progressing parade.

The addition of the American imperialists to the war games of Cao Family Village allowed for substantially less diversity than local renditions from the *Romance of the Three Kingdoms*. The role of Uncle Sam and the American soldiers was rather limiting. "Hello. Hello," Uncle Sam and the soldiers would repeat. "Okay. Okay. Okay." After suitable repetitions of hello and and okay, and many dramatic displays of cowardice, Uncle Sam and the American soldiers would throw up their arms and fall helplessly to the ground. *"Wo touxiang,"* they would all shout in a torrent of giggles. "I surrender."

Predictable and limiting though the role may have been, Yuxian reveled in playing Uncle Sam. The top hat and cape and white powdered face were departures from his standard war attire, and the slab of paper pasted across his nose was a touch of reality that rendered the role particularly satisfying. And nothing was more fun than the hellos and okays and falling helplessly on his back, convulsed in giggles, in abject comic surrender.

Few would have guessed that the little boy who had so thrilled to the role of Uncle Sam would finally eschew the military and follow the political path to glory. No one could have known that the same Ni Yuxian who had once so playfully succumbed as Uncle Sam would find himself one day as a supplicant before the American consulate in Shanghai in flight from arrest by the government he had so repeatedly challenged.

• • •

Ni Yuxian was barely four years old when the Communists took over his village. It is one of his first memories of being alive.

When his family saw the Guomindang forces fleeing and heard that the Communists soon would come, they joined the stream of country folk fleeing from the villages across the Huangpu River into the international settlement of Shanghai. In times of trouble, everyone believed, the international settlement would be protected.

So enchanted was Yuxian by the bright lights and the high buildings of the city, so fascinated was he by all its cars, that he barely sensed the danger or felt his parents' fear. It was the first time the little boy had been to the city.

When they returned to Cao Family Village, the Nationalist flag had already been lowered from the village primary school and the red, five-starred flag of the Communists had been hoisted in its place. The family courtyard and the road in front had been occupied by Communist troops, nearly a hundred men in all, and their horses. Doors from scattered houses throughout the village had been removed and lined up in the courtyard to serve as the soldiers' beds. Most of the soldiers had been in the Nationalist army just a few weeks before. They spoke the northern dialect unintelligible to the people of Shanghai, but even without listening to their speech, it was easy to tell that the soldiers were not from Shanghai but the north. The whole courtyard reeked of garlic, which the more fastidious southerners never ate precisely because it reeked.

The soldiers took a liking to little Yuxian, often sharing their garlicky food with him and riding him around the courtyard on the backs of their horses. They were polite to the Ni family, too, and everyone concluded that the PLA soldiers were much better than those of the Guomindang.

Not long after the Communist army arrived, a military committee was established to oversee the transfer of political power from the Guomindang to the Communists. It was then that the Cao Family villagers discovered there had been an underground Communist Party cell in the area for years. In Cao Family Village, they learned, Zhu Bing had long led the local underground.

Zhu Bing was one of the few villagers to have been educated. He had had six years of schooling, graduating from lower middle school at the same time as Ni Jizhong. He knew a little bit of science and history and some geography, too—like where Europe was and how many countries there were in the world. He may even have studied a little foreign language. So rare was education in the Shanghai countryside that six years of education entitled him to wear the long, high-necked robe of the scholar.

Zhu Bing became head of the military committee for the whole district. He collaborated with other local underground party members in identifying local suspects.

It was after Zhu Bing became head of the military committee that the executions of village leaders began.

•   •   •

There are those, looking back, who remember the early years after the communist takeover with a special fondness, as the "golden years" of Chinese socialism. China, after all, was finally united and at peace after two long and debilitating wars—first the Japanese invasion that began in 1937 and then, following right on its heels in 1945, the civil war between the Nationalists and the Communists. Indeed, China had not known real peace since its defeat at the hands of the British during the Opium War more than a century earlier. The Opium War had opened up an era during which foreign powers nibbled away at China's sovereignty, never really colonizing it but never leaving it fully in peace, either.

Shanghai owed much of its vibrancy and richness to foreign powers. It had been not much more than a lazy fishing town when it was forced to open itself as a treaty port following the Opium War in 1840, when first the British, then the French and other Europeans, and finally the Japanese came in to establish internationally governed settlements aloof from Chinese law.

The country had been rent internally, too, first from the massive Taiping Rebellion that lasted from 1850 to 1864 and left some 30 million dead and then from the gradual but inexorable corrosion of dynastic authority that followed. When the Qing dynasty collapsed of its own weight in 1911, neither Sun Yat-sen, the father of the ill-fated new republic, nor Yuan Shikai, who tried first to govern the country as a republic and then attempted to install himself as a new emperor, were capable of uniting China under a single, stable government. China disintegrated into a series of competing warlord satrapies.

Chiang Kai-shek was ultimately able to establish a tenuous new central authority, but even his new government was quickly rent asunder first from the ongoing threat of the Communists, then by the Japanese invasion, and later by the rampant corruption and galloping inflation he seemed unwilling or unable to stop. Many Chinese welcomed the new communist government as the only alternative to the evil the Guomindang had become.

With the country united and at peace, and so many people brimming with hope at what the new government might bring, the communist takeover ushered in a new era of optimism and cooperation. Socialism, finally, might be able to solve the problems of economic underdevelopment and political inequality that had mired China in backwardness even as the West had prospered.

But what for some was a new epoch of euphoria and hope and

was genuinely heralded as "liberation" was for others a nightmare of terror and fear. The communist takeover was followed in the rural areas by an often violent consolidation of political power and a massive land reform that at once redistributed land and property from the rich to the poor and often witnessed the execution of those deemed to have been landlords, Guomindang collaborators, or village leaders.

•   •   •

In the Cao Family Village, the communist takeover was peaceful. Its rule was consolidated by force. The optimism that swept some sectors of Chinese society with "liberation" did not extend to the Cao Family Village—or at least not to the Ni family who lived there. Ni Yuxian's childhood was filled with terror and with incidents of unforgettable cruelty.

It is the trials and the executions that are Yuxian's ineradicable memory of the times.

When the trials began, the children of the village were torn between an overwhelming curiosity to witness the spectacle and terrified at what they might see. Attended by tens, hundreds, and sometimes by thousands of people, the trials were held in schools or in sports stadiums, in public parks or open fields. Sometimes, the better to dispose of the bodies afterward, they were simply staged on the grounds of a cemetery.

The trials were simple. The verdicts had been determined in advance. With the accused standing silently, heads bowed, a party cadre would stand before the audience and recite the names and the crimes of those about to be punished. Often, the verdict was death. The punishment was carried out immediately.

Families of the accused were not allowed to attend the trials, and many of them were too frightened even to wait outside. But Yuxian and his little playmates sneaked into meetings where the families did wait outside, not daring to weep, standing next to the cheap caskets of thin white wood or woven reed matting that would enclose the bodies of their husbands or sons once the bullet went through the head. When families were too frightened to come, the bodies were simply dumped in mass graves or left in the open to be eaten by wild dogs.

The memory of the execution Yuxian witnessed has haunted him all his life.

Yuxian often accompanied his maternal grandmother to the

bustling marketplace at Zhoudiadu. While she shopped for vegetables and household necessities and chatted with sundry neighbors and friends, he sat in a little bookstall, looking at comic books and teaching himself to read.

It was around the time of the lunar new year in February 1950 and a light rain was falling the day Ni Yuxian and Grandmother Xu witnessed the executions.

The marketplace was particularly crowded at this time, as villagers from all around prepared for the feasts that accompanied the most important holiday of the year. Just as the rickshaw that was transporting Yuxian and his grandmother approached the village school on the outskirts of town, the road became crowded and noisy, the milling throng excited. Grandmother Xu suddenly became agitated. "Faster," she urged the rickshaw driver. "Faster, don't stop."

But the crowd was too thick. The rickshaw could not get through. Little Yuxian stood up in the carriage to see what was happening.

Just before him, only a few yards away at the edge of a field, a dozen or so men were kneeling in the dirt, their hands tied behind their backs with rope. They were thin and young—none could have been more than thirty years old—and their clothes were tattered and patched. They wore black cloth shoes and no socks.

Three soldiers from the People's Liberation Army, their legs tied from the ankles to the knees in cloth strips that were said to prevent fatigue on marches, stood behind one of the young men, Hausers in hand. The executions had already begun. Three or four men lay in the mud, and the mud was stained red with their blood.

As Yuxian stood up to look, he saw a gun being held directly to the base of the condemned man's skull and watched as the shot was fired. The man fell over like a rock. The young boy had not known that a bullet could have such force. The man's head hit the dirt in front of him.

"He looked like a chicken when it dies," Ni Yuxian remembers. Blood was flowing from his mouth and his head. "The man didn't stop breathing. He couldn't die. His legs just kept kicking—rapidly kicking. I could see that this guy was in agony. He wore such poor clothes, full of rips, and he was so thin his ribs were sticking out. But the thing that made the most lasting impression was that as his legs were kicking, his shoes fell off. It was so ugly—all that blood coming out of his head."

Just next to the man who was having such a hard time dying, Yuxian saw local peasants, uneducated and almost as poor as the men who had been shot, lined up and hovering over the men who had already died. They were using bean curd skin, thin as paper but very strong, to scoop out small pieces of the dead men's brains. As they put the human brains into their mouths, the people watching were spellbound and frightened. "*Ze, ze, ze,*" was the sound they made.

The people eating the brains were frightened, too. They were eating the brains for their health. Uneducated villagers in traditional China often sought strength from eating the brains and drinking the blood of executed criminals. Lu Xun, China's preeminent twentieth-century writer, had satirized such practices in his short stories.

"Something is wrong with those men," Grandmother Xu gasped, increasingly desperate as they remained stranded in front of this scene. "Don't look."

She grabbed little Yuyu, trying to shield him from the sight with her body. "Back up," she shouted to the rickshaw driver, "go back." As the rickshaw backed slowly out of the crowd, Yuxian could hear the gun continuing to fire, one shot at the back of each head.

"You mustn't think about it," Grandmother Xu had instructed her young charge as they headed back toward home. She began chattering about other things, telling him the stories he most loved to hear, such as how the emperors all came from the stars and how the big-nosed blue-eyed foreigner, Yuan Shikai, had tried to usurp the throne.

But the stories his grandmother told that day would not erase the little boy's memory. He remained afraid. He never knew what crime the men who had been executed committed, or whether they had committed any crime at all. But he knew they had died a cruel and agonizing death and that they had been helpless to resist. In war, he thought, at least soldiers have a chance to fight back.

It was his first confrontation with evil, his first discovery of a world that was savage, brutal, and unfair. "I didn't want the world to be like that," he recalls. Later, when prudence dictated that he turn away, Yuxian continued to insist on staring evil in the face.

• • •

It was not long after this event that Cao Yuanming paid a special visit to the Ni family home. Cao Yuanming had been one of the village leaders—the head of the *bao*, responsible for overseeing one hundred families.

Most people who had held any leadership positions under the Nationalists had the good sense to flee. The village was wary about what communism would bring, and the route to Hong Kong was still open. Cao Yuanming had thought of escaping, but his wife was reluctant. Even as the executions began, Cao Yuanming continued to hope that his position as a lesser leader would win him a reprieve.

Accompanied by his big black dog, Cao Yuanming came that evening especially to see little Yuxian. Villagers knew that eldest male children were possessed of special, almost mystical, insight, that they could often see the future and predict the truth. Ni Yuxian, as not only the eldest son but as one well known to be specially endowed, could be depended upon to see the future with particular clarity. Word of the little child's fortune had been shared throughout the village. Neighbors had already taken to calling him *xiao da hao*—"little man of extraordinary powers."

"*Xiao da hao*," Cao Yuanming addressed the child, "is Uncle Cao going to die?"

"Of course Uncle Cao is going to die," the child responded without hesitation.

Cao Yuanming's face froze and his skin went pale.

Xu Fengzhen grabbed her young son and took him into an adjoining room. "How could you say such a thing to Uncle Cao?" she demanded.

Two days later, when troops from the People's Liberation Army came to round up people from all over the Pudong area, they came to Cao Yuanming's home, too. They roped him together with other prisoners and took him across the river to Longhua Park. The park had been transformed, serving simultaneously as gigantic outdoor prison and execution grounds.

Not long thereafter Ni Jizhong saw Cao Yuaniming's name in the newspaper on the list of local village leaders who had been executed.

He took his young son by the hand and together they went to extend their condolences to the dead man's widow.

Arriving in the Cao family courtyard, they were greeted by a remarkable sight. "She has gone crazy," Ni Jizhong muttered when he saw the scene before them.

Many people were standing about outside the Cao family

house. In front, in the courtyard, was the casket containing Cao Yuanming's body. Cao's wife was addressing the assembled group. The voice of Cao's widow, though, was the voice of a man, and everyone recognized it immediately as the voice of her husband. The villagers all knew that when a person died, his soul could— and often did—enter another's body, particularly if the deceased had unfinished business at his death. "I am Cao Yuanming," his wife was saying. "I have committed no crime. I am innocent."

"Brother Jizhong," she said to Ni Jizhong when he entered the courtyard, addressing him in her husband's voice and holding out her hand, "I suffered such a miserable death. And I was innocent, you know."

• • •

Public executions continued around the Cao Family Village throughout 1950, the first year following the arrival of the Communists. Reading the newspaper lists became a daily ritual in the Ni family household. Every evening, Ni Jizhong would share with the family the news of which of their acquaintances or friends or local notables had been killed. Many of the villagers continued to be drawn by some combination of curiosity and fear to witness the shootings.

Not just the actual opponents of the new regime were executed but potential ones, too. Fear pervaded the village, as friends and neighbors were imprisoned or taken away to labor reform camps. One evening they would be there in the village, having dinner with family or friends, and the next day they would disappear, sometimes not to be heard from for years. Often, the reasons seemed minor, like listening to radio broadcasts from the United States.

One of the Ni family relatives was arrested for listening to American broadcasts.

When the call had gone out for villagers to turn in their short-wave radios, the relative had failed to comply. When he denied having listened to foreign broadcasts, the police refused to believe him. That the radio had been dusted was certain proof he had been listening to American broadcasts. For this crime, the relative spent twenty years away, the first ten in prison and the last on a labor reform camp in Anhui Province.

The families of those sent away instantly become both destitute and pariahs. In the early 1950s, most women of Cao Family Village were ordinary housewives, not yet in the habit of earning a living. Their family property was confiscated when their husbands were arrested—or any of it that might fetch money, such as gold, jewelry, and fine furniture. Because they were wives of counterrevolutionaries, other villagers feared contact with them. No one would talk to them, let alone come to their aid.

Often such a woman would divorce her imprisoned husband in the hope of finding another man willing to support her and her children. But such a woman was not at all desirable from the potential husband's point of view. Her new husband was usually so impoverished, so uneducated, and so generally unattractive that no other woman would want him.

The lessons of the executions and the imprisonments were clear. If anyone did anything to oppose the communist leadership, he too could be executed or sent away.

Guansheng became outspokenly anticommunist. "You see that clock's cock?" he would ask, pointing to the pendulum of the family's grandfather clock. "I once knew a man so rich he made ten thousand yuan with every swing of that cock. But he was poor compared to Mao Zedong. Mao is the biggest landlord of them all and the biggest capitalist, too. He's taking all our land, all our property, and making it his own."

But Yuxian's parents were frightened of such talk and frequently warned their son against talking too much. "It's too dangerous," they would say. "If you talk, you'll be locked up."

The little boy felt it strange not to be able to speak the truth. Silence was not a lesson he learned well, and often he insisted on speaking out when the emperor wore no clothes. The child, after all, was invulnerable and imbued with the power of life and death. He saw the truth even when adults could not.

Most adults in the village feared for their lives, however, and hence would not dare to oppose the new government. During the campaign to suppress counterrevolutionaries in 1952–1953, more people were arrested and some were executed. By then, however, the lessons of 1950 had been learned. Fewer people were killed, and the new wave of executions was less visible, less highly publicized.

Before, no one in Cao Family Village had thought too much about political leadership. Local leaders were fellow villagers sometimes a little better educated and often more worldly-wise, but really not greatly different from anyone else. Village leaders had cooperated with the Guomindang less from any well-articulated sense of support than simply because the government was the government in power. No one ever quite understood why the Communists executed so many village leaders. With all the older leaders executed or gone, however, the nature of village leadership changed. When Cao Yuanming had visited his fellow villagers, he was sometimes accompanied by his dog. When the new village head went to pay a call, he went like an official of old, whose arrival had been announced by the beating of a gong and whose path had been cleared by the shooing of bamboo rods. He came accompanied by a large entourage—the deputy head of the village, his secretary, the head of the militia, the representative of the women's federation, and four or five young activists trying to ingratiate themselves with the local powers. The villagers were afraid.

2

The primary school in Cao Family Village was a peaceful place, dappled with gardens and dotted with elegant, old-fashioned, wood-lined buildings centered around a series of courtyards. The grounds had once served as home to the richest landlord in the area. At the age of six, bookbag casually slung over his shoulder, Yuxian walked through its gates filled with the same naive aplomb, insatiable curiosity, and irrepressible exuberance that he brought to his childhood games and village performances. Impervious to rules and accustomed to creating dramas with himself at center stage, the six-year-old boy soon came into conflict with school authorities. The responsibility of Chinese educators was to tame the likes of Ni Yuxian.

Yuxian, though, would never be easily reined, making instead virtue out of conflict. At school, the little boy discovered in himself new and previously unsuspected talents.

Trouble was not long in coming. The first incident of note centered around a small dog.

When Teacher Chen was startled one morning to have her lessons insistently interrupted by the sound of a barking puppy, she was not surprised to discover that the sound was emanating from the vicinity of Ni Yuxian's desk. Yuxian had recently acquired a habit of nurturing small animals. He had traveled some distance to obtain the blond and white long-haired *Shih Tzu* that had accompanied him to school that day. Teacher Chen ordered Yuxian to stay after school to discuss the breach of rules.

"So, Yuxian, you have brought a barking puppy to school," Teacher Chen began gently. She handed him a piece of the gold-colored, hardened rice that sticks to the bottom of the pan when the grain is cooked too long and which can then be used to make sizzling rice soup. The rice cake had been dipped in sugar.

The little boy had never tasted anything so delicious. "This is my punishment?" Yuxian wondered as he munched on the sweet.

"Maybe you can explain why you brought the puppy to school," Teacher Chen encouraged the boy.

"Oh, yes, of course, Teacher Chen, I can explain," Yuxian responded fervently. He was beginning to like this teacher. "The puppy is a living creature and deserves to continue living. But if I didn't bring him to class with me, maybe some cruel person would find him and beat him to death. Or maybe the puppy would run away and get lost and starve to death. It is my responsibility to protect the little creature, you see. Without me, it might die. I had to bring it to school." Yuxian was brimming over with sincerity.

"Yuxian should become an orator when he grows up," Teacher Chen told Yuxian's parents when she delivered the child to his home. "He speaks very persuasively. He is very smart."

Teacher Chen's remark left a deep impression on Yuxian. His first open confrontation with authority had been satisfyingly successful. For defying the rules, he had been rewarded with the most delicious treat he had ever tasted and praise that swelled his heart. The teacher had discovered a previously unrecognized talent. The naughty boy began cultivating the gentle art of persuasion. He would not turn rebel for several more years, but his naturally incorrigible instincts had received unexpected nurturing.

Yuxian's time in primary school was a tug-of-war between recalcitrant pupil and exasperated teachers, with the young boy devoting most of his energy to inventing anew the age-old tricks of the mischievous schoolboy. His teachers lamented the young boy's misplaced creative energy, arguing that if he devoted to study only a fraction of the time he indulged in pranks his grades could be the best in the school.

Putting frogs in the teacher's chalkbox was Yuxian's favorite and most frequently repeated prank, a trick that was certain to draw a scream from the teacher and gales of laughter from the students, with Yuxian laughing most heartily of all. The young boy was also fond of tying young girls' pigtails to desks and suspending brooms over doors such that the broom crashed to the floor when the teacher came in. He reveled in putting caps under young girls' chairs and listening to them scream at the bang that exploded when they pushed the chairs back. Once he managed to paste the answers to a test on the teacher's back.

As the child grew, he learned to seek allies in his frequent clashes with school authorities. His transformation from independent prankster to leader of a minor boycott was directed against the opposite sex.

"This is embarrassing," Yuxian complained the day their teacher explained the principles of folk dancing, where everyone was expected to hold hands in a boy-girl, boy-girl circle. "I don't want to hold hands with a girl. I don't want to dance."

Impulsively, he decided to organize a boycott. "Let's all refuse," he urged his fellow males. "Let's all not dance." His schoolmates equally impulsively agreed.

"It's feudalist not to want to dance," the teacher chided when the sulking boys confronted her with their decision. "If you don't dance, you will be punished."

Authority naturally prevailed. The boys danced. Only Yuxian continued to refuse.

"You are the youngest in the class," the teacher admonished him in frustration, "but your thinking is the oldest. How can you be so backward?" She nicknamed him Lao Wangu—Old Diehard. The name—and the attitude—stuck.

Not easily dissuaded, Old Diehard persisted in his organizational efforts, his defiance of authority, and his antagonism toward girls. His first major, organized rebellion was also directed against the opposite sex. It began, and was defeated, on the first day of Yangsi Junior Middle School.

Set magnificently amid verdant, well-tended gardens and stately old pines, its low, tiled bungalows serving as classrooms, Yangsi Middle School was also located on the estate of a former landlord.

The separation of the sexes within the classroom was a hallowed principle in rural China, where even the consent to educate females was a modern phenomenon. Yuxian was well settled into middle school before he had spoken a single word to any contemporary female besides his sister. But the new homeroom teacher, Li Fojiao—Li Who Believes in Buddhism—was a particularly progressive man. Having spent many years in Hong Kong, he even wore a necktie. Buddhist Li returned to his native Shanghai after 1949 to make his contribution to the fledgling revolution. On the first day of middle school, he defied tradition by assigning boys to sit with girls.

Yuxian was indignant. This was a matter of honor. He would not sit with a girl.

To act alone, however, was difficult. Yuxian needed the unified cooperation of his fellow males. Never doubting his ability to lead, he quickly discovered that his indignation was shared. At recess, the boys made a pact not to return to class until Buddhist Li reinstituted the boy-boy, girl-girl arrangement.

The bell rang. The puzzled girls drifted back to the classroom as the boys waited outside, uncomfortably shifting from one foot to the other, staring at the ground, stealing embarrassed glances.

"Why aren't you returning to class?" Buddhist Li inquired.

"We don't want to sit with girls," their spokesman, Ni Yuxian, replied. "We've decided not to go back until boys can sit with boys and girls with girls."

Teacher Li was angry. "You're just trying to get out of studying, aren't you?" he mocked them. "I'll give you five minutes. If you are not all back in your proper seats by then, you will be expelled."

As the clock began ticking, the boys looked hesitantly around. They were not sure how long five minutes was, but knew it would be over quickly. They were terrified of being kicked out of school. Yuxian's oratorical skills were useless. In a flash, he was left alone in the schoolyard.

Teacher Li was still standing near the entrance to the school. He was furious. "So you aren't going in?"

"Not unless you'll change my seat so I can sit with a boy."

Buddhist Li slammed the door with a loud bang. Yuxian could hear the teacher shouting. "If you don't listen to me, you'll be punished," he was yelling. "I'm going to have that old diehard Ni Yuxian kicked out of school."

Yuxian was miserable. He had been kicked out of middle school on the very first day of class. He slung his bookbag over his shoulder and turned to begin walking home.

After a few steps, the door of the schoolroom flew open and Teacher Li strutted briskly out, grabbing Yuxian by the collar. Lifting him off the ground, feet kicking, Teacher Li half pushed and half carried his recalcitrant charge back to the classroom. He threw the young boy onto the seat next to a young girl. Yuxian bounded up from his seat like a basketball. Teacher Li put his hands on the child's shoulders and forced him down again. Yuxian bounced back up. Teacher Li forced the boy down a third time.

"Yuxian is infected by feudal thought," Buddhist Li lectured the class, hands on Yuxian's shoulders. "If he persists in his resistance, if he won't obey his teacher, then I am going to tell his parents and he won't be allowed to come to school."

"Forget it." Yuxian surrendered, settling into his chair, as Buddhist Li continued his sermon. Yuxian stole a glance at the girl sitting next to him. The hapless young thing was ugly. He took out a small knife and carved a line across the bench. For months, he would say not a word to his benchmate, delivering her a determined shove of the elbow whenever she strayed too close to the line.

The energy Yuxian had once devoted to individual pranks was now channeled into organizing his fellow males in an ongoing war between the sexes, with battles alternating between aggressive avoidance and outright bullying. His efforts to organize his fellow males to boycott feminine contact continued.

Before the school's annual observance of the founding of new China, celebrated every October first with a huge bonfire on the playground and singing and dancing that lasted until the wee hours of the morning, Yuxian and his six best buddies took a solemn pledge that they absolutely would not dance that night with girls. But as Yuxian was playing the harmonica and the older students were holding hands as they danced in a huge circle around the bonfire, he noticed from the corner of his eye a couple of his pledgemates sneaking into the circle. They joined hands with girls.

Quickly he organized his fellow holdouts in a minor kidnapping of the offending friends. Sneaking up on them from behind, the young boys clamped their hands over their buddies' eyes and dragged them into a dark and empty classroom. Pulling down their friends' trousers, they slapped red paint on the offenders' behinds. "Traitors," they yelled as their friends struggled to get away.

The partygoers were still in high spirits well after midnight. In the early morning hours, Yuxian and his friends decided to sleep in a classroom rather than venture home in the dangerous, ghost-infested dark. As they moved the desks together for beds and lay down to sleep on the hard wooden tops, an unmistakable buzzing began. The room was infested with hungry, merciless mosquitoes. The boys chose mischief over sleep.

Removing the curtains from the classroom windows, the boys wrapped the sheets around their bodies in the style of Buddhist monks, ends draped over their shoulders, using the wicker baskets that were used as trash containers as hats. Stumbling and giggling and clinging to each other for protection, they made their way furtively to the old pillbox that stood within full sight of the playground. Tripping over their monk costumes and losing their baskets several times, the boys finally managed to crawl on top of the pillbox. Adjusting their robes and straightening their baskets, they linked arms and began chanting the Buddhist prayer. *"Amituo Fo. Amituo Fo. Amituo Fo. Amituo Fo."*

Their presence went unnoticed by those still gathered around the bonfire. Then, after ten minutes of determined chanting, a cry went out. "Ghosts!" someone yelled from the crowd. "Ghosts! Look!" Looking in the direction of the pillbox, everyone saw the ghosts swaying suspended above the ground, chanting the Buddhist prayer. The group around the bonfire remained frozen. "Call the police," someone finally yelled.

"Yes, call the police," the others chimed.

The ghosts had disappeared by the time the police arrived, which only added credibility to the story. The appearance of ghosts was the talk of the school the next day, and from then on, everyone knew that the schoolyard was haunted.

• • •

In time, Yuxian developed his persecution of the opposite sex and the exasperation of his teachers to a fine art. Tao Yuefang was one of his favorite targets.

Tao Yuefang had taken a liking to Yuxian, her sentiments being displayed by accidentally brushing against him as she walked by his desk or bumping into him from her desk just to the rear of his. Believing at first that the physical contact was accidental, Yuxian paid no attention. When he realized that the accidents were actually flirtations, Yuxian was indignant. "Don't you have any face?" he demanded of the young girl in a self-righteously loud voice. "This is really embarrassing." Tao Yuefang blushed a bright red.

Tao Yuefang's demeanor, in fact, was one of perpetual embarrassment. She kept her chin low, and forced her brow into a slight frown, filling her eyes with a slight look of pleading whenever she spoke. Her tiny voice retained a childlike naiveté that Yuxian contemptuously was convinced was false. Yuefang loved to sing, and while she brushed aside compliments with a demure display of modesty, she knew—and wanted everyone else to know—that she sang better than anyone in the class. The displays of modesty, Yuxian knew, were also false.

Yuxian chose the occasion of the music competition to wreak revenge on Tao Yuefang's flirtations.

The whole class gathered together on the day of the competition, and Tao Yuefang was the first to perform. Her hands clasped modestly together at her waist, chin tucked in to just the right measure of innocence, the young girl's clear, sweet voice began an earnest folk song. A soft smile of self-satisfaction spread across her face. She really did sing beautifully. Suddenly she was interrupted by a cacophony of sound—a male chorus simultaneously imitating the long, low howling of wolves, the yapping of dogs, the bleating of sheep, the oinking of pigs. A few clucked like chickens and some bayed like donkeys. It was a veritable Old MacDonald's farm.

"Stop this," the music teacher ordered, banging her fist on the table. "Stop this at once." The giggling chorus broke up.

"Try it again," the teacher instructed Tao Yuefang, having admonished the male chorus to remain silent. Shaken, Tao Yuefang paused. Tentatively she began, her voice less certain, her eyes anxiously searching the faces of her male classmates. Gradually, she picked up confidence. Her sweet voice continued without interruption. Then, suddenly, the wolves began to howl, the pigs began to oink, the lambs began to baa, and the donkeys started to bay. Tao Yuefang was mortified, in tears. The music teacher, having lost all control over her class, rushed to find Buddhist Li.

Order once more was restored. Buddhist Li stood by and gently encouraged Tao Yuefang to begin her song again. But Tao Yuefang was so shaken that she could not go on. Class was dismissed.

Outside in the schoolyard, the boys were jubilant with victory, recounting their conquest with gales of laughter and recaps of their oinks and clucks and howls and yaps. Suddenly Tao Yuefang came dashing out, flailing into the assembled group, heading straight for the ringleader. Crying loudly, she grabbed on to Yuxian, hugging his body and shaking him on the one hand and scratching at his face on the other. Honor prevented him from striking a girl, but the boy dodged her first this way and then that as she continued her unrelenting attack. Then, as she lunged at him again, Yuxian dodged and Tao Yuefang was sent sprawling on the ground.

The young girl was howling loudly. When she began lunging at Yuxian again, the other boys grabbed her arms.

"What do you think you're doing, beating up on girls?" Buddhist Li demanded, rushing upon the scene.

"I didn't hit her," Yuxian insisted in self-defense.

"No girl would hit a boy," Buddhist Li retorted. "You hit her.

You will have to do a self-investigation after class today. If you don't recognize your mistake, you'll be expelled. The whole class will stay to hear you."

"I absolutely did not hit her," Yuxian declared at the meeting. He looked around desperately at his male classmates who had witnessed the fight, hoping that one of them would come forward in his defense. No one dared to speak.

Then, from the back of the room, Wang Weidi stood up. Wang Weidi was three years older than Yuxian and the tallest girl in the class. She was a champion basketball player, and her Mandarin was the best in the whole county. Her father was the head of the local police station and the respect accorded to him extended to his daughter as well. She was the leader of the Young Pioneers.

"Teacher Li," Wang Weidi began, "Yuxian didn't hit Tao Yuefang. Tao Yuefang hit him. I saw it."

Buddhist Li was momentarily stunned. Wang Weidi would not lie. "Oh," he stammered. "Well. Good. Then let's forget this. But next time, let's not have any fights with girl students. Okay, Yuxian, you can come to class tomorrow."

Yuxian had been saved by a girl.

• • •

Yuxian's transition from family to school was a time of transition for China, too, as the remnants of Nationalist power were destroyed and the Communists began consolidating their rule and building a new social—and socialist—order. The Ni family would never look back on the early 1950s as the "golden years," and they would never appreciate communist rule, but life for the Nis nonetheless improved under the new order.

Ni Jizhong got work at a small medical clinic in the market town of Zhoudiadu owned and run by his teacher, an old and highly respected doctor of traditional Chinese medicine. For the first time in his life, he had a steady, predictable income. Food was not abundant, but the family no longer went hungry. The family rarely ate meat or fish or eggs, but they had vegetables and rice. Yuxian often had no real clothes of his own. He wore his father's old, hopelessly large shirts to school. But he no longer wandered the streets naked.

There were undercurrents of tension. Just a few short years after Ni Jizhong joined the clinic, word came that it would be nationalized. The owner, Jizhong's teacher, fled in anticipation to

Taiwan. When the clinic was indeed taken over by the state, the communist government appointed as the director the son of the man who had once been the largest brothel owner in Shanghai. The son was cut from the same fabric as the father, an uncouth and uneducated lout devoid of any qualification to run a medical clinic. By right, the man deserved to be in jail.

When the opportunity came to raise the matter with the local authorities, Ni Jizhong did. The accusation caused considerable uproar, and as the decision hung in the balance, so did Dr. Ni's job. But the investigation proved the justice of Ni Jizhong's allegations. The scoundrel was dismissed from his post and sentenced to eight years in jail.

Justice did not always prevail. Good and decent people kept coming under attack.

One of Yuxian's cousins, Ni Yuzhang, had been orphaned at an early age. Yuzhang's mother had died when he was just an infant, and his father had died of sheer poverty during the Japanese invasion. The child was sent to an orphanage run by American missionaries. After 1949 the Communist Party had found him and sent him to normal school. Ni Yuzhang had become a middle school teacher.

Ni Yuzhang seemed a real natural for the party's propaganda efforts. Having gone from such dire and hopeless poverty to becoming a middle school teacher, he was a perfect candidate for "comparing the bitterness of the past with the sweetness of the present." With the Korean War in full swing, he could give anti-American testimony, too, explaining how cruelly had had been oppressed in the American orphanage.

Ni Yuzhang was called to speak at a public rally.

"Tell us how you were oppressed," the voice encouraged him as he stood on the stage before the assembled masses.

"But I wasn't oppressed," Ni Yuzhang replied.

"Of course you were oppressed," the voice encouraged him gently. "You were in an American orphanage."

"But I wasn't oppressed. My father had died and my own brother wouldn't even take me in. The American missionaries took me in."

"But they exploited you. Tell us how they exploited you," the voice urged him.

"No, they didn't exploit me. They gave me food. I was never hungry. They gave me an education. After I graduated from their middle school, I was able to go on to normal school. Everything I am I owe to the missionary school. They were kind to me. They didn't exploit me.''

Ni Yuzhang was a failure. He was labeled a reactionary and lost his job. But he was unrepentant. He continued to maintain his own, independent viewpoint. After he lost his job, he just stayed at home, reading books and painting flowers. He would not talk to other people. To the party cadres, he was sarcastic when others were obsequious. He laughed in their faces. He had a strange character. He liked to speak the truth.

"The Communist Party deceives people," Ni Yuzhang said bitterly to Yuxian one day when the two were alone. Yuxian was forbidden by his parents from meeting his cousin.

"Yuzhang is dangerous," Xu Fengzhen would say. "He's going to get himself locked up the way he talks."

But Yuxian was enchanted by the man who liked to speak the truth. His cousin's influence on the young boy's character was deep. Yuxian also developed a propensity for criticism and telling the truth.

• • •

In the fall of 1956, when Yuxian was eleven years old and beginning his first year in middle school by defying Buddhist Li's liberal seating arrangements, party policy began tilting in a more and more liberal direction. Within the top leadership of the country were some who feared that the harsh and repressive policies that had accompanied the consolidation of power were alienating the educated sectors of the society, that support for the party's cause among intellectuals was less than wholehearted. When the people of Hungary stood up in revolt in the fall of that year, the Chinese Communist Party drew lessons of its own. Unless intellectuals in China were permitted, indeed encouraged, to voice their dissatisfaction, the lid they had placed on dissent might someday blow.

The party began publicly encouraging intellectuals to voice their criticisms of the party's policies. "Let one hundred flowers bloom, let one hundred schools of thought contend" was the new slogan across the land.

In Yangsi Middle School, the teachers and upper level students were encouraged to speak their minds, and at Ni Jizhong's clinic, too, everyone was called upon to to offer criticisms of the party.

The campaign was slow in getting started. With so many people already having suffered so grievously for merely minor transgressions, even the most singularly discontented would not be so foolish as to give voice to their malaise. Many were afraid of a plot, fearing that the party was merely trying to identify the malcontents and would later call them to task.

But the party's encouragement continued through the winter of 1956–1957 and into the spring. "The more you criticize the party, the more you love the party," one slogan eagerly admonished. "Give you heart to the party—criticize the party," prodded another.

As a junior middle school student, Yuxian was not expected to understand or participate in politics. He and his classmates looked on from the sidelines.

Gradually, they saw big character posters beginning to appear outside the school cafeteria. The criticisms were petty complaints— as light as chicken feathers and garlic skins. "The classrooms don't have enough light," read one. "The party branch secretary doesn't show sufficient concern for the students' health," criticized another. "The cafeteria lines are too long. We have to wait too long for our food." "Some party leaders do not participate in physical labor like they are supposed to." "The party leaders do not pay enough attention to the well-being of the teachers."

Only a handful of the bravest really dared to speak out. "Why does China have to pay back all the money the Soviet Union gave us to fight in Korea?" a particularly daring student asked, one of the few to introduce issues of international relations. "Why does the Chinese leadership recognize Outer Mongolia as a separate country? Isn't Mongolia a part of China?" asked another.

The big character posters by Zhou Zhian and Si Xiongmao were hardly noticed at the time. "The party leadership really should study harder," wrote Si Xiongmao. "If they study harder, they won't make so many mistakes in teaching."

"I have so many children," wrote Zhou Zhian, "and not enough grain to feed them. Could the party leadership increase my family's grain rations?"

At his clinic, Ni Jizhong had also written a big character poster about the question of rice rations. Ever since the party introduced grain rationing in 1954, the family had been short of grain. "Don't tell anyone," Xu Fengzhen had implored the children when they had to supplement their rations with black market grain, bought surreptitiously from peasants who sneaked illegally into the village at night. "If you tell, you'll be locked up." But during the blooming of the hundred flowers, with such strong and persistent encouragement to speak out, Ni Jizhong thought the time had finally come to introduce his complaint.

· · ·

Then suddenly, overnight, in the summer of 1957, the blooming of the hundred flowers came to a grinding halt. The antirightist campaign began. Across the breadth of China, sincere and honest people who had spoken out at the party's encouragement were called to task, and many of them—some 500,000 in all—were labeled rightists. Work units throughout the country were given quotas—each unit had to find between 3 and 5 percent of its members guilty of being rightists. In many units, where people had remained reluctant to speak out, rightists were hard to find. But because success in socialist China lay in fulfilling and overfulfilling the quotas, enthusiastic party leaders found that rightists had to be invented.

The injustice of such inventions was compounded by the nature of the Chinese system of justice. "Rightists" who recognized their "crimes" and openly repented were given leniency. Those who did not were meted the harshest of sentences. Many of those who were singled out merely to fulfill the quota refused to recant, convinced of their own innocence, even within the perversion of logic that made an antirightist campaign possible at all. Often, it was these innocents who suffered most. Many of those who spent ten or twenty years in labor reform camps were guilty only of insisting on their own integrity.

There were many types of rightists and the punishment varied widely. At best, a rightist might be demoted and suffer a reduction in income, although even such an apparently mild rebuke carried with it the psychic pain of ostracism. At worst, rightists were incarcerated or sent to distant labor-reform camps where many of them remained for ten or twenty years.

The movement was not long in coming to Cao Family Village. Yuxian sensed something was wrong when his parents stopped coming home after work. He watched as his father became thin and anxious. Then one day, one of his teachers asked, "Yuxian, I have heard there have been lots of big character posters attacking your father. Is he a rightist?" The teacher was in charge of the school newspaper for which Yuxian had recently written an article.

The young boy had decided to become a journalist and had turned his energies to writing. If his father were a rightist, the little boy would no longer be allowed to write.

"I don't know," the puzzled boy responded. He didn't know what a rightist was.

"Father, are you a rightist?" Yuxian asked his father when next they met.

"No, son," Jizhong replied. "At least not yet." But everywhere in the clinic were big character posters attacking the doctor, accusing him of opposing the party's system of rice rationing. Every day, he continued seeing patients from early morning until early evening, stopping work only to attend the struggle sessions against him where day after day he was forced to answer the charges. Xu Fengzhen knew that her husband could be arrested any day.

Family relations suffered. The tension that Jizhong struggled ordinarily to keep in check would sometimes burst forth uncontrollably, and sometimes his anger was directed against his son. Yuxian loved playing the harmonica but did not have enough money to afford one of his own. Without telling his family, he had sold a small brass footwarmer that had lain unused for years, using the proceeds to purchase his coveted harmonica. Jizhong was furious when he found out. Taking a bamboo rod, he began beating his son, sobbing uncontrollably. "How dare you do this to me?" he demanded. "At the clinic, people are always angry with me, investigating me, criticizing me, struggling against me. My heart is already unhappy enough. My life is already miserable, can't you see that?

"But I never thought I would see my own son turn bad. You are becoming like my father, aren't you? He took everything we had and gambled it away, and now you are taking the family's things and selling them. What meaning do you think my life has after all this?"

"You just don't understand," Xu Fengzhen accused Yuxian when his father's emotion was spent. "Why did you choose the time when your father is most unhappy to do such a terrible thing?"

Yuxian was deeply shaken by his father's outburst—not by the beating but by his father's uncontrolled weeping over what the child regarded as an inconsequential, trivial matter. He began to sense how profound was his father's misery and knew in some inchoate way that the source of Jizhong's unhappiness lay with the Communist Party and its method of rule.

In the end, Ni Jizhong was not actually declared a rightist. He was labeled "one who stands on the side of the rightists." But he was never fully trusted again and his income was reduced from 180 to 135 yuan a month. Yuxian was able to continue his work as a reporter.

Others were not so lucky. Ni Yuzhang, the cousin whom Yuxian so admired for his insistence on telling the truth, was among the first to be locked up. He stayed in jail for a whole decade, released only in 1967 when the Cultural Revolution was at its height. Two years later, he was locked up again. Ni Yuzhang had remained a man who spoke his mind. He died in jail.

With the antirightist campaign in full swing, Yangsi Middle School underwent a major change. The old principal, who was simultaneously both head of the school and leader of the Communist Party Committee, was replaced. Xia Shengyu, the new principal and party secretary, was an old army man, a Korean War veteran, and not even a university graduate. He was sent not to teach but to enforce party policy. The atmosphere in the school was transformed. Secretary Xia was brutal to the rightists.

Under Xia Shengyu's direction, Zhou Zhian, the teacher who had complained about not having enough grain to feed his family, and Si Xiongmao, who had less than full respect for the teaching capacities of Yangsi's party members, were declared rightists. Their income was cut from one hundred yuan a month to twenty, and they were no longer allowed to teach. Instead, they were assigned the most menial and backbreaking labor the school authorities could devise. Teacher Zhou was assigned basic janitorial duties— cleaning the school toilets, weeding the grass, and pulling heavy carts. Yuxian had never seen people fall so quickly, never witnessed such a dramatic transformation of character and fate.

He often saw his former teacher wearing a straw hat so old it was coming unraveled, tattered clothes that even a beggar might have thrown away, and cloth shoes without socks, toes sticking through. Teacher Zhou worked in fear, his head bent down, eyes on the ground, not daring to look at anyone. "Right, right, right," he would repeat to anyone who spoke to him. "Yes, yes, yes," he agreed to any criticism leveled against him. If a rightist failed to exhibit the proper attitude, he could be branded a counterrevolutionary, an even more serious label, and one that led often to prison. Sun Dayu, a noted professor at Shanghai's Fudan University, had been downgraded from rightist to counterrevolutionary and consequently imprisoned when he had not shown the proper attitude upon being labeled a rightist.

With his head bent down, sweeping the streets, Teacher Zhou was often the target of curses. The children who had once been his pupils came often now to spit at him, and his own children were often beaten, too. Teacher Zhou's wife had gone mad shortly after her husband was declared a rightist, and she could no longer take care of the children. So they trailed after their father as he went about his appointed chores—their clothes like rags, barefoot even in winter, hair down to their shoulders, dirty, skinny, the snot running freely from their noses. The father suffered his humiliation in silence, gently wiping his students' spit from his face and dutifully continuing his chores even when his children were beaten and blood poured from their dirty noses. Principal Xia taught the schoolchildren not to sympathize with teachers like Zhou Zhian or his children. The more such men were made to suffer, he argued, the better. To demonstrate sympathy was to show that you were also a rightist and therefore bad.

There were those who did sympathize with teachers Zhou Zhian and Si Xiongmao and others like them. But they lacked the courage to say so. Most people felt great relief when the antirightist campaign was over—relieved that they had escaped being labeled themselves and thankful that they had not made any criticisms of the party or that their criticisms had been mild enough to be ignored.

● ● ●

It was his hatred for Secretary Xia that propelled the young Ni Yuxian from exuberant naughtiness and minor rebellion against the opposite sex toward his first blundering political act.

Secretary Xia was a strict disciplinarian with the students. If, during assembly, a student misbehaved, the principal would order the child to stand up for the duration of the meeting. In the morning and at noon, when the students returned from lunch, he would stand at the entrance to inspect them as they entered—vigorously cursing those who were late or improperly dressed or otherwise in violation of the rules.

Word quickly spread from the school to the village homes of the particular fondness the new principal exhibited toward the pretty girl students, whom he often invited into his office for friendly chats. Not long after his arrival, the mother of two young girls was forced to withdraw her daughters from school after the girls confessed that Secretary Xia had fondled their breasts during one such intimate chat. Against a party secretary, in the midst of an antirightist campaign, the young girls and their widowed mother had no recourse. To confront the party secretary was to risk being labeled a rightist.

Yuxian's active dislike for the new party secretary began one afternoon when the principal ordered him to throw away the Popsicle he had been eating when he entered the school gates after lunch. Yuxian refused. "I am the principal," Secretary Xia yelled at the boy, who continued with deliberate nonchalance to lick his Popsicle. "I have a right to tell you not to eat the Popsicle."

Yuxian continued his defiant licking. "Why should I throw it out? I bought it."

"Take it away from him," Principal Xia ordered the two student monitors.

Yuxian began sauntering toward his classroom.

Principal Xia overtook him and went directly to Buddhist Li. "Yuxian is truant today," he informed Teacher Li. "He is not allowed to go to school." Yuxian stood nearby, his eyes following the principal's every move, a wry, mocking smile on his lips. Secretary Xia's eyes met the young boy's and held. The hate was instantaneous and mutual.

The boy knew from books that Mao Zedong, exalted throughout the land as the country's great leader and teacher, had also been a rebellious youth, in frequent opposition to his teachers and the school authorities. Yuxian decided to follow in the party chairman's footsteps, forming a "young people's party" for protection against the likes of Secretary Xia and unfair teachers. He wrote a party constitution, the most important tenet of which was its mutual help clause. If teachers or the principal treated any of the signatories unfairly, they all had the obligation to help, to work together to oppose the injustice and to protect each other from harm. Seven of Yuxian's fellow male classmates signed. Together they swore an oath of secrecy. No one was ever to know about their young people's party. They were at least vaguely aware that even among children, only one party, the Communist Party, was permitted in China.

One day after class, Buddhist Li quietly and privately called Yuxian into his office. The teacher was concerned. "Yuxian, do you recognize this?" Buddhist Li asked, showing him a copy of the secret young people's party constitution.

"Yes, I recognize it," the young boy admitted. Yuxian knew immediately who had tattled. He had recently confronted one of his fellow signatories and accused him of stealing his harmonica. The frightened boy must have told.

"Why would you want to do this?"

"We wanted to cooperate and work together. We thought this was a good thing."

"But do you know what kind of thing this is?" Teacher Li continued. His voice was strained. Yuxian knew that the man was frightened. This was an extremely serious matter. "If you were an adult and tried to form a secret party, you would have your head chopped off. How many people know about this?"

"Only a few. Only the people who signed."

"Don't tell anyone else then. This is finished now." Teacher Li paused. His hands were trembling. "You must promise me you will never try organizing such a thing again. We'll say this was just a joke. You were just playing, weren't you?"

The little boy nodded.

"Do you promise never to do this again?" Teacher Li demanded.

"I promise."

Teacher Li lit a match and burned the constitution of the young people's party. Afterward, he called each of the signatories in one by one and extracted from each a promise never to tell and never to try to form such an organization again.

• • •

The antirightist campaign was followed quickly in the fall of 1957 by the campaign to eliminate the four pests. Throughout China, hundreds of millions of people were mobilized to rid the country forever of sparrows, rats, mosquitoes, and flies.

The first stage was devoted to the attack against sparrows.

The campaign was a great event at the Yangsi Middle School. Classes were canceled for three days running as students thronged in jubilation to the countryside, riding in groups on their bicycles, quilts tied to the rear, to make their contribution to the cause. Each student carried something that made noise—an old can and a spoon were the most frequently used implements—and a long bamboo pole. Scientists had calculated, correctly the students were soon to demonstrate, that a sparrow will die from exhaustion if it is forced to fly for more than two hours without an opportunity to perch.

At the appointed time, continuing for more than two hours without stop and extending for miles and miles around, mayhem reigned as students and teachers and peasants, too, beat their spoons and sticks against tin cans and cups and enamel basins and cooking pots, yelling all the while. School bells chimed and factory whistles blew, as families, factories, and sundry work units gathered en masse on roofs, beating and stamping and yelling. On the ground, they waved their bamboo poles in the air, and the boys climbed trees, beating the birds away with the poles, destroying nests and robbing them of their eggs.

For hours, the sky was aswarm with millions of the haplessly flapping creatures. No one had ever imagined that the world contained so many birds. Indeed, after a couple of hours, the exhausted birds began dropping from the sky like rain, not only sparrows, of course, but other flying feathered species as well. People began falling, too, and Ni Jizhong and his fellow doctors worked for several days almost around the clock setting the bone fractures that resulted when tens of excited and enthusiastic sparrow killers tumbled from buildings and trees. After three raucous days of bird fighting, the Yangsi middle schoolers returned with quite a haul—and millions throughout China feasted on sparrows for several days to come.

The campaign continued for months after the initial frenzy of activity. Students were assigned a daily quota of pests to kill, and classes competed with each other to fulfill and overfulfill their quotas. Rats were the best catch, because according to the system of equivalence, one rat was equal to two sparrows and to one hundred flies or mosquitoes. Students were required to present the teacher with one bird or its equivalent each morning. A rat thus filled two days' quota. Buddhist Li began homeroom each morning with each child emptying his pockets, presenting the previous day's grimy take. Actually, it was not the rats or birds themselves the students were required to present. The offerings were rather the tails of the rats and the claws of the sparrows. Only mosquitoes and flies were expected to be delivered intact. By the time class began, Teacher Li's desk was covered with rat tails and sparrow feet and hundreds of dead flies and mosquitoes.

The foul creatures became precious to the children, who spent most of their after-school hours in ingenious pursuit of the pests. A lively trade developed, too, as children bartered flies and mosquitoes and rats. The particularly industrious and successful hunters went into business for themselves, selling rat tails and sparrow feet in return for candy.

After his initial outburst of enthusiasm when classes were canceled for the great sparrow kill, Yuxian's interest in the movement waned. Often, he preferred buying his daily pest quota with candy rather than spending the hours necessary to trap a rat or kill one hundred flies or mosquitoes.

• • •

The campaign to wipe out the four pests was only a minor prelude to the much grander and more ambitious movement that followed. Intimations of something called the Great Leap Forward had begun in 1957 when Party Chairman Mao Zedong had visited Moscow and hinted that China was about to launch a program of industrialization so powerful and rapid that the country would be able to catch up with and then overtake Great Britain within fifteen years. Moreover, China was to industrialize not through the introduction of new technology or the application of scientific methods to solve the country's problems, or even through attempting to increase the educational level of its vast population. Rather modernization was to be achieved through the mass mobilization of the country's precious manpower—"three years of struggle for ten thousand years of happiness," the saying went. Suddenly the Chinese population, which had once been considered overly large, was regarded as too small. Means had to be devised to free up labor power for the task of industrialization.

In the countryside, the small and medium-sized collectives that had been formed in the mid-1950s were amalgamated almost overnight into huge, gigantic communes. Men who had once worked in the fields were assigned to industrial work as women with no farming experience were left to tend the crops. To free women further from household chores, huge mess halls were established, where food was free and plentiful for all. Communism, that utopian system where each gives according to his ability and receives according to his needs, was said to be just around the corner.

The Great Leap Forward was sheer utopian fantasy, destined to fail.

Schoolchildren, too, were mobilized in the great and patriotic endeavor. The foundation of industry was said to be steel, and thus the focus of the Great Leap Forward was on producing more steel— not only in the factories designed to produce steel but in schools and hospitals and back alleys, too. This was the era of the backyard steel furnace. Even the "old mamas" who had been housewives all their lives and had never participated in heavy labor stood over the backyard furnaces for hours each day, fanning the fires with their paper and sandalwood fans—partriotic devotion to their country's modernization that won them especially effusive praise.

In Ni Jizhong's clinic, the staff rotated between medical work and producing steel. Dr. Ni saw patients during the day and stayed at the hospital until late at night, stoking the hospital steel furnace. Xu Fengzhen, too, performed her nursing chores by day and did steel work by night. Once again, the parents rarely were home and the children were bereft of adult supervision.

Classes at Yangsi Middle School were halted so everyone could engage in the production of steel, with classes divided into specialized work groups, the shifts working nonstop around the clock because the fire in the middle school's furnace could not be allowed to go out.

The city of Shanghai has long been a major producer of Chinese steel, and one of the largest of the complexes is located in Pudong, along the eastern bank of the Huangpu River just adjacent to the Cao Family Village. At night, when the steel factory is in operation, the river bank looks from a distance like a sea of fire, and the air is so polluted with black soot that the lungs clog and a white shirt turns dark in a matter of minutes. As the movement to produce steel gathered momentum, this factory became Shanghai's focal point for receiving the coke and pig iron and other raw materials which were then distributed to the city's backyards. Day and night, boats pulled alongside the factory docks, and trains pulled into the yards, delivering endless supplies of raw materials. Day and night, in an infinite variety of makeshift transportation, the people of Pudong came to gather the raw materials to feed their voracious backyard steel furnaces.

At Yangsi Middle School, Yuxian was assigned to the brigade that gathered the coke from the Pudong steelyards.

Each morning at six o'clock, when he and some thirty of his classmates arrived at school, they were given ten cents for lunch and fifteen carts that required two students each to pull. It took them four hours to cover the ten miles between their school and the steelyards, including the time where everyone had to help, pushing cart by cart, to cross the three old-fashioned camelback bridges. The dirty, exhausted, and famished boys usually completed their run, delivering the coke to the schoolyard, by about five in the afternoon.

The school's furnace was set up in a corner of the playground. Around the clock, week by week, it produced brick-sized, hole-riddled lumps of something that everyone agreed euphemistically, because politics dictated, to call steel.

Every Friday afternoon, the school's gates and walls were pasted with the double happiness symbol that usually signifies a wedding, while the drums rolled and the gongs sounded announcing the "happy news report" student assembly. Principal Xia would gather the students together to announce the wonderful news that the school once more had fulfilled and overfulfilled its quota for steel production.

"This week," Principal Xia would begin, clearing his throat and reading cadrelike from a carefully prepared text, "the students and teachers of Yangsi Middle School have listened to the great call of our beloved Communist Party. Together, we have overcome great difficulty." His speech was given to dramatic pauses, as he rose on his toes. "We have all worked very hard at our great task of steel production, at the great task of catching up with and overtaking Great Britain industrially in fifteen years. Today, we want to make this joyous report to our beloved party. This week Yangsi Middle School has not only fulfilled the quota of steel production, but we have overfulfilled it."

The drums would begin rolling and the gongs sounding when Principal Xia reached the part about overfulfilling the quota. Sometimes he would announce that they had surpassed the quota by 100 percent and sometimes by as much as 200 percent or more, depending on the tenor of the times. No one ever bothered to measure how much of the so-called steel Yangsi Middle School had actually produced. Secretary Xia took his cue from the newspaper and radio reports which were also joyously proclaiming the fulfillment and overfulfillment of steel quotas, complete with human interest stories of people who had not slept for weeks or returned home for months the better to devote themselves to the glorious task of steel production.

Everyone—not just in Yangsi Middle School but throughout the country as well—had known all along that they were producing useless globs of something that had no right to be called steel. The lumpy, holey globs were as useless as garbage. But no one publicly said a word. At home, to his parents, Yuxian would say, "Those steel lumps are just garbage."

"Don't ever say that outside this house," his parents would plead. "Never."

A generation later, when Yuxian's own children began attending Yangsi Middle School, the steel globs still stood in the corner of the playground, so worthless no one had even bothered to cart them away.

After months of frenzied production of something declared by fiat to be steel, Yangsi Middle School moved into the next stage of the movement. The school was to become economically self-sufficient. Many of the girls began learning to make clothes. The boys studied carpentry. Yuxian joined a haircutting class, and Buddhist Li became his first customer, enthusiastically praising the child for the amateur haircut that stuck out in odd places, some hairs long, some short. Teacher Li wanted to join the party, and this Great Leap Forward was a time to demonstrate unflagging and unquestioning devotion to the party cause.

Following the movement for self-sufficiency, Yangsi Middle School turned to making revolution in the countryside, where the Great Leap Forward was also in full swing and the focus was on producing more rice. In November, fourteen-year-old Yuxian was assigned to a group of students who were sent to the countryside to live and work on one of the newly formed people's communes, arriving just in time to help with the fall harvest and to begin devoting their energies to preparing the fields for the next planting. The commune was a day's walk away from Yangsi, and the students and teachers set off together with not much more than their quilts, a little money, and the coupons they thought would entitle them to get rice from the peasants. They lived in dilapidated old houses, wallpapered in crumbling newspaper, sleeping on a straw-covered floor.

The revolution in education had spread to agriculture, too, and new plowing and planting techniques were being introduced throughout the country. The process began with deep plowing. In some parts of the country, fields were being plowed as deep as men were tall, but in Yuxian's commune, they were only plowing three feet below the surface. Plowing, though, was merely a euphemism for what was happening to the soil. There were no tractors or machines in Yuxian's commune, and no water buffalo either.

The process of turning up the earth had to be done with shovels, exhausting, back-breaking labor, which had to be completed quickly in order to plant the new crop in time.

The new soil that had come from three feet down was unfertilized and devoid of nutrients, a problem that advocates of deep plowing said could be solved by burning straw, trash, or anything else that might ignite, on the surface. After the fire, through a combination of the revolutionary new method of close planting and a generous application of the the nightsoil ordinarily used by peasants in those parts, the land, enthusiasts promised, would produce not merely bumper crops but crops surpassing in magnitude the wildest imaginations of the practical-minded peasants.

* * *

At the end of each day's exhausting work of digging deep and planting close, the students from Yangsi Middle School gathered at the edge of their fields to hear their dauntless and irrepressible enthusiastic political instructor make another "good news" report. The *People's Daily*, the nationally circulated newspaper of the Chinese Communist Party, and Shanghai's own *Liberation Daily*, from which the instructor often read, were full of news of the high-yield satellites—units that were producing wondrous amounts of steel and rice. Seven hundred catties (one catty equals 1.1 pounds) of rice per mou was a very good yield in ordinary times, and a thousand catties per mou was about the highest the most fertile land ever produced. But newspapers suddenly began reporting areas that had produced 3,000 catties per mou, 5,000, then 10,000, 30,000, 70,000. Soon reports were coming in of areas producing more than 100,000 catties per mou.

Every day, every week, every month, the official Chinese press reported national output of steel and grain climbing to ever-more astoundingly high figures. Yuxian and his classmates learned about fields where the rice crop was so thick and plentiful that an egg placed on top of the plants would not drop through, where the fields were so lush that even the few rats remaining after the campaign against the four pests could not crawl through.

It was difficult for Yuxian to believe these enthusiastic reports, sitting as he and his classmates were while listening to them at the edge of fields where the rice was being smothered and starved to death. Between the unfertile topsoil and the ill-advised method of close planting, the rice seedlings were either not coming up at all or were withering at an early stage. The rice crop in Yuxian's people's commune was going to be a disaster. The papers and the political instructor were full of deceit.

Food had never been plentiful in the people's commune where Yuxian was working, and no special provisions had been made to feed the young students. The heavy exertion in which they were engaged from morning until night required an additional allotment of calories, but their food was never enough. Mostly, they ate sweet potatoes, their rations being calculated on the basis of one catty of rice equaling two catties of sweet potatoes. But sweet potatoes digest much more quickly than rice, and the teenaged children were often hungry.

As Chinese new year, the spring festival of February 1959, approached food in the commune was running out. The students could no longer be fed. The hungry students were sent home.

After a day of walking, quilts on their backs, dizzy and weak from hunger, they arrived at Yangsi Middle School to be fed the biggest meal they had received in months—one bowl of rice and one steamed bun each. It was the most they would eat at one sitting for several years. The "three bad years" had begun.

Suddenly, at the state-controlled markets, there was nothing available to buy. On the black market, a slice of fried bread that had once cost five cents suddenly cost a whole yuan and was made mostly of chaff rather than flour. A catty of sugar that had cost one or two yuan now cost twenty or thirty. A bowl of rice with a little vegetable and a little oil—a precious commodity indeed—sold for ten yuan and required hours of waiting in line. When Chinese new year arrived, and the Ni family of eight celebrated the largest feast of the year, they ate only rice and half a pound of rotten pork.

It would be more than twenty years, after demographers had analyzed the census of 1980 and compared the statistics gathered then with figures gathered in several other earlier efforts, before the magnitude of the three bad years would be fully understood.

From the beginning of 1959 to the end of 1961, somewhere between 25 and 30 million people above and beyond the norm died in China—most of them infants and children under seven, the very elderly, and men over forty. It was the worse famine not merely in Chinese history but in the history of humankind.

It was a disaster that could have been avoided had the Communist Party of China, under the leadership of Mao, not persisted in its utopian fantasy, had the peasants been permitted to plow and sow in the age-old manner. The famine could have been prevented, too, had the Chinese leadership not been so preoccupied with face. The amount of rice China shipped during those years to the Soviet Union in repayment for debt was about equal to the shortfall that would have made the difference between hunger and starvation.

Cities were hit less hard during the famine than the countryside, and the larger cities suffered less than the smaller. Food riots in areas of concentrated population would have been politically disastrous for the party leadership, so every effort, including the importation of foreign grain, was made to keep the cities supplied.

Still, there was hunger in Shanghai. The Ni family and their neighbors were hungry.

And hunger wreaks havoc on the human character. Its effect is an overwhelming selfishness, a callous disregard for others in one's struggle for individual survival. Family relations are profoundly strained in such times, and the Ni family, like many others, nearly disintegrated during the three bad years. There was only rice to eat but never enough of that, and no way to divide it equitably among such a large family. To stretch the rice and fill the stomach, the Nis, like families everywhere in China, made watery rice gruel. But quarrels would break out over its distribution. A ladle of rice scooped from the bottom of the pot yielded more rice than a ladle gleaned from the top. Those who were served first got more than those who were served later. How much more should the older children get than the younger? The children quarreled constantly, blaming whichever of the sisters cooked that night. The parents, absent until late every night at the clinic, had no way to mediate.

Finally, the family decided to distribute the rice dry to each member of the family according the ration determined by the state. Each member would fend for himself in cooking. Yuxian frequently went to eat at the home of his best friend, where the two of them made rice gruel together and managed to settle the distribution problem with relative good will.

Life was most tenuous during the three bad years for the very young and the very old. The Ni family young managed to survive. Little Fenfen, the last of Xu Fengzhen's children, was born in 1959, shortly after the hunger began. Xu Fengzhen lost a great deal of blood when Fenfen was born and stayed weak and depressed for weeks thereafter. She had no milk and evinced little interest in the child. The five children she was already raising in the midst of famine were more than she could manage. Working as a nurse with her husband to supplement the income of the large family, Xu Fengzhen was often tired and frequently lost her temper with so many unmangeable little ones. Sometimes she even beat them with a switch. Yuxian often intervened on the other children's behalf, shielding the beaten child with his body, offering to serve as a substitute for the accused. He knew that as his mother's favorite, she would beat him less.

With his mother's lack of milk and her glaring indifference to Fenfen, Yuxian was afraid the cranky baby was starving to death. He credits himself with saving the baby's life. He pleaded with his mother to send the infant to his aunt—Xu Fengzhen's sister-in-law—who had also recently borne a child and who was rich with milk. Xu Fengzhen was adamant. "I would lose face," she insisted. Hungry and depressed, Xu Fengzhen made no effort to hide the fact that she did not care if the baby girl died.

Yuxian insisted. Hugging the infant to his chest, he wrapped her up and hung the child from his back, preparing to set out for his aunt's. The mother pleaded with her son. "If you send the child to her, then everyone will know I have no milk and cannot take care of my own children."

A compromise was reached. The baby was sent to a wet-nurse a day's bus ride away. There, the child was nurtured until she was able to live on the thin rice gruel that sustained the family through the crisis.

It was the elderly members of the Ni family household who finally succumbed to the crisis.

Life was hard for the Nis not only because food was so scarce and mouths to feed many but also because the family had been forced out of their old home when the campaign for making steel began. When the steel factory had first been built just next to Cao Family Village, Guansheng had been offered a great deal of money for his dilapidated house and the land around it, but Guansheng refused to sell. He did not want to leave his home and his village. In the frenzy of the Great Leap Forward, the factory was expanded, and Guansheng's property was confiscated, the family evicted. They moved temporarily to Zhoudiadu several miles away, living crowded for a time with Ni Jizhong and his family of six children in a single cramped room, Guansheng and his wife next door.

But Guansheng and his wife never could adjust to their new circumstances. It was the loneliness and the absence of a sense of belonging that affected them most. Taking an old couple out of the village where their lives had revolved for more than half a century was like taking fish out of water and expecting them to walk on land. All their friends, their whole system of social support, even the ongoing enmities and quarrels that were a part of the fabric of village life, evaporated overnight.

There was no canal behind the house anymore. Both drinking and laundry water had to be drawn from a well. One day, while Grandmother Ni was washing clothes, she began to feel dizzy after drawing a heavy bucket from the well. She collapsed over the basin where she was washing and died.

Guansheng died only a few months after Grandmother Ni. Without his wife, plucked from his village and his friends, the irrascibly exuberant old man was transformed. The light seemed to leave his eyes, and his heart became heavy. His spirit was broken. He no longer had reason for living.

"I am going to die," Guansheng told his sister one day. His head was still clear. Guansheng took a towel and soap and water and washed his face very clean. He took the corner of the towel and twisted it tight and small and cleaned out his ears and his nose. He splashed his body with water, changed his underwear, and lay down on his bed to die.

Ni Jizhong came and gave him acupuncture, herbal medicine, and encouragement.

"I am going to die," Guansheng repeated when he woke up again the next morning. Again, he washed his face and his ears and cleaned out his nose. He was weaker that day, so his sister helped him wash his body. He changed his underwear again, and lay down to die.

Ni Jizhong came back to give him more medicine.

All day Guansheng lay on his bed, so still he might have been dead. But he was still alive when Ni Jizhong came again in the evening.

Guansheng died that night. His sister could tell by feeling the old man's testicles. They had retracted into his body. "His five elements have disappeared," was how she informed Ni Jizhong of his father's death.

Yuxian was called in to stay with Guansheng's body while the rest of the family busied themselves with funeral arrangements. It was the first time he had seen anyone who had died in peace. Guansheng seemed to be asleep. His face had not changed, and when Yuxian touched the old man's hand and rubbed his body, he was still warm and supple. As the sun rose and shone across Guansheng's face, the last of the old man's *qi*—his vital life force—came gurgling up from his stomach. A sound escaped from the old man's mouth, and he seemed to move, to settle a little deeper into death.

The room began filling with people, remembering Guansheng. His transgressions were not easily forgotten, but Yuxian was reminded that, "When a person dies, you have to think of the good points, not the bad ones." Guansheng's sins had been forgiven years earlier, when the family had concluded that the gambling that had plunged them into poverty had also saved them from the wrath of the new communist government.

"He was a good man," Xu Fengzhen remembered. Still, she could not resist a few pokes at his faults. "He gambled a lot when he was young, and once he even took an ax to my door, but after liberation he stopped. Mostly he stopped, anyway. Several times, he said to me, 'my heart is clear now, you are a very good daughter-in-law.' Often I gave him good things to eat."

When his body was moved to the Taoist temple, Guansheng's descendants followed him, dressed from head to toe in white. His closest relatives—the two sons and a daughter, their spouses and children—pasted a strip of red paper on their shoes. He gained face in death because the number of his descendants was great.

At the temple, Guansheng was placed on a bed and his face was covered with a white cloth. A large, white drape hung from the ceiling to the floor just in front of Guansheng's resting place, separating the dead from the living and dividing the huge room in two. The Taoist monks chanted, speeding thereby the old man's soul to heaven. A plaque with Guansheng's name and the date of his death was attached to the drapery. In front of the drapery was an altar, on which were two white candles and offerings of fruit and cake. The room was fragrant with incense. On the floor in front of the altar was a pillow for kneeling, and off to the side was one small burner. As the monks chanted and the women wailed, Guansheng's descendants kowtowed before the altar one by one, paying their last respects.

Ni Jizhong, as the eldest of Guansheng's sons, was first. Clasping his palms together in front of his face, three times Ni Jizhong extended his hands upward, above his head. Holding his hands to his chest, he knelt on the cushion, then, arms stretched outward on the floor, he bent down and touched his forehead three times to the ground. He stood up, repeating the entire process three times. Ni Jizhong's younger brother was the next to perform the kowtow, then Guansheng's sister and his daughter. The wives of Guansheng's sons—Xu Fengzhen going first—were next. Yuxian, as the eldest son of Guansheng's eldest son, led his generation in the elaborate ritual. The neighbors and Guansheng's friends from the teahouse he frequented came one by one to bow—bending forward three times from the waist in lieu of the elaborate kowtow.

Throughout the ceremony, the hands of female relatives were busy in a constant rhythm, fashioning tinfoil-covered red paper into ingots and tossing the ingots into the fire—thereby assuring Guansheng of sufficient money in the afterlife. They wailed as they wrapped, voices and hands in syncopation, each woman sharing with Guansheng her own personal message, communicated for everyone to hear. "Oh, Guansheng," they wailed, "You are gone and we are alone. Why did you go without us? Why is your heart so hard? You have forgotten all about us, haven't you, Guansheng? Life is so difficult without you." The wailing and accompanying laments added to the dead man's face. Had no one cried, or had the wailers been few, the guardians of the netherworld might have suspected that Guansheng had not behaved well on earth. His path to a comfortable afterlife would have been tortuous.

Guansheng's sister, as the eldest of the women, wailed the loudest of all, and everyone agreed that she wailed the best. In the adulation paid to Guansheng in death, the sharing of food counted as the paramount virtue. "Guansheng, my elder brother," his sister cried, "You are such a good person. I still remember once, when we were young, and I had no rice to eat, you shared your rice with me."

The messages were not for Guansheng alone. Family feuds were argued over the corpse, with the disputants spewing forth their cases for the assembled to judge. In the babble of pleas, with five or six women wailing at once, only constant repetition guaranteed that one's argument would be heard.

At half-hour intervals, the wailing stopped for the participants to rest and recoup their strength, beginning again after a few minutes' rest.

Yuxian participated in the wailing, too. "What a filial grandson you are," Guansheng's sister complimented him. "You have cried so many tears."

Only Guansheng's daughter did not wail. His daughter had not forgiven her father for accusing her of greed when her mother's jewelry had been divided only months before. Her silence stood as open rebuke against her father to the guardians of life in the hereafter.

With the wailing and the kowtowing over, the monks burned paper effigies of the house and furniture Guansheng would need in the afterlife. They burned a paper boat, too, knowing that on land or in heaven, Guansheng at heart would always be a boatman. Then Yuxian held Guansheng's head and other male members of Yuxian's generation took the old man's feet, and transferred him to the wheeled cart that would roll his body to the crematorium.

The tears that flowed when the monks began pushing the cart were real, and the sound of wailing intensified as the white-garbed relations grabbed on to the cart, obstructing the monks in their appointed tasks.

Only Yuxian dared accompany the body into the crematorium, where five glass-doored ovens stood lined in a row.

He watched as the flames engulfed his grandfather's body, reflecting on what his grandfather's life had been. The old man had meant more to him than anyone else.

"Only yesterday, he was alive," Yuxian remembers thinking. "He had feelings and thoughts. He could taste and smell. Now he is dead, nothing more than a piece of wood. Everyone has to follow this road—no matter how long we live or what we do with our lives, whether we are rich or poor, respected or despised, Qin Shi Huangdi [the first emperor of the Qin dynasty] or Mao Zedong. We all finally end up here. We all become ashes.

"Even if all the world knows and remembers you as a great person, you no longer exist. When we die, we are all equal, no matter how great we were on earth. Who can distinguish this man's ashes from that man's ashes? Everyone's ashes are the same.

"And life goes by so quickly. Sixty years, and it is over.

"So what meaning does a man's life on earth have? Maybe it doesn't really have much meaning at all. How strange a person's fate. Once in every life, opportunity knocks, and what we do with that opportunity is an important question.

"If my grandfather had had an education, or if he had come from another family, he could have become a rich capitalist or owned lots of boats, or lots of land. He could have been rich. Even so, Guansheng had more opportunities than most. But he gambled most of them away. Others, he frittered away. He lost everything he ever had. He had a chance to go to Taiwan, too—or Hong Kong—just when the Communists were coming in. There, maybe he could have struck it rich. But he didn't want to go.

"I don't want to be like my grandfather when I die, to have lived a whole lifetime without ever having done anything worthwhile or interesting or significant. His life had no purpose. Every day went by like every other day without significance. Sure, life can be lived without purpose. But it is not enough.

"Most Chinese have no good reason for living. They just wander aimlessly through life. Look at my father, my uncle. Their lives are just for living—so their families can have enough rice to eat. My uncle has never even been out of Shanghai, and most people my grandfather's age have never even left Pudong. Lots of people in their whole lives have never been on a bus or a boat. Most of them have never even seen a train. After they turn thirty, most Chinese stop thinking about having fun or doing anything interesting—traveling, or going to a good movie, or reading a good book. So in Pudong, my grandfather is considered a special kind of person. He had a boat for a while and went to a few places and met different kinds of people and once earned some money. He rode in a car all around Shanghai, with his wife. He ate foreign food and used a knife and fork and that made him special. Even my father—he graduated from medical school, but he has never even ridden in a car. So everyone respected Guansheng—they thought he was really something."

Yuxian thought also of his own father's life. He respected his father. Jizhong had a strong sense of justice. He stood on the side of fairness. When he saw the poorly trained party doctors misdiagnosing patients, or dispensing improper medication, he never hesitated to criticize them and to intervene on behalf of the patients. He worked harder than any other doctor at the clinic, arriving earlier and staying later and seeing more patients than anyone else. At the end of a long day, after he had returned home, he never refused when people called on him for help. He never accepted money or gifts for his work.

But Yuxian still saw his father's life as meaningless. Jizhong had never recovered from the attacks against him during the antirightist campaign. He spoke out as a doctor on behalf of the medical well-being of his patients but he never spoke out against political injustice. If the party leadership said come, Jizhong came. If the party cadre said go, Jizhong went. He had no freedom, no real control over his life. He taught his son that speaking out against injustice, expressing one's own point of view, was dangerous. Passivity was the only safe road. But Yuxian knew that his father was not happy in his passivity. The pressures, the fears, were too great.

Yuxian watched as Guansheng's body slowly disintegrated into ashes. He cried. He grieved over the old man's remains. But mostly, there was a hollow, empty feeling inside him, a big open space that nothing could fill.

The monks scooped the few handfuls of the still-hot ashes that Guansheng's body had become, poured them into a heavy red cloth bag, and gave the bag to Yuxian. As Yuxian deposited the ashes into the wooden box that would house his grandfather's remains, he vowed to imbue his own life with a meaning and a purpose that his grandfather's and father's had never had. What exactly his life's purpose would be, or how to accomplish it, he had no idea at all. He was determined only that his life would be different.

•   •   •

Fourteen-year-old Yuxian faced his first major disappointment shortly after Guansheng's death. Most of his classmates at Yangsi Middle School passed the examination that placed them in a senior high school, guaranteeing their entrance into one of the country's leading universities. In the transition from junior to senior middle school, however, Yuxian remained at Yangsi. He still stood a chance of getting into university, but would have to compete in the nationwide entrance exams. For those he would need assiduous preparation.

For his failure to enter the college preparatory school, Yuxian blamed not himself but his father. Scholastic achievement was only one component of the selection process. Political background was another. Until the antirightist campaign, doctors like Ni Jizhong had continued to be respected by the new government. Intellectuals were considered necessary to the development of the country. With the move to the left that began with the antirightist campaign, social rewards shifted to those deemed to be imbued with revolutionary purity—workers, peasants, members of the Communist Party and their offspring. Children of intellectuals had to work harder to obtain the same rewards. Children of disgraced intellectuals had to work harder still. Jizhong had not been labeled a rightist when the country turned left in 1957. But to the leftist political authorities at Yangsi Middle School, Principal Xia in particular, men like Ni Jizhong who "stood on the side of the rightists" were barely distinguishable from the rightists themselves. Their children were suspect, too. The right to a university education was more than the likes of Yuxian deserved.

In the transition from junior to senior middle school, the mantle of responsibility for Yuxian's class passed from Buddhist Li—whose exasperation over the recalcitrant, rebellious, strong-minded young Yuxian was tempered by a strong measure of affection and respect—to a new teacher, Huang Guangrong. "Pockfaced Huang" the students called the man who came to serve as homeroom teacher, political instructor, and faculty head of the Communist Youth League alike. Pockfaced Huang was a candidate for membership in the Communist Party, and, at thirty, several years older than ordinary Youth League members. In the normal course of political progression, his candidate membership should already have been accepted. But there were unspecified "problems" in Huang's background. His membership was being delayed to give the young man the opportunity to prove himself worthy beyond question of the honor and responsibility. Huang's devotion to the party, its policies, and its individual members knew no bounds. "Whether you study well or not is not important," Pockfaced Huang instructed his class on the very first day. "What matters is whether you listen to the party, obey the party, become a docile tool of the party."

Politics assumed increasing importance during Yuxian's high school years, both because the students were older and the time had come to begin testing them and because, with the disastrous Great Leap Forward in full swing, the country was fully mobilized politically.

The political hierarchy of the class was not long in taking form. Of the forty students, four immediately became members of the Youth League—recognized by everyone as active loyalists to the party's cause and therefore head and shoulders in status above the rest of their would-be peers. The parents of Youth League members were all from the most politically "correct" classes—members of the Communist Party or workers who by some metaphysical definition had suffered in the old society and therefore owed unquestioning allegiance to the new. The responsibility of the Youth League members was to lead, and, indeed, on these four students and Pockfaced Huang, the futures of every other member of the class depended. The correct political standpoint of their classmates was a major concern, and ingratiating oneself with the Youth League members necessitated reporting on the political shortcomings and moral weaknesses of one's fellow students. In private, secret meetings, the chosen leaders reviewed the "little reports," constantly winnowing the trustworthy from the indifferent from the downright suspect, frequently calling their less worthy classmates to task in public criticism meetings, urging them to share openly with everyone their very innermost thoughts.

The most reliable and enthusiastic purveyors of the little reports were the five or six students who fell into the ranks of the activists—students whose goal was to join the Youth League and who therefore consorted with Youth League members and curried favor with Pockfaced Huang. The family backgrounds of the activists were more mixed, and some even had parents who were rightists. Among the activists were those who genuinely believed in the party's ideals of selfless giving and unquestioning obedience, who were honestly willing to sacrifice themselves for the good of others. But opportunism was the more frequent motivation for activism. Desperate to prove that they were different from their rightist families and revolutionary after all, hoping through political approval to find a place in a university, knowing that politics was the only route to success, students with suspect family backgrounds devoted the bulk of their energy to cultivating relations with the Youth League members and Pockfaced Huang, laughing when they laughed, smiling when they smiled, obsequiously attentive to the wants and anticipating the needs of those on whom their advancement depended.

Half the class, some twenty students, were middling sorts, not actively involved in the political posturing that was the route to success but not actively distrusted either. Included in this group were many students from "good" class backgrounds, whose parents were party members, workers, or peasants, but who had no particular ambitions and made no great demands on life. Students in this middle group were known to be obedient, if apathetic, listening to and following the party's directives.

Five members of the class were considered backward elements. Their fathers were landlords, rightists, counterrevolutionaries, or otherwise politically suspect. The backward students were either unwilling or unable to muster the enthusiasm for party policies that might have overcome—or at least neutralized—their stigma. They never quite understood why they were regarded as bad. But they were treated as suspect by the other students and openly looked down upon by the activists and league members. They were outsiders.

For some, there was honor in being an outsider, for as outsiders they saw more clearly the hypocrisy of those who so assiduously curried favor in order to get ahead. Outsiders more easily recognized the injustice of a system that defined as good only Youth League members or aspirants. They saw the absurdity of a political system that publicly propounded selfless service in the interest of the "people" while rewarding only those who shamelessly toadied to power, serving only their own political ambitions.

Ni Yuxian was the most backward of the backward students. He stood at the very bottom of the political ladder.

CHAPTER

3

Chinese life revolves in a complex array of circles. To dance in independent steps is to risk exclusion from the circle, and to be excluded is to be denied the very meaning of Chinese life. Ostracism is the highest form of punishment.

Expelled from the circle of Yangsi Middle School but forced to remain at its periphery, shunned by his teachers and fellow students alike, Yuxian was burdened with a sense of isolation and oppression. He bridled at his lack of freedom. But he remained defiant. Still believing himself a *xiao da hao*, a little man of extraordinary powers, and never doubting his own superiority and destiny, he continued to scorn those who regarded themselves as his betters, viewing the actions of his fellow students who so obsequiously fawned in the face of power—the Youth League members and activists—as nothing short of contemptible. He reveled in stories of commoners—Beethoven, Madame Curie, and Chopin among them—who refused to bow before kings. Obedience was not in Ni Yuxian's character. He regarded his own treatment as grossly unfair.

So imbedded in Chinese tradition is ostracism of the righteous that the upright exile is part of the national myth. The history of imperial China is replete with stories of moral officials who insisted upon justice during periods of corruption, placing the good of the country before personal advancement, confronting the ill-informed emperor with advice the leader did not want to hear. Such officials were often ostracized—stripped of their positions and sent for prolonged periods of internal exile to remote and isolated quarters of the land. Lauded in folkore as men of moral integrity and commitment to principle, praised for their courage in standing up for what was right, the exile came to serve as an exemplar of moral behavior. If the scorned scholar did not, like Qu Yuan, the most famous of them all, commit suicide to demonstrate his loyalty, he withdrew from society into a world of poetry and books, contemplation and painting, awaiting the moment when he could contribute to the polity once more.

Learning in his adolescence to admire the moral superiority and independence of the scholar in disgrace, Yuxian began to imitate him as well. His response to his own status as political pariah was to turn to the world of books and poetry contemplation, and painting. Yuxian became during his years of senior middle school a voracious reader. He devoured all he could of Chinese history and novels. He thrilled to Tang dynasty poetry, memorizing hundreds of passages, awestruck that the sentiments so eloquently expressed a thousand years before in circumstances so vastly different from his own could still carry such meaning. He marveled at his own ability actually to enter poetry and become one with poet and poem.

He read Western thinkers, too, philosophers like Locke, Rousseau, and Montesquieu, and became an avid student of the French Revolution.

He developed a special fondness for Russian novels, reading most of what had been translated into Chinese.

Yuxian was driven not merely by the insatiable curiosity that had possessed him since childhood but by a need to make sense out of the increasingly troubling contrast between the world as he experienced it and the world as it was so insistently described in official party and school accounts. In the midst of a famine where he and everyone around him was hungry, the press still took little note of the difficulties, continuing to glorify the already disastrous Great Leap Forward and shower praise on the man who was credited with initiating it.

Yuxian confronted the problem of memory, too. With the "liberation" of 1949, and the elimination of landlords and formation of collectives that followed, the lot of the peasant, so the party argued, had greatly improved. But Yuxian's own memories and the memories of the adults who influenced him were different. Certainly some landlords had been rich and the poor had been exploited before the Communists had restructured rural society, but war, not exploitation, had been the scourge. What had plunged so many in rich and fertile Pudong into poverty was the Japanese invasion and the civil war between the Nationalists and the

Communists, not landlords or the capitalist system. In the absence of war, yes, the pursuit of livelihood was a constant, grinding struggle, but so long as a man was not incorrigibly lazy or physically incapacitated—or an opium smoker or inveterate gambler—it was always possible to make a living—a much better living than anyone was making now. A peasant could raise vegetables, eggs, or watermelons and sell them for a profit in the city, and on the proceeds from even such a small business a family could eat reasonably well and have clothes to wear. During holidays, no matter how poor, everyone could buy a little something extra and special to eat. Even the poorest were never long without cooking oil. But it was impossible during the three bad years to buy oil. The Nis were reasonably lucky in that regard. Ni Jizhong occasionally administered his children small doses of the cod liver oil he was able to pick up at the hospital. For many of Yuxian's fellow villagers, life during the Great Leap Forward was worse than anything they could remember, including the Japanese invasion, which was as bad as their lives had ever been.

The party was standing truth on its head.

Even as individual experience and perception and memory cried out that the official version of the truth was not merely false but preposterous, the populace was forced to echo the party's version of reality.

1959 witnessed the start of yet another political campaign—a movement against "right deviationism"—criticizing those who had dared to describe the results of the Great Leap Forward as they had actually observed them. Peng Dehaui, the former Minister of Defense, was the primary object of the campaign, and while the letter that he had written to Mao criticizing the Great Leap Forward was not then made public, some of his criticisms were—like his argument that the backyard steel furnaces were a waste. But even as Peng's views were criticized, Ni Yuxian, and many of the people he respected, agreed that the former Minister of Defense had been right. The backyard steel furnaces had been useless. As a result of his daring to speak out, the press was accusing Peng—Douglas MacArthur's Chinese counterpart during the Korean War and chief negotiator at that time on China's behalf—of having been a spy for the American imperialists, colluding with them for decades. The accusations, Yuxian knew, were wild distortions of the truth.

Spurred by the falsehoods of the Great Leap Forward, Yuxian turned anew to the earlier antirightist campaign and read for the first time articles by leading rightists—men like Liu Binyan, the courageous reporter intent on reforming the system through exposing injustice and to whom twenty years later Ni would turn for help; Wang Meng, the idealistic writer who wrote about the disappointment of youth confronting the giant, intransigent bureaucracy; and Fei Xiatong, the country's leading anthropologist and advocate of a more balanced approach to rural reform. Now publicly disgraced and passing their lives in internal exile, Ni discovered these men to be thoughtful and reasonable patriots with the good of their country at heart.

The lesson of the political movement was reasserted once more. To criticize the party by telling the truth, even—perhaps especially—in the interests of the Chinese people, was to court ostracism, attack, or imprisonment. Silence was the only safe course.

• • •

So what was this Marxism-Leninism Mao Zedong thought? Every newspaper article, every statement from the mouth of an official or party member was filled with quotations from Marx and Lenin, Stalin and Mao, as though only by quoting from the socialist masters was any statement true. But Yuxian hated Marxism-Leninism Mao Zedong thought. He hated it for telling lies, and he hated Mao's insistence on dividing people into classes. Classes after all were the cause of the inequality and injustice that had thrown Yuxian to the bottom of the political ladder. But if the reality of the world around him and the reality as described by the party were so different then maybe the reality of Marxism-Leninism Mao Zedong thought was different, too. Yuxian set out to read the Marxist classics in the original.

A whole new world was revealed. The Marxism-Leninism of the Chinese press and of his teachers and officialdom was a perversion of real Marxism. Fundamental to Marxism, for instance, was the primacy of material conditions and the insistence that policy emanate from reality. But in the Great Leap Forward, objective conditions—of tried and tested farming techniques in the countryside, of basic production in the cities—were being ignored, with disastrous results.

Marxism argued, too, that the masses are the motivating force of history, not any great leader or savior. Yet in China, was not Mao Zedong being adulated as the great leader, the great teacher—the savior of the nation?

Through his reading of the Marxist classics, Ni Yuxian became a Marxist himself, finding in real Marxism a commitment to the truth and a hope for the future. "Whoever opposes the dialectic will receive the penalty of the dialectic," Engels had written. "If the Chinese leadership does not dare to tell the truth, if the leadership continues to speak falsity," Yuxian thought, "eventually they will receive the judgment of history."

• • •

Withdrawn as he was into the world of reading, Yuxian's grades not only improved, but in history and the humanities became among the best in the class, his closest competitors for excellence being his fellow pariahs, the other backward elements. Yuxian was led to the proposition that the system was worst to its best and its brightest, that individuals of ability and talent were inevitably cast to the bottom of the heap, bound there to clash with the authorities. He and his fellow backward elements became bosom buddies and eventually found in their political apartheid a certain freedom that had not seemed initially to exist. Excluded from the circle, trusted fully by no one, they formed their own small circle, expressing their opinions openly, defying authority and criticizing freely, with little fear of retribution. The school authorities had few means left to punish them. They were already outside the circle. The backward elements became known as the ones who dared to tell the truth.

• • •

Periodically, though, the school authorities found occasions to remind the backward elements where power lay.

One Monday morning, just as Yuxian was arriving at school, Pockfaced Huang sidetracked him, grabbing the boy tightly by the arm. "You're not going to class today," the political instructor commanded gruffly. "There are some people here who want to see you."

Yuxian was led to the school's party branch office, home to the students' confidential political files. Every educated Chinese has a file—a *dangan*—which begins in middle school and follows him through life, wherever he may go. No one is allowed to see this file, but everyone knows that all transgressions, major and minor, and many which might not even be true, are recorded there, to be resurrected should the occasion, such as a political campaign, require. Aspirants to party membership must be possessed of immaculate files, and whether behavior outside the norm has been observed and recorded in one's record is a perennial worry for those whose actions do not always fit the mold.

Yuxian had never entered the room that housed the files, and he remembers that the curtains were drawn, as though for a secret meeting. Principal Xia and several officials from the Public Security Bureau were glumly awaiting him.

Principal Xia slammed the door. "You'd better speak frankly here," he instructed roughly. "Tell the truth. We don't want any lies." Yuxian stood, facing the angry glares of the principal and the public security representatives. For two long minutes they continued to glare in silence.

"Do you know why we had you come here today?" one of the public security officials finally demanded.

"No."

"What is your name?"

"If you don't know my name, why did you call me in here?"

"Do you know what I'm doing here?"

"No, I don't know what you are doing here." Yuxian was tired of waiting for his invitation to be seated. He pulled up a stool and sat down.

"I'll tell you," the officer said. "I'm from the Public Security Bureau. You'd better answer my questions honestly or there'll be trouble for you."

"If you keep up this attitude and treat me like this, then I'm leaving," the defiant young boy responded angrily.

"Do you know who I am? Do you know what I do? Do you know what the Public Security Bureau is?" the officer yelled back, standing up and leaning forward across the desk.

"Yes, I know what you do. So you're the Public Security Bureau. But the Public Security Bureau are people, too, right? And I'm a person, too, right? If you want to ask me some questions, then ask them. But ask them politely. Stop treating me like some kind of criminal."

"You're suspected of being an accomplice in a counterrevolutionary incident," the officer responded, his head bobbing in self-righteous contempt. "We want you to tell us what you did last Saturday afternoon. If you don't cooperate we're going to lock you up."

"How can you lock me up if I haven't done anything wrong?"

the young boy insisted. "What authority do you have to lock me up? If you think you can just go around locking up whoever you want, you're wrong. You're disobeying the law."

The officer slammed his palm against the desk. "You arrogant brat," he yelled. "You'd better be careful. You're going to be sorry."

Yuxian stood up, opened the door, and slammed it loudly behind him, walking back to class. He heard the muffled yells of the public security officer demanding his return.

Pockfaced Huang was startled to see his student. "I'm not going to talk to them," Yuxian asserted, sulking into his seat. Huang left the room quickly to investigate, reappearing moments later with Principal Xia.

"What do you think you're doing?" the principal shouted, indignant. "The Public Security Bureau is trying to question you."

"I don't like their attitude. I don't like your attitude, either. You're supposed to be a teacher, and I'm a student. You're a human being, and I'm a human being. There's no need to treat me like this. That public security guy is treating me like a criminal. What have I done wrong? I haven't done anything wrong. If he thinks he can treat me like a criminal, he's wrong. I refuse to cooperate with him."

Pockfaced Huang became conciliatory. "Yuxian, your attitude isn't correct," he cajoled his recalcitrant student. "The comrade from the Public Security Bureau hasn't said you're a bad person. They're just here carrying out an investigation. They just want to know what you were doing Saturday afternoon. All you have to do is talk to him, tell him what you were doing."

"If he wants to know what I was doing, he can ask me politely. Anyway, I don't have to tell him what I was doing. It's my own private business. If he doesn't change his attitude, I won't talk to him at all."

That afternoon, the Public Security Bureau sent in a new team to interrogate the uncooperative Ni Yuxian. "Maybe our comrade was a little too severe," the new representative began by way of apology. "We hear you didn't get along so well with him. All we want to know is what you were doing Saturday afternoon."

"I went to the park with some of my friends."

"What did you do?"

"We played badminton."

"Did you do anything else?"

"No."

"Did you see anyone else doing anything bad?"

"No, we were just playing badminton."

"What about this?" The officer showed the boy a photograph.

"What about it? It's a picture of a tree."

"Look." Barely visible, hardly legible through the bark of the tree, someone had carved "Down with Mao Zedong."

"Did you do this?"

"No, of course not."

"Are you willing to guarantee that you were only playing?"

"Yes."

The public security officer wrote a few comments on the notes his assistant had been writing and shoved them in front of Yuxian, inviting the young boy to sign. Yuxian complied.

When Yuxian returned to class, his friend Ji Tie was sobbing, inconsolate. Ji Tie was another backward element, one of the five friends who had gone to the park that Saturday afternoon. While Yuxian had been questioned in the party branch office, the other four were being questioned, too.

"Why are you crying?" Yuxian urged his friend. "What's wrong? Tell me, Ji Tie."

"They accused me of writing a reactionary slogan," Ji Tie bellowed. "They made me write 'Mao Zedong, Mao Zedong, Mao Zedong' over and over and over again. They said I wrote Mao Zedong like the reactionary slogan on the tree. But I didn't carve the slogan on the tree."

The boys had not carved "Down with Mao Zedong" on the tree, and quickly, because the police found the real culprits, the matter was dropped.

But Yuxian never forgave Pockfaced Huang for the incident. Huang was the only person who had known the boys were going to the park that day, and he alone could have reported them to the Public Security Bureau.

Pockfaced Huang never forgave Ni Yuxian for his defiance, either. The sole responsibility the teacher had once entrusted to Yuxian—the organization of extracurricular activities—was taken away. That summer, when the entire class was sent to spend the summer vacation in militia training at an antiaircraft base, only Ni Yuxian and the daughter of a former landlord, the two most backward elements, were not allowed to go. The base, it was said, might contain military secrets, with which the two could not be trusted. Yuxian was delighted to stay at home. He spent his vacation reading. But Pockfaced Huang's intention had been to cause Yuxian to lose face, to isolate him further from his fellow students, to make it publicly known that Yuxian was not trusted by the party, the Youth League, or the school.

• • •

Pockfaced Huang meddled in affairs of the heart as well.

• • •

Puberty had struck Yuxian with a shock. One day, disrobing with his friends for a skinny-dip in the canal, he had been frightened to discover three thick brown hairs protruding from the region of his penis. Having failed in his several previous efforts to observe adult members of his own gender in the nude, Yuxian was engulfed by a fleeting moment of self-doubt, entertaining for a passing instant the possibility that something was wrong and that he was less than perfect. Quickly dressing, he set out for the public lavatories in a determined attempt to discover if other men suffered a similar affliction.

More perplexing still was the embarrassing and uncontrollable hardening of his private parts that began seizing him unpredictably while waiting in the cafeteria line for lunch. Comfort came finally from Guansheng, ever earthy but by then already fading, who bellowed with reassuringly hearty laughter when his grandson shamefully confessed one night to the bewildering changes that were marking his transition from childhood into adolescence.

Zhao Yuefang arrived at Yangsi Middle School not long after Yuxian's last skinny-dip in the canal and the embarrassments of waiting in line. The teenaged girl was tiny, pretty, and athletic— an accomplished gymnast. Her village had no senior middle school, and since home was nearly two hours away by bus, she lived during the week at school.

Yuxian's excessive attentions began the very first day the new student arrived. She had the same name as Tao Yuefang, and he was curious to discover whether two girls with the same name would also have the same personality. Yuxian's ongoing war against the opposite sex was about to come to an end.

He found that Zhao Yuefang liked to laugh and have fun. She had a naughty streak that the exuberant and rambunctious Yuxian found particularly endearing, and she liked to tease. Being one of the shortest in the class, she sat in the front row ahead of Yuxian, and the young boy delighted in the opportunity to smile at her whenever she turned around to look at what was happening behind.

"Why are you always looking at me?" Zhao Yuefang teased him once, beaming. She remembers feeling his attentions, his eyes boring into her back, even while facing the teacher.

"If you didn't turn your head around to look at me, how would you ever know I was looking at you?" he flirted back.

Yuefang was good at sports but not so good at history and literature—the areas in which Yuxian excelled. Yuxian began offering his help with her studies. He would come to the study room after dinner, and sometimes they would work together until late into the night.

One weekend afternoon, as he was returning home for the evening meal, Yuefang stopped him. "Yuxian, I have a problem," she pleaded. "Can you help me? It's Saturday and the cafeteria is closed today, so I don't have anything to eat." This was a test of Yuxian's devotion. To share one's rice in the midst of a famine, when everyone was hungry, was a gesture beyond the bounds of mere friendship. Yuxian promised to bring her some rice. Yuefang was somebody special.

Running to school with a bowl of steamed rice into which Xu Fengzhen had mixed a precious egg, Yuxian was still embarrassed to admit publicly his growing infatuation. He secretly put the food, still wrapped for warmth in one of his shirts, in Yuefang's desk drawer, informing the girl of his goodwill gesture in private.

"But Yuxian, I was just teasing," Zhao Yuefang exclaimed when she heard of his good deed. "The school arranged for our food. I didn't really mean for you to bring me rice." But the gesture had been made, its meaning clear. The two students talked that night not about their schoolwork but about life, about their families, and their different views of the world.

Not long afterward, when Yuxian was leaving the study room to return home, Zhao Yuefang and her girlfriend seized the pretext of stopping at a small shop for a snack to begin walking home with him.

"Why are you going home so early tonight, Yuxian?" Zhao Yuefang asked. It was already dark and the moon was very bright. This was the first time Yuxian had walked with a girl in the moonlight.

"I have to fetch water for my family," he explained. With no running water and no canal out back, the family had to draw water from a distant well, carrying it home suspended from carrying poles, in two big round jugs that held fifty pounds each. Yuxian was planning on making several trips that night. "Oh, then, we'll help you," the girls giggled. Yuxian thought they were kidding, but they really did help, even though they were not very strong. Time seemed to fly talking and walking with the girls. When they finished, Yuxian introduced his friends to his mother, and Xu Fengzhen presented each with a sweet mooncake, because the Mid-Autumn Moon Festival, when the moon is at its brightest and roundest, was approaching.

It was nearly midnight when Yuxian walked the girls back. The school gates were already locked. "I know a way," Yuxian assured them, and they sneaked around to the back where Yuxian saw them safely through a gaping hole in the fence. The adolescent boy was happy that night, walking home in the fading moonlight. He had a girlfriend now. It was no longer a secret, either.

Romance among middle school students was not condoned by school authorities. There were regulations against falling in love. During junior middle school, when two older students were discovered secretly going to a movie together in the city, Buddhist Li had organized a struggle session against the young couple. "What did you two do?" Buddhist Li had demanded in front of the entire class. "What bad things did you do?"

The couple, embarrassed and humiliated, denied any wrongdoing, but the whole class was called upon to participate in the questioning. "Did you bump noses?" the students kept demanding, relentlessly curious. Kissing is not a Chinese habit, and it would be years before the young people discovered that the romantic encounters in the foreign films they frequented, which invariably sent them into gales of laughter, involved mouths rather than the rubbing of noses.

Pockfaced Huang soon interfered in the budding romance between Zhao Yuefang and Ni Yuxian.

Yuxian's devotion to the harmonica had continued, and often he played for school events, serving as the accompaniment to the folk dancing that was the core of student performances. During the practice session for one such performance, however, Zhao Yuefang kept upsetting the dance. Whenever it came time for her to join hands with a boy and swing around together in a circle, she would balk. "I thought Ni Yuxian wouldn't want me to hold hands with another boy," she remembers. Yuxian, flattered, thought the problem would be solved by his staying away from the actual performance, letting one of his friends play the harmonica instead.

Only later did Yuxian learn that just before the high school dance troupe was to go on stage, after their costumes were on and their faces made up, Zhao Yuefang had thrown the whole schedule into turmoil by announcing that she would not perform. She still refused to hold hands with a boy.

Basking in the satisfaction of her singular devotion, Yuxian did not question Yuefang's handling of the matter, waiting as she had until the very last minute to announce her refusal to dance. So he was not prepared for Pockfaced Huang's response. Zhao Yuefang was asked to make a public self-investigation, a confession to the entire class. If not, Pockfaced Huang assured her, she would be punished, and the mark would go down in her *dangan*. With such a blotch on her record, she could face difficulties well into adulthood—in finding a work assignment, in getting into the university, and certainly in being admitted into the Youth League or party. Punishments like this were ordinarily reserved for the backward elements like Ni Yuxian. Zhao Yuefang was a middling element, and her father was a worker, of "good" class background, and a member of the Communist Party.

Yuxian did not believe that Zhao Yuefang would make the self-investigation or confess to her crime. He did not think the young girl had done anything wrong. To him, already outside the circle, his file no doubt already brimming over with details of his transgressions, with no thought of entering the party or Youth League, even the punishment did not seem so severe. As the meeting began, he still assumed that Zhao Yuefang would refuse to comply.

"Zhao Yuefang has to make a self-investigation," Pockfaced Huang began the meeting in no uncertain terms. "If not, she will be punished."

Zhao Yuefang stood up. Her face was red with humiliation, and her hands were trembling. She had never spoken in public before, and she hated the prospect. All eyes turned to Ni Yuxian as the girl began reading from the self-confession she had prepared. Was it not Ni Yuxian after all who had brought her to this awful state?

Yuxian was embarrassed, but also upset with Zhao Yuefang for having complied with Pockfaced Huang's demands. "I wanted her to be more brave," he recalls.

Pockfaced Huang and the Youth League students began pressuring Zhao Yuefang to end her relationship with Yuxian. "Your father is a member of the party," Pockfaced Huang would begin his conversations with the girl, "but Yuxian's thought, his behavior, is not good. Why do you want to be with him? He isn't good for you. You'd better watch out for him."

After Pockfaced Huang gave Zhao Yuefang a *C* in conduct, Yuxian received a message from his girlfriend, delivered through one of the students in the Youth League, returning all the letters Yuxian had written and asking that Yuxian return all of hers. "We can't talk anymore," Yuefang wrote.

After that, whenever Yuxian saw Zhao Yuefang, she would avert her eyes, pretending not to see or recognize him, as though they had never known each other and he was not even there. Often, when he returned to study hall after dinner in the evenings, Yuxian would notice Yuefang laughing and talking with the Youth League members. She would turn red and stop after realizing that Yuxian had returned, but to him it seemed as though Yuefang was switching her friendships from those considered most backward, like him and his friends, to those considered most progressive—the students Ni Yuxian most reviled.

Yuxian was angry with his one-time girlfriend. He thought that if she really liked him, she should not have succumbed to the demands of politics. She should not have been so afraid.

Zhao Yuefang remembers it differently. It was not the demands of politics to which she succumbed but the regulations against middle school students falling in love.

• • •

Months later, during the evening study hall, the gatekeeper who also manned the school's telephone suddenly burst into the quiet room. "Which one of you is Zhao Yuefang?" he demanded. "Come quickly. There's an important phone call from your family."

Zhao Yuefang did not come back to study hall that night, and she was not in school the next day. Yuxian could guess what had happened. Walking Zhao Yuefang home one day when the romance was just budding, he had met the girl's aged grandmother, already deaf and nearly blind. They had teased the old woman into believing that Yuxian was Zhao Yuefang's teacher. "Is Fangfang a good student?" the grandmother had wanted to know, referring to her granddaughter by her familiar name. "Oh, yes, very good, very good," Yuxian had assured the old woman, as he and Yuefang struggled to suppress their giggles. The grandmother had given him some corn.

Zhao Yuefang's grandmother must have died.

Knowing how much Zhao Yuefang loved the old woman, and worried that her loss would hit the young girl hard, Yuxian decided to write his former girlfriend a note.

"If I am not wrong," Yuxian began, "then your grandmother has died. I know this is difficult for you. But your grandmother was very old already. Everyone has to die. Don't be too upset. I am worried about you. You have my sympathy."

The summer vacation started before Zhao Yuefang returned to school. Ni Yuxian began indulging in his summer reading list. Absorbed in a book one afternoon, he heard a tiny voice beyond the courtyard gate calling his name. It was the five-year-old sister of Zhao Yuefang's best friend—the one who had been with her when they helped Yuxian carry the water. "My sister wants you to go to our house," the little child said. "She has something important."

Zhao Yuefang was at her friend's house, her eyes red from crying but looking fetchingly pretty in a new blouse and skirt of the same matching color of blue. "Are you still angry with me?" Zhao Yuefang asked.

"No, I'm not angry. But why do you dare to call me? Aren't you afraid that Pockfaced Huang will criticize you again?" Yuxian was dubious.

"I'm not going to pay attention to Huang anymore," Yuefang answered, her chin rising in the air to show her defiance. "I hate that old Pockfaced Huang. He gave me a C, but what did I do wrong? I was just a little close to you, that's all."

The romance of Ni Yuxian and Zhao Yuefang thus blossomed anew that day, in the summer of 1960. The next two years would be the most difficult in their young lives. Often there would be nothing to eat and they would be so hungry they sometimes could not believe they were still alive. But Pockfaced Huang never came between them again, and Yuxian would look back decades later and remember this as the finest, happiest period of his young and still-innocent first love.

• • •

Though forced to stand on the periphery of the circle, the best of Ni Yuxian's teachers continued to appreciate the young boy's quick intelligence and exuberant curiosity, encouraging him in his studies and sometimes even deferring to him in matters of knowledge. Even Pockfaced Huang, locked inextricably into battle as he was with this singularly difficult young charge, was willing to entertain the possibility that the boy might still, with work, be redeemed. When the People's Liberation Army began recruiting from Yangsi Middle School, Yuxian was allowed to take the medical tests. Even in the midst of hunger, the youth was strong as an ox, his health excellent. Pockfaced Huang was faced with choosing which two of the ten healthiest students should be allowed to enter the army.

Ni Yuxian knows that Huang pondered his decision at length, consulting with his superiors in the party. Ni Yuxian's political thought was problematic, but he could not really be considered bad. Maybe if he were to spend some time in the army, closely supervised, subjected to a rigid discipline, the young boy might change. Maybe the boy would turn out all right. At Yangsi Middle School, though, the boy's disruptions were sure to continue. He was already beyond the control of his teachers. With a year of senior middle school left to complete, Ni Yuxian was offered the opportunity to enter the army.

Yuxian's family was delighted. With a son in the army, the family's standing would change. Ni Jizhong's status as an intellectual and his label as one who had stood on the side of the rightists did not serve the family well in these troubled times. But with a son in the army, they would be transformed overnight into a high-status revolutionary family, respected by all.

There was a practical reason as well. The family was still hungry. Yuxian, as the oldest son, was entitled to twenty-seven catties of dry rice a month. But still he was hungry. In the army, he would get forty-five catties of rice a month. He could eat his fill. His battle with hunger would be won.

Yuxian was less enthusiastic about the prospect of joining the military, but he was curious to know what such a life would be like. He decided to accept.

Just before leaving for military training, on his last day of class, the circle at Yangsi Middle School was opened to permit Yuxian to join once more. For the first time in years, he felt as though he belonged, that his political problems were not so serious after all. The whole class gathered together to send him and his classmate, Yang Guoli, off, and everyone had his picture taken with the two comrades from the People's Liberation Army. Pockfaced Huang even made a brief speech about how glorious it was to serve in the army and presented the young soldiers with gifts of Chairman Mao's *Selected Works*. They sang patriotic songs and then gathered to wave the two young soldiers farewell.

Honor redounded to the entire Ni family as well, because in China, as the saying goes, when one member of the family makes good even the household chickens benefit. Relatives and neighbors from all around came to congratulate Xu Fengzhen and Ni Jizhong, and everywhere the walls were pasted with the big red symbols of double happiness. The girls from Yuxian's class, Zhao Yuefang included, came to wish the young soldier well, and Xu Fengzhen invited everyone inside. When the car came that night to pick up the young recruit, the whole neighborhood gathered in front of their gates to wave good-bye. Face and honor were gained all around. The Nis had become a revolutionary family.

• • •

The first night in the army, at a temporary base not too far from his family's home, Ni Yuxian ate meat and eggs and vegetables—and several bowls of rice—until he could eat no more. It was the first time in nearly two years had eaten until he was full.

The next morning when he donned his new uniform and walked to Zhao Yuefang's house to say good-bye, the children along the street addressed him as "uncle." He and his girlfriend had their picture taken together for the first time ever, thus further sealing their relationship.

The young couple did not talk much as Zhao Yuefang slowly walked Yuxian back to camp. "Be careful," were the only words she could muster, tears in her eyes, when they parted.

No one saw them off that night, when Yuxian and five hundred other new recruits piled into several open boats that waited along the banks of the Huangpu River. Their secret destination would not be revealed until they arrived.

As the boat slipped silently past the Bund, its solid Western-style buildings rooted mutely behind the tree-lined park that hugged the river, Yuxian knew he was beginning a new life. What kind of life or where it would lead, he did not know. It was the first time he had ever left Shanghai. He was sixteen years old.

• • •

The army delivered on its promise of food. Gold Mountain they called the dilapidated, disheveled old temple complex nestled by the edge of the sea far to the south of Shanghai in Jiangsu Province, just at the border of Zhejiang, where the new recruits were sent. Yuxian's new company commander was particularly enterprising in matters of the stomach, and the entrepreneurial spirit with which he carried out the call for military self-sufficiency had resulted in a life of plenty for his men. The company used sophisticated tools to farm vast plots of land. They raised pigs and chickens and grew a multitude of vegetables, and the men made their own delicious bean curd. So abundant was the food that it was dished into the soldiers' washbasins rather than the standard-size bowls, and oil was so plentiful they could eat *youtiao*, the deep-fried semisweet crullers for which the south is famous, every day and still make a profit selling the leftovers to soldiers from other squads. Most of the new recruits had been hungry when they arrived. For the first few days—until they had become completely satiated and were assured that food would always be plentiful—the refectory tables were the scene of near-pitched battles, as the young boys grabbed what they could to eat, elbowing others away, wolfing down their food without regard for decorum or their neighbors' needs.

With food so plentiful, the company was a magnet for hungry people with claims to a military connection. The local cadres from the surrounding countryside were frequent guests at the company commander's table, where the delicacies of the banquet fare were unsurpassed for miles around. Demobilized soldiers who had been sent to become leaders in their native villages used alleged "refresher courses" as an excuse to return to camp, which allowed them also to partake of the company's meals. After a month of refreshing, considerable encouragment had to be brought to bear to force the demobilized soldiers home. Even Ni Jizhong and Xu Fengzhen, worried about their sixteen-year-old son during in his first separation from the family, were guests at the captain's table during their visit to Gold Mountain military base. It was the furthest the couple had ever been from Shanghai, and they dined better than they had—or would—in years.

Emaciated wives of the noncommissioned officers were drawn to the camp occasionally, too. Yuxian once met the wife of his platoon leader, not yet thirty but looking old enough to be the leader's mother, a filthy mess of skin and bones in black peasant garb, her trousers held up by a rough hemp rope tied around a skinny waist, her whole image harkening back to the famine-ridden days of the past that Yuxian had seen only in photographs and had thought were gone forever.

The gulf between the abundance of the military and the hunger of the countryside was vast.

As a senior middle school student with much more education than the average, often nearly illiterate, peasant recruit, Ni was assigned to a wireless radio squad that spent much of its time operating in local villages, often in peasants' homes. In the countryside, meeting with the farmers, observing their difficulties, he was shocked to discover that the hunger he had experienced in Shanghai was plenty compared to the lot of the simple villagers. Confronted daily with the reality of poverty, he determined to do a private sociological investigation into the situation in the countryside. Chairman Mao had first called upon Communist Party members to conduct such investigations during the late 1920s, when famine and oppression were leading the Chinese peasants to revolt. "No investigation, no right to speak," Mao had written in 1929. Ni Yuxian's research would grant him the right to speak out against injustice. He wanted to know what families were eating and how much, what their incomes were, whether they were in debt, and whether their lives really were better now than before "liberation." He wanted to know about the relationship between the peasants and the cadres, how much the cadres earned and whether they worked in the fields or simply sat and gave orders from their desks. He wanted to know about the former landlords and how they were faring.

The peasants around Gold Mountain were mired in a poverty that Yuxian had earlier not even imagined possible. Their staple food was not rice or even coarse grain but wild grass mixed with coarse grain. They never ate meat, and there was no sugar or oil. At best, the peasant could indulge in some beans and squash and an occasional green vegetable. Even the pigs in Shanghai ate better than the average peasant on Gold Mountain.

The peasants lived in dilapidated straw huts without electricity and devoid of any furniture save a couple of rude chairs. There were no wells, so the water had to be fetched from streams—not for bathing or laundry, certainly, but for drinking and cooking. The people were filthy, soap unknown, hands, faces, and bodies black with dirt. The latrines were open pits beside the huts, and sanitary conditions were abominable. Clothes were homespun. No one in the villages had ever actually bought cloth. Most were already so in debt to the commune that a whole lifetime would not be long enough to pay back the loans.

Yuxian was confronted anew, but at a more frightening level, with the discrepancy between what he read in the party reports and his experience of everyday life. The books he continued to read still described how poor the peasants had been before liberation and how happy and prosperous they had become with the advent of socialism. But Gold Mountain had not greatly changed. To call the peasants happy, to describe them as prosperous, was a cruel and capricious mockery. They were poor. They were hungry.

Perhaps Gold Mountain was an exception. Perhaps this particular area was especially poor. Perhaps there were reasons. Yuxian needed to make further investigations.

One evening, Ni Yuxian noticed Xiao Liu, one of his new army friends, crying over a letter he had just received. The next day the friend did not participate in the platoon's activities. When the two were together in their barracks that night, Yuxian asked Xiao Liu what was wrong.

"My whole family has starved to death," his friend replied simply. Xiao Liu was from Anhui, the province just west of Gold Mountain base and one of the poorest in the nation. Soon Yuxian began to notice other of his fellow soldiers weeping when they received letters from home. He began questioning his comrades. Their stories were always the same. The families of the soldiers were starving. Many were from Anhui.

Figures released decades later would reveal that Anhui was the worst hit of all of China's provinces during the three bad years. Two million people died. The famine there lasted longer.

Yuxian tried to piece together a picture of hunger. Later he would visit Anhui himself.

There was no grain to eat in many villages from which his fellow recruits had come, and people had turned first to eating leaves, wild grass, the straw from their roofs, and finally the bark from trees. In some cases, the countryside was so denuded and people so hungry that they had been forced to eat dirt mixed with water—after which they quickly died. Sometimes, people were so weak they lacked the strength to gather the wild grass that might at least have kept them alive.

Yuxian interviewed the soldiers who had returned from visiting their families. The soldiers were sent off with bread and flour to distribute to their relatives but had to carry loaded guns to protect themselves on the trains. Hungry peasants with knives were killing for food.

The returning soldiers told of whole villages dying of starvation, of people so weak there was no one to dispose of the bodies, of the dead in their homes, in the streets, littering the hillsides where ordinarily they would have been buried, of skeletons and rotting corpses, of hungry, hungry ghosts. In Shanghai, in Gold Mountain, people were dying of diseases associated with hunger but rarely of hunger itself. In Anhui people were starving to death by the tens and hundreds of thousands.

But the officials, the local cadres, had enough to eat. At harvest time, the officials had made certain to collect enough grain to see themselves and their families through.

In ordinary times, the guilt for agricultural catastrophe in China rests with the weather—or war. Farming in China is prescientific, but it is based upon folk wisdom handed down over countless generations, on an understanding between the peasant and his land in which, as Vaclav Havel has pointed out with respect to his own country, "everything was bound together by a thousand threads of mutual, meaningful connection." The peasant was responsible to his land like a mother to her child, and if nature was sometimes capricious, betraying those who had nurtured it so well, this only proved that heaven moves in mysterious ways.

But the weather in Anhui and Jiangsu Province where Gold Mountain was located had not, Ni Yuxian insists, been particularly out of the ordinary in recent years. The calamity that Ni Yuxian was witnessing had not been dictated only by heaven. It was the invasion by the party and the arrogance of its revolutionary new farming techniques that had so upset the balance. With the organization of the villages into people's communes, the peasants who knew their land best had been denied their relationship to it. Decision-making over daily details of farming life—when to plant, how, and where, how much of what kind of fertilizer to apply, when to work and when to rest and when to have meetings, how much grain each person would eat, how much a peasant would receive in cash and how much in kind, whether to grant sick leave—was usurped by the party cadre "superiors." The land, but not the people who farmed it, had in turn rebelled.

With the emphasis of the Great Leap Forward on industrialization, men who all their lives had been responsible to the soil had been taken out of the fields to work in industrial pursuits, and women whose responsibilities had been closer to home were sent to till unknown fields. Because the reported, but grossly falsified, yields were so enormous, fertile land was often taken out of cultivation altogether, with a consequent drop in overall agricultural output. The new methods of deep plowing destroyed the topsoil faithfully nourished over the centuries, and plants smothered to death from the overcrowding of close planting. Accumulated generations of experience had taught the peasants which crops grew best in which fields, but the new structure of the communes assaulted that natural agreement as well.

When mess halls were introduced in the fall of 1958, the peasants had been encouraged at first to eat to their hearts' content, sometimes stuffing themselves on five meals a day and often competing to see who could eat the most food. But even with the bumper harvest that year, food was only adequate, not abundant, and many places had gorged themselves into hunger.

With the press continually announcing one fantastic success after another, and the ongoing attacks against Peng Dehuai and the right deviationsists who had dared to report the truth, local cadres were under pressure to report that everything was fine. No local official wanted to fail. As their cadres reported ever higher and higher—but completely fabricated—yields, the peasants were taxed at the fabricated rate. Grain that would have been adequate for sustenance was taxed away.

Man, not the weather, had upset the balance, and everywhere people were dying. Where, Yuxian wanted to know, was the party's sense of responsibility? The party was letting people starve.

What was most remarkable to Ni Yuxian was the fact that even knowing the cadres were wrong, certain that their decisions were ill-advised and would bring disaster to them all, the peasants remained docile, compliant, unwilling to oppose the party. The toiling peasants had become mere screws in the party machinery. "If they wanted you to die, you died," Yuxian asserts. "If they wanted you to live, you lived." The peasants were willing to starve to death rather than disobey the party.

Why such quiescence in the face of unremitting disaster? Compliance to authority—shattered periodically by spectacular and bloody outbursts of rebellion—had been ingrained into the Chinese peasant from time immemorial. Yuxian speculated also that the early campaigns orchestrated by the party had taught the peasants well. Fear was the underlying basis of their compliance. The peasants had participated themselves in the struggle sessions against the landlords, and they knew the price of opposing party policies. To oppose a cadre's opinion or to challenge party policy was to oppose the Communist Party itself; to oppose the Communist Party was to risk becoming a counterrevolutionary. To be labeled a counterrevolutionary was to risk execution, for counterrevolution was a capital offense. If a counterrevolutionary were allowed to live, he would suffer all his life. The lot of the ordinary peasant, marginal even in the best of times, was difficult enough. Once labeled a counterrevolutionary, the work points and grain rations that were a major determinant of a peasant's standard of living would be reduced his whole life long to the level of subsistence, and he would become as R. H. Tawney's classic description of the Chinese peasant, standing perpetually in water up to his nose, threatened always by the smallest ripple. In the organization of labor, the counterrevolutionary would be forced to continue working when other peasants were allowed to rest. At the end of the day, when the other peasants were allow to return home, the counterrevolutionary would be forced to stay. The whole family would suffer the unbearable humiliation and indignity of ostracism. For the uneducated peasant, there was no escape to poetry, painting, or books. To be a counterrevolutionary was to be denied any semblance of humanity. To have little and to be threatened with less is a powerful goad to compliance, the sense of deprivation being relative rather than absolute. Better to risk dying of hunger than oppose the party and live as a counterrevolutionary. Never before in the history of China had a government possessed so much power.

Yuxian's heart went out to the frightened, simple, illiterate folk who listened dumbly to the cadres' orders, acting so faithfully in accordance with their directives, never raising a question. The reality of the countryside around him, the reality of the power exercised by the party over simple folk, stood outrageously at odds with Ni Yuxian's Marxist-Leninist ideals. Marxist-Leninist philosophy propagated the happiness and well-being of the people, a life without exploitation, where individuals were free to make their own choices, to follow their own paths, to choose their own destinies.

How could a sixteen-year-old soldier save so many millions of starving people? The sense of power instilled in infancy was with

Ni Yuxian still. The adolescent boy, feeling himself responsible for the hungry masses of China, believed he could save his country. The highest leaders must be informed. Perhaps Chairman Mao did not know about the catastrophe sweeping the land. Maybe he was being deceived by unscrupulous advisors and the lower-level cadres. He must be told.

Ni Yuxian decided to write a letter to Chairman Mao.

He was aware of the potential danger inherent in writing. In imperial times, commoners had no right to petition the throne, and even ministers criticized the emperor at grave risk to their positions and their lives. Former Minister of Defense Peng Dehuai had been vested with the right to petition the emperor but was still being persecuted for the letter he had written to Chairman Mao criticizing the petty bourgeois fanaticism of the Great Leap Forward and the people's communes.

Good intentions were not sufficient protection from attack. Yuxian included a poem in his letter. "I am like a newborn ox that does not yet fear tigers," he said. But he avowed his willingness to suffer personally on behalf of the Chinese people.

The letter was divided into three parts. In the first, Yuxian reported, Maoist style, on his sociological investigation into the situation in the countryside, describing the poverty and hunger, the starvation and death that were everywhere around. "The situation is extremely serious," he gravely admonished.

In the second section, in language dripping with the vocabulary of Marxism-Leninism, he analyzed the underlying reasons for the disaster. The party was ignoring objective material conditions, he argued. A given piece of land can only produce so much. But everywhere the party was deceiving itself through wishful thinking, acting according to what it wanted to be true rather than on the basis of reality itself.

Finally, Yuxian presented his solution to the problem. The communes should be broken up, he argued, and the fields returned to the farmers, with the right to till the land free of interference guaranteed for a full ten years. The peasants, and not the party cadres, should decide what to plant on the land, and farmers should retain the right to choose whether to sell their agricultural produce directly to the state, on the open market, or to keep it for their own livelihood. Peasants should be allowed to raise chickens and pigs freely, as many as they liked. Taxes should be eliminated altogether to give the farmers time to recoup, and if the state could not afford to forgo tax revenues completely, taxes should still be drastically reduced. Only thus could the countryside overcome the terrible crisis.

The letter took him two weeks to write and was thirty pages long.

In the dark of night, after the barracks was asleep, hiding under a blanket and reading by flashlight, Yuxian shared the lengthy document with his three best friends. The content of the treatise, they all agreed, was absolutely correct. Whether to send it to Chairman Mao, however, was a question of dispute. Only Yang Guoli, Yuxian's classmate from Yangsi Middle School, agreed that the letter must be sent.

"I know it's dangerous," his friend argued. "But we have to be responsible to the peasants. If you don't take responsibility, who will? If Chairman Mao really does read the letter, if he knows the true situation, then the results just have to be good. The policies will change." His other friends were not so sure, frightened of the possible outcome if somehow the letter should fall into less than sympathetic hands, failing to reach Chairman Mao.

Secrets are not easily kept in the crowded conditions of a primitive army barracks. While Yuxian was perfecting the Marxist prose of his letter and copying it once more for final dispatch, he received a series of visits from his military commanders.

"I want to see what you have written," the company commander said to Yuxian. "That is an order."

Yuxian's conflict with the company commander had begun almost the moment the raw middle school recruit had arrived in the camp. Yuxian's enthusiasm for the life of a soldier was wanting. When reveille sounded at six thirty in the morning and the troops had two minutes to make their beds, fold their quilts, wash their faces, brush their teeth, dress, and line up in formation outside, yelling and being yelled at all the while, Yuxian refused to be hurried. He resented being roused unexpectedly in the middle of the night to go out on surprise maneuvers. The transformation from student into machine, the abrogation of his personal freedom, the necessity of submitting to orders, had been distressing.

The uneducated company commander particularly resented Yuxian's devotion to reading. "There is someone among us," he used to say during meetings, scrupulously avoiding names, "who thinks that studying Chairman Mao is not enough, who likes to read other books, too. But there is no need to study anything but

Chairman Mao. A whole lifetime is not enough time to understand Chairman Mao completely. There is someone among us whose tail is very arrogant. If he doesn't reform himself, he's going to be in dangerous trouble." When, after the first four months in the army, most of Yuxian's fellow recruits were promoted to two-star privates, Yuxian still had only one. His military promotions would not come quickly.

• • •

"You have no power to command me to show you my letter," Yuxian had responded to the company commander. "This is a private matter."

"A soldier has no private life," the captain snapped. "A soldier's job is to obey the orders of his superiors."

"How can you expect me to show you my letter? I have my own thoughts. I have the right to write my own letters. Those rights are protected by the constitution." Ni Yuxian was angry.

Yuxian's political instructor also came to meet with him, taking a more conciliatory tack. "Just show me the letter, Yuxian," he tried to persuade. "If there are no mistakes, then you can send it. If there are, we'll help you correct them. Think of your future, Yuxian. You're a smart guy. Maybe some day you'll have the chance to get into the party. Don't do something now you may later regret. Show me the letter." If the letter were declared at the central level in Beijing to "have problems," Yuxian's military commanders would be in trouble for harboring a counterrevolutionary in their midst.

Meetings were called, the whole company attending, to dissuade Yuxian from sending the letter.

"Yuxian has written a letter to Chairman Mao," the company commander began one such meeting. "This is an anarchist act.

"We are responsible for Ni Yuxian, so we want him to give us the letter. But he doesn't trust his own leaders. He doesn't believe that what he does is our responsibility. This is dangerous." Most of the soldiers agreed with their commander, and many tried to persuade Yuxian not to mail the letter. In fear that Yuxian would sneak to the post office, he was prohibited from leaving camp. His fellow soldiers were assigned to watch him.

Yuxian bided his time.

One Sunday afternoon, relaxed and off-guard during their weekly respite from military discipline, his fellow soldiers temporarily forgot their responsibilities. Yuxian managed to get to the post office to mail the letter—one copy to Chairman Mao, one to the Central Committee, and one to the party's theoretical journal, *Red Flag*—return receipt requested.

A few weeks later, the receipts came back. Chairman Mao's office had received his letter. Only then did his superiors know for certain that the petition had been sent.

Yuxian began steeling himself, preparing his family and friends for the trouble he knew would come. "I have done something very dangerous," he wrote to his parents and to Zhao Yuefang. He even wrote to Wang Weidi, the female student who had defended him against the injustice of Buddhist Li's attack. "I wrote a letter to Chairman Mao," he explained, "criticizing the Great Leap Forward."

• • •

A meeting was called. A team had been sent to Yangsi village to learn more about the soldier's family circumstances and to investigate his record in school. "Some people think they are really smart," one of the commanders began the meeting. "Some people even think they are so educated they know more than their leaders. But in fact, people like this are the type who make mistakes. These people are the type who have had trouble with the school authorities. These people have even been in trouble with the Public Security Bureau." Yuxian's name was never mentioned in the repeated references to "some people," nor was the letter to Chairman Mao brought up, but his fellow soldiers all turned to Yuxian while their leader talked. "Some people" could only be Ni Yuxian.

Ni Yuxian was demoted, relieved of his duties on the wireless squad, and detailed to onerous training in heavy artillery.

Relations with his platoon leader deteriorated. One evening as the men squatted together on the earthen floor, gobbling down the last meal of the day, the platoon leader walked over to Ni Yuxian and kicked the young soldier's bowl from his hands, spilling the food, laughing. There was no apology.

After the platoon leader had settled back on his haunches to begin eating his own dinner, Yuxian stood up and slowly, deliberately, walked over to the man. He planted his shoe against the platoon leader's bowl and kicked it out of his hands and up in the air. "What the hell do you think you're doing?" The platoon leader stood up.

"You knocked over my bowl."

"I didn't do it deliberately."

"If you didn't do it deliberately, you should have apologized."

"Fuck you."

The company commander intervened. "I command you to take the platoon leader's bowl and replace his food," he bellowed.

"I don't accept your command," Yuxian responded with contempt.

"Ni, I swear, from Nanjing to Beijing, I have never seen the likes of you," the captain yelled back. "If you don't obey me, then I'll have you court-martialed. I'm going to have you locked up."

"Okay. Lock me up."

Yuxian managed to smuggle his harmonica into the rude room where he was incarcerated, two gun-toting soldiers standing guard outside. The gay and lively songs he played served to lift his sagging spirits, and he knew his comrades liked to hear romantic songs about love that blossoms in the spring, folk songs, and Russian love songs. Time in his makeshift prison passed more quickly when he played the harmonica.

"I forbid you to play the harmonica," the company commander ordered the captive when he visited his room that night. The military leadership had never appreciated Ni Yuxian's music. During the performances the military staged for the variety of official holidays that dotted the calendar year, Yuxian was invariably called upon to play a few pieces. But the songs of love and romance that were his specialties and that set the soldiers in the audience stamping their feet, humming and clapping along, were an anathema to the officers whose duty it was to maintain discipline and discourage the flowering of love. When Yuxian once insisted on playing Russian folk songs even in the face of China's growing dispute with the Soviet Union, the officer corps had stood up and left in the middle of his performance.

"I've never seen any regulations that say a prisoner can't play the harmonica," the ever-defiant prisoner responded. "I'm locked up so I can't go anywhere, right? What's wrong with me playing the harmonica?"

The next day, even as the soldiers performed their war maneuvers, the sound of Yuxian's harmonica continued to waft through the military compound.

The prisoner was freed shortly thereafter. The company commander had lost too much face.

But the punishment that Ni Yuxian most expected—expulsion from the military—did not come.

•   •   •

Instead, he was transferred after his prison release for a three-month stint in a sparsely populated mountainous area of Anhui. Life in the mountains was simple and poor—primitive, in fact—communications so sparse that party policies found few means to intrude, so isolated that the last outsider anyone could remember had passed through some ten years before. People's communes had never been established in that backward mountain hideaway, and the peasants had never heard of grain rations or backyard steel furnaces or deep plowing or catching up with Great Britain in fifteen years. They had never even heard of Great Britain. Military leadership was lax there, too, so life for the troops was freer. The soldiers spent much of their time catching fish and shooting the wild animals that inhabited the place, wandering and talking openly—a welcome respite from the disciplined life at camp.

It was when wandering in to one of the mountain village that Ni walked into a small hut to find a man in his forties lying dead on a bed, his body bloated from starvation. Two children were in the room, too, one already dead, another dying.

•   •   •

Newspapers never reached the mountains, so Yuxian knew nothing of the changing world situation until new year's of 1962 when he and his company returned briefly to Shanghai. Yuxian read then a lengthy article in the *People's Daily* by Albania's Enver Hoxha criticizing the Soviet Union. He deduced thereby that relations between China and the Soviet Union had further deteriorated. Khrushchev had recently set forth his principles of peaceful coexistence, arguing that war between the Soviet Union and the United States, between East and West, between developed and underdeveloped, was not inevitable, that peaceful competition between the superpowers was possible, that even the transition from capitalism to socialism within each country could be accomplished without violence.

Khrushchev's principles were anathema to militant, mobilized China, and the country's response to the Soviet Union's overtures of peace was quick and virulent. Only through violent struggle will the world be transformed, the Chinese press averred. The transition from capitalism to socialism will not—cannot—be peaceful. The death knell of capitalism and imperialism has begun but even as the end draws near, the hegemonist, imperialist superpower, the United States, will strike out in war against countries like China, struggling toward socialism. Taiwan, that lackey of American imperialism, situated just across the straits from Fujian Province, is about to launch an attack on China with the full complicity of the United States and American arms. War—nuclear war—is inevitable.

But China has nothing to fear from nuclear war, Chairman Mao asserted. If we lose half our population, we still have 400 million people. We will still be the largest country on earth. Why should we fear nuclear war? If people die, what does it matter?

Still, China must prepare for this impending nuclear war. The country must be prepared to fight. Ni Yuxian's company was put on war alert. Time was of the essence.

Beginning in early 1962, Ni Yuxian and thousands of other young soldiers began engaging in a massive construction project designed to ensure that the army high command would survive the coming nuclear holocaust.

The task of the soldiers was to move a mountain. Shovelful by shovelful, they burrowed into the mountain, carving out a catacomb of rooms that would both be protected from nuclear bombs and safe from radiation once the attack was over. The military high command would be housed there, and preparations were made for them to remain for up to ten years if necessary. The rooms would be well-furnished with electricity, wood paneling, and carpets, and the underground military headquarters would be equipped with the most modern communications facilities. Ten years' worth of grain would be stored there, and the nation's gold would be housed in the mountain, too. The underground Great Wall, the soldiers called the mammoth project.

It was backbreaking, exhausting, dangerous work, carried out with no modern machinery, relying almost exclusively on the manual labor of thousands of young coolie soldiers. From above, the rocky mountain was broken up, stone by stone, the boulders sent tumbling down to be molded by primitive knives into bricks of three different sizes, each stone brick an exact replica of the last. With water, the bricks were washed and rewashed and washed again, until the surface was as smooth as glass and not a speck of dust remained. Closer to the ground, hundreds more men worked carving out the mountain's insides, lining each room with the stone bricks, the wall of each compartment several feet thick, to prevent radiation from seeping in.

Clothes were reduced to tatters in a matter of hours working under such conditions, and because each man was allotted only two suits of clothing a year, they worked in their underwear, the skin of those tunneling out the mountain shredding, the flesh of those lugging the stones bleeding, and then finally turning to callus.

As the bowels of the mountain were gradually emptied, and the sculpting of the catacombs began, the haphazard wiring and the constant seepage of water rendered electrocution an ever-present hazard. Several soldiers were killed that way. They died, too, when stones from the top of the mountain came tumbling down on the workers below. One of the foremen, a friend of Yuxian's, died from a wayward rock around lunch one day. He had emerged from the catacombs to complain to the cook of his hunger and urge him to speed the food. The foreman settled down in frustration to smoke a cigarette while awaiting his noonday meal. The rock that broke his neck and killed him instantly hardly jarred him at all, and they found him there, cigarette still burning, staring peacefully ahead. They buried him in the mountain, two steamed buns by his side, to stave off the hunger that had gnawed his stomach at the moment of death.

The high command came to inspect the work being done on its behalf. Ranks had ostensibly been abolished within the Chinese military and the leaders wore no insignia, but the tailored uniforms and leather shoes of the officials made a mockery of their alleged equality with the scantily clad toiling soldier coolies. "Can the project be completed in time for October first and the celebration of the establishment of new China?" the high command wondered idly. "Of course we can finish by then," the military officers in charge of the project enthusiastically agreed. How could they refuse the high command? Careers were at stake. Was not the purpose of a soldier to obey?

Changes would have to be introduced into the work routine. At the current pace and with such primitive methods, the underground fortress would take well over a year to complete. One problem slowing progress was the necessity of clearing the soldier coolies from the base of the mountain when blasting and rolling the huge boulders from the top. Even taking precautions, occasional deaths, like the accident with the foreman, had occurred.

With a concerted effort of manpower to loosen the stones from the mountaintop and a "dare-to-die" squad willing to risk working at the bottom while the stones tumbled down below, precious time could be saved. Volunteers were needed to dare to die.

A meeting was called to present the dilemma to the troops. "According to present regulations," the political cadre explained, "we have to give a warning to clear the base area every time we blast the rocks from the top. But if we keep doing it this way, clearing everyone out each time we send down the rocks, we'll never finish the project in time for October first. So we're going to need some people willing to stay when we do the blasting—willing to die in order to complete the work on time. We need really progressive people for this. You're guaranteed membership in the party. Your families will be given a money reward, and they will become families of revolutionary martyrs. Everyone will recognize you as a hero."

No one volunteered.

"This project is just like war," the military command concluded. The young men were ordered to fight, the makeup of the dare-to-die squads—young men of peasant background, the oldest of whom was only twenty years old—being determined by the military commanders. No leaders were included in the squads.

The first dare-to-die squad was gathered together for a sumptuous last meal of fish and meat, with plenty of cigarettes and copious quantities of strong alcohol. Thus satiated with food and liquor, the young peasant soldiers were sent to their daunting task. Many of the men cried as they worked. From the top of the mountain, the blasters loosened the rocks and the boulders came tumbling down. One after one, the youth at the foot of the mountain were crushed, some to die, many to be badly injured.

There was a big meeting that night to commemorate the youth who had died. "They were heroes," the officers in charge all said. The financial payments to the martyrs' families were announced, determined by the size of the hero's family. A few families were to receive a hundred yuan, but most would receive double that. The families with many mouths to feed would receive four hundred altogether.

The next day the second dare-to-die volunteer squad was sent out, stomachs full and besotted with wine. They, too, cried as they worked and some were crushed to death when the rocks went tumbling down the mountain. They, too, were honored at a meeting that night.

A third group went out the following day, and the whole tragic drama was played out again. A pall settled on the camp. Morale was low. The men became insolent. They resisted work. Not even the military careerists had the stomach to assign volunteers after that.

Back at the Gold Mountain army camp, as a fresh new recruit, Yuxian had read training manuals instructing military commanders how to teach their men to be willing to die, how to convince soldiers that death does not matter, how to persuade the young that the death of a soldier is reasonable and not to be feared. The military takes its soldiers as war tools, not people, Yuxian had concluded.

The picture of the executions he had witnessed as a child by his grandmother's side, indelibly etched in Ni's memory, began reappearing unexpectedly to haunt him, together with a gnawing, inescapable, lingering suspicion that the men the Communist Party had killed that day were not criminals but ordinary villagers with no greater faults than most. Confronted now with official apathy in the face of massive starvation and with dare-to-die squads that deliberately sent young men to their deaths, another impression was building in Ni Yuxian's maturing mind. The lives of ordinary Chinese people—the people Yuxian knew and liked and saw every day, the people who made up the fabric of his life—meant little to the party which governed them.

So many people had died on behalf of the Communist Party, Ni reflected. The vast majority of them had been simple folk, uneducated people, peasant youth from the countryside incapable of understanding the great issues at stake, unable to comprehend why they were being sent to their deaths. Who had died during the civil war between the Nationalists and the Communists? Peasant youth, sixteen and seventeen years old, illiterate, uneducated, locked in a parochial world that did not extend beyond their market towns, ignorant of the cause for which they fought and died.

Who was dying by the millions during the three bad years as the cadres continued to eat their fill? Again the peasant masses, pliant and passive, the hapless victims of egregiously mistaken agricultural policies that flew in the face of centuries of peasant tradition. Why? So the party would not be forced to admit that its policies were wrong? So Chairman Mao, the modern-day emperor in whose name the disaster had been launched, would not lose face?

And who had been crushed to death when the boulders came tumbling down the mountain? Again, simple, ignorant peasant youth who would succumb without question to authority, even when it meant their death. And for what end had they died? So that a construction project to house the military high command during a nuclear war that would never come could be completed in time for National Day?

• • •

Ni Yuxian was often called upon during political meetings to read his government's attacks against Khrushchev's new theory of peaceful coexistence. The articles were so rich with historical allusions that the political instructor, whose grasp of history and reading ability alike were limited, was left befuddled and embarrassed. Yuxian's better education enabled him to cope with the questions that inevitably arose.

The more he read, the more Yuxian agreed with Khrushchev. What good was war for any country—the Soviet Union, the United States, China? How could mankind progress through war? Could any country really be victorious in a nuclear confrontation? War destroyed culture.

The ultimate price of the vast sums expended on war, on preparing for war, on building modern weapons, was the economic well-being, the welfare, the development of ordinary people, particularly in an underdeveloped country like China. How much money had been spent—no, wasted—on the underground Great Wall, and to what avail? How many peasant rice bowls could have been filled with the money poured into the whims of the military high command?

But the whole premise of socialism in China was violence. Without violence, there would be no socialism, and therefore, in the official logic of the day, to oppose violence was to oppose socialism as well, and hence to be a traitor. To favor peace was to be a traitor.

Yuxian favored peace.

But China would have war. Taiwan was poised across the straits ready to invade the mainland, and Yuxian's regiment was chosen to defend the motherland. In the fall of 1962, they were given orders to leave for Fujian. They had only a few weeks to prepare.

New supplies of modern weapons poured into the camp, and military drill was stepped up to ten hours a day. Since the war was expected to be nuclear, the maneuvers were conducted with the soldiers dressed in rubber suits and gas masks designed to protect them from the radiation following the blast. At the end of a hot summer day, the soldiers would empty two cups of water from the feet of their rubber suits.

In an effort to whip up hatred for the enemy and prepare the soldiers psychologically for battle, political training was also intensified, with frequent sessions comparing the bitterness of the past under the reactionary Guomindang government with the sweetness of life in the present. The focus was on how cruelly the Guomindang, in collusion with the landlords, the capitalists, and the American imperialists, had oppressed the Chinese people. Photographs of poverty and war were one means of proving the point. But with so many soldiers from poor peasant backgrounds, the living testimony of their own family experiences could prove persuasive indeed. The peasant soldiers were asked to share the stories of their lives with their comrades, relating the poverty and oppression their families had suffered in the past.

But not all the soldiers understood their instructions, and some had no great sense of time. When their talk of bitterness and poverty focused on the present and on the starvation that had so recently stalked their families and their villages, the political instructors had to revert to the photographic method of proving the point.

As the war clouds gathered and the time approached for the troops to depart for battle, the families of the soldiers were permitted to visit the camp to wish their sons good-bye. Ni Jizhong and Xu Fengzhen came to say good-bye to Yuxian, and the company commander, knowing this might be the last time they saw their eldest son alive, treated them again to a sumptuous meal.

Zhao Yuefang came, too. "Yuxian," Yang Guoli had said to Yuxian one afternoon in the middle of maneuvers, "there's a girl here to see you. She's as pretty as a flower." Yuefang's visit was an act of bravery. She had never ridden on a train or left Shanghai before, and she traveled alone without her parents' knowledge.

His military superiors were gravely displeased and threatened to punish him, but Yuxian left camp to be with his girlfriend. The two sat for hours, talking on a park bench. "I miss you so much," Yuefang told her boyfriend. "I'm so worried about you." The couple had never sat so close together, and Yuxian reached out to touch her hair. He was so happy to see her, so pleased she had come. "We will get married later when I am out of the army," he assured her. Yuefang jumped when he tried to take her hand. Yuefang stayed alone that night in a tiny inn, the cost of which ate deep into Yuxian's salary of six yuan a month. The next morning, he saw her off at the train.

"I was so happy to see you," Yuefang wrote her boyfriend immediately after she returned home. She had always found it easier to write her innermost thoughts than to say them out loud. "No matter what, I will wait for you. I love you so much. I really do want to marry you." Yuefang wrote him every week, and Yuxian carried her picture in his wallet.

He would have carried her picture off to battle. But mere minutes before the troops, fully prepared and dressed in battle gear, were to climb aboard the trucks that would transport them to the front, the orders for their departure were delayed. One month went by and then another and another. Ni Yuxian never went to Fujian. The nuclear war was indefinitely postponed.

The letters from Yuefang became less frequent, more distant. She had passed the college entrance exams and had begun her studies at East China Normal University. Yuxian missed her terribly, ached to see her, to talk to her, to share the jumble of thoughts that were rumbling through his head—about war and death, about pretense and reality, about his own responsibilities to his country and his people, about his love. He had to find a way to return to Shanghai.

One afternoon during military maneuvers, the rocket he was directing misfired. Yuxian's hand was badly mangled. He would have to go to Shanghai for medical treatment.

Ni Yuxian was beaming when Zhao Yuefang emerged from class to find him waiting. The young woman was surprised, but Yuxian soon sensed that she was not entirely pleased. Walking through the campus, Yuefang seemed nervous, preoccupied, ill at ease, glancing around this way and that to see if they were being observed. The tryst did not unfold as the young romantic had fantasized.

Over a simple dinner of steamed bread and vegetables served in a tiny, open-air restaurant, the young woman haltingly, hesitantly, began to speak. Yuefang was not blessed with the same gift of expression that Yuxian had discovered so early in himself. Her communications had always been more sensory than verbal. "My classmates would criticize me if they knew we were in love," the young woman said, pausing to gauge her boyfriend's reaction. He attributed her reticence to that painfully sweet shyness that inevitably develops between two young lovers after so many months of separation. "My political instructor would be unhappy, too," she continued awkwardly, focusing hard on a steamed bun. "University students aren't supposed to fall in love. They say we're still too young. We're supposed to concentrate on our studies."

Yuxian was growing puzzled.

Walking toward the small village on the outskirts of campus, he and his girlfriend stopped at the stone bridge that spanned the village canal. The young man's heart was still brimming, and he wanted to assure Yuefang again of his love. Dusk was gathering. Few people were about. He reached out to touch his girlfriend's hand.

Yuefang pulled away. "Can't we talk about something else?" she insisted, confused. "If anyone saw us like this, they would think it was bad. We're still too young to think about love." The young woman was uncomfortable, close to tears.

"Okay, so we won't talk," Yuxian responded, angry but still stoic. "Do you still want to write letters?"

"We can write, but we have to write less than before."

Yuxian's world suddenly turned upside down. Yuefang was completely different. Her love seemed to have evaporated into thin air, and he could not understand why. How could she have changed so much, so quickly? Just a few months before, when she had come to say good-bye, the couple had been so warm, so affectionate, so certain of their love. Her letters had been so full of her devotion. They were not too young. At Yangsi Middle School, they had been younger still. Studies, or school regulations, were hardly sufficient excuse. Yangsi Middle School had had regulations, too. Had not Pockfaced Huang tried to interfere in their romance? They had been brave enough to chart their own course.

No, Yuefang's rejection must be due to her new status as a university student. As one of the select few to partake of a higher education, naturally she would look down upon such a lowly soldier as he. His usual self-confidence suffered a bitter blow. "Forget it," Yuxian thought to himself angrily, in wounded pride. "I absolutely will never come to see her again. Never, ever will I write her another letter."

"Fine," he replied curtly. "I'll be going now." Ni Yuxian turned on his heel and never looked back.

• • •

At Gold Mountain military base, his head swam as he paced the city wall overlooking the beach. A strong wind was blowing that day, and the waves were high. Yuxian's heart, he remembers, was as turbulent as the sea, the hurt so intense he imagined he was going crazy. His romance with Zhao Yuefang was over. He would never see her and never write again. But neither would he ever allow himself the humiliation of being looked down upon. Staring disappointed and angry into the ocean, he contemplated his future once more, committing himself afresh to the accomplishment of great and glorious deeds. If Yuxian had failed with Zhao Yuefang, he could still prove himself to the world.

• • •

Lei Feng died in 1962—crushed to death by a telephone pole while he was directing a backing truck—shortly after the breakup of Zhao Yuefang and Ni Yuxian. The entire army was mobilized to learn from the twenty-two-year-old soldier whose highest ideal had been to become a rustless screw in the Communist Party's machine, a docile tool of the party. Lei Feng's good deeds—secretly washing the dirty laundry of fellow soldiers, sharing his food with the hungry, helping old ladies cross the street, donating his meager salary to the needy—became immortal when his diary, a veritable catalogue of his charitable acts and spilling over with testimony to his selfless devotion to the party cause, became an overnight bestseller. No soldier in military history had been more frequently photographed. There were pictures of Lei Feng driving tractors and cleaning cars, studying the works of Chairman Mao both in solitude and with friends, darning the socks of his fellow soldiers and sewing on their buttons, helping workers build and repair their houses, holding umbrellas in the rain and helping old people with their luggage onto trains, speaking out in righteous indignation against reactionaries, counterrevolutionaries, rightists, and other varieties of antisocialist bad eggs, receiving his numerous awards for being a model soldier. The frequency with which Lei Feng's likeness appeared in public was rivaled only by that of Mao's, but the variety of the soldier's poses was substantially greater.

As his unit mobilized to study Lei Feng, Ni Yuxian was confronted with a dilemma. He was suspicious of the dead soldier from the beginning.

That Lei Feng had performed a multitude of good deeds was admirable, to be sure, and his devotion to helping others was worthy of emulation. Grandmother Xu's early admonitions on the value and necessity of performing good works were the essence of Yuxian's moral dictates. In the face of famine and government deceit, Yuxian's devotion to his grandmother's teachings had taken on the quality of a religious cause.

But the dead soldier was vapid, without a brain of his own. The soldier had deliberately sought out his political instructor, obsequiously exposing his political thought, pressing to know whether he had made any progress, and inquiring with concern what further subordinations to the party were necessary to perfect himself. Entrance into the party was Lei Feng's highest goal, confirmation that his conquest of self and his search for perfection were complete. On the party's birthday, Lei Feng had recorded his thoughts in his diary. "Dear Party, great party, you are my mother," he wrote. "Without the party, I would not exist, my life would be so bitter. My life, all that I am, was given to me by the party. For the party I will struggle. Dear Party, I always want to obey you. Whatever you ask me to do, I will do. If you want me to climb a mountain of knives and swim an ocean of fire, I will. Only then am I worthy to be a member.''

On one page, adulation was heaped upon the party, on another the interchangeable words of religious devotion were directed to Chairman Mao.

Yuxian suspected Lei Feng of ulterior motives. Every day of this selfless screw's diary contained an entry about yet another good deed. But it appeared as though Lei Feng had done those good deeds so others would know, faithfully reporting each act of charity to his political instructor, asking him to read his diary, in the hope that through good deeds he would gain entrance to the party. But if every good deed is directed toward personal ends, can the deed really be considered good? Does not a good deed performed for the sake of reward become false?

The photographs were the most damning evidence against the soldier. How did it happen that a professional photographer was on hand, snapping away, every time Lei Feng spontaneously performed a good deed? How was it that in the candid shots of those unpremeditated acts of generosity, Lei Feng was invariably situated front and center, face to the camera, smiling? There were even photographs of Lei Feng before he had entered the army. No photographer had ever recorded for history the dangerous work of constructing the underground Great Wall or the good deeds helping the peasants that Yuxian and his fellow soldiers had performed. No one had ever photographed them doing anything. Clearly someone had decided to make Lei Feng a model even before he had joined the ranks.

Yuxian would never become Lei Feng, the cog in the wheel, the rustless screw, the docile tool, the obedient slave. He would refuse on principle to keep a Lei Feng diary and would eschew reports to his political instructors. Ni Yuxian's good deeds would go unrecorded. But he would emulate the dead soldier's self-discipline, his kindness, his willingness to help. He would imitate that part of Lei Feng who did good deeds. Yuxian wanted to be a good person, respected by others. Above all, he wanted to win back the respect he had lost when Zhao Yuefang had left him. Perhaps, by becoming a living model of Lei Feng, he could even win back Zhao Yuefang herself.

Yuxian began leaving the army camp each day for the neighboring village, searching for good deeds that needed to be done. "Do you have enough water today?" he would ask the peasants whose water supply depended on carrying heavy jugs from the stream. Helping the villagers carry heavy loads became his specialty. He wrote letters for the illiterate villagers, and for many of his fellow soldiers, too, and secretly sent money to the hungry families of his comrades from Anhui.

So vast was the change in the young man that his superiors could not help but notice, and so greatly did his merit build that the political instructor wrote a letter to Ni Jizhong and Xu Fengzhen complimenting them on their son's progress.

The fervor of Ni Yuxian's devotion to good deeds presented his superiors with something of a dilemma, too. The nature of the young man's progress was troubling. Yuxian still had no desire to join the Youth League or the party. He evinced little respect for his superiors. Politically, he had made no progress at all.

Word of the change that had taken place in Ni Yuxian, and of the dilemma that transformation had posed, reached the battalion-level political instructor—an intelligent and educated man, well-versed in Marxism-Leninism Mao-Zedong thought, who had always liked Yuxian and had long taken a special interest in the lad. Despite his political disagreements with Ni, Colonel Sheng knew that soldiers with the young man's intelligence, curiosity, and sheer ebullience were rare, and the political instructor respected the youth. What a benefit to the party to welcome such a young man to its ranks! He decided to talk to the soldier.

"Xiao Ni," the political instructor began, addressing the soldier familiarly as "little Ni." "You have read so much Marxism-Leninism. You're such a smart guy. The party really needs people like you, you know." The instructor paused. Yuxian was already obviously skeptical. "You need to think about trying to get into the party. You need to think about being better to your superior officers, about cultivating your relationships with them. You need to remember that the party is always right and that you should always obey the party. If you do, Xiao Ni, if you follow the party, obey the party, become a member of the party, then you could have a very bright future. You could become a cadre someday, Xiao Ni. If you don't follow this path, I'm afraid one day you'll make a big mistake."

Yuxian was cautious. "Our viewpoints are different," the young man began, cautiously formulating his reply. He liked the political

instructor enormously. He appreciated the special interest the officer had shown. He wanted to be polite. "You think that progress
means getting into the party, becoming a cadre and an officer. But
I don't agree. I don't think a person's status should be determined
by whether someone is a member of the party or not. I don't
believe that the only honor is being a member of the party. 'Progress' is whether one understands things correctly, whether one's
viewpoint is correct."

Yuxian knew the instructor was disturbed, but the floodgates
of his thoughts were opening and he plunged recklessly ahead.
"And there's another thing. I believe people should be equal. I
don't like all this unequal status, with party members considered
superior. Here, I don't agree with you, Colonel Sheng. I know that
you are an officer and I am only a lowly soldier, but still, to me,
we are equal. In terms of our human rights, we are equal. In
today's society, most people wouldn't consider us equal. Most people think party members are superior to others, that people who
come from the 'correct' background—workers, peasants, sons and
daughters of party members and cadres—these people are superior.
It's not just that I don't agree. I think this viewpoint is wrong. It
seems to me, for instance, that a person's status could be low but
that person's political viewpoint could still be correct. And by the
same token, even party members, persons with high status, could
have incorrect viewpoints."

"Xiao Ni," instructor Sheng responded gravely, "your viewpoint is very dangerous, you know. This is capitalist thought. What
you are talking about is capitalist democracy, capitalist notions of
equality. The party doesn't want people who think like this."

In the gathering darkness, the two men sat together in silence,
their mutual affection and respect as deep as the gulf that separated
them. The elder man spoke first. "I want to tell you something,
Xiao Ni," he began quietly, measuring his words. "I want you to
remember what I say forever. In our country, if a person leaves
the party, that person will surely be defeated."

"But I believe in truth, in justice, Colonel Sheng. For me, truth
and justice are the most important things."

"Today, our two viewpoints are not the same," the officer
replied, standing up. He was a big man, nearly six feet tall. "But
I want you to think about our conversation today. Think about
what I have said. I'll come back and talk to you after awhile. I still
hope someday you will join the party."

The meeting was over. The two men shook hands, as they always did.

• • •

Politically flawed though he remained in the eyes of the party, Yuxian continued doing good deeds, and so remarkable was the transformation of the young soldier, so large the change in his self-discipline and motivation, that he became, despite his political weakness, a model in the study of Lei Feng, a paragon for others to emulate. When the movement to study Lei Feng spread from the military into the rest of society, and military commanders were sent to schools and offices to lecture about how to learn from Lei Feng and to describe the remarkable transformations that might be expected, Ni Yuxian was one of the examples of the miracles the study of Lei Feng might reap.

Sent to lecture to a political study class at East China Normal University, Yuxian's political instructor naturally chose as his favorite example of transformation the story of the young soldier named Ni who was as smart as any university student and had read as many books. Since studying Lei Feng, soldier Ni had become a new man.

"That soldier, Ni, that you talked about," a blushing coed began, addressing the political instructor after class, "what is his full name?"

"Ni Yuxian."

"How do you write it?"

The political instructor wrote the ideographs of the young man's name.

"He's my classmate from Yangsi Middle School. Could you take this picture to him?" She handed him the photograph of the political study class taken to mark the occasion of the army officer's visit. "Could you tell him it is from Zhao Yuefang?"

"Ni Yuxian, one of your classmates asked about you after my lecture," the political instructor teased the young soldier when he handed the soldier the class picture. "Maybe you should write to her."

Yuxian was troubled, his festering wound reopened. The loss of Zhao Yuefang's love had propelled him in this new and virtuous direction of trying to emulate Lei Feng. But the anger and the pain were still too deep. The romance, he concluded, would not work. He did not write.

A week later, he received a letter from Zhao Yuefang's best friend, the young lovers' frequent emissary. "She still hasn't forgotten you, Yuxian," Yuefang's friend wrote. "She wants me to try to convince you to write her. She wants to get back together with you."

Yuxian was in turmoil. Again, he pondered his romance. "It just won't work," he thought, "not after everything she said. I can't get back together with her."

He wrote a letter to the friend. "Yuefang said before that she couldn't have a boyfriend while she is a university student. She's still a university student, so how can she want me back? I won't write."

• • •

The campaign to study Lei Feng was an ideal testing ground for selecting new party members. After nearly three years of military training, the time had come to reward a few of the recruits who had joined the army with Yuxian. A small select handful who had so emulated Lei Feng that they too had become docile tools of the party, rustless screws in the party machine, selflessly working on behalf of the party, the people, and socialism, could expect at the close of the movement to be welcomed into the party ranks.

Of the ten or so soldiers in Ni Yuxian's company competing heart and soul for entrance, two—Pei Xingling and Chen Yunghu—were chosen by their superiors to be rewarded at the culmination of the campaign. The two were widely reviled by their fellow soldiers whose aspirations were more modest and who hated the hypocrisy and toadying to power that the quest for party membership so frequently entailed. Pei Xingling was the object of particular opprobrium.

Pei was demure to the point of coy, and the thrust of his hips lent a slight feminine swagger to his gait. His hands were a bit too expressive and the way he flattered his superiors seemed to Ni and his friends to be downright flirtatious. His relationship with the platoon leader, they felt, was beyond the bounds of propriety. They cavorted almost like lovers, the leader often tickling the soldier, who would giggle and squeal like a girl. Pei Xingling was referred to almost universally as Da Guniang—Big Girl.

Big Girl Pei was given to histrionics in his public demonstrations of loyalty. At meetings to praise the party, where soldiers were encouraged to pledge their willingness to die on the party's behalf, Big Girl could actually bring tears to his eyes and send them flowing copiously down his cheeks as he related all the party had given him and pledged his willingness to serve the party unto death.

"Before liberation, we had no food to eat," Pei would begin one of his dramatic presentations. "The poor peasants were oppressed—oppressed by the landlords, oppressed by the Guomindang. But the Communist Party came and liberated us. The Guomindang was overthrown. The landlords were overthrown. Without the Communist Party, just think, we would still be slaves. We would be beggars—like my father and my grandfather."

Emotions would begin building at this point in his speech. Tears would fill his eyes.

"But the party, the party sent us to school, gave us an education. Now the party has sent us to the army, given us the great honor of becoming soldiers."

The crescendo building, the tears would begin falling. "Oh great, glorious, and correct Communist Party, oh great leader and teacher Chairman Mao, how I love you! How grateful I am! I am willing to die for you!" Emotions spent, the climax reached, Big Girl Pei would seat himself again in triumphant self-satisfaction.

A seasoned observer of Big Girl, Yuxian viewed Pei Xingling's tears—indeed much of the young man's life—as a melodrama played to the party leaders for the calculated purpose of obtaining party membership and hence his own advancement. On the job, when they were involved in the dangerous work of constructing the underground Great Wall, for instance, Pei's muscles would tense, sweat pouring from his brow, when the party leaders were there to observe. When the party leaders left, the slackening in Pei's work was perceptible. When dangerous tasks had to be done, like going deep into the catacombs where several had been electrocuted, Pei Xingling found excuses to remain behind. The contrast between the cowardice of Big Girl Pei in the field and his public protestations of heroic self-sacrifice, his frequent pledges of his willingness to die, was glaring.

Worse still, Big Girl was in the habit of secretly informing on his fellow soldiers. He was the one who had told the superiors that Yuxian was writing a letter to Chairman Mao, and he had once reported that Yuxian kept some bullets stashed in the satchel he kept by the side of his bed. Mostly, though, Big Girl informed on his competitors for the few spaces available in the party ranks.

Often the facts of his secret reports were twisted. When Yang Guoli—Yuxian's friend from Yangsi Middle School—ran out of money one month, Pei reported that Yang had spent the money on candy. But Big Girl knew that Yang Guoli, learning from Lei Feng but modestly refusing to let his charity be public, had secretly sent the money to a famine-struck family of one of his fellow soldiers from Anhui.

Like Lei Feng, Pei Xingling both kept a diary detailing his good deeds and made certain the good deeds recorded there became known to his fellow soldiers and officers alike. All the help he ever gave, every cent he ever sent to families in distress, was proudly reported at public meetings.

As the movement to study Lei Feng crested, the unit set aside a full two weeks in July 1964 to review its fruits. Pei Xingling and Chen Yunghu would be admitted into the party as part of the closing ceremonies. Three problems would be explored during the fortnight of meetings—the relationship between the military and ordinary Chinese people, the relationship between the army and the government, and finally, the relationship between the military leadership and ordinary soldiers. Relations between the officers and their men were presumed to be so good that only half a day of the two-week period was set aside for that discussion, and Ni remembers the officers insisting that the meeting would be free, open, and democratic. The leadership seemed unaware of the irony of holding a democratic discussion after months of teaching that the party was infallible and the function of soldiers was to obey, that soldiers were meant to be docile tools of the party and rustless screws in its machine.

"This meeting is to be conducted completely democratically," Ni remembers the political instructor assuring the assembled soldiers as he called the meeting to order. "We want you all to speak freely and raise whatever problems are on your minds. No matter what you say, there will be no repercussions—no big sticks, no putting on hats, no pulling the pigtail. No matter what criticism you raise, it won't be treated as a political mistake."

The meeting was desultory, aimless, boring, the occasional complaints raised by the soldiers minor and trivial. Saturated with the virtues of Lei Feng, the soldiers were not accustomed to democracy. They had been trained in unquestioning obedience. The political instructor's encouragement to speak out was not enough to undo months of military practice—or years of social conditioning.

A half day might even to be too long for the soldiers to air their complaints. The young men began shifting on their stools.

From the back of the room, Ni Yuxian raised his hand. He stood up.

"Actually, there are a couple things I'd like to talk about today," he began casually. "I'm concerned about what kind of people are getting admitted into the party—and also about the question of keeping a Lei Feng diary.

"I think the type of person to be admitted into the party ought be one who really does his work well, who really does selflessly serve all the people, someone who is not two-faced." This was his first major address to so large a gathering, but years of practice in persuasion at Yangsi Middle School were good preparation. He sounded relaxed, natural. "Who has been invited to fill out the forms for party membership this time? Pei Xingling and Chen Yunghu, no? I don't think these two guys satisfy the party's requirements for membership. In order to get into the party, they have done dishonest things. They coddle up to the party leadership, they write in their Lei Feng diaries and give it to the leadership to read. But when they do good things, is it really because they want to do good things or are they just doing those good things so they can tell the leadership and get into the party? Why do they have to write every good thing they do in their diaries to show the leaders? Why do they have to make sure everybody knows all the good things they have done? This isn't right."

The atmosphere in the meeting was changing. Lined in a row behind a table at the front of the room, the party leadership sat rigid, immobile, transfixed. The political instructor scribbled in his notebook. The soldiers were suddenly rapt.

Ni continued. "About Chen Yunghu—it's fine that he wants to join the party. It's great. But every night, he gets the platoon leader hot water to wash his feet. If the platoon leader's health isn't good, or if occasionally Xiao Chen wants to get him water, okay. But does he really have to do it every day? This is really kissing ass. And, anyway, why does the platoon leader let him do it? There's something abnormal about these guys' relations with the leaders." A collective look of concern registered on the faces of the party leadership.

"We have all heard Big Girl Pei's diary, right? He says that the platoon leader and the political instructor have been better to him than his own father. How could these two men be better to him than his own father? Pei is just trying to make these leaders think that he's the best, most obedient soldier in the world. But if he's just saying all this to get into the party, really, it's disgusting."

So daring were the words, the soldiers had difficulty believing their ears, but a few were beginning to smile and nod in agreement.

Big Girl Pei began crying loudly.

"Come on, Big Girl," Yuxian demanded sarcastically, "take out your diary and read it so we can all hear." Big Girl Pei cried more loudly still. Yuxian sat down.

The leadership core, incapacitated by disbelief, had watched the soldier's performance in stunned silence. The speaker's political supporters were also silent, needing time to collect their thoughts. Then hands began shooting up and other soldiers, especially the new recruits from Anhui, yet to be fully socialized into military discipline, rose to speak in support of Ni Yuxian's condemnation of the party's choices. They were country lads, uneducated and inarticulate, ill at ease with public speaking. Their condemnations were short, direct, and to the point.

"I've worked alongside Big Girl," one young recruit recalled. "He won't do the hard work. If he thinks something is going to be dangerous, he's the last in line to do it. These two guys shouldn't be allowed into the party." The deputy political instructor continued diligently taking notes, his face wearing the look of someone forced to confront a malodorous object.

One after another the soldiers rose to burst out their opposition to the party membership of Big Girl Pei and Chen Yunghu. When the time came to adjourn, many others were still waiting to be called. "We'll reconvene after lunch, at one o'clock," the party secretary assured the soldiers. "Everyone will have a chance to speak. Don't worry."

The party secretary called an urgent meeting of the party branch. At one o'clock, as the soldiers gathered in the elementary school auditorium that was serving as their assembly hall, the party meeting was still in session. At two o'clock, they were still waiting. At three o'clock, the leadership emerged to announce that the soldier's democratic meeting would be postponed until the following morning.

The atmosphere at the camp was tense. The soldiers who ordinarily laughed and kidded together were silent, waiting. The officers had had no reason to expect more than trivial complaints, certainly no cause to believe that their selections for party membership would be challenged. A means would have to be found to reassert their authority.

After dinner, the party leaders began calling the platoon leaders and deputy platoon leaders, the party aspirants and activists, one by one for private meetings.

Xi Shenfa, Yuxian's deputy platoon leader, good friend, and party aspirant, called Yuxian aside to report on his own meeting. "You have to promise never to tell I told you this," a nervous Xi Shenfa urged. "I'd be in terrible trouble if you did."

"The leaders started by asking me what I thought of your speech, and I told them it wasn't bad, that what you said was right. 'Most of the soldiers agree with him,' I said. 'Maybe he comes on a little strong, but still, we all think he's right.'

"But the political instructor told me I was too simple," Xi continued. "He said I don't understand you, that you are very complicated, that you have an ulterior motive. He said that you are trying to incite the soldiers to oppose their leaders. He reminded me of the letter you wrote to Chairman Mao. He said the letter is revisionist. He said that the party central committee has just sent down its ruling saying that the letter is revisionist and that you are a person with problems."

Hearing that his letter had been declared revisionist, Ni Yuxian knew in some vague, inchoate way that his career in the army was finished. No revisionist could have a future in the military. He would never be promoted, never be trusted, never be given any position of responsibility. Colonel Sheng was right. Yuxian had made a big mistake. The price would be high.

"You're the deputy platoon leader, Xiao Xi," the political instructor had continued his conversation with Xi Shenfa. "We leaders trust you. You absolutely cannot stand on the side of Ni Yuxian. Tomorrow we're going to have another meeting. We hope you'll get up at the meeting and criticize Ni Yuxian's mistakes. We're doing this for you, Xiao Xi. We don't want you to make any mistakes. You do want to get into the party, don't you Xiao Xi? This is your opportunity. Show us you stand on the side of the party." Xi Shenfa was frightened. He wanted to join the party. He did not want to lose his chance.

Yang Guoli was also called to a meeting with the deputy political leader. The leader repeated the same admonition he had delivered to Xiao Xi.

"But this isn't fair," Yang Guoli had responded, furious. "When you called that meeting, you said that you wanted to hear the soldiers' opinions, that no one would be punished even if they said something wrong. Didn't you say there would be 'no big stick, no putting on hats, no pulling the pigtail'? You did say that, didn't you?" The young man was yelling at his superior with the unfairness of it all. "And now you say tomorrow we're going to have a meeting to criticize Ni Yuxian? This is deceit. Most people won't agree with you anyway."

"Come now, Comrade Yang. Are you really so confused?" The deputy political instructor was solicitous. "Do you know what kind of person Ni Yuxian is?"

"Of course I know what kind of person Ni Yuxian is. I went to school with him for five years, didn't I? We've been together here in the army for nearly three years. We've worked together. He's my best friend. He's a good person."

"Do you know he wrote a letter to Chairman Mao?"

"Yes, I know he wrote a letter. I read the letter. It was a good letter. Really good."

"Yang Guoli, do you still want to get into the party? You know, if you want to get into the party, I could be your sponsor. But if you're like this, I can't agree to your entering the party."

"Of course I want to enter the party, but I still can't agree with this," Yang Guoli responded. "What you're doing and what the party requires aren't the same. You asked us to speak out and you said there would be no big stick. Isn't this a big stick? Ni Yuxian's writing that letter and this thing are completely different anyway. Why are you putting them together?"

"Ah, Yang Guoli," the political instructor responded patiently, as though Yang were a child too young fully to comprehend. "You just don't know. You don't understand. It's just that Ni Yuxian has problems. His family has problems. Remember, Yang Guoli, what you do tomorrow, what you say tomorrow, has a lot to do with your future."

• • •

At the meeting the next day, the number of military officers sitting behind the table at the front of the room had grown. The superiors were serious and well-prepared.

The deputy political instructor orchestrated.

"Yesterday, at our meeting, Comrade Ni Yuxian said a few things, raised a few questions about the matter of new party members," the deputy noted in opening. "He dared to raise his opinions, and that is good. But whether his opinions are right or wrong, whether he described the situation correctly, today we have lots of comrades who want to talk about this question. So we have decided to extend the meeting time to a whole day." The heads behind the table bobbed in agreement.

"Now we'll ask people to talk."

The platoon leader, to whom Chen Yunghu daily brought water for washing his feet, was the first to speak.

"Yesterday, when I heard Comrade Ni Yuxian's speech, I thought it was very strange," he began, scratching his head in puzzlement. "Why should we have this problem in the army? Other people know that these two comrades' work is good, their relations with their leaders are good, they often write in their diaries, they want to get into the party, they stand on the side of the party. All this is good. So of course the party branch decided to let them enter the party.

"But there are people—people like Ni Yuxian—who deliberately say that these two comrades aren't good. This isn't a simple question. There is struggle inside the army today. There is a struggle between the advanced and the backward people, between the revolutionary people and people who are not willing to be revolutionary. There are struggles between people who are willing to listen to the party and people who are not willing to listen. This struggle—it's clear—this struggle is very ferocious. Some people think that we only have class struggle in society, that there is no class struggle within the army. But yesterday, circumstances demonstrated clearly that there is class struggle within the army. Yesterday, Ni Yuxian deliberately attacked the party. Today, at this meeting, we want everyone to talk about what Ni Yuxian did, about why he said what he did. What is his class standpoint? Comrade Ni Yuxian himself has to think about that, about why he did what he did."

To accuse Ni Yuxian of attacking the party, to bring up the question of class standpoint and class struggle, was to put the meeting on a different plane. After first concluding in 1956 that classes and class struggle had ceased to exist with the advent of socialism in China, Mao Zedong had then reversed his analysis after observing the enthusiasm with which so many had criticized the party during the hundred flowers campaign. Classes and class struggle continue to exist even under socialism, he had asserted. By

September 1962, he was arguing that sometimes class struggle would be sharp. Class enemies would not be tolerated.

The next speaker moved the question of Ni Yuxian more decidedly in the direction of class struggle. The content of Yuxian's criticisms of the party's choice of new members was largely ignored. The mere fact of criticizing a party that regarded itself as infallible and preached unquestioning obedience was sufficient cause for him to be branded an enemy. "When Ni Yuxian accuses our two comrades of being despicable, when he accuses them of kissing ass, what this means is that he himself is standing on the side of the enemy," the speaker argued. "And because Ni Yuxian has taken our two comrades as an enemy, we in turn take Ni Yuxian as our enemy."

One by one, party members and aspirants to the party stood up to declare Yuxian the enemy. Pei Xingling spoke in self-defense. "Yesterday, Ni Yuxian's speech wasn't just a criticism of me. In fact, he was criticizing the party leadership, the party organization. He accused me of writing a Lei Feng diary. But in fact, everyone knows that writing a Lei Feng diary is a way of respecting our leaders. Our superiors have asked us to keep Lei Feng diaries, they have educated us to do this. So if Ni Yuxian opposes me writing in my Lei Feng diary, he opposes the party leadership."

Chen Yunghu was next. "I think that Ni Yuxian's speech had another purpose," he said. "Ni Yuxian's thought and our thought are not the same. What we think is good, he thinks is bad. What we think is bad, he thinks is good. Last year he wrote a letter to Chairman Mao. At that time, our company commander educated him, helped him not to write that wrong, mistaken, letter. But Yuxian thought he was so great, he thought he was better than the party. He didn't listen to his leaders. So he wrote a completely revisionist, reactionary letter. If Ni Yuxian doesn't change his standpoint, he will be very dangerous. The army can also have counter-revolutionary elements in its ranks."

The company commander who had frequently criticized Yuxian for reading so many books when a single lifetime was not enough to study Chairman Mao followed. "I want to say a few words to the comrades who supported Ni Yuxian yesterday," he said. The soldiers were tense. Not merely Yuxian as spokesman but those who followed him were in danger of being attacked as enemies. "Ni Yuxian really thinks he's something. He thinks because he's got a little bit of education he's really special. But it's not so difficult to understand why his viewpoint is so wrong. In the fifties, his father launched an offensive against the party—a real assault. So—you comrades who followed Ni Yuxian yesterday—you've got to be careful. If you follow him, you'll make mistakes. This is a question of supporting or opposing the leadership. Today, lots of comrades have talked in agreement with the leadership. They don't agree with Ni Yuxian's viewpoint. This is good. It means their consciousness is good, their eyes are clear. We can see that most of the comrades still listen to the party. This is good."

Yuxian had sat, listening to the mounting criticism, becoming increasingly agitated. He feared that if he did not publicly defend himself, he would be declared a counterrevolutionary. He stood up, demanding his right to speak. "I want to answer the criticisms my comrades have made against me," he interjected, his outward calm belying his anger. "Every soldier is supposed to be given the right to speak." No one moved to stop him. Ni Yuxian continued.

"The first question I have is for the political instructor. Do you still take me as a comrade, or have I become an enemy? On the one hand, you address me as comrade, but on the other you say that I oppose the party and that means that this soldier has become an enemy, that this thing is class struggle. So my first question is whether you really think I am the enemy.

"I want you to stop twisting my words, too. Chen Yunghu said that I said that writing in his diary and kissing ass were contemptible. I didn't say that. I said it was disgusting." The sarcasm was beginning to show. "He said I wrote a reactionary letter to Chairman Mao, but how does he know it was reactionary? He's never even read the letter. I'd like to add accusing me of writing a reactionary letter when you haven't even read the letter to my list of things that are disgusting. According to our constitution, I'd like to remind you, I have the right to write Chairman Mao a letter expressing my viewpoint. Mao Zedong has not said my letter was reactionary, so how can you say it was reactionary?

"And as for the platoon leader, he also twisted my words. He says I'm contemptible. Well, you're contemptible, too." The anger was spilling over, reason and caution tossed to the winds. "Your wife is in Anhui, isn't she? She's ugly and poor. I've seen her. I saw you, too, when you went to Shanghai, playing around with those two Shanghai girls. And when your wife came to visit you, you beat her every day. Her face was black and blue. Isn't this contemptible? You've done contemptible things, too." Rarely is the content of political dispute in China confined to matters of principle. Issues of personal morality, as Ni Yuxian would later discover to his own detriment, are often called upon as final proof of political perfidy.

"You bring up the question of my father. My father is a doctor who really does serve the people. Every day from morning till night, he serves the people. He sees patients, he cures their illnesses. No one has ever said he is a bad person. And besides, my father and I are two different people. What does my father have to do with whether what I said yesterday is right or wrong?

"The second question is that I think it's a mistake for you to take this meeting as class struggle. You said yesterday that every soldier had the right to raise his opinions, that there would be no big stick, that no one would be called to task. But what you are doing now is precisely using a big stick against me. Chairman Mao said not to take internal contradictions among the people and make them into antagonistic contradictions between the enemy and the people. But what you are doing today is taking my friendly opinions and making them into contradictions with the enemy. But this is wrong, absolutely wrong. And I want you all to know that if you keep doing this, I'm going to report you. I'm going to report you to your superiors and to their superiors and to their superiors all the way up to the central committee if that becomes necessary. Because what you are doing here is oppressing the people, oppressing people's right to speak out. When I talked yesterday, I was bringing up the facts. Everyone knew they were the facts. And now you take me as a counterrevolutionary. If you take me as a counterrevolutionary, who else will ever again dare to speak out? How can the party ever correct its faults? If you continue to act like this, no one will ever believe you, no one will ever trust you, you'll just keep deceiving the people and the legitimacy of the party will get less and less."

His anger spent, Ni Yuxian sat down. The scratching of the political instructor's pen against his notebook was the only sound in the room. The silence seemed interminable.

Finally, Yang Guoli raised his hand. "I want to speak." He hesitated. The young man was agitated. "I have listened carefully both to our superiors and to Ni Yuxian. I have thought a lot about what has been said here. I think I have to tell you my true thoughts." Yang Guoli paused again. His future was at stake. What he was about to say could destroy his chance to join the party.

"Last night, the platoon leader secretly came to me and told me to stay away from Ni Yuxian. But, I'm sorry, there is just no way I'm going to stay away from him. What he says is right. It's you who are wrong. You can't tell people to talk and then punish them for what they say. You say he's reactionary, but when I think about what he says, how is he reactionary? He's been in the army for three years now. He's done dangerous work. How is he the enemy?"

Again, the atmosphere in the meeting changed. One by one, soldiers—especially the young recruits from Anhui—stood up to agree with Yang Guoli and to support Ni Yuxian. They brought up new problems, too—the arrogance with which the officers treated the soldiers, the lavishness of their lifestyles, how shamelessly the party aspirants curried favor with their superiors. One soldier revealed that Pei Xingling had given the political instructor an expensive wristwatch as a bribe for getting into the party. As the soldiers' disaffection grew more and more apparent, as it was clear that there were more revelations to be made, the chairman intervened.

"Comrades, time is running out," he began. "We need to do a little research and decide whether we should have another meeting later."

"No," the audience roared. "Let's continue the meeting now. People still have things to say. Look at all the hands that are still up."

The meeting continued. As dinnertime approached, the chairman again took the floor. "Comrades, this has been a very long and lively meeting," he said with well-feigned enthusiasm. "It's good that everyone is speaking out so openly. But dinnertime is approaching. Let's stop for dinner and meet again tomorrow. Comrade Ni, is that okay?"

The meeting was in Ni Yuxian's hands. "Do you agree, Comrade Ni? Can we break for dinner?"

"Sure," comrade Ni replied. "We all have to eat."

The evening meal was a lively affair, the soldiers clustering into small groups to review again and again the details of the afternoon meeting. About a third of the soldiers—some of them true believers and others upwardly mobile youth who knew the rewards to be reaped from sycophancy—continued in their unqualified support for the leadership. Another group sympathized with the criticisms leveled against the party leadership and the two aspirants to membership but knew the price of disobedience and the truth of Colonel Sheng's warning that he who leaves the party will surely be defeated. Dissatisfied, they were uncomfortable but would remain silent. Another third were both disgruntled and potentially vocal. Some, like Yang Guoli, were frightened but principled, and would speak out in the belief that the party was fallible but perfectible, if only its members could be persuaded to confront and correct their faults. Others, like the raw and uneducated peasant recruits still innocent of the machinations of power and ignorant of the consequences of dissent, were less sophisticated and more forthright in their disgruntlement, easily mobilized by a leader like Ni.

The dissidents were in the minority but not much dissension was necessary to undermine the leadership of the party. The officers knew that their hold over their men was slipping. The legitimacy of their leadership and of the system by which new members were recruited depended upon universal tacit agreement to ignore the hypocrisy upon which the system was based. With that hypocrisy exposed, the system itself could crumble.

After dinner, the party leadership convened another urgent meeting, summoning soldiers one by one into their offices, trying to gauge the extent of disaffection within the ranks. Ni Yuxian was the last to be called. He knew as well as the leadership and better than his supporters what stakes were really involved. The leadership was facing an incipient insurrection.

Colonel Sheng accompanied the company-level political instructor in speaking to the ringleader. "Ni, at this meeting, giving your opinions, you spoke well," the political instructor, now excessively polite and conciliatory, flattered the young man. "We aren't saying you made mistakes. Our idea is—why don't we just forget this thing? Let's just end the meeting. What point really is there in continuing?"

"Xiao Ni," Colonel Sheng continued, "you could persuade the other soldiers to forget this. Let's not keep bringing up all these criticisms."

Ni Yuxian believed that in fighting back, he had saved himself from the label of counterrevolutionary. But he also knew that if he continued his criticisms, he would not only be declared counterrevolutionary but the soldiers who had supported him would suffer, too. Yang Guoli would never get into the party. His fellow agitators—innocent and ignorant country bumpkins—would also be labeled and expelled from the circle. No one would ever come to their aid and they would never understand why. Yuxian was not prepared to carry the matter to that extreme. He was not suited for this army life, that he knew. Pressing his point was useless.

• • •

The regiment commander opened the meeting when the troops were assembled together again. "At the last meeting, lots of people raised many different opinions," he began. "This is a good thing. A very good thing. This means that we're developing democracy. Ni Yuxian in particular brought up some criticisms. He criticized the leaders. He dared to criticize the leaders. And this is a good thing, too, not a bad thing.

"Of course, we can't say that what Ni Yuxian said was right. But Ni Yuxian has the right to criticize other people and other people have the right to criticize Ni Yuxian. Everybody has the right to criticize everybody here. But now, after all these criticisms, the time has come to unite. We want to continue doing our work well, don't we? And if we don't listen to the leaders, how can we do our work well? So I hope we won't talk about this anymore, eh?" The colonel cast his glance in the direction of Ni Yuxian. The eyes of the soldiers were on him, too. Yuxian's nod was barely perceptible. The dissident soldier remained silent.

"So we won, Yuxian," Yang Guoli greeted his friend enthusiastically after the meeting.

"Like fart we won," Yuxian responded gruffly. "Just you watch, Guoli, you're not going to get in the party, I tell you. And I'm going to be leaving here pretty damn quick."

• • •

Two weeks went by.

The political instructor came to visit Ni Yuxian again. "We've decided to let you return home," he said simply, without elaboration, offering no explanation for the decision. "You'll still be working for socialism," the instructor added lamely.

"If you hadn't told me, I would have made the request myself," Yuxian replied, seeing no need to inquire into the basis for the decision. "I know it's not suitable for me to stay here. When am I supposed to go?"

"In three days. This gives you time to pack."

"I don't need three days. I can leave tomorrow." The camp had already begun mobilizing for the meetings that would attack

Ni Yuxian's erroneous thinking and bring those who had supported him to task. The dissident soldier was anxious to be on his way.

• • •

Only one piece of unfinished business remained. Yuxian would be required to sign the final evaluation of his military performance, the evaluation that would be placed in his *dangan* together with the second, secret, party evaluation which he would never see.

Yuxian was handed his evaluation. "Comrade Ni Yuxian has been in the army for three years," it began. That he was still being referred to as comrade was a good sign. Had the high command decided to label him a counterrevolutionary or reactionary, he would never be addressed as comrade. "During that time, Comrade Ni has been active, responsible, enthusiastic," the report continued. "He really likes to study—reads a lot of books, understands a lot. Willing to help other people. Active politically. Leads a simple life. No male-female problems. Really active. Work had a lot of accomplishments."

Every evaluation begins with a few well-placed words of praise. Political futures were determined by the equally necessary words of criticism that followed. "He is proud and arrogant, puts forth his own private criticisms without listening to the critcisms of others. We hope that after he leaves the army, he will become more disciplined. We hope that he will fill his head with Mao Zedong's thought. He needs to reform his thought so he can become a man of use to his people. If he does this, he has a future."

The undisciplined, free-thinking soldier could not object greatly to the evaluation. He had escaped being labeled, which was most important, and the criticisms were not too severe. He signed the form, knowing all the while that the signature was mere charade. The most important record, the one that would affect him the rest of his life, was the one he would never see.

The cook prepared a special meal that evening—four dishes altogether—for Yuxian and his three best friends. Even as the soldier packed—a few items of clothing, his extra pair of shoes, his toothbrush and toothpaste, his soap and washbasin, and his accumulation of books—the meeting criticizing Ni Yuxian's mistakes, the meeting that would begin to reestablish the officers control over their men, was beginning. As he wrapped his belongings in a quilt, suspending the bundle from a carrying pole, Yang Guoli and Xi Shenfa, who had shared so many party secrets with their wayward friend, came to say good-bye. Yuxian removed the red insignia from his cap and took off his shoulder lapels. His days as a soldier were over.

Standing at the door of their barracks, his two friends waved good-bye. Gu Jiabing, Yuxian's closest political and intellectual soulmate, who had also shared in the farewell dinner, had disappeared. No one would accompany him on the hour's walk to the bus station. The meeting evaluating Ni Yuxian's mistakes would continue into the night, and Yang Guoli was being asked to make a self-criticism for the support and loyalty he had shown his high-school classmate.

Walking in solitude through the quiet, darkened streets, heavy carrying pole slung over his shoulder, Yuxian was suddenly overcome with emotion. He had been at the army camp for more than three years. The education he had received was more valuable and would be more long-lasting than any knowledge he had learned from books—and more distressing, too. He had been brought face to face with the overwhelming poverty of the Chinese countryside and with the incompetence and indifference of local party leadership. He had seen human misery and human greed and the corrupting influence of power. He had been transformed, he thought, from adolescent to man and was proud, even in his disgrace, that he had been a good soldier. The young man was saddened, filled with the sense that something important had been lost. Expelled from the circle again, he felt empty. After three years of sharing his life with so many comrades, not a soul had come to see him off.

Looking up at the sky, at the stars and the moon, another thought entered his head. He was free. For the first time in three years, he could go wherever he wanted to go. He could do what he wanted and not have to ask for permission. There were no platoon leaders or officers to obey. He could sleep late in the morning and he would never have to line up in a row again. He did not have to go to artillery practice or ever look at another cannon or rocket. For three years, he had been a machine. Now, the sky and the world seemed vast, and Yuxian felt like a bird, soaring high.

From a simple house that faced the road, a door opened and a young soldier emerged. "Yuxian, where have you been? I've been waiting forever." It was Gu Jiabing. "Your bundle is so heavy with all those books. I came to help you carry them." Gu Jiabing had sneaked away from camp on the pretext of buying soap.

"I brought you a copy of *Dream of the Red Chamber.*" For months, Yuxian had wanted to buy the most famous of all of China's traditional novels, but the cost was an extravagance he could not afford. Yuxian was moved by his friend's gesture.

Ni Yuxian and Gu Jiabing had shared their books in those three years and exchanged ideas about every matter under the sun. Witnessing the inexorable constriction of his countrymen's thought, from a lively mixture of superstition and practicality, fatalism and the work ethic, to the same predictable dull-gray mouthing of the party line, Yuxian had concluded that the brain atrophies if not indulged in frequent exercise. He had no greater fear than that his own brain might lose its capacity to think. When individuals refuse to speak out publicly for fear of retribution, Yuxian reasoned, the brain can still remain conscious and relatively agile so long as it continues to think and occasionally to share those thoughts with others. But once silence becomes the norm, the brain becomes indolent and begins to lose the capacity to function. When the brain begins to lose its function, the original fear that compelled it initially to silence is also forgotten. Instead of focusing on the large and momentous and meaningful questions, the energies of the brain are diverted to minute details and minor problems, as though the world were merely a mass of small and bothersome details. Immersed in the details of daily life, the brain shuts down and begins to atrophy.

Ni Yuxian saw his countrymen as a mass of atrophied brains mired in petty, meaningless detail. Outwardly whole, these individuals still laughed and cried, worked and played. They continued to make love and raise families and in all obvious respects were normal. But having lost the capacity for thought, and not even knowing that they were not free, they remained crippled, not just unwilling but unable now to think.

In the rigid discipline of the camp and the intrusion of the military into all one's thoughts, it was to Gu Jiabing that Yuxian most frequently turned to keep the cells of his mind nimble, active, and alive. He had an insatiable need to share his ideas, to turn them over and hold them to the light, to examine them from every conceivable angle, however ordinary or bizarre, conventional or iconoclastic those ideas initially seemed. Discussion was the best way to nourish and clarify thought. A good thought left unspoken, Ni Yuxian feared, might die. Once the two soldiers had spent hours trying to decide whether, if a bank burned to the ground, the money was lost to the state forever or whether it could be replaced simply by printing new bills.

Ni Yuxian took off his soldier's cap and gave it to his friend. Gu Jiabing's own cap had become something of an eccentricity. He wore it constantly, night and day, through heavy artillery maneuvers and reading in his room in the evening. It was grimy, encrusted with sweat and dirt and oil.

The two said good-bye. "Come visit me and my family in Shanghai," Yuxian called to his friend as the bus pulled away.

"I will. I promise."

Gu Jiabing never made the visit. The regiment finally did go to war after all—not with the militant public fanfare with which they had prepared to fight the nuclear war across the Taiwan Straits but silently and in secret, in Vietnam. Gu Jiabing did not want to go to war. Like his good friend, he believed in peace. He had never regarded the United States as an enemy. He liked the Americans, in fact.

Since the government never admitted that its troops were in Vietnam, and Gu Jiabing wore the uniform of a North Vietnamese soldier, his parents could never openly admit that their son had been killed there. "He died in the course of his work," was all they were allowed to say. His family never saw their son's body, either. Gu Jiabing was buried on the battlefield sometime in 1965. He remains inadequately mourned, another hungry ghost haunting the land.

• • •

The release that had flooded Yuxian as he experienced the first taste of freedom upon leaving Gold Mountain military base was fleeting. He was not in fact free. In August of 1964, at the time of his demobilization, job assignments in China were the monopoly of the state. All employment was determined by the government. The veterans' affairs bureau of Shanghai was responsible for finding him a job.

Military service was one route to success in China, a training ground for lower-level cadres, and the attraction of the army for many young men was precisely in the career opportunities it afforded. After several years of rigorous discipline, most soldiers were ready to enter the party and serve it loyally for life.

Soldiers from the rural areas often returned to their native villages to assume responsible positions of local leadership, gradually working their way up the political ladder. Urban youth with a middle-school education could expect relatively comfortable positions in the city, serving as lower-level cadres in the Public Security Bureau or the post office, teaching middle school, or becoming deputy managers of factories or large shops. They were eligible to take the university entrance exams, and with a university degree could expect to climb even higher up the ladder of success.

Yuxian's fate was different.

His reputation had preceded him to the Shanghai Veterans' Affairs Bureau. "You've got problems," the bureaucrat informed him after locating Ni Yuxian's file. "Your unit says you didn't return the insignia from your cap and your shoulder lapels. They also say you may have some bullets stashed away somewhere. I can't give you a job until you give everything back."

Keeping a few bullets and a set of their military insignia as souvenirs was a custom among soldiers, the regulations prohibiting such keepsakes being regularly overlooked. Fearing that a recalcitrant, impetuous, demobilized Ni might someday find occasion to impersonate a soldier, his superiors had demanded, and received, his insignia before he left the Gold Mountain camp.

"I don't have my insignia," Ni retorted testily. "I gave them back when I left." After three years in the army at six yuan a month, feeling all the while like a tool of his superiors' whim, having tasted just briefly the flavor of freedom, Yuxian was exasperated to discover that he was still in the army's grip. "Check with my platoon leader if you don't believe me," he challenged the bureaucrat. "I don't have any bullets, either. Search my house if you want. Search everything."

"But I can't give you work if you don't give those things back," the confused but loyal bureaucrat replied.

"Tell me, how can I give them back to you if I don't have them?"

It was a standoff. In no rush to begin work, Yuxian returned home to wait.

• • •

Summer vacation was well underway, and most of his middle school classmates had returned home from their second year of college. Yuxian began renewing old acquaintances, happy to see his friends, but regretting that he had sacrificed college for three years of military life.

Chopping vegetables one afternoon for the family's evening

meal, he became aware of a figure lingering quietly outside the courtyard gate. He went to investigate.

It was Zhao Yuefang, standing with her brand new Phoenix brand bicycle, blushing bright red in embarrassment. There had been no communication between the two former sweethearts for nearly two years.

Seeing her so confused and embarrassed and pretty, Yuxian was suddenly overcome with forgiveness. Perhaps he had been too harsh. They had once been so much in love, and she had already apologized, told him she wanted to get back together.

"Oh, so it's you," he said, walking to the gate, wiping his hands on a towel. "What are you doing just standing there? Why don't you come in?"

"I didn't know whether you'd want me to."

"We're old classmates aren't we? Old friends? Come on in, sit a while."

Repressing his normally irrepressible curiosity, Yuxian never raised their earlier breakup, never asked why she had not wanted to see him anymore, ignoring the passing thoughts that there might have been someone else. He preferred to believe that a proud young university student simply could not countenance love with a lowly foot soldier.

Later, he would claim to regret having taken the problem and wrapped it up so tightly, storing it out of mind's reach. But in the summer of 1964, his on again–off again romance took flower and blossomed once more.

• • •

Two weeks later, he was called back to the Veterans' Affairs Bureau.

"You're getting work," the bureaucrat explained. "But if you're ever caught with any bullets or with those insignia, it's your responsibility. Your case has been assigned to the handicrafts bureau in your county. The factory where you'll be working is very close to your home."

There was no worse job than with the county-level handicrafts bureau.

In the Chinese hierarchy of work, urban work is better than rural work and state-owned industry is better than collectively owned industry—or county-level handicrafts. The handicrafts industry, in fact, stands at the lowest rung of the ladder.

For Ni Yuxian to be assigned to the handicrafts industry in his native county was even worse.

When Ni Guansheng and his extended family had been forced during the backyard steel campaign in 1958 to leave their native Cao Family Village and move to Yangsi, the full and long-term implications of the change were not yet apparent. The tragedy then had been the loneliness and rootlessness of being forced out of their native place.

Administratively, Cao Family Village was located in suburban Shanghai and hence was a part of the city. Yangsi Village was simply a small town in a rural county. At the time of the move, the only difference the family could discern from the distinction was that in Cao Family Village their ration of cooking oil was five ounces a month. In Yangsi Village, it was only four. But during the three bad years, when they moved, even that difference did not matter. There was no oil at all.

In fact, however, once Guansheng had registered his household in Yangsi, the entire extended family and the generations to come were condemned to remain in perpetuity in rural China. Over the years, as the system of household registration became entrenched, and as ever-more regulations were introduced to govern the system, the urban-rural distinction, so minute in the beginning, grew wider and wider.

Educational opportunities in the rural areas were significantly contracted. The quality of rural middle schools was generally lower than that of urban middle schools and hence the probability of a rural middle school graduate succeeding in the nationwide competition for entry into universities was low.

Income differences were substantial, with workers in large, state-run industrial urban factories both earning a higher salary than a worker in a small rural factory and receiving a generous welfare package that often surpassed their salaries in value. The lowest urban wage in 1964 was thirty-six yuan a month; but ration coupons permitted the worker to buy rice, meat, eggs, and cooking oil at subsidized prices. His housing was virtually free, and medical care was also free, widely available, and relatively modern. The lowest rural factory wage was twenty-six yuan a month, the welfare benefits modest, and housing a family responsibility. State investment in handicrafts was negligible, and salaries and benefits were at the very bottom of the scale. Working conditions were primitive.

Yuxian watched glumly as the official from the Veterans' Affairs

Bureau completed the form that outlined his fate: "Ordinary worker, Quansha county, handicrafts factory, twenty-eight yuan a month, possibility of increase to thirty yuan after six months probation." Stamping the form with the official seal, without which no slip of paper in China has authority, the bureaucrat handed Yuxian the form. For a young man who had once aspired to enter the university, who wanted to accomplish great deeds and to make something of himself, who, in ordinary circumstances, could have expected after his military service to spend a year in the city, working on the one hand and preparing for the university entrance exams on the other, the assignment was a bitter disappointment, the three years in the army not merely a waste but a personal disaster. The dejected youth turned to leave.

"Are you going to the factory right away?" the bureaucrat asked.

"Yes, I guess I'll report today," Yuxian answered dully. The factory, and his home, were still a four-hour bus ride away.

"Would you take this, then, and save me some trouble?" The bureaucrat began fishing absentmindedly through the voluminous files cluttering his desk. "Ni Yuxian. Ni Yuxian. Here it is." The file was thick.

It was his *dangan*, the personal file that was destined to follow him wherever he went. Individuals were not allowed to carry their own files. Such transfers were always handled by party officials within the respective personnel departments. This military bureaucrat was lazy, already tired of the complexities and complications of Ni Yuxian's case.

The bureaucrat sealed the fat envelope with the paste of ground rice and water that dries as solid as cement and stamped the closure with the official seal, guaranteeing thereby that the contents could not be opened without the knowledge of the recipient.

Yuxian's heart began pumping wildly, the blood rushing to his head. By the time he boarded the bus that would carry him back to Quansha county, he was trembling. Rice paste may be as solid as cement, but the paste takes a long time to dry. Yuxian wanted to open his file, to read what was written there, to predict his future from what was written about his past. Looking at one's file was absolutely forbidden, illegal. For all the trouble he had already brought to himself, Yuxian had never knowingly done anything illegal. Opening his file, reading it, would be his first deliberately illegal act.

Trying to appear casual, looking out the window at the passing countryside, he began fingering the envelope. The closure was still wet. His heart was beating so loudly he feared others might hear, and the blood was pumping so hard against his ears his head was about to explode. He was terrified. He should not look. He should not open the file. It was against all regulations. But imagine knowing what the file contained! Imagine knowing what his superiors had been writing all those years! The corner of the closure gave way easily.

Slowly, the envelope sitting on his lap, his eyes busy trying to gauge whether his fellow passengers were observing him, certain first that they were all looking, had discovered his crime, then believing they had not, feigning indifference to his surroundings, his index finger began cautiously making its way under the seal. The paper gave way with little resistence. The envelope was open.

The ride to Yangsi Village was excruciatingly long. Yuxian did not dare to look at the file. He hardly dared to move, scarcely permitted himself to breathe, fearful that with the slightest movement his secret would be revealed, or the files would tumble on the floor for everyone to see.

Yuxian's little sister was the only one at home after a ride that seemed to last a lifetime. "Have you eaten?" she greeted her big brother.

"I'm not hungry. Little sister, you have to help me. Guard my door. Don't let anyone in. I have something I have to do. Promise?"

Behind the closed door of the upstairs bedroom that he shared with his two younger brothers, Yuxian opened his file.

His whole life spread out before him.

Every transgression he had ever committed was recorded there, many of which had long since faded into the dark recesses of the mind. His insolence during the Popsicle incident with Principal Xia was noted, and the chorus of "Old MacDonald's Farm" when Tao Yuefang had tried to sing. The confrontation with the Public Security Bureau over who had carved "Down with Mao Zedong" in the park received a lengthy description, and Pockfaced Huang had noted with concern Yuxian's potentially bad influence on Zhao Yuefang. Pockfaced Huang, who still came frequently to visit Ni Jizhong, citing his relationship as teacher to the doctor's son as a reason for receiving free medical care, seemed to have taken special pleasure in recording the young boy's sins.

Ni Jizhong stood accused as well—of having opposed the party during the hundred flowers campaign and thus of being someone who stood on the side of the rightists. The father's political standpoint was offered as a powerful explanation for the sins of the son.

The most important and damaging reports were from Ni's military commanders. Ni Yuxian's thought, the military report said, was frequently mistaken, and he often opposed the party.

"Ni Yuxian's thought is capitalist thought," one entry read. "In 1962 he wrote a revisionist letter to Chairman Mao. In it, he opposed the three red flags—the Great Leap Forward, the people's communes, and the backyard steel furnaces. He also advocated the reintroduction of free markets and private plots and the right of families to raise chickens and pigs and to engage in subsidiary sideline production."

Considerable evidence of Ni Yuxian's capitalist thought was advanced—the fact that he was well-educated and liked to read books, that he played love songs on his harmonica, and that he took a bath once a week, clear indication that he was a hedonist, selfish, a seeker of comfort and pleasure, and a coward. His commanders had frequently criticized him for his habit of taking a weekly bath and using soap to boot. Soldiers were not supposed to fear dirt. A soldier afraid of dirt would also surely fear hard work and be unwilling to die for his country. To be clean was to set oneself above and apart.

Yuxian was particulary surprised to read Colonel Sheng's report. "Ni's thought is not just mistaken," wrote the man who had taken such a special interest in him, warning against the consequences of leaving the party. "His thought is full of big mistakes, and he is potentially dangerous. I haven't figured out where this thought comes from—maybe from reading too many Western books—but it's systematic." Yuxian had thought those conversations were private. The report was a betrayal of trust.

Despite his mistaken, capitalist, and revisionist thought, the soldier was not to be discarded as hopeless. In the final instructions to the political cadres who would be responsible for the young man after he left the army, the military commanders pointed out that Ni ought not to be treated as a counterrevolutionary. "Don't lock him up," the military warned, "just try to educate him."

Ni Yuxian found little solace in the fact that he was not yet a counterrevolutionary. Confronted with the stark reality of his file, he knew that his future was doomed. Growing up, even as a soldier, the young man had still believed that merit in the end would be rewarded. So long as he continued to work conscientiously and hard, to perform his tasks well, so long as he remained honest, Yuxian believed he could still accomplish something, become someone, make a contribution to society. Seeing his file, however, he knew that political standpoint was the primary determinant of success. Today he might merely be a young man with problems, but tomorrow, in one of the political campaigns that he knew would continue to sweep China in a series of waves, Yuxian would surely be singled out. He was too easy a target. Moreover, with a record like this, he would never be allowed into college. He would not even be allowed to take the exams.

He was angry. He hated the system that insured that every detail of his life would follow him forever. He hated being condemned merely for being his father's son, the offspring of a man who stood on the side of the rightists. He hated the system that required obsequious flattery to get ahead, that could dictate what books you read and what songs you sang, that took cleanliness as evidence of degeneracy and cowardice. He was overcome by a sense of oppression, like a slave in chains to the system. He longed to break free of the shackles. He wanted his independence and freedom. He was a tool, not a person.

He was angry with himself, too—angry for ever having trusted his superiors, for sharing his iconoclastic views, for believing in his powers of persuasion, for thinking that others, like Colonel Sheng, really were interested in sharing ideas or concerned about his welfare. He knew that if, from that day forward, he were completely to surrender his self, if he were to give up completely his penchant for the truth, perhaps someday he could be a minor cadre. Nothing more. To get that far, he would be forced to dissemble. Deceit was the only way to win.

He searched the folder for a list of its contents. There was none. With no record of what the file contained, then no one would ever know what materials had been removed. Page by page Yuxian began removing the damaging evidence.

The file was nearly flat when he completed his work. His high-school grades were still there. He could be proud of his academic achievements. He added the letter the political instructor had written congratulating his parents on how well their son had studied Lei Feng. The military report that bore his signature, praising his enthusiasm on the one hand and criticizing his arrogance on the other, remained. The file was flatter than one might expect for a nineteen-year-old youth who had served three years in the military. To protect his secret, Ni Yuxian counted on the generally haphazard administration of most county-level handicrafts factories and the fact that the files of his uneducated fellow workers would also be rather sparse.

Mixing ground rice with water, Yuxian sealed the file again, and so clever was his workmanship that the two sides of the official red seal were perfectly aligned. No one would ever know that the file had been opened. He would report to the factory the next day.

Staring into the fire into which he was feeding the incriminating evidence, he felt like a criminal, overcome with guilt. His measures of self-protection had been drastic, and so unheard of was his crime that he had no idea what the punishment might be. Burning his file was the most important thing he had ever done in his life.

• • •

"What in the world are you doing with this thing?" his new boss asked in amazement when Ni Yuxian presented his file the next day.

"The comrade at the Military Affairs Bureau asked me to give it to you," Yuxian replied innocently, pretending ignorance.

"That guy must be off his rocker. It's okay. This has nothing to do with you. That guy just doesn't understand the rules."

Yuxian's record was clean. His past was behind him. He could start a new life, from scratch. Some people were offered only one opportunity in a lifetime. Ni Yuxian would be offered many.

CHAPTER

5

Like rural enclaves everywhere along the Yangtze River delta, the villages of Yuxian's youth fairly burst with energy—the cacophony of their shops a testimony to the ingenuity and inventiveness of China's rural small-scale producers. Within the new Marxian framework, however, those same villages came to be regarded as embodiments of petit bourgeois capitalism. The owners of the shops and tiny factories that gave the villages character could hardly be placed in the same category as landlords or rich capitalists, whose wealth was far greater and who depended on the sweat of the laboring class. But no one ever doubted that the petite bourgeoisie, if given the chance, would seize the opportunity to become landlords, rich capitalists, and exploiters themselves. The foundation of capitalism, after all, was still private ownership. The declaration of socialism in China depended in the end on gathering even the hard-working, long-suffering, self-interested petite bourgeoisie into the fold.

And so, as socialism in China was consolidated in the mid-1950s, the once richly patterned texture of small-town public life became subordinate to the desiderata of socialist equality and socialist industry. As industry expanded from the city of Shanghai proper east to Pudong, whole villages along the river were razed, Cao Family Village among them, the canals filled in, trees felled, burial mounds leveled, vegetation destroyed to make room for smoke-belching factories, crowded one on top of the other—symbols of the country's modernization. Way had to be made, too, for the workers who labored in the new factories. On the razed land, now parched and dry, scores of "new workers' villages" were built. Rectangular, soulless, gray concrete structures several stories high, each an exact replica of the next, decay seemed to set in even before the buildings were complete, burdening the houses with a depressing look of listless decline even before the first tenants had moved in. The new workers' villages were unremittingly, uncompromisingly ugly, devoid of even small traces of the color and vibrancy that had once been the hallmark of village life. Public life took on the same dull quality of sameness.

The party's answer to the cacophony of small shops was consolidation. Socialism in rural towns meant bringing the confusing jumble of separate small producers—the manufacturer of belt buckles and the man who made barrettes, the local crafter of garish costume jewelry and the man who fashioned and repaired umbrellas, the doorknob maker and the woodcutter—together under the same roof, all working together to produce, often not very well, the same thing.

It was to such an amalgamation that Ni Yuxian was sent in the fall of 1964. There were three hundred workers in the factory then, most of whom were former "little bosses," past members of the petite bourgeoisie who had once owned and managed their own small shops—or the sons and daughters of those who had. They included in their midst two ordinary party members, in addition to the three who governed the factory, one full-fledged former large-scale capitalist, one rightist, and "three bad elements"—one of whom was a "historic counterrevolutionary" who had previously, so it was said, worked for the Guomindang. With so many once independent and independent-minded small bosses and their children mixed together under Communist Party control, human relations within the factory were complicated, duplicating much of the complexity that characterized relations in the villages themselves. Most workers treated the factory's three party leaders—the factory head, the party branch secretary, and the cadre responsible for personnel—with a deferential respect born in no small measure of fear. Like most such county-level amalgamations, the factory seemed destined to muddle along indefinitely like a low-grade headache without major upheaval or upsetting outbursts of human drama.

Ni Yuxian, young, healthy, well-educated, and strong, was assigned to the storeroom where the electric gadgets that were the factory's specialty were dispatched each day, carted away on the rear of bicycle-drawn carts owned by peasants from the nearby communes whose incomes were increased substantially with the money they earned transporting locally produced goods. Yuxian's job, because he was educated, was to record the flow of shipments, and, because he was strong, to move and pile the boxes on the back of the peasants' carts. It was not a particularly demanding job, and from the very start he was able to spend much of each day immersed in reading.

• • •

Politics intervened unexpectedly a bare two months after Yuxian began working. The socialist education campaign descended upon the factory with the arrival of a "four cleans" work team—the party branch secretary of one of the city's middle schools accompanied by five students from local Shanghai universities. The work team immediately dismissed the factory leadership pending further investigation and took over administration themselves. The task of the work team was to "clean up the class ranks" from the top—the factory's party leadership—to the workers at the bottom.

The socialist education movement was both an outcome of the calamitous Great Leap Forward and the precursor of the Great Proletarian Cultural Revolution to come.

Twenty years would pass before China's leadership would acknowledge the massive famine that had claimed the lives of some 20 to 30 million people in 1959, 1960, and 1961, preferring to refer euphemistically instead to the "temporary difficulties of the three bad years." To this day, the party has never recognized that the disaster was in any way related to the egregiously misguided agricultural policies introduced by the country's highest leaders during the Great Leap Forward. Responsibility for the disaster, when it is assigned at all, has been blamed on the worst weather in over a hundred years—drought in some areas and floods in others—the precipitous withdrawal in 1960 of Soviet experts, together with their blueprints for modernizing China's factories, and the basic-level cadres in the communes and factories whose job it had been to implement the ill-advised policies emanating from the top.

Calamities everywhere provide occasion for corruption, as those whose power is unrestrained provide first for themselves and their own and then turn to profit-making at the expense of the poor and the powerless least able to protect themselves. The Chinese famine of 1959–1962 was no exception, as Ni Yuxian had learned during his stint in the army, and many of the same basic-level cadres who—whether out of ignorance, fear, or opportunism—

blindly followed the party's stupendously foolish policies also ensured that they and their relatives passed the crisis with a minimum of discomfort.

One purpose of the "Four Cleans" Socialist Education Campaign was to investigate and "clean up" instances of corruption among the basic-level cadres—to expose and bring to justice the small handful of party members who may have embezzled funds, juggled the account books, or otherwise been the beneficiaries of ill-gotten gains. The campaign was also the first practical test of Mao's evolving theory that classes, class contradictions, and class struggle continue to exist even under socialism. Not only could unrepentant, unreformed landlords and members of the bourgeoisie be expected to continue their quest to overthrow socialism and regain political control, Mao was beginning to argue, but even once reliable and trustworthy party members could be politically corrupted, transformed into pernicious carriers of the disease of capitalism.

The Socialist Education Campaign thus demanded that party members and masses alike be investigated to determine where their real sympathies lay, and the class labels that had been assigned to everyone in the earliest years of party rule were to be reexamined and adjusted. Perhaps a few landlords had escaped detection in the early 1950s, mistakenly being labeled middle peasants or members of the petit bourgeoisie instead. These hidden landlords would have to be rooted out. Maybe with the lenient and liberal policies introduced in the wake of the "three bad years," new class enemies had emerged, with some members of the relatively benign classes having been transformed through force of opportunity into active counterrevolutionaries. People who had spoken out too stridently in criticism of the party would also have to be called to task.

Corruption within the ranks of the party would be thoroughly investigated, but the investigation was a double-edged sword. If there was corruption within the party which claimed near-infallibility, surely that corruption included only a very small handful of the party's total numbers, and its roots must trace to society itself. The moral integrity of the masses had to be investigated, too. If there was corruption within the party, surely there was corruption among the masses. If cadres had been guilty of stealing, workers surely were not without crime. Sexual transgressions would be scrutinized, too, illicit affairs exposed, adulterers and philanderers publicly punished and condemned.

The conscientious work team sent to Ni Yuxian's factory vowed to delve deeply into all manner of transgressions. They constructed a small wooden box and promised the factory workers that secret, unsigned criticisms revealing hitherto unknown problems about anyone in the factory would be thoroughly and seriously investigated. In a workplace where tension was constant and antagonisms stood just beneath the surface, the encouragement of the work team provided fertile opportunity through truth and slander to open the wounds of long-standing grudges.

The atmosphere in the factory turned tense.

•   •   •

Yuxian was struck with an underlying sense of unease. If he were to become a target of serious investigation, the work team would surely discover that he was a young man with problems.

His concern was fleeting. Not only did the investigation focus on those who had been with the factory nearly since its inception, but Ni Yuxian's recent service in the military bestowed on him an aura of revolutionary legitimacy. The army under the command of the new Defense Minister Lin Biao, with Lei Feng as its shining example, had become the organizational model for all other sectors of Chinese society to follow. Ni Yuxian's *dangan* was crystal clear and even contained the letter of military praise about how well he had studied Lei Feng. The ordinarily irrepressible troublemaker was quickly declared a "dependable element."

After four months of detailed and determined investigation, the four cleans work team was unable to unearth any great problems with the factory leadership. The party cadres were permitted to return to work. Most of the former little bosses, the one-time petit capitalists, were determined to have been transformed through hard work and proper attitude into proletarian workers, and their class labels were therefore changed in recognition of their status as loyal citizens of socialism. A few miscreants were unearthed. One man originally classified as a member of the petite bourgeoisie was discovered to have been a hidden landlord instead and was thus relabeled. The divorced wife of a rightist was declared a bad element when her chastity was called into question. Lonely and impoverished, with several children to support on her meager wages at the handicrafts factory, her unsuccessful efforts to find a new husband were said to have been determined and far-reaching. The enterprising, hard-working peasants whose bicycles had transported goods from the factory were deemed to have been following the capitalist road, their services dismissed.

• • •

In his new, cherished, and potentially fragile status as a dependable element, Ni Yuxian quietly seized the opportunity to pursue his own ends. He wanted to go to college.

When the leader of the factory labor union, anxious to serve his workers in a new, creative, and innovative fashion, decided to establish a small library, Ni Yuxian, as the most educated and intellectual of the workers, was appointed to buy the books that would lay the foundation for the project. Yuxian naturally bought a sizable collection of the picture and comic books he knew the workers would appreciate, but at the huge New China Bookstore on Shanghai's crowded and bustling Nanjing Road, he turned to indulging his own tastes in Shakespeare, Turgenev, Dostoevsky, and a variegated selection of other Western writers.

The manager stopped him at the cash register. "These books all have problems," the man remonstrated. "They are for university students and professors—intellectuals. Workers are supposed to stick to Mao Zedong."

"I represent the workers in my factory," Yuxian retorted haughtily. "We workers will decide for ourselves what we read."

The manager, puffed with education and authority, phoned the party secretary in Ni Yuxian's factory. "You can't read these books," he commanded. "They're bad. They're for intellectuals."

"If they're so bad, then why are you selling them?" the party secretary demanded angrily, insulted that the supercilious manager should think that intellectuals could be trusted with books that ordinary workers, the vanguard of the revolution, could not. "Ni Yuxian has our fullest confidence. We have entrusted him to buy our books."

With confidence in him thus fully established, Ni Yuxian presented the party branch secretary with his own long-term plan. He wanted to take the university entrance exams, and in order to study for them he needed full run of the Shanghai library. Ordinary citizens were given only minimal access, their permission to read confined to those books that were safe, politically innocuous, and therefore "open." Ni Yuxian wanted the right to read the *neibu* or "internal" books. For that he needed a cadre's pass.

"Can you guarantee you'll pass the exams?" the party secretary inquired dubiously. To succeed at the university entrance exams after having left middle school a year before graduation followed by three years in the army and another at factory labor was virtually unknown. Such were the rigors of the examination system that a combination of high native intelligence and several unrelenting years of full-time study and preparation were ordinarily necessary. The manager risked losing face should permission be granted and the factory-sponsored candidate fail.

"I think I can pass," Yuxian responded honestly.

The party secretary wrote a letter of introduction granting him library privileges.

For the next several months, Yuxian went weekly to the city library, checking out both the orthodox books that would serve to bring him success on the college entrance exams and the secret books that continued to provide him the jarring contrast between the world as it was officially interpreted by the Chinese press and party officialdom and the world as it was written about by philosophers and pundits who wore glasses of a different tint.

By spring 1965 he was prepared to take the exams. To register, he needed his factory's approval.

"You need to give the party secretary a few gifts," a worldly Xu Fengzhen admonished her son, encouraging him to follow the path through the "back door," without which little in China gets done. The bananas, apples, and eggs she placed in the basket for her son to deliver to the party leader cost more than half of Ni Yuxian's monthly salary. Ashamed, discomfited, and for once at a loss for words, the young worker-who-would-be-student, the youth who ordinarily so vehemently despised the hypocrisy and flattery in which so many of his countrymen indulged, called one Sunday afternoon on his leader, laden with gifts.

"Why are you giving me all this?" the leader exclaimed in mock refusal, delighted and with every intention of receiving the offering. "The committee has already met. You can take the exams."

Yuxian took the exams. Against all odds, he passed.

But academic achievement was only half the university entrance equation. Political purity was the other. The education ministry sent a small team to the factory to investigate Ni Yuxian's political record.

His *dangan* was too clean. Something was missing. A young man who had spent three years in the military, who had been a model in the study of Lei Feng, and who was so well regarded by his factory superiors, should surely be a member of the Youth League. Why was this Ni Yuxian not a member? What stain in his past was being hidden?

The party secretary was not there the afternoon the Education Ministry investigators arrived. The ministry representatives spoke with the official in charge of personnel instead. Relations between Yuxian and the personnel cadre were strained. Called upon by the four cleans work team to criticize their own cadres, the workers had been reluctant to raise the issue that had been a rich source of factory gossip for months. Once the work team departed, the workers would once more be at the mercy of their original party leaders, and no one wanted to jeopardize his future standing. Everyone knew, however, that for months the married personnel manager had been busy pursuing a liaison with one of the female factory workers—a young activist and Youth League member with aspirations of joining the party. As the party member in charge of her case, the personnel cadre frequently invited her to his office, where the glass windows lining one wall stood as an open invitation to curious workers witnessing the cadre's unwelcome but persistent advances. The story circulated that the cadre was promising to divorce his wife, offering the young woman the dual bonus of marriage to him and entrance into the party if only her resistance ceased.

Egged on by a group of young workers who were vigorously, openly opposed to the liaison and encouraging her instead to pursue the recently demobilized young soldier, the young woman's own propensity to romance lay in the direction of Ni Yuxian. Several times she had invited him to the movies, and even today, twenty-five years later, during my own visit to the factory, she still remembers Ni's factory identification number and could recall their conversations in full detail. Her eyes took on a certain mistiness when discussing him, and she glowed with pride in showing the storage room where once he studied and worked. Ni Yuxian encouraged their friendship but refused the romance, or so he now alleges, not out of loyalty to the girlfriend his workers did not know he had but because romantic competition with the party leadership while his chance to enter the university still hung in the balance would have been foolish in the extreme. Besides, the young man had developed an appreciation for feminine good looks and the young woman had not been blessed with beauty.

The personnel cadre, however, had been blind to Yuxian's indifference, imagining himself locked in a dramatic love triangle that he was determined to fight and win. The arrival of the investigators from the Ministry of Education provided an excellent opportunity to divest himself of his competition.

"There's really nothing wrong with Comrade Ni's politics," he assured the investigators. "His political thought is just fine. He's a good worker, too. No problems at all."

"So why isn't he in the Youth League?" the investigators pressed. "Isn't it a little peculiar that a demobilized soldier, such a good worker, so good politically, should still not have joined the League?"

"No, we want him in. Really. He'll join. It's just—you know we've been so busy since Comrade Ni joined us, what with the four cleans and everything. The work team has been here and we haven't been able to do any real political work of our own for months. The party secretary just hasn't gotten around to it, that's all."

"Can you have the party secretary write a letter to that effect?" the investigators demanded.

"Sure." Indeed, the party secretary did write such a letter, guaranteeing Ni Yuxian's immediate entry into the Communist Youth League.

Ni Yuxian never joined.

• • •

Months went by, and Ni heard nothing about his university admission. Then one evening, returning home from work, his two little brothers ran out to greet him as he biked up the small lane to their house. "You failed," they giggled, dancing around his bicycle. "Their said your grades weren't good enough. You didn't make it to college."

Yuxian rushed home. Ni Jizhong was standing proudly at the door, letter in hand, smiling. His brothers had been teasing. "They're letting you go to university," his father said. "The Shanghai Maritime Academy."

The Shanghai Maritime Academy.

Yuxian was struck with a momentary twinge of disappointment. His first choice had been the Peking University Department of Chinese, Fudan's Department of Journalism in Shanghai the second. The Maritime Academy had been last on his list of preferences and a distant third to the two leading institutions of higher education in China. Then, remembering why he had listed the Maritime Academy, he was mollified. The Academy had been established to train skilled and absolutely dependable personnel to accompany the foreign-owned ships that China would be renting during the interim when the country's foreign trade and commerce were expanding more rapidly than its capacity to build its own ocean-going vessels.

Yuxian's dream of traveling abroad was as old as he could remember. Growing up in Pudong, the music of whistling ships was always in his ears, their mournful echoes and busy toots at once comforting and compelling. As a child, he and his friends had found a special place along the Huangpu where one of the canals met the river and the paddy fields ended just where the muddy shore began and the steps of the water buffalo unwittingly uncovered clams that the young boys gathered for dinner. Far off in the distance was the Shanghai known to the West, the Bund, with its solid modern buildings and the harbor lined with oceanworthy boats. Nearer to view were the mysterious, noiseless junks, gliding as they had for centuries between river and canal, square sails unfurled. It was to this spot that Ni Yuxian and his friends, and later his little brothers, too, came to think the thoughts and dream the dreams that were forbidden in the mundane life of their everyday world. Sitting for hours along the banks, watching the comings and goings of the busy Shanghai harbor, joining his friends in gathering clams and the flotsam and jetsam, the beer cans and condoms the foreign ships left in their wake, Yuxian had often dreamt himself a stowaway, escaping his own country for the mystery and expanse of foreign lands.

Some of his friends from middle school, who had once sat gazing there with him, did escape. In 1962, as the famine lingered and the Chinese government turned a blind eye to the crowds of people flocking to the border between southern Guangdong Province and the British colony of Hong Kong, tens of thousands, several of Ni Yuxian's classmates among them, had simply walked across the wooden bridge into the British-administered New Territories. By 1965 they were returning to visit relatives, wearing ties and Western-style jackets and looking very rich indeed, singing the praises of freedom and of the riches to be made through the opportunities afforded by capitalism.

As Ni Yuxian's own dissatisfaction and disillusionment took

root and grew, as he began dimly to be aware that the dreams he had dreamt for his future might never come true, his longing to travel had settled somewhere in the pit of his stomach, returning like hunger to nag again and again. That oppressively hot summer, waiting for the university results to come in, he had often gone to his special spot along the banks of the Huangpu River to be soothed by the sights and sounds of the harbor. Often while contemplating his future he had been reminded of the ancient myth of Hou Yi and of the ten suns that had once filled the Chinese sky.

Once upon a time, many centuries ago, almost before anyone could remember, there had been not one but ten suns in the sky. The earth's rivers and lakes had all dried up and the seas were in a perpetual state of boil. The season was always summer, and no wind ever blew. The land was so parched that no plant or tree could grow, and there was no food to eat. Humans and animals everywhere were perishing.

Hou Yi came to save mankind. Taking his bow, he shot nine arrows into the sky, destroying all but one of the suns.

With only one sun, the rivers and the lakes and the seas returned, time on earth was divided again into four seasons, the wind blew again, and crops and trees flourished together with humankind. So grateful was humankind, the people crowned Hou Yi king, but the one-time hero became corrupt, betraying the people's trust through excessive indulgence in women and wine.

For Ni Yuxian, China in the 1960s was like the world before Hou Yi had saved it—hot, oppressive, windless, and dominated by the sun. There was no freedom—of speech or of thought—and no way to be a real individual with separate interests and desires and goals, no way really to make something of oneself. The ever-heroic side of Ni often imagined himself the modern-day Hou Yi, shooting the suns from the sky and becoming the savior of humankind. But China in the 1960s had only a single sun—the man known as the red, red sun in everyone's hearts—Party Chairman Mao Zedong. Maybe rather than saving mankind, Ni Yuxian could simply escape the oppression of the sun. The Maritime Academy would be his route out. After five years of study, he would be able to go abroad.

• • •

Bicycling home at breakneck speed one hot summer afternoon in 1965, Yuxian was nearly bursting with joy. He had just finished his last day at work in the factory. Life was about to begin anew.

The opportunity he had created when he destroyed his incriminating files was about to come to pass. In a couple of weeks, his life as a university student would begin.

The young man indulged himself for one last time in his favorite childhood danger. As a tractor rattled noisily by, pulling behind it some four empty carts, he latched on to the last cart with one hand and with the other extracted his harmonica. Handlebars free, he began to play. Yang Guoli's little sister was one of those who had watched dumbfounded the crazy antics of the harmonica-playing bicyclist careening wildly down the street behind a smoke-sputtering claptrap of a tractor. "What kind of juvenile delinquent is this friend of yours?" she had asked when her brother introduced them later. "He's no delinquent," Yang Guoli had roared with laughter, "He's just one of the happiest guys in the world—and one of the bravest, too."

Playing "Auld Lang Syne" on his harmonica as the tractor dragged him along, Ni Yuxian thought he was bidding his last farewell to Yanggao Road. He had no intention of ever returning that way again.

But such is the nature of Chinese fate that the individual will return at least once in his lifetime to those places that have served as significant turning points, and those places will serve again as a crossroads. He would return again to Yanggao Road just as in entering the Shanghai Maritime Academy he was returning to the spot that had earlier been a major turning point in his life. The Shanghai Maritime Academy was located on the same street and just opposite the military camp where Yuxian had spent his first night in the army some four years earlier, just before he and the five hundred other recruits had set out in darkness for the secret destination that turned out to be the Gold Mountain base. Military service had been the first major turning point in Ni Yuxian's still young life. The Shanghai Maritime Academy would be another.

•   •   •

As party policy began moving perceptibly toward the left and Mao's dictum on the inevitability of class struggle came to be repeated with ever-increasing frequency, the atmosphere within China's universities began to change. Academically, the primary focus of education at Shanghai Maritime Academy was English, necessary preparation for the communications the students would have with foreigners on the high seas and in their future ports of call. But politics, in fact, had come to command the academy. Not only was the country itself increasingly politicized but students who would ultimately assume responsible positions on ships that would traverse the globe had to be politically reliable beyond any shadow of a doubt.

Zhen Fanrong was responsible for assuring the political purity of Ni Yuxian's class. The epitome of the proletarian intellectual, a study in the triumph of red over expert and of ideology over expertise, he was, as Ni Yuxian describes him, a gentle, cultured-looking man, the elegant dignity of his bearing a startling contrast to the simple dark blue jacket of the worker, patched and threadbare, in which he was invariably garbed. When discussing the great leader and teacher Chairman Mao, Zhen's face filled with reverence and awe. In reading party directives, brimming as they were with concern for the proletariat and adulation of the poor peasant masses, indignant at the cruel exploitation to which the poor had been subjected in the past, the teacher's voice rose in outrage against the evils of capitalism, ringing in pride with all the good that socialism had wrought.

The first lesson he taught his new class was the lesson of gratitude—gratitude to the party for the privilege of a university education, a privilege reserved in the former class system for the children of the tiny minority of the wealthiest exploiters and an opportunity even under socialism which only some 4 percent of middle-school-age youth were offered. As he read from the report detailing the costs to the state of educating a single university student, calculating the days of peasant toil incorporated into four years of college, he wept in gratitude for the party's generosity in nurturing a new generation of university-trained intellectuals, crying out in love for the party, nearly moving his class to join him in tears.

Zhen's devotion to his students knew no bounds, and he could be seen intruding himself eagerly into any small group that collected to chat, interrupting the conversation to ramble enthusiastically about the glories of socialism, the Communist Party, and Mao, eagerly reporting to his party superiors any wayward thought he might have detected in his charges. Even the party loyalists among the students—and the vast and overwhelming majority of students were proudly and enthusiastically loyal—found the man disturbing. Ironmouth Zhen they called him, and groups into which he intruded learned silently, wordlessly, like beads of rain upon a window, to scatter with his arrival. So thick was his skin that he was forever unaware of the catalytic process of dispersal and regrouping his presence precipitated.

The Maritime Academy had admitted few accidents into its midst. The politics of its students had been carefully checked, and most came from "good" class backgrounds—their parents were workers, peasants, and party cadre. Only Ni Yuxian's military service, the glowing recommendations he had received from his factory, and the purity of his personal file had permitted his admittance.

His political troubles were not long in coming. With the new policy of class struggle gradually gaining momentum, every unit would need its own class enemy. Ni Yuxian became a natural and deserving target.

After his students had all stood to evince proper demonstrations of gratitude to the party and the state for the opportunity to attend university, Teacher Zhen's political study class moved on to revolutionary show and tell. The class was broken down into small groups where students were invited to compare the bitterness of their past with the sweetness of the present, detailing for all to hear how painfully their parents and their parents' families had suffered in the old society, how well they were faring now.

Yuxian's schoolmates were enthusiastic participants in the process, each student spending some twenty to thirty minutes immersed in the telling of his family's previous degradations. Indeed, there were stories to be told. The class was made up of sons—and four daughters—of the formerly poor and downtrodden, and socialism had treated them well. Yuxian waited for the others to speak.

Li Buoyu was one of the first and one of the best. His family had been poor peasants, and his patched and faded peasant garb, his worn cloth shoes, testified to his village roots and the persistence of his poverty. Li's gratitude to the party and to Chairman Mao, his devotion to the revolution, knew no bounds. "When I first came here, I didn't even know the ABCs," the young man recalled, laughing at his earlier ignorance. "But now I can say 'I am a student' in English. After studying the thought of Chairman Mao, I understand how important it is for me to study English for the sake of the revolution—for the sake of the world revolution."

The instruction he had received from Professor You Mingli received particularly effusive thanks. Trained in one of the American missionary colleges established in China during the 1930s, You Mingli was fluent in English and devoted to her students and had often through the years been selected as a model teacher. Through her nurturing, many of her pupils were selected as "three good students"—good in thought, good in health, and good in studies. Li Buoyu was not alone in his praise or his gratitude. Professor You was widely respected and admired.

Yuxian listened, growing ever more apprehensive, as others spoke, hoping time would run out before his turn. He could relate how impoverished his family had been at the time of his birth, explain to his classmates that there was not a grain of rice in the house when he, Ni Yuxian, entered the world. But the roots of the family's poverty would be difficult to explain. No one had ever claimed that the Nis were poor because they had been exploited. The war with Japan and Guansheng's insistent character defect— his obsessive, compulsive gambling—had plunged the family into the depths of poverty. The way the Nis told the story, it was not communism that had saved Guansheng but Guansheng's compulsive squandering of the family's wealth that had saved the family from the wrath of the Communists. By the time the country was "liberated," his personal reform had been so successful he could no longer even be classified as poor. His small shop along the banks of the Huangpu entitled him to membership in the commercial class. He had been labeled a member of the petit bourgeoisie.

Ni Jizhong's status was even more problematic. Struggle, hard work, and devotion to his profession aside, he had attended medical school and become a doctor at a time when only the sons of landlords and rich capitalists could afford the astronomical costs— or so present political convention asserted. Indeed, Jizhong had sold a plot of his dead mother's land, reserved for that purpose since his birth, to pay for his education. By 1965 the present for the Nis was far better than the worst of their past, but it was not nearly as prosperous as the best the adults in the family could remember—or as good as they imagined it could be. How could Yuxian's family claim to have been exploited—and saved?

He stumbled through his family's complex past, downplaying as best he could the reasons for poverty and the family's conviction that it was Guansheng who had saved them from the Communists rather than the Communists who had saved the family from anything. Ironmouth Zhen took silent note of the young man's politically unorthodox tale.

Zhen was a conscientious teacher, constantly endeavoring to keep his students involved, the classes lively, the contents germane to the pressing issues of the day. Each political study session was devoted to a different topic, and students were asked to share their opinions on the issues at hand, opinions which in turn were expected faithfully to reflect the prevailing political line. The teacher faced a built-in contradiction between the goal of imbuing his classes with spark and verve and the need to direct his students' thinking into a common mold. The outspoken and independent Ni Yuxian provided a welcome and unexpected solution.

The question of individualism fell early on the agenda of topics and was naturally expected to be held up for attack. Like Lei Feng, who had snuffed out all traces of individualism (a term often preceded by the adjective "bourgeois") to become a docile tool of the party, so Chinese everywhere were being called upon to sacrifice themselves for the good of the party and the state.

It was not that Ni Yuxian did not agree that the goal of selfless sacrifice was a noble ideal. He simply thought that the ideal was often not carried out in practice. "Some people are motivated by individualism," he insisted in class. "Chairman Mao, Communist Party members, lots of people, work in the interests of the revolution, the people, the country, not for themselves," he pointed out, "but there are still people, even within the university, who have not yet accepted the education of the party, who still study for their own selfish ends, for individual reasons. This is a fact. We cannot deny this fact. So here in our school, we have to educate these people so we can all learn to work selflessly."

Ironmouth Zhen invited Ni Yuxian into his office after class. The boldness with which the young man spoke had given him cause for delight.

"Ni Yuxian, you used your own independent thought today in class. You did not have to rely on other people's opinions. We like this kind of independent spirit here." The teacher smiled benignly at his student. "Did you hear what the other students were doing? They were all imitating each other. They didn't use any of their own analysis. So your way was really good."

Yuxian was puzzled. His independent analysis should not be receiving such effusive praise from the man who prided himself in slavishly following the party line, who had willingly sacrificed to the party cause his own capacity for independent judgment.

"What—you know—we're having a big meeting for the whole class in a few days, you know," the teacher began haltingly, cautiously, stumbling over his words. He was uncertain at first how to coax his student's cooperation. "You could really help out there, you know—if you wanted to." The teacher was trying to sound persuasive. "How about if you let everyone hear your own independent viewpoint? How about if you spoke before the class—about your views on individualism? This would really be a good education for everyone."

Yuxian was suspicious. He hesitated. He was ill at ease with this man. But he really had no reason not to trust the overly enthusiastic revolutionary teacher. "Oh, I couldn't talk in front of so many people," the student who blossomed before groups, who prided himself on his ability to sway audiences, responded with disingenuous modesty. "I wouldn't know what to say."

"Oh, no need to worry about that," Teacher Zhen encouraged. "Just say what you said today. It'll be good practice, good experience for you." The teacher was friendly, gentle, almost humble.

"But I'm afraid I might say something wrong. Really, I have no experience." Somewhere not yet come to consciousness was the premonition that he was being trapped.

"No problem, Ni Yuxian. I'm your teacher. You won't get into trouble. There won't be any big stick or pulling the pigtail, no matter what you say. We just need you to help us a little, that's all. We want to have a lively discussion—and having you talk to us would be so much better than just having the teacher talk—or having all the students saying the same thing. Don't you agree, Ni Yuxian?" Ironmouth Zhen spoke with such fervor, such honesty.

Ni Yuxian, reluctantly, agreed to speak.

Three hundred students were gathered in the auditorium when Yuxian presented his speech on individualism, outlining his views on the gap between the real and the ideal. "Historically," he began, having done a little homework in preparation, "many Chinese scholars and intellectuals have been motivated not by selfless love of society, not by self-sacrifice, but by individualism, pursuing their own private ends. But their scholarship, their books, have been no less good because their motivation was selfish. Some of China's best books, some of our country's most renowned academic accomplishments, have been undertaken for selfish reasons. The same is true of the study of foreign languages—what many of us are studying here now. It's entirely possible to become fluent in a foreign language for selfish reasons. Anyone can study very well, very conscientiously. A person can still study well without a thought at all about the Communist Party or revolution.

"But the problem is that selfishness is a bad motivation for study," the student continued, bringing his speech to its logical conclusion, returning, he thought, to the accepted view. "China is a socialist country. We're all supposed to work for the good of everyone, and if we're just concerned about our individual selves, then it's not socialism. Individualism is not a good motivation for studying under socialism. We have to study for the good of society, not just for the good of ourselves."

That surge of self-satisfaction he ordinarily felt on ending a speech never appeared, overtaken instead by a lingering sense of concern. Despite his concluding argument that study ought to be selfless, he feared that pointing out the real motivations for study might have been a mistake. He was gratified when a number of students complimented him on his analysis, saying that his speech had helped clarify their own thoughts.

Yuxian was not prepared for what happened the next day.

Ironmouth Zhen's demeanor was stern as he opened the class. "Yesterday, Ni Yuxian raised a number of his own views about individualism," he began, apparently troubled. "But after class, a number of students came to speak with me. They were very dissatisfied with what Ni Yuxian said. They thought his viewpoint was wrong. Today, in the interests of democracy, we want to give the comrades who disagree with Ni Yuxian a chance to speak." He called on the student secretary of the Youth League.

The young man, never a polished speaker, was anxious to end his presentation as quickly as possible. "Yesterday, Ni Yuxian said that individualism is a motivation for study," he began woodenly. "His purpose was to say that individualism is good. But indiviualism is not good. It is bad, so Ni Yuxian is wrong when he says individualism is good." Abruptly, the Youth League secretary sat down.

"Why did Ni Yuxian say that individualism is good?" one of the student party members stood up next to inquire rhetorically. "We all know that individualism is bad. So why does this one student insist that individualism is so good? Because Yuxian wants to take the capitalist road. He wants to leave socialism and go the capitalist road."

One by one, the leaders of the Youth League rose to condemn Yuxian, arguing that he had called individualism good and accusing him of taking the capitalist road. When the class period was over and others had not had a chance to speak, Ironmouth Zhen agreed to extend the criticism session to the following day. Again, the party and Youth League members, the activists and aspirants to party membership, stood up one after another to deliver variations on the theme that Ni Yuxian had declared individualism to be good and that hence he was reactionary, taking the capitalist road.

At the end of the second session, Zhen delivered his summing up.

"These two meetings have been very good," he began enthusiastically, complimenting the students. "Very good. Lots of students have taken the correct standpoint and stood on the side of right. We have heard some good, strong criticism here in the last couple days, too—criticism against individualism and against capitalism. This means that our party's education has been correct and that our students—the vast majority of them—are good. It shows that the vast majority of the students are willing to follow the road of the party and our great leader Chairman Mao.

"There really is a class struggle in our society now," he continued knowingly, almost conspiratorially, wagging his chin. "I realize that some of you students want to think that inside the school— here at the Maritime Academy—there is no class struggle—that class struggle is all out there, in society." He raised his arm and gestured into the distance, smiling indulgently, understandingly, at the mistaken youth who might think that class struggle was all somewhere in the direction of his arm. "But when you see a situation like we've just seen in the past couple days, I know that you can all now understand that there is also class struggle right here within our own university. Capitalists try to hide themselves, you know, try to disguise themselves. They're afraid. But eventually the capitalists show themselves. Their capitalist thought just bursts out for us all to see. So those people who have criticized this capitalist thought in the past few days—these people are good, what they said is good.

"So you students have all received a very good education," Ironmouth Zhen continued brightly, gazing out with pride upon his class. "Those among us who need to be educated are naturally the very first among us to make mistakes. Don't think this is strange. Since there is class struggle in society, there is bound to be class struggle within the university, too. The strange thing is that the very people our party nurtures, the very person our party is cultivating, the very person our party is educating, still opposes the party, can still say that individualism is good. This person was in the army—in the army, mind you—for such a long time, receiving so much of our dear party's education." Ironmouth Zhen's voice was rising in indignation now at the ungrateful individualist.

"Why, after so much education, does he still have this thought? Why, after the party has nurtured him so long, does he still believe individualism is good? We are going to have to find out why. He is going to have to make a self-criticism. He is going to have to dig deep into his thought and find out where those mistakes come from. He is going to have to look into his family past, into his class background, and discover the influence of his family on this thought. He is going to have to tell us what books he has been reading—what bourgeois, capitalist books he must have read—to have become such an individualist. He is going to have to dig deep and do a thorough self-examination." Ironmouth Zhen was beginning to ramble, enveloped in self-satisfaction. "How could it happen that the party gave this student so much education and still he can say that individualism is good? This is reactionary thought. How can this student say . . ."

"Teacher Zhen," Ni Yuxian interrupted, standing up, "you keep talking about 'some people,' 'this student' who says individualism is good, who has reactionary thought. You are talking about me. Why don't you use my name? Why do you keep saying 'there is someone'? Look at all the students sitting here listening to you. Everyone knows you're talking about me." For two days, Ni had sat on the very last row of the large auditorium, writing every word in his notebook, looking down with a growing sense of betrayal and anger at the scene being enacted below.

"When I hear you today, I feel as though you are an actor in a play and I a member of the audience. What you are doing today completely changes my feelings about you. That time, just after school started, when you read the article about how the party had nurtured us, about how the party was giving us all an education—remember?—you cried, Teacher Zhen. You cried. The tears were streaming down your face. You read with such emotion, such love for the party. And I believed you. I thought you were real. I thought those tears were real. But today, when I see how you have behaved, I know that was completely false. But—oh, excuse me—that performance doesn't have anything to do with today, does it?

"Today, I want to talk about two questions. First, I want to say that I think that there is absolutely no mistake in what I said in that last meeting. Everything I said is absolutely consistent with Marxism-Leninism Mao-Zedong thought. There are people in our society who are motivated by individualism. This is an objective fact—an objective fact that we have to recognize. For us students, for intellectuals, our goal should be to discover the truth. This is how our studies make progress. If you say that individualism doesn't exist, that everyone's goal in studying is only the good of society, then why do we have to have thought reform movements in the first place? Why do we have class struggle? Surely we don't have to have thought reform because our thought is already perfect. We don't have to study Mao Zedong because our thought is already correct. If there were no need to change, then we wouldn't need class struggle, would we, Teacher Zhen? So whose thought is wrong? What you are saying, Teacher Zhen, is opposed to Chairman Mao's thought. If you are looking for class struggle, then maybe we'd better start by criticizing Teacher Zhen's point of view, huh?''

Yuxian was testing a new style of argumentation he had first employed in the army, one that he, and others, too, would later develop into a perverse political art, mingling arguments of principle with nasty personal attack. Merely defending oneself against verbal assault was not sufficient. One's accuser had to be attacked as well. The political battle could be won only by proving that the accuser rather than the accused was the real opponent of Mao. It was a tactic that demanded considerable skill, requiring the victims to become more conversant with Maoist thought than those who served as his chosen exponents, nimbly able to pluck the proper Maoist quotation from the whole panoply of the chairman's works, unhesitatingly parrying one Maoist aphorism with an equally apt retort. The party chairman had been a lifelong prolific writer and one who reveled in the contradictions of the world. He could persuasively be quoted to support just about any position.

''But if Teacher Zhen's thought has problems, that's perfectly natural, isn't it?'' Yuxian continued. ''Everyone's thought has problems. No one is perfect. So we have to help the person with problems, right Teacher Zhen? We have to discuss the problems according to the three principles—no big stick, no putting on caps, no pulling the pigtail, right? When a person has problems, there is no need to accuse that person of being a reactionary, is there? There is no need to overthrow such people, is there Teacher Zhen? So this is the first thing I want to say. I wasn't wrong.''

As Ni Yuxian pressed his relentless parody, his voice alternately ringing with sincerity and dripping with sarcasm, Ironmouth Zhen stood at the front of the room, the blood drained from his face, stunned. He was the political instructor, above reproof. No one had ever dared challenge him. No one. He was a revolutionary. He was a loyal member of the Communist Party. He believed in Marxism-Leninism Mao-Zedong thought. He loved Chairman Mao. He had devoted himself heart and soul to the party, to the education of his students. His job was to criticize others, not to be criticized himself. During the antirightist campaign he had been the first to stand up in indignation to speak out, identifying and attacking the miscreants. He had risen in righteous criticism of the antiright deviationists, the opponents of the three red flags, the revisionists. No one had been more thoroughgoing in his efforts to root out corruption and class enemies during the socialist education campaign. Futures were in his hands. Never had anyone criticized him.

"The second thing I want to bring up is this," Yuxian continued, unrestrained. "Today, yesterday, in class, the people who criticized me—the league members, the party members—it's clear you were all prepared. You said I am a reactionary, a capitalist, a poisonous weed. You all want to struggle against this Ni Yuxian. You want to criticize his mistakes. You take me as some kind of reactionary element.

"Well, again, let me say that what I said was not wrong. There were no mistakes in my talk. But why did I say what I did? Lots of you students, I bet, don't know, do you? The teacher—Teacher Zhen—asked me to help him. He wanted me to help him conduct this class well. He wanted me to talk. When I told him I was afraid of saying something wrong, he said that this was all according to the three principles—no big stick, no cap, no pulling the pigtail. He said my independent thought was very interesting, so he wanted me to talk about it. So if what I said is really reactionary—and I don't think it is—then it is something Teacher Zhen told me to say. He encouraged me to spew forth this so-called poison. I didn't want to. I was afraid of saying something wrong.

"So Teacher Zhen knew this Ni Yuxian was reactionary, but he deliberately encouraged his student to talk this reactionary talk. He wanted you—his students—to hear this reactionary talk, to receive this reactionary's education. This is strange, isn't it? Why? Why did he do this? Teacher Zhen, I want to ask you. Why did you do this? This is all something you brought on yourself. So how about

you delving into your own past and solving the riddle and answering all these questions? If you can't answer the riddle, no one can.
If you use this method to turn your own student into a reactionary,
then how can any of us ever feel secure? None of us will talk,
none of us will tell you our real thoughts because we'll all be afraid
of being reactionary. Isn't this dangerous? Do you really want us
to tell lies? I hope you'll answer this question."

Yuxian sat down.

The auditorium had turned silent as Yuxian spoke, his voice
resonating to every corner. Zhen was dumbstruck. Every other student he had ever criticized had capitulated immediately, often in
abject apology, confessing his faults. Ironmouth Zhen was facing a
situation for which there was no precedent, and one he had no
idea how to handle. He was incapable of responding. His party
superiors had to be consulted first. No student had ever been so
rude. No student had ever accused him of deceit. Deceit? He who
loved the party so!

The auditorium remained in stunned silence.

"I want to say a few things," the muffled voice of a young
woman began haltingly. She stood up. The voice belonged to Li
Shaoqing, the student deputy chair of the university-wide Youth
League and daughter of one of the city's most respected and highest-
ranking party members. Zhen's breath began escaping in short,
slow puffs of relief. Li Shaoqing was a friend, dependable. She
could be counted on to defend him. Li was scheduled to enter the
party soon and she would not want to take any chances with her
membership.

"I completely agree with Ni Yuxian's speech," she began.
Teacher Zhen, for all his attention to the details of student life, had
failed to note that Li Shaoqing had been helping Yuxian as he
struggled, hopelessly baffled, to learn the ABCs of English. A minor
flirtation had developed between the two. "What Teacher Zhen did
was completely wrong." A startled look of wounded anger glim-
mered on the political instructor's face, and a few students began
nodding, smiles slowly spreading across their faces. "When Ni
Yuxian spoke originally at the meeting, he never said that individualism was good. You've twisted his words. He said that, yes, indiviualism is something that exists. It is an objective fact. But he said
we have to overcome individualism. He said it was a bad tendency
that we have to learn to fight against. Teacher Zhen deliberately
took what he said and twisted it so he could criticize him. More-

over, he organized other people to criticize him. We had a meeting. Both the party and the Youth League members met, and we were all given instructions on how to criticize Ni Yuxian. This was all deliberate."

As Li Shaoqing concluded her speech on a pitch of high anger, she received a hearty round of applause. Hands began shooting up everywhere. Teacher Zhen had been rendered mute, incapacitated. Unable to call on the eager students, order broke down as they began standing up in turn, so many wanting to speak, and all of them supporting Ni Yuxian. No one, not even the students who had originally spoken out so vociferously against Yuxian, came to the defense of the increasingly flustered and beleaguered Zhen. The truth had been exposed for all to see, and not even the opportunists were prepared to oppose the truth.

Regaining his composure, Zhen quickly brought the meeting to a conclusion. "Our student Ni Yuxian raised lots of opinions today, and not a few students seem to agree with his point of view. So we have two different kinds of opinions here. There is no way to decide today who is right and who is wrong. We'll have to ask the party leaders to join us next time to solve our little dilemma, huh? The party will tell us all what to do. We'll continue to rely on the party."

The university-wide director of politics at the Academy came to visit Ni Yuxian that afternoon. He had already talked to Teacher Zhen and wanted to hear the student's side of the story. An old, uneducated Red Army veteran, one of the survivors of the party's epic Long March, what Jiang lacked in education, he made up for in experience. He was both respected and feared, a simple and honest man, a party member who really did have the good of his country and people at heart. After hearing Ni Yuxian's side of the story, he held meeting after meeting, talking to as many students as he could. He rendered his verdict. Ni Yuxian had said nothing wrong. His viewpoint was reasonable. There was no need to criticize him.

• • •

"We need to talk," Teacher Zhen sidled up to Ni Yuxian after Jiang's decision was announced, "privately."

"It was a misunderstanding, Xiao Ni." The teacher's tone was friendly, conciliatory, apologetic. "We both misunderstood. You didn't really mean that individualism was good, so I was mistaken.

But I didn't deliberately mean to do you harm. So let's forget it, okay? I wasn't wrong, and you weren't wrong. Let's stop all this and unite together for the revolution. How about it?"

Ni Yuxian was not easily assuaged. "Teacher Zhen, I don't want to continue struggling with you. But what you did was deliberate. It wasn't a misunderstanding. I just hope that in the future, you won't do this to me again."

"Xiao Ni, you really know how to talk." Teacher Zhen answered wryly, immediately becoming serious. "You've read lots of books. You're very smart. If you listen to the party, if you follow the party, then there's a lot of work for you to do in the future. But I have to tell you Xiao Ni, I have to warn you. If you go in the wrong direction, if you don't follow the party, someday you'll make a big mistake." Ni Yuxian had heard those words before.

The teacher became fatherly, putting his hand on the young man's shoulder. "I really do hope you'll obey the party, do lots of important work for the party."

"Thank you for your concern," Yuxian replied solemnly, a bite to his voice. "I am still young and there are lots of things I don't understand. I hope in the future you will stick to educating me and not accuse me of being a counterrevolutionary."

The teacher was still embarrassed. "It was a misunderstanding, Xiao Ni. A misunderstanding." He patted the young man on the back again. "It's over now. Let's forget about it. Don't put all this in your heart." The two shook hands.

The enmity would last for twenty years.

• • •

Despite the political director's support, Ni Yuxian was kicked from the circle again, joined over time by a growing number of others as the demarcation between party members and political activists on the one hand and the not-to-be-entirely-trusted on the other was painted in ever-deepening hues. Li Shaoqing was the next to suffer ostracism, her solidarity with the troublemaker excluding her from membership in the party.

Jin Ji followed shortly thereafter, duped into Ironmouth Zhen's trap during studies of Lin Biao's speech on "Long Live the Victory of People's War" in much the same manner as Ni Yuxian had been. China's list of foreign enemies had been growing, with only North Vietnam and Albania still being counted firmly among the ranks of its friends, and war again was regarded as inevitable. China's victory was assured, the students were taught, not through superior weaponry but through the force of its 800 million people armed with the thought of Mao Zedong. Mai Xiande, an illiterate peasant soldier, was paraded as a new Lei Feng, a model of the triumph of man over weapons. During a violent encounter between the navies of the mainland and Taiwan, Mai Xiande had been struck on the head with a shell fragment, his skull cracked open, brain exposed. As the legend was told, the man had fought bravely on, being delivered to the hospital in a coma only after collapsing when the battle was done. Waking days later, the first words to spring from his lips were "Long live Chairman Mao."

Living models proved riskier than dead ones, however. Mai Xiande's role as a nationwide hero was terminated when the effects of his brain damage became impossible to avoid. The man was aggressive and belligerent to the point of violence, a lewd and flagrant womanizer, completely unpredictable. As the Shanghai Maritime Academy was hailing him as a hero and the hope of China, the Beijing officials charged with designating models were being forced to confront the fact that their model was crazed.

Called upon to discuss why a population mobilized not with modern weapons but with the thought of Mao Zedong could defeat both the United States and the Soviet Union in war, Jin Ji, the son himself of a military man, dared to present a contending view. "We shouldn't be so sure we could be victorious over enemies like the Soviet Union and the United States," he admonished one afternoon in Teacher Zhen's political study class. "The United States and the Soviet Union are large countries, and they are modern and economically developed. But China is backward; our technology is outdated. We don't have modern weapons. We aren't really so strong. Maybe we wouldn't be victorious. I think we should be talking about peace with the Soviet Union and the United States."

Ironmouth Zhen recognized an opportunity when he saw it. Jin Ji later told Ni Yuxian the teacher had taken him aside in private just before the whole class, three hundred strong, was scheduled to meet again. "Help me out," Ironmouth Zhen had cajoled the student. "You can even take what you said and make it a little stronger. Exaggerate a bit—for effect. Lots of people feel the way you do, Xiao Jin. They just don't say it. Don't be afraid to exaggerate. After it's over, we can say that those weren't really your thoughts, that you exaggerated so we could have a chance to explore the problems more widely."

Jin Ji did exaggerate when he stood up before the gathered assembly. "China's policy of opposing the Soviet Union is incorrect," he declared in no uncertain terms. "In fact, much of our country's foreign policy is wrong. The Soviet Union's policy is the right one. We should try to coexist peacefully with the Soviet Union and the United States. There is no way we could win a war."

Jin Ji was labeled a revisionist for the speech he made that day and was forced to make a series of public self-criticisms before the entire class. In contrast to Ni Yuxian, whose words had been deliberately twisted to benefit the occasion, Jin Ji could not claim that the contents of his speech had been misinterpreted. By the terms through which the Chinese people were divided and labeled, he was indeed a revisionist.

As the struggle sessions against him continued, he became disoriented and confused. "The viewpoint I expressed was not completely my own," he would repeat lamely, afraid to come out forcefully to attack Teacher Zhen. "Teacher Zhen made me talk like that." Some people presumed that Teacher Zhen had provoked the whole thing, but others worried that Jin Ji had been a little mentally off balance from the start. No one of fully sound mind would so openly, so thoroughly, subject Communist Party policies to attack. Most people, though, agreeing that the contents of his speech had been revisionist beyond a doubt, thought that his crime was great and his public self-reproof not sufficiently strong.

The winds of the Cultural Revolution had begun to blow. Political mistakes were no longer being forgiven. Jin Ji's revisionist label stuck.

• • •

The portents of an impending political movement were everywhere, as Chinese society poised, increasingly tense, for what most believed would be an extravagant replay of the earlier antirightist campaign. The first major omen at the Shanghai Maritime Academy came in the form of a play about that period. All students were required to attend, and lengthy discussions followed.

Yuxian and his friends had been to many movies but never to a play, and the mere fact that the whole class was organized to attend lent the drama an aura of particular political importance.

As the curtain rose on a typical but unnamed university, the audience was introduced to a panoply of villains in the form of the college faculty, learning that despite lip service to socialist ideals, the vast majority of teachers still believed deep in their hearts in freedom and democracy and hence were unrepentant, unreformed capitalists—enemies of the people. Too cowardly to speak openly for themselves, the capitalist democratic university faculty had deceived their students—innocent, naive, and confused—into speaking out on behalf of their views. Only one particularly perceptive and courageous student—and (naturally) the adults on the university party committee—were sufficiently clearheaded to recognize the faculty as class enemies and the students as their unwitting dupes. When the faculty could contain themselves no longer and began speaking out directly on behalf of freedom and democracy, their dangerous antisocialist views were brilliantly defeated in debate with the upright party committee and the one student whose thought remained pure. The play ended as the antirightist campaign was beginning, with the most recalcitrant of the rightists being taken away to prison—newly exposed spies and people with "overseas connections" among them. The students, seeing the light at last, wept openly and long, vowing to reform themselves and to follow the party forever. The curtain fell with the admonition that while the antirightist campaign of 1957 was over, the rightists had not accepted defeat. Rightists, the audience was assured, will inevitably attempt to stage a comeback, and new struggles and new campaigns against them will necessarily follow.

The school waited for the impending campaign.

Traditional titles—Mr., Mrs., Professor—suddenly fell out of fashion, as "comrade" became the only acceptable form of address—posing difficulties in communication for many faculty members, including several of the most senior professors, who clearly stood outside the ranks. School dances, tinged as they were with the color of bourgeois decadence, were halted, and coffee shops, so blatantly Western, began serving Chinese-style tea instead.

The opening salvo came in November of 1965 with the publication of an article by Yao Wenyuan—a decidedly leftist political theorist from Shanghai, later destined to rise together with Mao's wife, Jiang Qing, to the height of power in Beijing, only to be overthrown and arrested at the time of Mao's death in 1976 as one of the Gang of Four. Ostensibly a literary critique, the article was an attack against a play, "Hai Rui Dismissed from Office," written in 1961 by Wu Han, a widely respected liberal historian and playwright who had thrown his lot with the Communist Party to become a vice-mayor of the city of Beijing. "Hai Rui Dismissed from Office" was about a real—and well-known—figure from the Ming dynasty, one of those legendary and exemplary scholar-bureaucrats who, as minister to the imperial court, had had the courage to speak out in support of the common people and against injustice at a time of widespread corruption and moral decay. Among Hai's proposals had been the suggestion that land be redistributed from wealthy landlords to poor and landless tenant farmers. For his forthright views, the stubborn and misguided emperor had dismissed Hai Rui, exiling the minister to the remote southern island of Hainan where the righteous Hai died still waiting for vindication.

The right to political criticism has always been constrained in China, and political battles have often been fought indirectly, through opaque allegorical tales. Yao Wenyuan had read Wu Han's play as political allegory, seeing in the morality play an attack against China's latter-day emperor, Mao. Hai Rui, in Yao Wenyuan's view, was not, or at least not merely, Hai Rui but Peng Dehuai, the former Minister of Defense who, in his open letter to Chairman Mao, had criticized the Great Leap Forward—and hence, by extension, Chairman Mao—for petit bourgeois fanaticism. Hai Rui's advice to redistribute land from the rich to the poor was in fact a call to break up the communes formed during the Great Leap Forward and to redistribute land to the peasants—to return, in short, to capitalism. Wu Han was accused of being a counter-revolutionary.

Wu Han's presentation of Hai Rui is generally regarded today as a historically accurate portrayal of the facts. To this day, many Chinese believe that the playwright's intentions were precisely to write about Hai Rui and that the historical lessons for the present were unintentional—or at least not so decisively clear. Mao Zedong himself had praised Hai Rui and encouraged scholars like Wu Han to study and write about him. Wu Han's intentions will never be known. Shortly after Yao Wenyuan's attack, he like Hai Rui before him, was dismissed from his post and arrested, dying at the height of the Cultural Revolution in October 1969 from torture and medical neglect.

The viciousness of Yao Wenyuan's attack, with its insistence that Wu Han was a counterrevolutionary and the self-righteous presumption that Yao Wenyuan alone stood on the side of truth, was disturbing. In the past, artistic freedom had been greatly restricted, and people had been puzzled, often confused, when movies that seemed so powerfully to sing the praises of the Communist Party and socialism came under official attack for their alleged antisocialist views. But now the cage in which intellectuals were allowed to fly was shrinking smaller still, the penalties for spreading one's wings were increasingly severe. To side with Wu Han, or to disagree with Yao Wenyuan, was to risk being labeled reactionary oneself. Newspapers were filled with articles supporting Yao Wenyuan and attacking Wu Han. Guo Moruo, philosopher and writer, leading noncommunist sycophant of the party, publicly denounced all his previous works as "poisonous weeds."

By May the press began talking about a "Great Proletarian Cultural Revolution," and the Shanghai Maritime Academy began mobilizing for the drama of the impending antirightist campaign, a spectacle that promised to be an even more concerted effort to ferret out the unrepetant, unreformed intellectuals who continued to take the capitalist road.

The battle lines were drawn.

Party members and political activists were energized with excitement. In ordinary times, the 10 percent of the university population who made up the internal apparatus of party control devoted considerable effort to worrying about the class backgrounds, the past transgressions, the political deviations, and the sexual peccadilloes of the 90 percent of the people under their control. Their major responsibility was to be suspicious and secretive, prying, petty, and narrow. It was their job to believe that class enemies were everywhere, plotting conspiracies behind every door, planning imminent counterrevolution. Despite the lavish flattery on which they fed, party members were usually feared and often hated, sometimes ostracized by those over whom they exercised power.

The daily rewards of institutionalized suspicion were not insubstantial. Party members were proud to be members of an elite and privileged class. There was satisfaction to be derived from power over the daily lives of others, from the overt and often obsequious subservience they were routinely accorded.

Some of the benefits were economic—less in the form of higher salaries than in the better housing, the official banquets, the out-of-town trips, and the many gifts that ordinary folk felt compelled to present to help guarantee that they stayed on the right side of the political fence.

Political campaigns were the logical imperative of the politics of institutionalized suspicion, proof that work had not been done in vain, that suspicions were indeed well founded. Without the political campaign, evidence against the politically suspect could only lie dormant in personnel files, wasted, biding time until it could be used publicly to discredit class enemies—often those who had been least obedient and obsequious in the face of power. Thus the small group of people charged with controlling the lives of the majority lived from political campaign to political campaign, waiting until the information they had collected could be brought forth publicly to discredit those they deemed to be class enemies. Party members and political activists welcomed the Great Proletarian Cultural Revolution. Political transgressions could be brought to public light. Party committees everywhere would be given quotas of followers of Wu Han to fill—and attack.

Political campaigns were welcomed, too, because they served as the route to promotion for upwardly mobile cadres, an opportunity for those waiting to join the party to prove their loyalty and devotion beyond any shadow of a doubt. Political campaigns were the career equivalent of war to the general or battlefield promotion to the ambitious enlisted man.

Already well-acquainted with the meaning of previous political campaigns, the faculty at the Maritime Academy, particularly those who had been persecuted earlier, who were Western—or Christian—educated, or who had family ties abroad, were tense, knowing they would be the first targets of attack. Like lambs waiting for the slaughter, they went through the motions of life in dread, waiting for the inevitable knock on the door.

• • •

On June 1, 1966, the students and faculty of the Shanghai Maritime Academy listened rapt to the nationwide broadcast of the big character poster that Nie Yuanzi had posted on the wall of the student cafeteria at Peking University. Students, faculty and party administrators alike began to get a glimmering that this "Great Proletarian Cultural Revolution" was not a mere repeat of the anti-rightist campaign. An event of far more earth-shaking proportions was unfolding. Nie Yuanzi had not stopped with an attack on Wu

Han. She had gone on to castigate the Communist Party governing committees of both the city of Beijing and of her own university. The attack was unprecedented. In the decade and a half of communist rule, no lesson had been better learned than that the party was immune from attack, that to attack the party was to invite the label of rightist or reactionary or counterrevolutionary or worse and to guarantee punishment of the harshest order. All of China looked to Beijing as the epitome of Communist Party governance, the model for governing party committees at all levels of society to follow. Among institutions of higher education, Peking University had no superior; its party leadership was presumed to be impeccable. Yet here, on nationwide radio, unquestionably sanctioned by the very highest levels of party power, most probably by Mao Zedong himself, was a scathing attack on the epitome of Communist Party leadership.

Within days, both the Beijing Municipal Party Committee and the president of Peking University as well as his closest associates had been overthrown. Not only the intellectuals and the rightists were coming under attack. The Communist Party itself was being challenged.

Ironmouth Zhen was befuddled. "This is really amazing," he confessed to his class as they began studying Nie Yuanzi's big character poster as it was printed on the front page of the *People's Daily*. "This cultural revolution is really going to be big. It won't be over quickly."

Ironmouth Zhen was right. China was about to implode upon itself. The Cultural Revolution would last a full ten years, plunging the country into chaos, rending the very fabric of Chinese society. During its course, the majority of the Communist Party politburo and the majority of the larger Central Committee would be purged—the giants of the communist revolution, the men who had led the party to victory, who had stood together on the podium over Tiananmen—the Gate of Heavenly Peace—to proclaim the establishment of a new People's Republic of China. Some, like head-of-state Liu Shaoqi and one-time propaganda minister Tao Zhu, would die from torture and medical neglect, ignored by their lifelong comrades who alone had the power to save them. The power struggle at the pinnacle of the party elite would be duplicated at every level, from top to bottom, of the hierarchy, leaving the ruling party in shambles, rendering governance impossible, the whole country adrift.

China's elite educated class, the intellectuals of the universities and research institutes, newspapers, magazines, and publishing houses, would be singled out everywhere as enemies of the people, condemned at best to years of manual labor in rural labor reform camps, subjected to torture and unnatural death at worst. How many died the world may never know. At least a million. Probably more.

The country's educational institutions, particularly those at the middle school level and above, would be closed for years, and if they did reopen relied on Mao Zedong's collected writings as their basic and most important texts. It was to the country's youth that Mao turned to lead the attacks against the party and the intellectuals, and in the frenzy of wanton destruction and violence with which the young obliged, China became Lord of the Flies come true. After turning against their teachers and the party leaders, the student organizations splintered into factions. The youth of China turned against themselves, and pitched battles, fought with real weapons and lethal bullets, broke out in cities throughout the country.

The army would ultimately be called in to restore order and reestablish control, and millions of the country's youth, sixteen and seventeen years old, would be separated from their families and shipped to remote and impoverished areas of the countryside where many stayed for a full decade and more, often eking out only the barest existence. Then, in an episode proving once again that truth is stranger than fiction, Lin Biao, the Minister of Defense and Mao Zedong's hand-chosen successor, touted as the party chairman's closest comrade-in-arms, turned against the man he would one day succeed, plotting a coup and the party chairman's demise. When the plot was discovered, Lin commandeered a plane and fled to the Soviet Union, crashing mysteriously en route—so the story is still officially told—in Outer Mongolia, killing all persons on board.

Mao Zedong's wife, Jiang Qing, and her three close associates from Shanghai, together to be labeled later as the Gang of Four, usurped power beyond all ability or reason, as Jiang Qing seized the opportunity to carry out vendettas stemming from real or imagined slights already decades old.

At its most violent, the Cultural Revolution spanned a mere three years, from the summer of 1966 until 1969, continuing as a period of routinized repression and listless, sullen terror until the fall of 1976, the death of Mao, and the arrest of the Gang of Four. Its wounds continue even now to fester.

Ultimate responsibility for that tragic episode in the history of man's inhumanity to man rests with Party Chairman Mao, though opinion will forever remain divided between those who would accuse him of a megalomaniacal quest for power and those who believe he had the good of his country at heart, that it was the means he used that went somehow tragically awry. Mao the revolutionary shared with young Ni and millions of others, too, a profound distaste for the entrenched bureaucratic power and its attendant abuses the party had amassed unto itself. How profound the discontent against the party, how close to the surface the anger festered, how violent would be the catharsis unleashed when Mao called on the Chinese to rebel, how destructive of the social order, no one in China could have known.

When it began, the sanctity of the Communist Party was still so deeply imprinted on the Chinese psyche that the logic of the Cultural Revolution was simply impossible to grasp. The logic in fact was simple. If the party leadership in Beijing was suspect, then so was party leadership everywhere. If the party committee at Beida, as Peking University was colloquially known, was unfit to lead, then the party leadership at every other institution of higher education—and in middle and primary schools as well—would also be called into question.

Even if some did grasp the logic, implementation of that logic would not be easy. At the Shanghai Maritime Academy, as in other universities throughout the country, the party committee was still firmly in control of the school and of the whole gamut of its political activities—and hence of the Cultural Revolution itself. The university party committee could hardly be expected to turn against itself. Its members responded in time-honored fashion, the only way they knew how. Like the police commissioner in *Casablanca*, they began rounding up the usual suspects—the rightist intellectuals of the past, their alleged crimes now modified to fit the new situation. They were accused of being representatives and followers of Wu Han.

Classes were canceled as the party committee at the Maritime Academy went into high gear, meeting until late into the night, culling evidence from the personnel files of teachers known to have rightist tendencies, writing big character posters themselves, and meeting with the party members and activists among the students to pass on evidence of their teachers' crimes and to determine who should come under attack. The student cafeteria was the designated spot for hanging the big character posters everyone was encouraged—subject to final approval by the party committee—to write; and the student-run radio station maintained a steady broadcast of news and reports from Beijing and Shanghai alike.

Department by department the student activists met to determine which of their teachers to single out for attack. Rarely were the choices difficult. The most senior professors, educated as they had been in the old society, had invariably also been influenced by the reactionary Guomindang or by the American imperialists, and hence were inevitable scapegoats. So was anyone who had been labeled a rightist or who had come from a landlord or capitalist family.

There was no refuge from student attacks. When the moment came, a bevy of the teacher's own supercharged, revolutionary pupils would burst in to drape a huge placard around the teacher's neck and place a tall white duncecap upon his head, both inscribed with the teacher's alleged crimes—counterrevolutionary, landlord, capitalist, running dog of the American imperialists. With tens of his students leading the way, shouting slogans calling for the downfall of the reactionary enemy, the teacher would be led in humiliation, white-faced and trembling, on a street parade through the campus grounds to be spit upon, cursed, and mocked. The homes of the victims would be ransacked as students searched for proof of the counterrevolutionary crimes and exemplifications of the teacher's bourgeois lifestyle. Damaging evidence was confiscated and carted away.

You Mingli, the Christian-educated English teacher who had so often been praised as a model, was in the first group of teachers to be attacked, and Li Buoyu, the poor peasant's son who had been the first of the academy's students to be admitted into the party, once so lavish in his praise of You, was the first to rise up in accusation, charging his teacher with being an imperialist, a running dog of the American capitalists, and opposed to the Communist Party, Chairman Mao, and socialism. The public humiliation of the most arrogant and narcissistic of the senior faculty, professors puffed with the sense of their own importance and known for the contempt they had once demonstrated to the vast majority of the university community, invariably brought rounds of applause and hearty laughter from the curious, gawking crowds.

Called upon to to participate in their own deprecation, many faculty took an active role in their own humiliation. Not only was resistance no use but it could also serve as an an invitation to even more vicious attack. More importantly, many under attack accepted their guilt. Kicked by virtue of their background from a circle which they often desperately wanted to join, the fear of ostracism and the need to belong, and the power of the Maoist utopian myth, compelled many to confess their guilt, to doubt not the party, their attackers, or the objectively repressive political system, but themselves. Teachers at the Shanghai Maritime Academy could often be seen striking at steel-wired trash cans with their fists, kicking with their feet, while yelling such self-accusatory slogans as, "I am a capitalist, a reactionary, a counterrevolutionary"— whatever label happened to fit. In the interim between attacks and self-criticisms, the faculty was kept busy cleaning the university latrines.

Orderly government collapsed. The police, once charged with maintaining public safety, could provide no protection. To harbor a political renegade was to risk being attacked oneself.

•   •   •

The depth of his own dissatisfactions caused Ni Yuxian faster than others to grasp what the Cultural Revolution might actually be about. He witnessed the humiliation of his teachers from the sidelines, disturbed at the inhumanity of his fellow students, outraged that those who had once fawned upon their superiors could so quickly, so effortlessly, and so viciously turn against them. But gnawing persistently at the edge of consciousness was the suspicion that this was not what the Cultural Revolution was meant to be about, that the significance of Nie Yuanzi's big character poster, calling for attacks against the university party committee, was being deliberately ignored. At the Maritime Academy, the party committee itself was leading the attacks.

Li Shaoqing, whose work at the university broadcasting station had continued even after her political problems began, finally raised the question that turned the Maritime Academy's Cultural Revolution around. Two weeks after the publication of Nie Yuanzi's big character poster, at an afternoon meeting of their first-year class, Li Shaoqing stood up to share a problem she had been unable to resolve. "There is something I would like to talk about," she began. "A few weeks ago, after we started the Cultural Revolution here, the party committee came to the broadcasting station with a list of students' names—thirteen names altogether. They said that these students had problems—that they were reactionary—so they are not allowed to participate in the Cultural Revolution. So if they send articles to the broadcasting station, or want to put up big character posters on our blackboard, they are absolutely not allowed.

"But is this correct?" Li Shaoqing wondered before the assembled class. "They are students. How can you say they are reactionary? Who says they are reactionary? Is this really the meaning of the Cultural Revolution? Are not all students supposed to be allowed to participate?"

Li Shaoqing sat down to await the answer to her questions.

Ni Yuxian was amazed. "Is what you just said really true?" he whispered to his friend.

"Yes, it's true," Li Shaoqing assured him.

"Am I on the list?" he asked.

Li Shaoqing nodded.

Ni Yuxian rose to his feet. "The name list is absolutely reactionary," he said, indignant. "Why shouldn't these students be allowed to criticize? Only because the party committee is afraid. They are afraid we'll accuse them of being rightists. But we students are still young. We've grown up under the party's education. How can we oppose the party that educated us? If the party committee tries to control us like this, they're just trying to scare the students, and this is pointing the Cultural Revolution in the wrong direction. I really oppose this thing—this black name list.

"There's something else, too, about the party committee's control. Why do all the big character posters have to be approved in advance by the party committee? Doesn't everyone have the right to criticize the capitalists? Not to give everyone this right is to opposed Chairman Mao's line. We are supposed to be criticizing the party people in authority taking the capitalist road. But the party committee isn't letting us criticize. They're taking the direction of the running dogs."

Hearing no response from the party committee and encouraged by his fellow students, Ni Yuxian decided to press his point. He would write a big character poster addressed to the party committee and display it for everyone to read.

"What Does the Incident of the Broadcasting Station's Black Name List Tell Us?" he titled his missive accusing the party committee of trying to divert the Cultural Revolution from the real goal by attacking the faculty and prohibiting deserving students from participating in the unfolding movement. "The party committee should apologize for its actions," the big character poster argued, threatening that if the committee refused to recognize its mistakes, its members could be accused of undermining the Cultural Revolution.

But permission to post big character posters was still in the hands of the party committee. "You can read your big character poster to class, Ni Yuxian," the party instructed, "but we can't let you post it. It would have a bad influence. It's opposed to the party leadership. You still have to follow the party. You can't oppose the party."

Yuxian read his proposed criticism to his class. "I want to go ahead and post this," he explained. The party members and activists—eight students in all—naturally sided with the party committee's conclusion that the message was too provocative to be publicly displayed. Thirteen students agreed both that the contents were correct and that the article ought to be posted. The supporters copied the piece in elegant calligraphy. Fourteen students, with Ni Yuxian's name heading the list, added their signatures.

At eleven o'clock the next morning, Ni Yuxian and a coterie of friends went to the student cafeteria to put up the big character poster. Several representatives of the party committee were waiting.

The party spokesman was polite. "Maybe you shouldn't put up the big character poster, Ni Yuxian," he coaxed, gently. "Foreigners come to the cafeteria, too, you know. We don't want them to see this, do we?" The traditional Chinese dictim against washing dirty linen before a foreign public was strong, and the academy had a handful of students from North Korea and Albania.

"But we want all the students to see it, and this is definitely the best place. I have to hang it here," Ni responded emphatically. "If you don't agree, I'm going to do it anyway."

"Okay, Yuxian," the party representative relented. "How about this? You hang up the poster inside for half an hour. After half an hour, take it down."

Yuxian made a quick calculation. It was then eleven fifteen. Lunch would start at eleven thirty when students would begin streaming into the cafeteria. The party secretary had not specified during which half hour he could hang the poster. If he waited until eleven thirty, and the poster stayed up until noon, most of the campus would have had a chance to read it.

"Okay," Ni Yuxian agreed.

Yuxian and his friends waited until a little after eleven thirty, just as the rush of students into the cafeteria had reached its height and the canteen was filling up. Then, with great dramatic flourish, and to a hearty round of cheers and applause, they unrolled their poster and hung it from the screen at the front of the cafeteria where movies were shown. The students flocked around to read, and most approved of the contents. Before the half hour was over, new and supportive big character posters had gone up, demanding that the party committee publish the black name list and demanding to know who had been responsible for composing it. That afternoon, and well into the evening, more and more big character posters went up. The Cultural Revolution at Shanghai Maritime Academy had entered a new phase. The party committee was under attack.

The president of Shanghai Maritime Academy was a natural, almost inescapable, target. The logic of the Cultural Revolution made him so.

Even after the shortage of educated party memebers had catapulted Xu Jian into a position of academic leadership, the middle school graduate and former primary school teacher continued to shun ostentation, embarrassed by the accoutrements of status. The chauffeur-driven car that picked him up at his home in the center of Shanghai each morning for the long drive across the river, through the Huangpu tunnel and on to the Shanghai Maritime Academy, arrived invariably at the campus brimming with the sundry university employees and students he had spotted en route wending their way on foot. Much of his day was devoted to hearing the laments and solving the problems of campus workers and teachers in difficulty. When a worker's family had many mouths to feed and not enough grain to go around, Xu Jian never chastised the parents for their failure to practice birth control. Instead, he sought to help, providing work on campus to a teenage son or donating his own rice coupons to the family in need. In his quest for new and better ways of management and education, he frequently traveled to investigate how other universities were organized, usually accompanied by several interested students. Always available to hear student suggestions and complaints, his own respect for education and the educated had earned him the gratitude and admiration of faculty and students alike. An avid gardener, campus beautification—in the form of trees and shrubs and flowers—was one of his favorite ongoing projects. The university's architecture had little aesthetically to commend it, duplicating as it did the dull gray drabness of the new socialist villages that were springing up all over Pudong.

Far from suffering from a belief in the infallibility of the party, Xu Jian had been troubled by the many mistakes he had seen the party commit—most recently and most notably during the Great Leap Forward. In the early 1960s he had been formally exonerated from the suspicion that he had harbored sympathy for Peng Dehuai and been part of an antiparty clique hostile to the ranking authorities in Shanghai, but his appointment as president of the Maritime Academy was nonetheless a demotion, a signal that he was not entirely trusted by the Shanghai powers that be.

His position with the university combined with his political proclivities to render Xu Jian a necessary and natural target. With Peking University as the example for universities throughout the country to follow, revolutionary administrators, faculty, and students everywhere were expected to review the credentials of their own top leadership, attacking and overthrowing those small handfuls of "party persons in authority"—presidents especially—who were "taking the capitalist road." Just as Beida president Lu Ping had been attacked and removed from office, so university presidents everywhere would be forced to step down.

Shortly after Ni Yuxian's big character poster, the first group of student rebels stormed Xu Jian's office, demanding to know his position on the Cultural Revolution. "If the university party committee has committed mistakes," the president had calmly replied, "then surely you revolutionary students have the right to criticize us." The angry students, anxious to make revolution and frustrated that the president had been so conciliatory, had smashed the glass that covered his desk, shattering it over the floor.

But the most formidable challenge to Xu Jian's leadership came not from the student rebels but from the party committee itself.

Although Xu Jian was president of the Shanghai Maritime Academy, he was not the most powerful man on campus. Nor, as the party had come to consolidate its control over higher education and authoritative decision-making had been vested in party committees separate from and higher than the academic administrative structure—the president, deans, and department chairmen—was he expected to be. Chen Qi was the first party secretary of the academy and the man upon whom power, by virtue of office, devolved.

But Chen Qi was already in his sixties when the Cultural Revolution began, the veteran of one too many internal power struggles. Looking forward to peace in his declining years, he had come to savor the comfortable life, learning the Daoist art of withdrawal by falling quietly asleep during party meetings and devoting most of his ostensibly working hours to reading the newspaper, drinking tea, and playing badminton and cards—preferably with pretty young women. The seal of authority remained in his hands, and he alone was responsible for the round red stamp that lent all major university decisions their authenticity, but Chen seemed bemused and quite content to pass the headaches of decision-making over to the ambitious and active Wang Hua who had arrived in the early 1960s to serve as his deputy. Power at the Maritime Academy inhered more in individuals than in the roles they were assigned.

Manipulative and single-minded, Wang Hua's efforts to expand his power had focused on matters of personnel, and over the years he had gradually ensured that key party positions were staffed with people loyal to him. Wang Hua was not known for the empathy he displayed to faculty or staff. He was feared more often than respected.

In mid-June, when Ni Yuxian fired the opening challenges against the academy's party leadership, the differences among the ranking officials were regarded as matters of style and personality rather than of deep political schism. As the message from the center became unavoidably clear, when there was no longer any doubt that the main purpose of the Cultural Revolution was to root out party officials who were "following the capitalist road," the unity of the academy's leadership was shattered, undermined from within.

Wang Hua took the lead.

Quickly grasping that the Cultural Revolution would be another opportunity for the upwardly mobile to climb a few rungs up the ladder and understanding early that the campus party leadership would inevitably come under attack, the ambitious deputy secretary acted out of self-protection, a finely honed instinct for survival, to ensure that the criticisms were not directed against him. Some of the ranking leadership would have to be sacrificed to the students' revolutionary demands. Wang Hua maneuvered, so his detractors alleged, to throw Xu Jian out like meat to hungry dogs.

The first big character poster calling for the overthrow of Xu Jian presented a side of the president the workers and teachers who admired him had never seen. Written by a leading political commissar and close associate of Wang Hua's, the poster asserted that in a private meeting of some fifty university army veterans held on August 1, 1966, to commemorate Army Day, Xu Jian had viciously and scathingly opposed the Cultural Revolution. "Xu Jian demanded that those who have criticized him be called immediately to account. He is deliberately inciting students to struggle against each other," the poster asserted. "The Cultural Revolution was meant to liberate the masses to struggle against politically corrupt party leadership. Instead, Xu Jian is suppressing the Cultural Revolution by calling for a struggle against the masses. Down with Shanghai Maritime Academy President Xu Jian!"

The open attack against the maritime academy president was a university event of unsurpassed significance, bringing all other activities to a halt. Opinion was deeply divided. Campus workers and most of the teachers, appreciative of the interest Xu Jian had bestowed on them over the years and immune to the jockeying for power that kept the party committee perpetually in motion, were nearly unanimous in their support of the president. The great bulk of party members and aspirants, owing their positions and their futures to Wang Hua and knowing that someone in the leadership would have to be sacrificed, were quick to turn against him. The voices raised calling for the overthrow of Xu Jian, demanding a struggle meeting against him so the outraged masses could make their accusations known, came mostly from within the party.

The many supporters of Xu Jian were at a grave disadvantage. His alleged attacks against the students and the Cultural Revolution had taken place at a closed meeting of military veterans, and the truth of what had been said there was of paramount importance. If Xu Jian really was attempting from behind the scenes to mobilize the students to struggle against each other, if he really had asserted that those who had criticized him had to be called to task, then he could, within the governing revolutionary logic of the day, indeed be accused of opposing the Cultural Revolution and hence of being a counterrevolutionary. The president could be defended only if evidence could be presented that the allegations of the big character poster were false, that he had not in fact spoken those words. The military veterans who knew, however, were silent.

The struggle remained unresolved, and because the dispute was within the very party committee charged with deciding issues of conflict, no means were available to settle it. The campus was leaderless, adrift. The Shanghai municipal authorities dispatched a work team to investigate.

The work team, naturally, called a meeting. With the participants in the August 1 gathering of army veterans sitting on the stage as witnesses, and an agitated audience of students and staff filling the large auditorium to overflowing, the work team sat themselves behind a large table to serve as the court charged with determining whether the allegations of the big character poster were true.

The meeting did not initially further Xu Jian's cause. The college president was not without defenders among the military veterans, but those who rose to speak on his behalf were unskilled and unconvincing speakers, stammering out their support without clear presentation of the facts. Many in the audience owed their positions to Wang Hua and hence could be expected to support their patron by attacking his enemy.

As an army veteran and a participant in the original meeting, Yuxian sat on the stage, following the proceedings in growing anger, frustration, and disbelief. He had not meant his big character poster attacking the college party committee to include Xu Jian. He knew the college president as a man of rare integrity, one of the few ranking party cadre genuinely deserving of respect. He remembered well what Xu Jian had said on August 1 and was anxious to come to the president's defense.

But Xu Jian's detractors were well-organized. Noting the preponderance of Wang Hua's appointees standing ahead of him in line for the microphone, Yuxian calculated that the time for adjournment would arrive before his turn to speak. He listened to Wang Liming, fellow student and demobilized soldier who had also attended the army meeting, rail against the college president. "When Xu Jian spoke out in favor of attacking the students," Wang Liming was asserting, "his hands were shaking, his voice was trembling. He was almost hysterical, like he was crazy. Then Xu Jian criticized Wang Hua. But Wang Hua is the deputy party secretary here. Attacking him is the same as attacking the party. Xu Jian is against the party."

Ni Yuxian could bear the falsity no more. He handed the chairman a note.

"I have a terrible stomachache and am going to have to leave to visit the doctor," he wrote, "but I have something very important to say. Can you give me my chance before I leave?"

The chairman waited until Wang Liming had finished berating the president. "There is a Comrade Ni Yuxian who is ill and will have to leave early," he said, interrupting the proceedings. "Comrade Ni, where are you? Come forward, we want to give you a chance to speak."

Yuxian's illness was nowhere in evidence as he began addressing the audience.

"Wang Liming's speech was really funny," he started casually, feigning puzzlement. "Strange, in fact. I was at that meeting, too, from beginning to end, sitting just across from President Xu, not more than a yard away. My eyesight is excellent, and I could see him very clearly. My hearing is perfect, and I could hear every word he said. But Comrade Wang was sitting in the back of the room. He wasn't even wearing his glasses that day. Are my eyes and ears really so bad and Wang Liming's so much better? I never heard President Xu say anything about attacking the students. I never saw Xu Jian's hands shaking or noticed that he was hysterical. Why is it that Wang Liming saw and heard those things and I did not?

"Besides, trembling hands are a matter of health, not a matter of politics. If his hands were shaking, maybe President Xu was sick or cold—or frightened. But that has nothing to do with his political stance. Just now, while Comrade Wang talked, did you see that white spit dribbling out of the sides of his mouth? Do we want to say that he was hysterically foaming at the mouth, attacking President Xu? No, it's just that white spit dribbles out of his mouth when he talks. It's a bodily matter, not a political one, no?

"But why did you talk this way, Comrade Wang? Why are all these people attacking President Xu? Because you support Wang Hua, who represents the party, and everyone assumes that because Wang Hua is the party secretary, he must be right. But what is this Cultural Revolution about anyway? Peng Zhen is the party secretary of Beijing and Chairman Mao has said that he is wrong. Liu Shaoqi and Deng Xiaoping are the highest of all party secretaries, and Chairman Mao has said they are wrong. Just because someone is a party secretary doesn't make him right. That is why our great leader Chairman Mao has launched this Cultural Revolution.

"I'm talking today to oppose Wang Hua, and I want to tell you why. I was at the meeting when Xu Jian spoke. He did not call for attacking the students. We talked a lot about military matters. At the end of the meeting, after President Xu had spoken, he turned to Wang Hua and asked him openly, 'Do you agree with what I have said?' and Wang Hua said clearly, 'Yes, I agree.' Now Wang Hua says he agrees with the big character poster attacking President Xu. But that poster is full of falsehoods. Wang Hua knows the big character poster is false. Wang Hua is two-faced. One day he agrees with this, the next day he attacks. Do we really want our party secretary to be two-faced, dishonest, deceitful? Of course not. Chairman Mao says we should seek truth from facts. But Wang Hua is is opposed to seeking truth from facts. He is deliberately trying to deceive you. I say that Wang Hua is opposed to Chairman Mao, opposed to Chairman Mao's thought."

The audience was still applauding as Yuxian left the stage and walked the length of the auditorium on his way to the health clinic. Hands reached out to congratulate him. "Good talk, thanks a lot," they said. "That really needed to be said." "Boy, did Wang Hua ever lose face."

"Quiet, please," the work team chairman kept repeating, reminding the audience of the meeting's ground rules and the fact that the work team was still serving as a court. "Please, please, no applause.

"The situation must be as Comrade Ni Yuxian described it," he mused out loud when the applause had finally subsided. The tumultuous response convinced the work team that Ni Yuxian had told the truth. The meeting was adjourned.

But Xu Jian was not saved by the revelation that the big character poster against him was false. Truth was not of great import in the unsettled struggle for power. Campus opinion remained irresolvably divided between those who supported Wang Hua and his followers and those who sided with the college president. The entire party leadership at the Shanghai Maritime Academy, Xu Jian and Wang Hua included, was forced to step down. The Cultural Revolution was entering a new stage. Throughout the country, ranking party committees, accused of following the capitalist road, were being dismissed. New governing bodies, known as revolutionary committees, were to be democratically elected and to consist of a cross section of reliable party cadres and representatives of the masses. The remaining task of the work team at the Maritime Academy was to organize the election of the new revolutionary committee.

• • •

At the grass-roots level of his own thirty-student class, dominated as it was by party members and loyalists and those most familiar with his temperament and general unorthodoxy, Ni Yuxian's popularity was mixed. The students had to vote twice before choosing him, fifteen to thirteen with two abstentions, to stand for election to the university-wide revolutionary committee. At the university level, however, everyone remembered Ni Yuxian's speech attacking Wang Hua. Of a thousand votes cast, Ni won 860 and thus was elected with the highest number of votes to the new thirteen-member Revolutionary Committee henceforth designated to govern the school. The seal of authority passed from Chen Qi, Wang Hua, and the party to the new democratically elected committee. At twenty-one years old, ever-rebellious Ni Yuxian was suddenly in a position of power.

His responsibilities were vast, the demands on his energy, time, and goodwill nearly ceaseless. Universities, like work units everywhere in China, are self-contained and all-encompassing units, the lowest and most basic level of party control, education constituting only a small fraction of overall activity. Universities not only provide those associated with them—faculty, students, administrators, and workers alike—with the basic necessities of life, but the benefits of association are virtually impossible to obtain elsewhere. The university guarantees its employees a minimum wage and lifetime employment, reasonably comfortable retirement, medical insurance, and child care, housing for mere pennies a day, and a host of services and benefits ranging from free movie tickets, watermelons, and sightseeing excursions to yearly visits to distant relatives. Students at graduation rely on the university party committee to find them employment, and once assigned there is no escape. Jobs—and work units—are for life. The Chinese work unit thus provides permanent security at the price of a perpetual state of dependency. And because the benefits offered are both basic and scarce, university party officials responsible for administering, managing, and authorizing the myriad details of everyday life reap tremendous individual power. Opportunities for corruption are rampant, and the ubiquitous favoritism and abuse of authority result in an inevitable division between the beneficiaries of party largess, who offer their loyalty in return, and the many who are convinced the party has treated them unfairly and who therefore live with a myriad of pent-up personal antagonisms, grievances, and slights, hardly daring to dream of a day when they might spew forth their anger in protest.

In 1966 the power of the party committee was so great and deeply entrenched that the democratically elected Revolutionary Committee of which Ni Yuxian was a leader was never fully accepted as the legitimate governing body of the university. The campus remained sharply divided between party loyalists who continued to see the Cultural Revolution as a new variation of the old antirightist campaign, with its primary targets the bourgeois intellectuals and their few sympathizers in the party, and those disgruntled, dissatisfied subjects who hoped that the Cultural Revolution was really an attack on the party itself and on the abuse of power and petty corruption that had come to characterize it. The substantial body of party loyalists at the Shanghai Maritime Academy who refused on principle to accept the authority of the new Revolutionary Committee established instead a "Mao Zedong Thought Headquarters" to voice opposition to what they viewed as an antiparty clique, blaring their dissenting views from morning to night on loudspeakers liberally dispersed throughout the campus, answered with equal clamor through the competing loudspeakers of the opposition.

But with the seal of authority and responsibility for financial disbursements in the hands of the new Revolutionary Committee and permission still required for even the most mundane of activities, even the party loyalists were often at the mercy of the newly elected committee. Cars, buses, and trucks were under the committee's control, and it was responsible for distributing the paper for big character posters and the red armbands that became the symbol of rebellion for both sides of the ongoing political struggle.

The greatest worry of the new Revolutionary Committee, however, was not the petty details in which they were daily immersed but the seething undertone of violence that threatened the campus more ominously each day. The Revolutionary Committee may not have been regarded as fully legitimate by the university community it served, but its leaders were nonetheless vested with a measure of responsibility for how the Cultural Revolution unfolded on the university campus. The newly formed Red Guards were threatening to go on a rampage.

On August 18, 1966, when a million wildly cheering students from Beijing's middle schools and universities, garbed in military dress and sporting armbands that identified them as Red Guards, gathered in Tiananmen Square in the heart of the nation's capital, the message they received from Party Chairman Mao Zedong had been "to rebel is justified." Introduced to female middle school student Song Binbin—"Polite Song"—the party chairman had chastised the young rebel for her name. "We don't want 'polite,' " the party chairman had said. "We want war." Song Binbin obliged by changing her name to Song Yaowu—"Song Wants Violence"— and is widely rumored to have engaged in violence herself. For millions of young people throughout China, Chairman Mao's review of the Red Guards on August 18 stands as the day when the permission to engage in violence was officially granted, the checks against adolescent rebellion were openly unleashed, when the thin veneer upon which civilization ordinarily rests was deliberately stripped away.

The Red Guards were an elite group, their membership confined to the sons and daughters of the "four good" categories— workers, peasants, soldiers, or revolutionary party cadres—and their sympathies generally coincided with those who viewed the Cultural Revolution more as a new antirightist campaign than as an attack against party abuse. But young people everywhere wanted to join, and as membership expanded the level of violence—and fear—escalated considerably.

Beginning in Beijing and then spreading contagiously to cities throughout the country, young Red Guards took to the streets in a wild and wanton rampage of putative revolutionary activity. The Cultural Revolution was touted to the young as an attack against China's traditional, allegedly "feudal," culture, and the young hence turned to smashing the "four olds"—old culture, old customs, old ideas, and old habits. Cultural artifacts preserved for posterity over the centuries and once lauded with pride as symbols of China's rich and glorious past, were destroyed. Buddhist temples, deemed the seat of traditional superstition, were looted, religious relics smashed. Wooden shop signs, carved with the melodious names that had often graced shop fronts for centuries, were torn from their moorings and burned, the names of stores and streets changed to render them more revolutionary. Traffic signals were revolutionized, too, with red lights serving as signals to go and green to stop, creating havoc when the message of the revolution in traffic control failed to be universally heeded.

People were attacked, too. Those whose dress was not properly proletarian were accosted on the streets, and many older citizens and suspected representatives of the bourgeoisie were beaten. Some were beaten to death.

On the campus of Shanghai Maritime Academy, the response to the formation of the Red Guards was electrifying, sparking a new wave of humiliating street parades and struggle sessions against the allegedly bourgeois and "rightist" faculty, and subjecting them once more to the tribulation of the house search—the ransacking of hearth and home in an effort to find evidence against the suspected and accused.

The possible crimes of the intellectuals were many, the rules of evidence wide. A proclivity toward feudalism was witnessed in their possession of traditional-style porcelain and furniture, artwork, calligraphy, and religious artifacts, and because these traditional objects were deemed feudal and therefore exemplifications of the "four olds," the Red Guards had the right—indeed the revolutionary responsibility—to destroy them. Countless numbers of China's privately held precious artifacts, perserved through the centuries, were thus forever lost. Gold, jewelry, and watches, even photographs of individuals in Western garb, were deemed proof of one's capitalist past and present bourgeois proclivities. Foreign books and university degrees obtained abroad were taken as evidence of collusion with the foreign imperialists, subjecting the owner to the risk of being accused as a spy. People with newspapers dating back to the Guomindang era, even when those papers were lining trunks or used as backing for picture frames and hence had long since been forgotten, were accused of longing for a return to the past and thus were labeled reactionary. Diplomas and documents bearing the seal of the Guomindang government brought similar accusations. Letters and diaries, even marginal notes on books, were confiscated to be examined for their political, presumably antisocialist, content.

What was not destroyed was confiscated, the list of confiscated contents filled out in triplicate—one for the owner, one for the local police, and one for the work unit responsible—the evidence delivered for storage to the Revolutionary Committee or the local police station. Few complained if their list of confiscated goods was shorter than the number of items actually taken away, the unrecorded items pocketed by the Red Guards themselves. Not wanting to risk being implicated as members of the bourgeoisie, most people were anxious to appear poorer than they really were.

The homes of most party members and activists were immune from the search, but all five members of the Maritime Academy's party committee, Wang Hua and Xu Jian especially, came under attack, brought frequently to public struggle sessions—the Mao Zedong Thought Headquarters taking the lead in organizing the attacks against Xu Jian and the opposition Red Rebels leading the struggles against Wang Hua, each group trying to prove itself more revolutionary and more Maoist than the next.

However lofty the revolutionary and socialist ideals of the Cultural Revolution may have sounded in Beijing, few participants ever transcended their own parochial experiences in giving voice to their dissatisfactions. The grievances that spewed forth when the bonds were loosened were petty and personal, grudges held in check while the party was still in control, cloaked primarily for revolutionary legitimacy in the Maoist rhetoric to which both sides of the debates studiously adhered. When sixty-one-year-old illiterate worker Ding Foshan became a leader of the Shanghai Maritime Academy revolutionary rebels opposed to party leader Wang Hua, the man rose at a struggle meeting to hold aloft his tattered cotton padded jacket, many years old and filthy, as evidence of Wang Hua's oppression of the masses and of his counterrevolutionary stance. "Look at this jacket," he demanded of his audience. "Our country has been liberated for seventeen years, but I have worn this old jacket for more than a decade and still can't afford to buy a new one. I don't even have enough money to send my kids to school. My life is worse now than it was before this so-called 'liberation.' But when I asked Wang Hua to help me, to give me a little extra rice to feed my family, he refused. He asked me why I had so many kids. Wang Hua is terrible to us workers, just like the capitalists in the old society."

Outraged followers of Wang Hua accused the old worker of being a counterrevolutionary. After all, the system Ding was criticizing was socialist, and to criticize socialism was to criticize the revolution and hence to be counterrevolutionary. But fellow revolutionary rebels, believing that socialism inhered in the dictatorship of the proletariat, of which Ding was decidedly a member, sympathized with Ding Foshan and his plight, viewing Wang Hua as a "capitalist roader" and counting the worker's grievances as revolutionary. The reason Wang Hua had refused to help poor Ding, they argued, was that he was opposed to the proletarian revolution and hence to Chairman Mao, as witnessed not only by his failure to help but also by his less than enthusiastic support for this Cultural Revolution.

The decisive proof of Wang Hua's counterrevolutionary heart came at the end of one of the struggle sessions against him when he was asked to stand and shout the requisite slogans—"Long live the Great Proletarian Cultural Revolution," "Down with Liu Shaoqi and Deng Xiaoping," and "Long live Chairman Mao"— with which such meetings were always concluded. Instead of shouting "Long live Chairman Mao," the party secretary had actually yelled "Down with Chairman Mao." He slapped himself on the face in astonishment immediately thereafter, and there were those who thought that the counterrevolutionary slogan had been a slip of the tongue and that Wang Hua had been the victim of his own nervous tension. But the slip was used by his enemies as a powerful weapon against him.

With each side waving the red flag and quoting Chairman Mao with equal conviction and similar persuasion, the academy was bereft of any means of solving its problems of party leadership. The more intractible the problems of party leadership, the greater the number of struggle sessions against the party leaders, as those under attack were forced to stand outside for hours in the oppressively hot August sun, listening to the taunts and jeers against them. Their health was a matter of increasing concern. Tempers flared.

The new Revolutionary Committee was powerless. With no one to stop the marauding Red Guards, the house searches expanded from faculty with genuinely suspect pasts to ordinary teachers who had nothing against socialism or the Communist Party. Those teachers, too, were beaten, their possessions destroyed. The faculty came to plead before the Revolutionary Committee for protection against such wild and wanton attacks. After proclaiming a set of rules forbidding searches without the committee's approval and prohibiting violence against individuals and the destruction of personal property, the central party newspapers in Beijing began praising as revolutionary what the teachers viewed as wanton and unnecessary violence, and the Revolutionary Committee's rules for peaceful revolution were rendered null and void.

• • •

Deep in the Chinese psyche is the belief that only recognized authority stands between order and chaos, that peace is maintained not through the mediated observance of mutually agreed upon rules but through a strong and authoritative leader whom everyone agrees to follow. Episodically, throughout Chinese history, when leadership has failed, *luan*—chaos—the situation most feared by Chinese, has followed, the society gradually disintegrating first into confusion, then to turmoil, and finally to violent, bloody, and terrifying internal war. The Cultural Revolution became yet another such historic descent. At the Shanghai Maritime Academy, too, in the absence of recognized authority, the campus began degenerating into anarchy, uncontrolled and unpredictable—a situation of *luan*.

Then Guan Foshan, a professor of French with alleged previous ties to the Guomindang, hanged himself from a plumbing pipe after suffering the indignity of being locked in the toilet when the Red Guards searched his home. Ni Yuxian and many of his like-minded colleagues were afraid that if the *luan* continued, further deaths would follow—that another faculty member would commit suicide or that one day a teacher would die from a Red Guard beating.

When a call went forth from the Cultural Revolution Small Group in Beijing for university students to leave their campuses to travel at the state's expense in "great revolutionary linkups" to other parts of the country to share their revolutionary experiences, Ni welcomed it with relief. If the campus could be emptied of students, the violence would subside.

On September 15 Chairman Mao would be holding what was being feted as the last of his reviews of the Red Guards in Beijing's Tiananmen Square. What better way to begin the great revolutionary linkups than with the entire student body of Shanghai Maritime Academy assembled in the heart of the nation's capital, the seat of revolutionary government, the home of the chairman himself! The Shanghai municipal authorities had allotted the school only two hundred free tickets, but after days of negotiations with the railway bureau and the maritime authorities, Ni Yuxian was able to secure an additional three hundred train tickets and five hundred places aboard a boat bound for Tianjin, just two hours away from the nation's capital by train. All the students could visit Beijing.

When the students left their campus in the first week of September, joining tens of thousands of others from around the country similiarly traveling to pay their respects to Chairman Mao, the trains were so crowded they could only be exited and entered through the windows, and students were jammed in the aisles and sleeping in the overhead luggage racks. A visit to the bathroom counted as a major victory over the crowds. In a triumph of the Chinese bureaucratic imperative, Ni Yuxian and his colleagues managed to establish an "office" on board, and the students reached their destination without major mishap.

The Beijing Red Guards—offspring of the "four good" categories and many of them sons and daughters of Communist Party cadres—were patrolling the train station, puffed with the arrogance of adolescent authority, inspecting the students as they left the trains. The class background of the out-of-towners was a matter of gravest concern, and students whose parents were intellectuals or rightists, landlords or counterrevolutionaries, reactionaries, bad elements, or otherwise suspect were subject to beatings and immediate deportation home. Yuxian was uncomfortable on principle with the ceaseless investigations into class background, and necessarily so because his father's status as an intellectual put him at the lowest level of the political ladder. Yuxian relied on the fact that he was a demobilized soldier to save him from attack.

The streets of Beijing, too, had been taken over by the young Red Guards. Quiet terror reigned. At the headquarters of the Communist Youth League, Ni witnessed the ongoing political spectacle organized by the Red Guards to humiliate its director, Hu Yaobang, and two of his deputies, Hu Qili and Hu Keshe—the "three Hus," as they were called. Regularly, every half hour, the Red Guards forced the three Hus, their bodies covered with newspapers on which the attacks against them were written, to crawl onto a stage on all fours, barking like dogs in three different tones to symbolize their crime of having been running dogs of the foreign imperialists. (At the end of the Cultural Revolution, Hu Yaobang would be made general secretary of the Chinese Communist Party, the highest-ranking party official in the land, only to be removed a decade later for his too-liberal views. His death from a heart attack on April 15, 1989, would spark another massive student revolt.)

Yuxian talked with many Beijing Red Guards, middle school students fifteen and sixteen years old, who bragged proudly of the people—landlords and rich peasants, bad elements, counterrevolutionaries and rightists—they had beaten to death with their belts. The crematoria in those days were so busy that the dead had to wait in line to be burned.

But the students' parade to Tiananmen Square was handled by the People's Liberation Army with admirable military precision. The pupils from the Shanghai Maritime Academy left their dormitory on the outskirts of the city at six o'clock in the morning, school flags unfurled, singing revolutionary songs, marching for two hours along the wide boulevards of the capital before finally arriving in the square to take their place near the middle of the huge expanse at the foot of the Monument to the Revolutionary Heroes. With the Great Hall of the People on their left, the Revolutionary History Museum on their right, they were impossibly far from the podium atop Tiananmen—the Gate of Heavenly Peace—where Chairman Mao and the other party leaders would stand. At nine o'clock, when the loudspeakers rang with the music of the "East Is Red," everyone knew without being able to see that their great leader Chairman Mao had arrived. Half a million students rose to their feet in song, arms raised high, holding Chairman Mao's Little Red Book aloft, singing the "Internationale," and listening without comprehension as Chairman Mao's designated successor and closest comrade in arms, Defense Minister Lin Biao, spoke a few impossibly accented words. Then Mao Zedong's car slowly circled the square, as soldiers from the People's Liberation Army locked arms to hold back the crowd of frantically pressing students, the progress of the Chairman's route being followed by those from within the square by the shouts, the screams, the calls of "Long live Chairman Mao," the frantic leaps into the air, as the motorcade went by.

Ni Yuxian never actually saw Chairman Mao, able only to make out the few cars as they circumnavigated the square. Troubled by the displays of fervent, frenetic, religious adulation his fellow students exhibited before the man become emperor become god, he remained silent as the square reverberated again and again, louder and louder, with the shouts of "Long live Chairman Mao."

It was like watching a play.

• • •

After receiving the blessing of their great leader Chairman Mao, the students of Shanghai Maritime Academy fanned out, small group by small group, in their great revolutionary linkups to diverse parts of the country. Ni Yuxian, as responsible person on the Revolutionary Committee, helped with the arrangements. Two groups were organized to duplicate the Communist Party's Long

March—the year-long epic retreat from the revolutionary base area in the Jinggan Mountains in southern Jiangxi Province to the town of Yenan in northern Shaanxi Province, where they established a new base area from whence the revolution was ultimately successful. Beginning in October 1934, the exodus had taken the Communist Party some six thousand miles on foot through some of the most difficult and hazardous terrain in China or the world. It had begun with some one hundred thousand men and a handful of women. Only twenty thousand survived. By imitating the Long March of the Communist Party heroes, the young who had never participated in a revolution hoped to become revolutionary themselves.

The students returned to Tiananmen Square to begin their Long March with as much fanfare as could be mustered, and Yuxian delivered a pep talk to send them on their way. "Your Long March is really a good idea," he encouraged them. "You'll be able to see how the peasants live and understand more about their needs and better understand Chinese society." Each participant was given an army uniform, a pair of walking shoes, and a hundred yuan—a substantial sum in those days, almost four times Ni Yuxian's monthly salary in the factory. Everyone carried a thermos of water, a straw hat as a shield from the sun, and an allotment of rice. Those in the lead carried a red flag emblazoned with the name of the Maritime Academy and a portrait of Chairman Mao, held aloft.

Only Red Guards, whose family backgrounds were "good," were allowed to participate in the Long Marches, and Ni Yuxian was therefore prohibited from joining. But he marched with them for the first day, returning to Beijing after seeing them on their way. Making virtue of necessity, he claimed to have witnessed enough of peasant misery during his stint in the army and to have marched enough for a lifetime then, too. He saw no reason to participate in a new long march. He decided to go sightseeing instead.

Zhao Yuefang was waiting for Ni Yuxian in Beijing, and on his return they set out on their own, more romantic, great revolutionary linkup, traversing the country by boat and by train, visiting the most famous historic and scenic spots, reading the big character posters and informing themselves of the unfolding revolution along the way. For millions of young Chinese, the Cultural Revolution was an unparalleled opportunity, the only one they would ever have, to sightsee their country—for free.

Ni Yuxian and his girlfriend headed north, traveling by cargo boat, sleeping on the floor, constantly interrupted by representatives of the police and the military inspecting school permissions and letters of introduction. Visiting Dalian, Harbin, Jilin, Shenyang, and Changchun in China's northeast, where the weather was already cold and the food unappetizingly Russian, they borrowed padded jackets and shoes. Then they went south, traveling by train to Wuhan and taking the boat up the Yangtze River, through the magnificently beautiful three gorges, to Chongqing, then turning back to go further south still, to Guilin, winding by boat down the Li River, surrounded by breathtakingly beautiful, improbably peaked mountains that have served for centuries as the subject of Chinese landscape paintings.

The Red Guards hosted them, modestly but gratis, everywhere, providing the dormitory rooms and the food, and subjecting them also to endless inspections of class background and letters of introduction, the forms for which Ni Yuxian, as responsible person on the Revolutionary Committee, carried in abundance. The couple quickly learned that suspicion was best avoided if they presented themselves as relatives, and Yuxian began filling out Zhao Yuefang's letters of introduction with the name of his younger sister.

Sexual encounters among college students were not yet part of the lexicon of the Cultural Revolution, and revolutionary fervor, the crowded conditions of the hostels, and traditional taboo conspired to guarantee the couple's chastity en route. The closest Ni Yuxian and his girlfriend came to sexual dalliance was in Dalian, when Zhao Yuefang, as the only female in a crowded hostel, was assigned to sleep alone in a single room. In a strange city and unfamiliar inn, surrounded by militant young males, the naturally timid girl was afraid to sleep alone. Staying in the single room together with her boyfriend was much too risky, so Zhao Yuefang joined Yuxian, mask over her face, hair tucked up under an army cap, lumpy in cotton padded clothes, all traces of her gender erased, to spend a sleepless and nervous night huddled against her boyfriend in the corner of a huge dormitory room, ever fearful that in one of the many Red Guard interruptions during the night, the blanket that covered her would be snatched away, her sex revealed.

It was during their great revolutionary linkup that Ni Yuxian claims his later doubts about his girlfriend were sown. Traveling up the Yangtze with several of Zhao Yuefang's college classmates, the young man was standing alone one day, leaning against the railing of the boat, absorbed in the mountain scenery and his own thoughts, when one of Yuefang's friends came to join him. "So how are you and Yuefang getting along now?" the girl inquired curiously.

"Can't you tell?" Yuxian responded. "Everything's fine. We're getting along really well."

"Yes, I can tell. She's finally decided on you." The friend paused. "She doesn't want her other boyfriends anymore."

"Her other boyfriends?" Yuxian asked with a start.

"Yes, she's had two of them, you know. One was her class secretary. The second—the one until just recently, Huang Jinglong is his name—was her classmate."

"What is he like, this Huang Jinglong?"

"He's really very nice. Very honest. But his father was a capitalist, so when the Cultural Revolution started Zhao Yuefang thought that being a capitalist was bad, so she didn't want to be with him any more."

Yuxian had tried not to think about the two years he and Zhao Yuefang had gone without communicating. That she had had other boyfriends had barely entered his mind, so great to him would such a betrayal have been. That night, in Chongqing, he confronted her.

"You had a boyfriend before and never told me," he accused the young woman. "You told me that since you were a university student, you weren't allowed to be in love. So we separated. We didn't write each other for more than two years. But really, it wasn't because you were a student, was it? You had another boyfriend. I want you to tell me about this. I want you to tell me the whole thing. Otherwise, we'll just break up—forget it."

The tears had already begun spilling down Zhao Yuefang's face. "It wasn't that way," she began awkwardly. "Really. They wanted to be friends with me. They were the ones who came to me. We were just friends."

"But it wasn't just friends, was it? You tell me, tell me what kind of relationship you had."

Zhao Yuefang was sobbing. "We were friends. We went to the movies sometimes."

"What did you do there? What did you do?"

"We just watched the movie together."

"What else? Did you hold hands?"

"Nothing else. I'm sorry, Yuyu. Forgive me. Please forgive me. Can't you see? I came back to you. You're the best. You're the one I want."

"You just go back to Shanghai by yourself. I don't want to be with you anymore."

"No, Yuyu, please,." Zhao Yuefang pleaded. "Please forgive me. We were just friends. I won't do it again. Really, it's just you I want."

Yuxian's anger suddenly dissipated. He was persuaded, overcome with forgiveness and a feeling that he describes as democratic, that the young woman, after all, really did have the right to choose.

"Okay," he relented. "Let's just forget about it then. We won't talk about the past. We'll start again."

To this day, Zhao Yuefang insists that the story she told Ni Yuxian then was true, that the other boys were merely friends and that she had only been forced to suspend their relationship because of pressure from the school authorities against students falling in love. But Zhao Yuefang's alleged other boyfriends would haunt Ni Yuxian for years to come. A quarter of a century later the issue was still sensitive, and he would raise it to explain the difficulties in their relationship. In the fall of 1966, the couple returned together to Shanghai.

• • •

The Maritime Academy was in turmoil. Xu Jian had been kidnapped.

• • •

Most of the long marchers from the Shanghai Maritime Academy had never reached their destinations. Walking was tiring, after all, and the city youth got blisters on their feet. There was no place to bathe in the countryside, either, and often no way to cook their rice, which the students frequently ate nearly raw, which wreaked havoc on their stomachs. They often had to sleep in the open—or on vermin-infested straw mats in peasants' huts. All but the hardiest and most enthusiastic returned home by train after only a few weeks on the march, arriving back on campus several weeks before the return of Ni.

The authority of the campus party committee had collapsed,

and the Revolutionary Committee was barely functioning. Without authority, the seething violence Yuxian had earlier feared awaited only the students' return to begin its rapid ascent. The campus remained broadly divided into two main groups. Most party members and party loyalists continued their attacks on the traditional, safe targets—alleged rightist intellectuals, landlords, and members of the bourgeoisie—adding for the sake of the Cultural Revolution and their own protection and quest for power those rival party members they accused rhetorically of being ideologically unsound. The opposition revolutionary rebels, generally consisting of those who had never had any hopes of attaining even a taste of power under the socialist regime and who had often suffered abuse, both great and small, at the hands of the party, continued to welcome the excuse to rebel against their own, different versions of "party people in authority taking the capitalist road"—party members who had slighted or oppressed them in the past. But as time went on, as opinions fragmented and divided and became more refined, as more and more people come forth to participate in politics, and more and more people came to thirst for even a small savor of power, a myriad of smaller factions—"fighting groups," they were called—grew up within the two umbrella factions, each with its own ultrarevolutionary name, its own leadership, and its own favorite targets of revolutionary attack, and struggling not merely against the larger rival umbrella opposition but fighting also against each other over a myriad of irresolvable petty details. One-time friends became sometime enemies as factions divided and multiplied and alliances were forged and broken in ever-shifting configurations.

Nor were the fighting groups confined to the universities. With the call to leave the campuses and go out into society to attack the "four olds," with the encouragement to traverse the country in the great revolutionary linkups, student revolutionary activity had spilled over the campus walls and into the city itself, as the students from the Maritime Academy began making "revolutionary linkups" with like-minded students from other universities and then joining with those revolutionary young workers who were becoming increasingly restless tied to their daily factory routines while the more educated and privileged members of their age cohort took to the streets in a frenzy of political activity.

It was Ma Changyu, the leader of one such fighting group and a particularly energetic and ferocious young student, a party member of impeccably good poor peasant class background, who mustered some three hundred of the college's most militant rebels to kidnap Xu Jian and incarcerate him in one of the city's opera houses.

There were those who believed that Ma's vendetta against Xu was more personal than political. Ma Changyu's romantic proclivities had once been thwarted by the academy's president.

Ma Changyu had been betrothed to a country girl before coming to Shanghai to be seduced by the bright lights of the city and the daringly attractive young women there. But his rural girlfriend refused to allow herself to be jilted, and had written a letter to President Xu accusing her boyfriend of perfidy and urging the president to expel the young man and send him back to the countryside where he belonged. The president refused to send the youth home, but did attempt to make certain that he was properly "educated" about his responsibilities to his fiancée. Ma had never forgiven Xu Jian's efforts.

Ma and his faction naturally avoided such personal issues in explaining why they had forcibly removed Xu Jian from campus. Xu Jian was a capitalist roader, they argued, and the Cultural Revolution was a struggle against party people in authority taking the capitalist road. The president of the Maritime Academy and his defenders were undermining the Cultural Revolution. In the interest of the the revolution, the president had to be moved.

Xu Jian had been struggled against innumerable times on the Shanghai Maritime Academy campus, and the struggle sessions had often been humiliating and brutally abusive. But Xu Jian had his protectors within the university, and the attacks against him generally stopped short of outright violence. When the situation occasionally got out of control, when he was asked to kneel down and bend over from the waist, arms outstretched behind him in the position known as the "jet airplane," when his hair was pulled and he was kicked, his defenders in the audience could bring the excesses to a halt. "The Cultural Revolution is supposed to use words, not force," they would yell, "words not force!"

When Xu Jian was kidnapped, that protection ceased.

From captivity in the opera house, Xu Jian was brought out daily to be paraded through the streets of Shanghai on the back of an open truck, the route taking him regularly past his own home where his wife and son were dragged forth to watch the struggle against him, and then, horn blaring and insistent, on to the Bund, where the truck was invariably stopped in front of the Peace Hotel.

Forced to bend from the waist at right angles to his legs, burdened with the weight of a twenty-five-pound accusatory placard hung around his neck, the college president was regularly beaten, the beatings growing daily in severity. His family members feared for his life.

Xu Jian was a tough old cadre, and the more his detractors struggled against him, the more determined he seemed to become. The more determined Xu Jian became, the angrier Ma Changyu became. As the daily struggle meetings continued and Xu Jian still refused to recant or admit to his crimes, Ma Changyu began grabbing him by the throat, threatening to choke the president unless he confessed.

It was only when Li Pingxin, senior professor at Shanghai's East China Normal University, was beaten to death by his own students that Xu Jian finally grew desperate.

"Save me," he had cried out in fright to the curious crowd one afternoon as he was being driven on his daily street parade around the Bund. "Save me."

So infuriated was Ma Changyu that he kicked Xu Jian off the back of the truck, sending him tumbling onto the pavement, the heavy placard still around his neck, the truck speeding quickly away.

Xu Jian, shaken and badly bruised, was recaptured the following day, and the tortures against him were renewed.

Ni Yuxian returned to the Maritime Academy campus just at this stage of the the president's plight. The young man's childhood propensity to heroics was undiminished. He called an urgent meeting. "If we don't save him, our president my die," he argued. "Others have already died. We must act immediately."

Xu Jian's defenders, some four hundred strong, commandeered the university's entire pool of vehicles, rushing by cavalcade, horns blaring, to the Shanghai opera house.

"No beating," Yuxian admonished as he led his supporters into the building. "We don't want any violence tonight. We're just going to have a meeting with them to get this thing settled."

Red Guards from Peking and Qinghua universities, and a smattering of press representatives, were in the audience as the debate between the two sides, Ni Yuxian presiding, began. "What you guys are doing is fascist, taking our president and kidnapping him, treating him like this, beating him and not giving him food," he berated the opposition. "This isn't what the Cultural Revolution is supposed to be about."

The captors laughed in derision.

"You conservatives will be defeated," Yuxian admonished.

The debate lasted until the wee hours of the morning, with the kidnappers arguing that the Cultural Revolution was a struggle against landlords and the bourgeoisie and party persons in authority taking the capitalist road, and that Xu Jian qualified on all counts, and the college president's defenders accusing the kidnappers of beating their prisoner and denying him food, and detailing again and again the crimes of the university party committee and its unrelenting efforts to kill free debate and stifle the development of the Cultural Revolution. Wang Hua, not Xu Jian, was the real enemy, they argued. Ni Yuxian made certain that those who had suffered at the hands of Wang Hua were called upon frequently to pour forth their tales of injustice and woe.

The decision in the dispute was made by the visiting Red Guards from Peking and Qinghua universities, who, because they were from the capital of revolutionary activity, from the universities Chairman Mao had declared the most revolutionary of all, were therefore deemed capable of determining matters of revolutionary morality in Shanghai. Xu Jian's defenders were determined to have been right.

The Maritime Academy president and his colleagues were freed at around two in the morning, escorted to the waiting trucks by hundreds of their jubilant supporters. As the leader of the liberating force, Ni Yuxian stayed behind, like the captain of a ship, to be the last one out, only to be temporarily captured himself. The "dare-to-die squad" defending Xu Jian, tough and big and strong, found him later locked in a small room, standing alone in the center of a circle he had drawn with white chalk. "The Cultural Revolution Committee says to struggle with words, not with force," he was berating his captors. "Whoever steps across this line will be struggling with force and will be held responsible for whatever happens." The revolutionary rebels' dare-to-die squad dragged him to freedom through a window.

•　•　•

In the city itself, the slow descent into anarchy had begun.

•　•　•

When the students took to the rails in the great revolutionary link-ups, traveling the length and breadth of the country, the city of

Shanghai was suddenly flooded with poor petitioners from the countryside who had also availed themselves of the free ride. At the depth of the famine in the early 1960s, in an effort to ease the demand for food and prevent an outpouring of urban unrest, the Shanghai municipal authorities had shipped tens of thousands of urban dwellers to the countryside, promising, so those who were forced to leave believed, that they could return when the food shortage eased. Four years later, apparently forgotten by their original factory managers and by the Shanghai party committee, the rusticated one-time urban dwellers began descending on their factories and the municipal authorities en masse to insist on their right to return.

Workers within the city, many harboring long-standing grievances against the party leadership of their factories and many having been labeled or politically persecuted in times past, began rising up, too, first forming small groups of revolutionary rebels to press their accumulated grievances against the party committees within their own factories, and then, when the factory party committees insisted that worker rebellion would lead to an unacceptable decline in production, leaving their factories to take their cause to the Shanghai municipal party committee. The temporary contract workers in which the city of Shanghai abounded—the lowliest of all the urban employed in terms of education, pay, working hours and housing, medical and welfare benefits—were among the most vocal, insistent, and unruly in pressing their demands.

Having little experience in organizing, their lack of education and verbal underdevelopment working to their decided political and practical disadvantage, the workers began turning to the students for advice and help in arguing their proletarian cause. Alliances were formed, the first overt manifestation of which was in December 1966 when workers and students cooperated in taking over and occupying the offices of the *Liberation Daily*, the Communist Party–run newspaper for the city of Shanghai. In addition to their brawn, the workers supplied weapons, too— steel bars and crudely fashioned knives and spears straight from the factory floor. The possibilities for violence were commensurately enhanced.

The old guard in the Shanghai municipal party committee were attentive, even sympathetic, but finally intransigent in the face of worker demands. Students' classes might be canceled so the young pupils could take to the streets in rebellion, but production must go on. A worker's place was in the factory. Party leaders within the factory naturally agreed.

But the logic of the Cultural Revolution was not on the side of either the municipal party committee or the managers of factories. Just as the overthrow of Beida's president brought the leadership of every other university president into question, so the overthrow of the Beijing municipal party committee undermined the legitimacy of party committees in cities throughout the country, subjecting them to the suspicious scrutiny of the increasingly restive masses. One-time municipal party committee member Zhang Chunqiao, now promoted to the Cultural Revolution Small Group in Beijing charged with overseeing and guiding the unfolding movement, may have been immune from attack, but the other members were not. Lest the message be missed, Nie Yuanzi herself, the same political activist whose big character poster at Beida had unleashed the Cultural Revolution in early June, was dispatched to Shanghai to open the attacks on the two ranking members of the Shanghai municipal party committee.

Encouraged by Nie Yuanzi's attack and angered at the authorities' intransigence in the face of the unfolding workers' movement, a group of outraged workers, some three thousand strong, commandeered a train heading for Beijing, intent on presenting their demands to participate in the gathering rebellion to the Cultural Revolution small group in charge. The train was stopped less than an hour outside of Shanghai, before it reached Suzhou, but Zhang Chunqiao himself personally flew down to negotiate with the workers. One of the men he met that night, representing the militants, was Wang Hongwen, later to rise together with Zhang Chunqiao to the highest positions of power, falling together, too, as members of the Gang of Four. "We cannot let you go to Beijing," Zhang Chunqiao is reported to have explained to the disgruntled workers, "because if you go, workers from all over the country would also want to go to the capital to present their demands. But we will grant your basic requests. Workers can participate in the Cultural Revolution."

Overnight the number of revolutionary rebels in Shanghai's factories increased from the tens of thousands to a million, and the list of demands expanded, too. The Chinese worker's lot was secure, but his livelihood was modest and his income and standard of living had not discernibly improved in years. The workers resented the special privileges of both the high-ranking party cadres and the senior intellectuals, and they wanted higher salaries and better housing for themselves. Permission from Beijing granted, they began pressing their economic demands against factory party committees. The factory party committees capitulated. Anxious to keep their own jobs by following the dictates of the Cultural Revolution Small Group, the managers interpreted Beijing's decision that workers, too, had a right to rebel as encouragement to give in to the workers' demands. Factory administrators throughout the city began awarding bonuses, raises, and previously undelivered back pay.

There was a run on the banks. In the Pudong machine parts factory where Ni Yuxian once had worked, old worker Ah Xing claimed that for more than a decade his wages should have been forty yuan rather than the thirty-two he had actually received. He was awarded eight hundred yuan in back pay, more than the man had seen in one bundle in his entire life. Ah Xing could not sleep the night he went to the bank. He put the money under his pillow, then got up to count it, laughing and counting, laughing and counting, putting it again under his pillow, lying down, getting up, laughing and counting. The next day he spent half the money on a new bicycle for himself, a sewing machine for his wife, and new bookbags for his children. The rest he put back in the bank.

Ah Xing's experience was repeated throughout the city, and soon the banks had no more money to distribute. Workers everywhere were stopping work. Production ground to a halt. Transportation was stopped. Trains no longer ran, and foreign ships stood at the docks unloaded. Workers from factories throughout the city pressed their demands, banding together to threaten recalcitrant factory administrators that if their demands were not met, the electricity would be shut off, water stopped, garbage collection halted, and transportation services terminated.

New word came from Beijing—a reversal of the original interpretation of the worker's right to rebel. The workers' economic demands, the center asserted, were part of a capitalist conspiracy foisted on them by Liu Shaoqi with the intent of destroying the Cultural Revolution. The signatures authorizing banks to disperse money for workers' increased wages were capitalist signatures, and banks were prohibited from making such payments. The workers' economic demands were themselves capitalist-inspired and counterrevolutionary. Factory leaders who had succumbed to the workers' demands were party people in authority taking the capitalist road and would have to be overthrown.

Ah Xing was forced to give back the eight hundred yuan, and since the shops would only return ninety percent of what he had paid for the bicycle, the sewing machine, and the bookbags, he ended up losing forty yuan—more than a whole month's salary. Again he could not sleep. He cried for nights thereafter.

But the word from Beijing sparked a new wave of worker rebellions as factory workers throughout the city rose up to overthrow the "party persons in authority taking the capitalist road"—the factory managers who had succumbed to their earlier economic, counterrevolutionary demands. New factory managers, and new worker revolutionary rebel leaders, appeared everywhere. Revolutionary rebel organizations of workers proliferated, most of them under the broad overall aegis of the umbrella group headed by Wang Hongwen, supported in Beijing by Zhang Chunqiao. Factory managers were replaced by leaders of the Revolutionary Rebel Workers. The city descended still further into chaos.

The leaders of the new workers' revolutionary rebel organizations fared substantially better than the hapless Ah Xing. While vocal in their opposition to the special privileges so many party administrators had claimed, many of the revolutionary rebel leaders simply usurped those privileges for themselves, seizing the luxurious homes, the chauffeur-driven cars, and the substantial worldly goods of the leaders they had revolted against, thus transforming themselves overnight from ascetic and impoverished workers into cocky nouveau socialist riche. And because the luxuries of the former factory managers were not sufficient to satisfy the appetites of the growing numbers of revolutionary workers, the revolutionaries expanded their attacks to include other of Shanghai's privileged elite—the high intellectuals, the actors and sports figures, the former but still-privileged and wealthy capitalists, and those who depended on remittances from relatives abroad. The revolutionary rebels occupied their homes and confiscated their money and their cars. The Cultural Revolution was growing more complex.

As the movement became more complicated, so Ni Yuxian's attitude toward it grew increasingly ambivalent. He continued to despise Party Chairman Mao Zedong, viewing him as a cruel and barbarous dictator, devoid of humanity—a modern-day version of Qin Shi Huangdi, the ignominious founding emperor of the ancient Qin dynasty, who has lived in Chinese history as the evil dictator who burned the books and buried the intellectuals alive.

Ni Yuxian hated Mao's notion of classes and class struggle and resented the way he had continued the class struggle not only against the landlords and the bourgeoisie, long since defeated, but against anyone who deviated from orthodoxy.

But Ni was still of two minds about Mao. Mao's criticisms of the party leadership—of its bureaucratism, its special privileges, its abuse of power—resonated with Ni's own profound malaise. Had the Cultural Revolution been merely a struggle for power between Mao and high party officials like Liu Shaoqi and Deng Xiaoping, Mao could simply have removed them in the same way Peng Dehuai had been purged. But in mobilizing first students and then workers to struggle against "party persons in authority taking the capitalist road," in raising the issues of bureaucratism and special privilege, Mao Zedong was bringing fundamental problems of the Chinese socialist system, problems that the party itself had worked hard to keep hidden, out into the sunlight for scrutiny and criticism. The fundamental problem of the Chinese political system, Ni believed, was that the party had too much power and the people had none, that power, once granted, was forever. There was no routinized way of removing leaders who overstepped their bounds. The Cultural Revolution gave ordinary Chinese the right to rise up and overthrow corrupt and overweening power. Witnessing the workers' struggle sessions against their one-time party bosses, watching years of pent-up grievances and antagonisms come spewing forth unchecked, Yuxian knew his own dissatisfaction was shared, that the workers' anger was deep, their hatred real.

Thus in the Cultural Revolution, for all its violence and turmoil, and led as it was by people he despised, Ni Yuxian saw hope for changing the oppressive political system and for making it better, more democratic. He believed in a system that granted people the right to choose their own leaders and to dismiss them if they overstepped their authority. The democracy he envisioned was not capitalist but socialist, the type of democracy he thought Lenin had written about in State and Revolution, and the type of democracy that had once actually been implemented, or so the books he read informed him, in the Paris Commune.

The Cultural Revolution also provided Ni Yuxian the opportunity to become the heroic leader of men he believed he was destined to be. With revolutionary organizations proliferating every day, he began contemplating how to establish a different kind of organization, a commune modeled after the one in Paris, with himself at the helm. His idea was grandiose. With a Paris Commune established in Shanghai, he could begin propagating the principles of the commune, inviting like-minded rebels to join. The commune would grow, its guiding principles introduced to other cities, to the countryside, to the whole country, gradually transforming the political organization of all of Chinese society. Ni Yuxian would be the leader. He began sharing his ideas about a new Paris Commune with his friends at the Maritime Academy—with anyone who would listen.

The opportunity came one night with a visit from a mysterious Zhou Baoling. Zhou was second in command of Shanghai's largest faction of worker rebels, the faction headed by Wang Hongwen, the young worker become leader, protégé of Zhang Chunqiao, who would soon rise so quickly in the party hierarchy he would be referred to as the "helicopter" by his allies and detractors alike. Having lost to Wang in the struggle for leadership, Zhou presented himself as an idealist intent on transforming Chinese society, defeated by a political opportunist more intent on furthering his own power than building a new revolution. Zhou Baoling had heard about Ni Yuxian and his critique of the Communist Party, his views on the democratization of Chinese socialism, and his facility with words, and decided to seek the young man's cooperation in forming a new organization. One night in early January 1967, dressed in a bulky army coat, a surgical mask hiding his face to render him incognito, Zhou Baoling traveled to the Maritime Academy to present his proposal to Ni.

The two men hit it off well politically, and they agreed to work together to form a new organization. Founded on lofty ideals that eschewed the violence of the beatings and the house searches, their organization would be dedicated to transforming all of China into a Paris Commune. Four goals, drawn, they believed, from the experience of the Paris Commune, were to motivate them and their work: political power was genuinely to rest in the hands of the people; the people would democratically elect their own officials; officials would live without special perquisites at the same standard of living and with the same rights as ordinary people; and the people had the right to dismiss officials. They called the new organization the Shanghai Worker, Peasant, and Student Revolutionary Rebel Commune—the Revolutionary Rebel Commune for short.

One of the boundless number of curiosities about the interplay between breakdown and order during the Cultural Revolution is the fact that even when leaders were under vicious attack, even when they were in captivity, their decision-making authority remained largely intact. When Zhou Baoling and Ni Yuxian agreed to form their new organization, Zhou was holding Ma Tianshui, a besieged but still powerful member of the Shanghai city party committee, in custody. Ma agreed to donate fifteen thousand yuan in government funds to the Zhou-Ni organization, with most of the money going for the purchase of the red armbands that gave every revolutionary organization its identity. Ma even agreed to provide funding for a newspaper to propagate their views.

The new revolutionary commune took up quarters in the former Polish consulate, just opposite the massive Sino-Soviet Friendship Exhibition Center, and its leaders hung a sign with the name of their organization so huge that it could be read from blocks away. A factory made a seal so their documents could be stamped with a proper legitimizing chop, and they organized themselves very much the way the Communist Party was organized, with a standing committee in charge of day-to-day affairs, a larger representative committee responsible for general policy decisions, and ministries of propaganda and economics, education, finance, and personnel. Zhou Baoling headed the entire organization. Ni Yuxian was number two. Democracy notwithstanding, the leadership was selected by general agreement rather than through elections, the irony of the gap between their founding principles and the absence of elections apparently being missed. Zhou and Ni, after all, were the founding fathers of the organization and hence deserved to lead. Besides, Ni argues, the turbulent times rendered democratic elections impossible.

The ten thousand armbands they had ordered were distributed to their membership in a single day, so enthusiastically was the Revolutionary Rebel Commune welcomed, and the manufacturer could not produce armbands fast enough to satisfy the demand. Within days, the Revolutionary Rebel Commune had branches in all the districts of the city and in the surrounding suburbs as well, its membership extending to workers, students, and peasants alike. It was, in sheer numbers, the second-largest revolutionary rebel organization in Shanghai.

The Shanghai Worker, Peasant, and Student Revolutionary Rebel Commune was short-lived.

The Cultural Revolution was a strange and contradictory amalgam of control from the top and spontaneous outburst of pent-up frustration and anger at the bottom. When workers began participating in the Cultural Revolution in ever-increasing numbers and their demands were labeled "economism," many within the city disagreed with the label. But to disagree with the label was to disagree with Zhang Chunqiao, and to contradict Zhang Chunqiao was to contradict a leading member of the small group leading the Cultural Revolution from Beijing. To challenge the leading group in Beijing was to challenge the Cultural Revolution itself and hence to be counterrevolutionary.

But there was a precedent for such a challenge. Tao Zhu had been overthrown as a leading member of the Cultural Revolution Small Group. Admittedly, his demise had been orchestrated from Beijing, but the fact remained that he had been a member of the Cultural Revolution Small Group and had been successfully overthrown.

The Honggehui, the largest Red Guard organization in Shanghai, had become particularly dissatisfied with Zhang Chunqiao, convinced that he was an opportunist—foxy, crafty, a false revolutionary, seeking power at any cost. They were angered by his maneuvering to play one Shanghai rebel faction off against the other and disgusted by the arrogance of his insistence that he represented Chairman Mao. The Honggehui decided to make the challenge.

In need of evidence—damaging material from Zhang Chunqiao's past—they began sending scouts to various parts of the country, hoping to unearth information that would justify his overthrow. From Taiyuan came word that he had been a traitor. But then everyone was being accused of having been a traitor in the past, and one man's accusation without evidence was hardly enough to make a case.

The Honggehui decided to kidnap one of Yao Wenyuan's close lieutenants, Xu Jinxian, in an effort to extract damaging evidence from someone who surely would know the old man's deepest secrets. Xu Jinxian himself was considered by many to be an opportunist, late to the scene of rebellion and quick to attack the Shanghai party committee in the interests of his own advance. In the stealth of night late in January 1967, Xu was removed to the Fudan University campus, where the Honggehui was strong. The students demanded both that Xu recognize his own opportunistic faults and that he reveal Zhang Chunqiao's sordid past as well.

Zhang Chunqiao's response upon learning of Xu's kidnapping was swift and ruthless. Troops from the People's Liberation Army were sent to surround the Fudan University campus, bayonets at the ready, prepared, the students thought, to kill. It was a major move, an escalation of hostilities far surpassing any of the other struggles, the first time the army had been used during the Cultural Revolution.

The army, moreover, was unnecessary. Zhang Chunqiao's power was unassailable. A simple phone call to the students from him or one of his close associates would have been sufficient to secure the release of Xu. The students were outraged that Zhang had sent troops to their campus. The use of the army truly constituted suppression of the student movement. Those who had entertained doubts about Zhang Chunqiao's revolutionary integrity became convinced of his hidden perfidy, and those who had been indifferent to the man were suddenly filled with indignation. The Honggehui needed no further investigations of Zhang Chunqiao's past to begin shouting "Down with Zhang Chunqiao."

At the Shanghai Sino-Soviet Friendship Exhibition Hall just across from Ni's Revolutionary Rebel Commune headquarters, the Honggehui held a huge meeting, with Zhang Chunqiao and Yao Wenyuan—his close associate and the Shanghai ideologue whose attack on Wu Han had opened the Cultural Revolution—sitting in the audience, front row center. Over and over, rude and angry, the students demanded from a tense and sweaty but stolidly silent Zhang Chunqiao an explanation as to why he had sent the troops.

"What authority did you have to send the PLA to surround the students?" the Honggehui kept demanding to know. "Does Chairman Mao know what you did? Does the Cultural Revolution Small Group know? Did they agree?" If Zhang Chunqiao did not have the full backing from Mao and the Cultural Revolution Small Group, surely he would topple from power.

Zhang Chunqiao remained silent.

"Okay, then," the students decided. "If you can't answer us, then call. Call Beijing and the Cultural Revolution Small Group. We'll ask them whether they support you."

A handful of students disappeared with Zhang Chunqiao's secretary to call Beijing. Wang Li, himself a member of the Cultural Revolution Small Group, answered the secret number. "The situation still isn't clear," Wang waffled. "We have not yet decided how to treat this case."

The students were disappointed, but the meeting concluded in the early morning hours with the decision to hold a huge rally the next day in People's Square. They would publicly demand the overthrow of Zhang Chunqiao and Yao Wenyuan.

The Shanghai Revolutionary Rebel Commune faced a dilemma. Ni Yuxian was in favor of joining the call for the overthrow of Zhang Chunqiao. He had long been opposed to the man. He disliked him for his behind-the-scenes manipulation of one faction against the other. He was revulsed by Zhang's incessant invocation of Mao's name to bolster his own authority. "Comrades," Zhang Chunqiao would inevitably begin his speeches in Shanghai, "I come from Beijing. I represent Chairman Mao in saying hello to you all." Above all, Ni Yuxian opposed Zhang Chunqiao's power to determine who was revolutionary and who was counterrevolutionary. Whatever Zhang Chunqiao said was revolutionary. Whatever he labeled counterrevolutionary was counterrevolutionary, and the putative counterrevolutionary could be locked up. But calling out the army to attack the students was beyond the pale. To Ni Yuxian, opposition to Zhang Chunqiao's use of the military was a matter of principle. The Honggehui, to be sure, had its faults. But to bring in the military to suppress the students was an egregious error. If the military could be used at Fudan, it could be brought in anywhere in China to suppress students and workers. Whatever his earlier political record, using the PLA to quell the student movement was a provocation that destroyed Zhang Chunqiao's right to lead.

Zhao Baoling was more cautious. If the Revolutionary Rebel Commune were to attack Zhang Chunqiao and the Cultural Revolution Small Group later decided that Zhang was right, the Revolutionary Rebel Commune's days would be numbered. Zhang Chunqiao and Wang Hongwen had never approved of the Revolutionary Rebel Commune. The organization had been founded, after all, as an alternative to Wang Hongwen's rebel worker group, and its leadership was much too independent for the tastes of Beijing. To attack Zhang Chunqiao publicly, to call for his overthrow, was to invite being declared counterrevolutionary and thus to sound the death knell of the Revolutionary Rebel Commune.

Ni Yuxian's viewpoint dominated. The Shanghai Revolutionary Rebel Commune issued a manifesto arguing that the students' right to rebel had to be protected and condemning Zhang Chunqiao and the use of troops at Fudan.

Ni had miscalculated. The day after the manifesto, new slogans began springing up throughout the city, and the streets of Shanghai were filled with minibuses spreading the news of the Cultural Revolution Small Group's decision. The small group sided with Zhang Chunqiao. The massing of the army to protect Xu Jinxian had been correct. To oppose Zhang Chunqiao was counter-revolutionary.

In yet another political flip-flop, the atmosphere changed over-night. Zhang Chunqiao's power was immeasurably enhanced, and rumors began circulating that he was about to inaugurate a new form of government in the city.

On February 5, 1967, Zhang Chunqiao and Yao Wenyuan established the Shanghai People's Commune as the new governing body for the entire city of Shanghai. All other organizations were expected to pay obeisance.

The very name of Ni Yuxian's organization—the Shanghai Revolutionary Rebel Commune—constituted proof of its opposition to Zhang Chunqiao's Shanghai People's Commune. In the televi-sion announcement immediately following the establishment of the Shanghai People's Commune, the Revolutionary Rebel Commune was labeled a dissident, reactionary organization. Red Guards loyal to Zhang Chunqiao began harassing Ni Yuxian's Revolutionary Rebel Commune, propaganda loudspeakers blaring from atop their minibuses accusing its leadership of being reactionary, forcing them into constant verbal skirmishes. Some of the organization's mem-bers were arrested, accused of being counterrevolutionary, and taken away.

Then the Revolutionary Rebel Workers, Wang Hongwen's orga-nization, stole the huge nameplate that was hanging in front of the Revolutionary Rebel Commune headquarters, beating the com-mune members who tried to protect it. The theft was an act of war. The Revolutionary Rebel Commune prepared to fight. More than twenty trucks, each one easily holding some thirty people, waited ready to send the rebels off to battle as the commune mem-bers began arming themselves with iron clubs and knives, prepared to die. No one doubted that the confrontation would be violent and that the violence would result in deaths.

Ni Yuxian called an urgent meeting. "We're playing right into the hands of Zhang Chunqiao if we go out and do battle," he argued. "Nothing would make him happier than to see us attack the Revolutionary Rebel Workers. Then he'd really have an excuse to dissolve our Revolutionary Rebel Commune, wouldn't he? He could send us all to jail. And look what we'd be doing. It would be workers attacking workers, ordinary people against ordinary people. It's the workers who would die. Zhang Chunqiao is trying to pit workers against workers."

"Traitor!" someone yelled from the audience. "Whose side are you on anyway?"

"They attacked us, man," one worker stood up to declare. "They stole our signboard, beat up our members. What about our face? We can't let them get away with this. What are we, cowards? If we don't fight, they'll think we're all a bunch of sissies. We'd lose even more face. No. Fight. I say we fight."

The audience roared its approval. The members of the Revolutionary Rebel Commune were itching for battle.

"Wait a minute," Yuxian intervened. "Who's going to die? Workers are going to die. What good is that?"

"Coward! You're just a coward. You're afraid." Voices from all over the meeting hall joined in the accusation.

"No. I'll tell you what. How about this? How about if I go alone and try to negotiate with them, try to get them to apologize and get our sign back. If they agree, we won't fight. If they don't agree, okay, I won't oppose you. Just give me a chance to negotiate."

"Yeah, but what if they capture you? What do you do then?"

"I think I can persuade them."

"You can't go alone. Someone has to go with you."

Yuxian arrived at the headquarters of the Revolutionary Rebel Workers accompanied by a single burly bodyguard from the Revolutionary Rebel Commune. Only blocks away, the trucks were loaded with commune members ready to fight if the negotiations broke down.

"I'm the responsible person from the Revolutionary Rebel Commune," he introduced himself to the tough-looking youths standing guard at the entrance. "I've come to negotiate about the theft of our sign." A leader of the Revolutionary Rebel Workers appeared, surrounded by several sullen bodyguards. "I'm alone," Yuxian continued. "But there are a whole bunch of workers out there. They're angry, ready to fight. I want to avoid bloodshed. I want to talk, to negotiate this thing. Let's see if we can settle this peacefully, huh?"

Led to the spacious room that housed the factory's four huge red fire engines, Ni Yuxian was confronted with twenty or more burly, muscular workers, each wearing the hard hat of a fire fighter and stripped to the waist, muscles flexed, guns in hand.

"Please, comrades," Yuxian began addressing the sullen, ferocious-looking assembly, "please everyone take out Chairman Mao's book of quotations. We'll begin by reading together from Chairman Mao."

Everyone in China carried a copy of Chairman Mao's quotations, and everyone supported Chairman Mao. No one could refuse to participate in a group reading. To refuse to read Chairman Mao was counterrevolutionary.

A hard core of the bare-chested rebels refused to budge, staring sullenly at Ni Yuxian, guns and knives at the ready.

"Comrades," Ni Yuxian repeated, "please take out Chairman Mao's book of quotations. It is only appropriate that we begin by studying Chairman Mao."

Some took out their books but a few recalcitrants still would not be moved.

"Surely there is no one here who opposes studying Chairman Mao's quotations, is there? This isn't respectful, refusing to study Chairman Mao. Are there actually people within this organization who are opposed to Chairman Mao?"

The bare-chested musclemen put down their arms.

"Okay, let's everyone turn to page 251, the section on unity. Let's everyone read together. 'The unificiation of our country, the unity of our people and the unity of our various nationalities—these are the basic guarantees of the sure triumph of our cause. It is only through unity . . . that the enemy can be defeated and the national and democratic revolution accomplished. We shall soldily unite all the forces of our Party . . .'

"Good, comrades, now let's turn to page 291—'How should we judge whether a youth is a revolutionary?'

" 'How should we judge whether a youth is revolutionary? How can we tell? There can only be one criterion, namely, whether or not he is willing to integrate himself with the broad masses of workers and peasants and does so in practice.'

"I've come here to talk to you," Ni continued after the didactic readings. "Yesterday, some representatives of your organization stole our signboard and smashed it in two. They beat a few of our members. Our members are really angry. They want a fight. But if we fight, you know as well as I what would happen. Some of our members on both sides would be killed. Workers would die. Both sides would suffer losses. And for such a small thing. I don't want to see us fight. We're all members of the working class. We're all revolutionaries. Chairman Mao says we should unite and work together. I know it was only a few people from your organization who destroyed the sign. So maybe we could unite to find some way to solve the problem."

"Yeah, but some of your guys cursed us. That's why we smashed the signboard."

"Well, it wasn't right of our people to curse you. But cursing is no excuse for breaking and stealing our signboard, either. Both sides are going to have to recognize their mistakes."

The battle that day was avoided. The Revolutionary Rebel Workers agreed to repair the signboard and to hang it back up, and they recognized that the curses of the Revolutionary Rebels were not really sufficient provocation to induce the theft of the signboard.

But the provocations against the Revolutionary Rebel Commune continued. There was no escaping the fact that the commune had opposed Zhang Chunqiao. The very name of the commune continued to bespeak its opposition to the Shanghai People's Commune. Night and day the headquarters of the Revolutionary Rebel Commune was barraged by strident loudspeakers and the leaders were allowed no surcease from the constant accusations and bickering of their rival factions. The head of one of the branch offices was arrested and accused of being a counterrevolutionary, and when Ni Yuxian heard rumors that other arrests were impending and went to investigate, he barely escaped arrest himself, dodging his would-be captors and tricking them by a quick change of clothes. The Revolutionary Rebel Commune closed its office in the Polish consulate, its leadership, Ni included, going underground and incommunicado in a different part of town, trying against increasing odds to keep the organization going.

In the end, the Shanghai Revolutionary Rebel Commune had to disband. Shanghai was no place for an organization opposed to Zhang Chunqiao.

The standing committee called a memorial meeting for the organization. They were proud of its accomplishments, believing that in the four months of their existence they had genuinely lived up to the high ideals of the Paris Commune. They were proud of the propaganda work they had done, planting a few seeds of the democratic ideal in the minds of countless people of Shanghai, seeds that might germinate to blossom at another, more appropriate time. They were proud that in the midst of so fractious and bitter a struggle as the Cultural Revolution, they had stayed united around their common cause.

The commune staff were given letters of commendation, thanking them for their unstinting contributions.

Then Ni Yuxian and his colleagues visited the city government to inform the Shanghai leadership that the Revolutionary Rebel Commune was calling it quits, its members returning to their own work units. Zhang Chunqiao's idea of a people's commune had not worked either, and the new city government went by the name of the Shanghai Revolutionary Committee.

Then the entire Revolutionary Rebel Commune got together for a final farewell.

When the meeting was over, Ni Yuxian returned to the Shanghai Maritime Academy. He had not been back for months.

The Maritime Academy was in chaos. The student rebellion had expanded. No longer were attacks confined to the bourgeois teachers or to party members accused of taking the capitalist road. The myriad factions and fighting groups that had formed in the fall were deep into battle with each other. Witnessing the violence and finding in it no means of achieving his own political ends, Ni Yuxian for once eschewed the maelstrom.

But his appetite for politics was insatiable. He still had work to do. Political involvement had become for Yuxian what gambling had been for his grandfather Guansheng—an obsession.

Ni had welcomed Mao's attacks on bureaucratism and party privileges. But he still railed against the party chairman's insistence on using class struggle to oppress his enemies, bridled against the denial of freedom to those who did not faithfully pander to the party chairman and his representatives, hated the glorification of the dictatorship of the proletariat and its degradation of democracy. He was disgusted by the insistence, most forcefully expounded by Minister of Defense Lin Biao, now touted as Mao's chosen successor and closest comrade-in-arms, that one of Mao's sentences was worth ten thousand of anyone else's, that all truth was contained in Mao's Little Red Book, that reading anyone else was both pointless and antirevolutionary. Ni was haunted by Lenin's critiques of ultraleftism and of the cult of personality, his thoughts returning constantly to Lenin's writings on socialist democracy and the right of the people to select—and criticize—their leaders. The Russian revolutionary's paeons to the virtues of humility and his praise of the Paris Commune constantly intruded into Yuxian's consciousness. Perhaps Lenin could be used to rein in Mao. For all the adulation of Mao, he was still presented not as fully sui generis but rather as a man above men—simply the greatest Marxist-Leninist of his time. To use Lenin to criticize Mao, to use Lenin to criticize Lin Biao as the leading public adulator of Mao, could hardly be considered, or at least not legitimately, counterrevolutionary. Ni Yuxian decided to publish his own little red book—a little red book of Lenin's quotations, comparable in size and style and layout to Chairman Mao's but directed against the worst excesses of Mao.

It was a daunting and dangerous task.

The thirty-six volumes of Lenin's works in the Maritime Academy library were for "internal circulation" only and officially off-limits to a student like Ni. By virtue of his good relations with one of the librarians, however, he was able to borrow them all, tying them together with string and carting the load home by bike. For weeks he sat closed in his room, poring over Lenin, marking the pages containing potentially worthy quotes—several thousand of them in all—with long strips of paper. The librarian donated stacks of used library cards, and the Revolutionary Committee, with which Yuxian still had influence, agreed to allow a few of the "ox ghosts and snake spirits"—the faculty members they were holding in custody—to participate in the project. Between struggle sessions and street parades and writing their self-confessions, a few of the ox ghosts and snake spirits, delighted with the task, spent several months copying the voluminous quotes onto the library cards. Zhao Yuefang helped, too. Sorting through the cards, reading and rereading, choosing some, discarding others, arranging and rearranging, the outlines of a book began to appear.

The book of Vladimir Lenin's quotations was divided into thirty-three sections, covering topics that ranged from the Communist Party, class and class struggle, socialism and communism, to women, culture, and art—a perfect duplicate in style, size, and organizational content of the Little Red Book of Chairman Mao.

Paper for printing the book was expensive and hard to come by. Ni borrowed the money—a thousand yuan from the Maritime Academy revolutionary rebels opposed to Zhang Chunqiao, another thousand from the Fudan rebels, and yet another from the rebels at East China Normal University. The loans would be repaid with copies of the book. Zhao Yuefang helped him buy twenty reams of cheap wastepaper that he managed to transport home for safekeeping on the back of a cart.

But the most daunting task of all was finding a factory willing to risk printing the Russian revolutionary's quotations. Factories in the city of Shanghai were out of the question. Permission from the municipal revolutionary committee was required to print anything but Chairman Mao, and Zhang Chunqiao and Wang Hongwen were now firmly in control of the city. Ni Yuxian's mission was impossible.

Friends from a Red Guard fighting group opposed to Zhang Chunqiao introduced him to a factory in Jiangsu Province miles outside the city. Ni arrived to negotiate the bargain just after the revolutionary rebels had been driven out and the military had taken control. The book of Lenin's quotations, the new leadership decreed, would have to begin with Lin Biao's picture and a few apt quotations by the defense minister in praise of Mao. Ni Yuxian demurred. The purpose of the book, he took pains to avoid letting them know, was to criticize Lin Biao and the cult of Mao.

His comrades found another factory even further away, and Yuxian submitted his plan to them, arguing that since this was a book of Lenin's quotations, of course it was revolutionary. Suspicious, the factory's propaganda committee began making inquiries. "If the book is so revolutionary and you are from Shanghai," they wondered, "why are you not having it printed there? There are plenty of factories in Shanghai."

A telegram was sent to the Revolutionary Committee in Shanghai. "There is a student from the Maritime Academy named Ni Yuxian who wants us to publish a book of Lenin's quotations. Is this legal? Is this revolutionary?"

The answer came back. "No, this is counterrevolutionary and illegal. We are sending a group to investigate immediately." Ni fled in advance of the coming investigators.

Finally, though, Ni Yuxian did find a place willing to print his book—a small factory in the town of Jiangying along the railway line from Shanghai to Nanjing. He and his comrades spent another month in final preparation, checking and rechecking the quotations, returning to the original source to compare with the handwritten copies, making certain there were no errors. If a book of Lenin's quotations ran the risk of being declared antirevolutionary, a book filled with the leader's misquotes would be more antirevolutionary still.

The trip to Jiangying was fraught with danger. Political order had collapsed along the Yangtze River valley. Four rival Red Guard factions had carved the territory into separate, endlessly warring fiefdoms, their boundaries drawn by crude roadblocks—stones and road dividers strung across the roads. The army had been called in to "support the side of the left," and those factions so honored were being supplied directly with weapons. Rival factions were stealing guns. Warfare was constant, and permission for outsiders to enter was not lightly given.

Traveling in a three-wheeled motorized cart borrowed from the Maritime Academy, accompanied by two drivers whose pay for the dangerous ordeal would be coupons worth a hundred pounds of grain donated by a variety of friends, Yuxian had prepared for the journey well.

Garbed in the overcoat of an officer of the People's Liberation Army, and armed with letters of introduction from a variety of Shanghai's rival revolutionary organizations, Yuxian exuded the self-importance that is a hallmark of Chinese officialdom as their truck was stopped first by one rebel faction and then by another. "Out of the car. Stand at attention. What faction do you belong to?" the adolescent roadblocks would demand when stopping the truck. "Where is your letter of introduction?"

"Get your leader out here quick," Ni Yuxian would respond with pompous disdain. "We're from Shanghai. We're here on important business." The responsible person would arrive, inevitably, Yuxian was convinced, to be impressed by the revolutionary rebel from Shanghai. Just as the Shanghai rebels bowed to the authority of their elder brothers from Beijing, so the Jiangsu rebels looked to Shanghai for leadership. Once having determined that Ni was a revolutionary rebel from Shanghai, that he actually knew Wang Hongwen and had met and talked privately with Ma Tianshui, the Jiangsu rebels would insist that he join them for a banquet, the table laden with dishes of the meat and fish for which the land of milk and honey, as that part of Jiangsu has always been known, was justly famous. Ni Yuxian and his driver colleagues ate well in the two days it took them to traverse the fewer than one hundred miles from Shanghai to Jiangying—five full banquets in all. The Jiangsu rebels never had to pay for their food. Living under a reign of adolescent terror, the restaurant managers and shopkeepers gladly shared all they had in return for a guarantee of safety.

Arriving at the outskirts of Jiangying in the dark of night on the second day, they discovered that Jiangying, too, was divided into factions, and a pitched, armed battle was being fought at the bridge which served as the main entrance to the city. Scores of people had already been killed.

Ni Yuxian negotiated with soldiers from the People's Liberation Army who were observing the battle. "Comrades, comrades, attention please. Attention please," a military voice repeated over the loudspeaker from atop a van after the negotiations were concluded. "Please stop the shooting. Some friends have just arrived from Shanghai. Please given them safe passage."

The guns gradually quieted, and a squad of revolutionary rebel fighters led the three Shanghai men to a middle school that had been converted for the duration of the fighting to a hostel for one of Jiangying's contending rebel factions. The three spent an uncomfortable, sleepless night surrounded by guns and bullets and the hyperactivity of youth fresh from battle. Yuxian's greatest fear was not for his own safety but for the security of the twenty reams of paper. Despite the descent of the Cultural Revolution into armed violence, the most powerful weapon in the rebels' arsenals was still the persuasive power of the written word, and for that all sides needed paper, which was expensive and vexingly hard to come by.

The next morning, when an escort of Jiangying revolutionary rebels succeeded in delivering Ni Yuxian and his two comrades to the factory that would print Lenin's quotations, Yuxian was relieved, indeed delighted, to discover that his assistant in the factory would be a pretty young girl whose captivation with the young rebel from Shanghai was, Yuxian perceived, both immediate and obvious. Indeed, a pattern was developing. The "someone or something" he believed would always save him was almost invariably a pretty young girl. Yuxian took secret pride in the charm he held over the opposite sex and had learned to use that charm to his own political and personal ends.

Through the young girl's uncle, fortuitously also the head of the county revolutionary committee, Yuxian obtained the final permission to print his book, and the young woman agreed to help him in the final collating as the volume came off the press. They worked until the wee hours of the morning, the gunfire and violence that engulfed the town each night lending danger and excitement to their otherwise tedious task, fostering an intimacy that ordinarily might have taken months. One night, very late, when the gunfire began moving in the direction of the very building where they were working just as the young girl began to take her leave, Ni Yuxian easily persuaded her to stay with him for the night. Wrapped in a thick padded coat, her hair tucked up under an army hat in an effort to disguise her sex, the two cuddled together under padded quilts until the gunfire died down and the battle-weary youth began returning to the dormitory. Frightened at being discovered despite their precautions, the young girl sneaked out before dawn and was escorted home by a squad of revolutionary rebels, past the corpses of the town's young that still littered the streets.

In a week, Ni Yuxian's work in Jiangying was complete, ten thousand copies of Lenin's quotations, with his own anonymous introduction, bound in the same type of red plastic that covered the quotations of Mao. The two drivers returned to pick him up, and Yuxian was escorted back to Shanghai through the same treacherous territory. It was early February 1968. The process had taken an entire year.

Once home, he hid the books until he could contact potential buyers, hoping to insure that all ten thousand would be snatched up immediately upon going on sale. Vladimir Lenin's revolutionary credentials aside, Ni Yuxian knew that publication of the book could bring trouble. The more quickly the volumes were out of his hands, the less likely his role in the publication would be discovered. Several thousand of the books were distributed to the rebel groups at Fudan, East China Normal University, and to the Maritime Academy as repayment for the loans. Then the Maritime Academy student broadcasting station announced that a book of Lenin's quotations would go on sale the following day for forty-three Chinese cents a volume—half the price of Mao's. The entire printing was sold out in a matter of hours.

Early in the morning the day after the sale, just time enough for the authorities to have spent a sleepless night perusing its contents in search of its political import, big character posters began appearing all over the academy's campus. The publisher of Lenin's quotations was a counterrevolutionary, opposed to Lin Biao. Lin Biao, after all, had been responsible for the publication of Chairman Mao's little red book, and the chairman's quotations began with an introduction from his closest comrade-in-arms. Anyone with the audacity to publish a book of someone else's quotations without an introduction by Lin, no matter how respected a revolutionary that someone else might be, must be a counterrevolutionary. The Revolutionary Committee at the Maritime Academy asked the Shanghai municipal committee for instructions. In two weeks, the verdict was returned. Of course the publication of Lenin's works was counterrevolutionary. The criminal must be arrested.

At the morning devotions to Chairman Mao which all students were required then to attend, Ni Yuxian was arrested and incarcerated.

The jails had long since filled. Yuxian was locked in a large room on the campus of the Maritime Academy, guarded by one group of seven Red Guards during the day and another group of seven Red Guards at night. Just as the fiercest struggles of the Cultural Revolution took place behind the walls of one's own, self-contained work unit, with people one knew and saw every day, so it was the work unit where most punishments were meted out. Daily, Yuxian was brought before portraits of Chairman Mao and Lin Biao and ordered to bow his head, fall on his knees, and confess his counterrevolutionary crimes. The young man refused to confess. He never believed that he had committed a crime. He was ordered to write a self-confession. He transcribed the poems of Lu Xun instead—Lu Xun the great and acerbic early twentieth-century Chinese author proclaimed by Mao as the greatest revolutionary writer of all times. "These are counterrevolutionary poems," Yuxian's Red Guard captors declared, having been denied the opportunity themselves to read the works of their country's greatest writer. A special struggle session was organized to criticize Ni Yuxian's counterrevolutionary poems. "I didn't write them," Ni confessed at the last minute. "I memorized them. Those are Lu Xun's poems."

Captivity did not rest well with Ni Yuxian. He decided to escape.

• • •

One night in early March, when the winter chill of Shanghai had not yet lifted, he lay tense and still clothed under his cotton padded quilt, waiting until long after the heavy, regular breathing of the guards had assured him they were fast asleep. Slowly, stealthily, he lowered himself from his top bunk next to the window furthest from the door. He waited in stocking feet, shoes in hand, listening still to the steady breathing of his captors, gradually working his way to the door. The opening door was mercifully silent as he turned the knob. The prisoner made his way in darkness to the toilets that stood in a room just adjacent to the stairs. If anyone were to awake, if he were discovered now, he could claim that he was only paying a late-night visit to the bathroom.

The corridor was empty, silent. The whole building was asleep.

His eyes adjusting to the darkness, Yuxian worked his way down the stairs and onto the deserted campus. The walled grounds of the Maritime Academy were small and compact, and Ni Yuxian knew the place well. To attempt to escape through any of the gates would be foolish. The entrances would be guarded around the clock. Behind the dining hall, where waste was incinerated and the trash was collected, he put on his shoes, climbed atop a trash bin, flung himself over the fence, and began running as fast as he could.

In fifteen minutes, he was knocking on the door of Zhao Yuefang's house, whistling the way he often did to announce his arrival. "Just let me stay a few hours. I'll leave before dawn," Yuxian pleaded when Zhao Yuefang's father opened the door. Yuxian had been held incommunicado for nearly a month, and neither family nor friends knew exactly where he was. But he was being openly and vociferously denounced as a counterrevolutionary, and to harbor an escaped counterrevolutionary was to risk imprisonment oneself. Yuxian's future father-in-law was a Communist Party cadre, a loyal, stolid, and uneducated follower of the party's commands, torn between his loyalty to the party he loved and his obligations to the youth who was soon to become part of the family. Frightened, he let Yuxian in.

The representatives from the Maritime Academy banged on the door at five the next morning. "Ni Yuxian escaped during the night," the agitated spokesman blurted out while the escaped prisoner observed the interchange from a small crack in the attic storage space atop the central room of the Zhaos' antiquated peasant house. "Has he come here? Have you seen him? Do you know where he is? He's a counterrevolutionary, you know. If you know anything about him you have to report it. Otherwise you'll be in real trouble. If he's here, you've got to turn him over."

"No, no, I know nothing," Zhao answered, the anxious family gathered around him. "Nothing." The posse's collective vision scanned the room for the runaway, and Ni, still hidden from view, found himself staring straight into the eyes of one of his would-be captors. He watched as the man's gaze shifted to the shoes he had left at the foot of the ladder that led to his hiding place. He held his breath as he felt their eyes meet again.

The men were suspicious, but they did not search further. They left with the harsh admonition that the Zhaos report to the Maritime Academy authorities as soon as they got word of Ni's whereabouts.

"You've got to get out of here immediately," Mr. Zhao demanded when the men disappeared. "It's too dangerous for you to stay."

"Can you loan me a coat?" Yuxian asked Zhao Yuefang's brother-in-law.

"How can I loan you my coat? What if you get caught and they discover I loaned you my coat? Then I would have committed a crime, too."

Zhao Yuefang's father loaned him a coat and a bicycle.

As dawn was breaking over a bitterly cold and rainy Pudong, Ni Yuxian pedaled as fast as he could, head down, cap covering his head, to the ferry that would take him across the river and into Shanghai where he could lose himself in the crowds while he searched for refuge. He called several of his father's oldest and dearest friends, fellow doctors at the medical clinic where Ni Jizhong worked. One of them agreed to hide him in his mother's house. An old lady with no political involvements was hardly likely to raise suspicions.

Yuxian stayed hidden in the old woman's house for weeks, passing the time in solitude by reading and only rarely, in the darkest of night, venturing forth into the streets. He might have stayed there for months had it not been for the decision by the Honggehui to renew their attacks against Zhang Chunqiao.

Well over a year had gone by since the Honggehui had staged the first attack on Zhang Chunqiao. In the interim the group had neither disbanded nor reconciled itself to Zhang's right to lead. Their scouts continued to investigate the Shanghai leader's past, and by mid-April 1968, they were willing to renew their assault. Zhang Chunqiao had been a spy for the Guomindang, they asserted. He would have to be overthrown. Beginning on April 12, big character posters began appearing all over Shanghai attacking Zhang Chunqiao and calling for his immediate downfall.

In the ensuing three days, the anti-Zhang sentiment rose to a feverish pitch, spreading in epidemic proportions. Many who had stood solidly on Zhang Chunqiao's side in late 1966 openly turned against him, and when no word came from the center renewing its support for Zhang, the belief spread that Zhang was on his way out, that Beijing—Mao Zedong himself—supported the rebel attacks.

From the isolation of his hideaway, Ni Yuxian was thrilled to hear the news. If Zhang Chunqiao were overthrown, Ni would be freed. No one could prove he had actually attacked Lin Biao, but there was no denying that he had called for the downfall of Zhang. Besides, he had been incarcerated by the faction loyal to Zhang.

It was around midnight on April 15 when Ni Yuxian returned to Pudong and knocked at the home of a close friend and fellow student from the academy. "Ni Yuxian, what are you doing here?" his friend, frightened, demanded. "Where have you been? You escaped. You can't be here. What will happen to me if they know you're here? You're a counterrevolutionary. I'll be a counterrevolutionary, too. Please, Yuxian, please leave."

"It's okay. You're safe," Yuxian assured his friend. "No one saw me. No one knows I'm here."

"But what if they find out anyway? What will happen to me then? This is too dangerous, Yuxian."

"No, I won't tell. I'm the only one who knows, and I won't tell. Tell me about the calls for the overthrow of Zhang Chunqiao. I want to write my own big character poster."

Ni Yuxian did write a big character poster that night, demanding the overthrow of Zhang Chunqiao. Together with his terrified friend, he sneaked back into the sleeping Maritime Academy campus to post his latest political statement on the wall of the campus dining hall.

For three days the Cultural Revolution committee in Beijing remained silent as the attacks against Zhang Chunqiao continued to spread. From the sidelines, Zhang Chunqiao silently watched the spectacle as his enemies came forth in attack. On the fourth day, Beijing spoke. The attacks against Zhang Chunqiao were counterrevolutionary, traitorous, organized in fact by the Guomindang reactionaries, the proof being not only the open support for the attacks by the Guomindang in Taiwan but also because Chiang Kai-shek's brutal 1927 slaughter of the Communists in Shanghai had begun on April 12, the same date the big character posters against Zhang had begun. The traitors would be called to task.

As the dragnet went out for the arrest of the counterrevolutionaries who had called for the downfall of Zhang, thousands came forth to assert themselves duped by the alleged Guomindang reactionaries. The unfortunate dupes began public and vociferous mea culpas, literally falling on their knees and striking their breasts, kicking and hitting themselves, calling out to be forgiven for their foolishness. The city reeled as thousands were carted off to jail and the executions of Zhang's enemies began.

No one even noticed when Ni Yuxian returned to the Maritime Academy campus in broad daylight for the first time since his escape. Nor was Yuxian surprised to find his former captors among those kneeling on the ground, beating their breasts, alleging they had been duped into turning against Zhang, begging for forgiveness and swearing undying fealty to Mao and Zhang.

Ni confronted one of his kneeling captors. "Oh, so you're back, Ni," the man looked up in surprise, interrupting his self-flagellation.

"You want to lock me up again?" Ni mocked.

"No, no. That's over now. Let's forget it, huh?"

Ni Yuxian was free again.

•   •   •

With the spring of 1968, the Cultural Revolution entered a new stage. Fearsome *luan* had gripped the land, and order was proving impossible to restore. Ordinary rules of human behavior had ceased to have meaning. Enemies were seen lurking in every corner, ready to strike, and violence was glorified as the means to counter all threats. The mass fever was contagious, gripping the ignorant, the bored, and the angry, striking some primal chord reminiscent of nothing so much as the witch trials of the West and on the same continuum with the countless outbursts of mass peasant terror that have dotted China throughout its history. For two years, middle schools and universities had ceased to function as educational institutions, and the millions of students throughout the country who would otherwise have graduated and been assigned employment in those two years had been turned loose instead to their own devices. The Red Guard or revolutionary rebel factions to which many of them belonged continued to glorify themselves as political entities, but political principles had long since evaporated as the various factions turned against each other and the most minor and petty pretexts were conjured up as an excuse for battle. Many of the Red Guard and revolutionary rebel factions were nothing more than armed adolescent gangs defiant now of all adult authority, reveling in their bogus heroism, proclaiming their willingness to die for Chairman Mao, bathed in communal rituals, their behavior imbued with esoteric meanings.

In wonderment and awe, Ni Yuxian had stood on a train platform one day watching the public mourning ritual of one such cultural revolution gang, thousands of defeated Red Guards freshly returned from battle. At the head of the procession were the tens of dead, their comrades holding their blood-soaked bodies aloft for everyone to see. The wounded followed, aided, too, by their fellow rebels, and young female revolutionaries were honored to carry the occasional severed bit of a body—an arm or leg or a hand—as proof of the viciousness of the fight. Behind the wounded were the defeated troops, defiant and high spirited even in retreat. A few carried guns but their primary weapons of war were the razor-sharp sickles originally destined for Castro's sugar fields. They marched in perfect formation—one, two, three, four; one, two, three, four—alternately chanting time and yelling slogans of defiance and revenge. They were proud to have risked their lives and would be willing to risk death again. They believed they were dying for Chairman Mao.

Other youths had become part of gangs that were no less violent but devoid of even the pretense of political principle. The fear of theft, beatings, and murder was palpable. Adolescents had taken control of the cities.

In late 1968 the government began shipping educated youth, as unemployed middle school and university students were known, from the cities to the countryside in what was to become the largest forced migration in the history of humankind. Between 1968 and 1976, when the Cultural Revolution officially came to an end, some 12 to 18 million young people had been transferred to the countryside. While many were shipped to suburban communes on the periphery of their own cities, where food was plentiful and life reasonably comfortable, and where family visits were frequent, millions of others were sent to primitive and impoverished backward areas deep in the mountains or in the far hinterlands near the nation's borders, where life continued untouched by the twentieth century. They went voluntarily, of course, because all mass participation in China is, by official declaration, voluntary, and they went with great fanfare, red flags unfurled, brass bands blaring the music of revolution, a portrait of Chairman Mao inevitably leading the way. Two decades later, having stood the test and safely back in the cities, they would be proud of their capacity to survive, grateful

to the peasants for the help they had been given, wiser for the
lessons that poverty and backwardness had taught, certain that
unlike other city folk who had never experienced hardship or lived
in rural poverty they understood the real China, the 80 percent of
the Chinese people who were peasants. They would accuse the
younger generation—the generation of the eighties and nineties—
of being ignorant and soft.

But in the late 1960s, they went in loneliness and fear and
pain, believing they were being separated from their families,
friends, and homes forever. They passed their days in hunger,
barely able to eke out an existence, relying often on contributions
from home for the bare minimum to stay alive.

In the universities, those who remained behind became subject
to yet another experiment in governance as the Revolutionary
Committee that had once replaced the long since moribund party
committee was replaced by worker, peasant, soldier propaganda
teams. Taking over control and leadership of the university, the
worker-peasant-soldier propaganda teams were responsible for
investigating the whole gamut of internal university affairs—for
determining whether the attacks against the faculty and the party
members were justified in fact, for meting out punishment where
punishment was due, for determining who indeed was fit to lead.

But the worker-peasant-soldier propaganda teams were often
composed of crude and ignorant men, men inclined by tradition
and the influence of the propaganda of revolution to assume that
all intellectuals were evil and to accept as true even the wildest
allegations of corruption within the party. They were prone to use
violence as a means of settling scores. The state of *luan*, Chinese
say, allows evil men to come to the fore, gives evil men control.
That may be true, but more important still is the fact that the mass
hysteria that is also the product of *luan* provides undue opportunities for the ignorant and the rude, imbuing them with a conviction
of their omniscience and omnipotence, further testimony to the
banality of evil.

With the arrival on the college campuses of the worker-
peasant-soldier propaganda teams, the rules of incriminating evidence that had long since been stretched beyond the limits were
stretched further still, and fabrication became commonplace as the
gap between actual misdeed and alleged crime grew incredulously
wide. They launched a campaign to root out what was described
as a clandestine ultraleftist organization called the May 16 Group,

May 16, 1966, being the date the Communist Party Central Committee issued the circular launching the Cultural Revolution. The May 16 Group was alleged to be dedicated to the overthrow of the revered premier Zhou Enlai and was said to have tentacles reaching all over the country. Hundreds of thousands stood accused of crimes they could not possibly have committed, because in fact the May 16 Group had never existed at all.

To the violence and humiliation the students had meted out to their professors, to the attacks against party members alleged to be taking the capitalist road, to the bloody battles between rival revolutionary organizations, and the seething violence of the streets was added the violence of the worker-peasant-soldier propaganda teams—violence against students, intellectuals, and suspect members of the party. People labeled the reign of terror the "red typhoon" as thousands and tens of thousands were rounded up, many to be jailed and charged with the capital offense of counter-revolution, many more to be confined in their work units to undergo investigation. Tortured, or threatened with torture, tens of thousands began confessing to crimes they had never committed. The suicide rate soared.

Those who had not earlier questioned the Cultural Revolution began now to doubt. So adulated was Mao that few indeed seemed to have doubted him, but there were misgivings about a movement that was claiming so many of the country's innocent and good, and the authority of those closest to Mao began to be questioned. What right did Jiang Qing have to lead the Cultural Revolution, to speak for her husband, to determine the fate of so many tens of thousands of people? Through what authority could Zhang Chunqiao determine what was revolutionary and what was not? Why should he remain immune from attack when so many countless others were being purged? For what cause, really, were so many young in China giving their lives and why were they so willing to die? Was the violence really so necessary? When would it end? How many more would die? Would China, when it was over, really be better off?

Ni Yuxian was one who had begun to wonder, not only at the violence and turmoil the Cultural Revolution had unleashed but at the premises upon which it was being fought. Underpinning the Cultural Revolution, its fundamental raison d'être, was the assertion of a covert, decades-long struggle within the party between the capitalist line of one-time chief of state Liu Shaoqi and the socialist line of Party Chairman Mao Zedong. The Communist Party, it was said, was fairly riddled from top to bottom with followers of the capitalist road. Survivors of the Long March, the men who had made the Chinese revolution, the comrades who had stood with Mao on the podium over Tiananmen Square to proclaim the establishment of the People's Republic of China had conspired for years to overthrow socialism in China. But until the Cultural Revolution began, no one Ni Yuxian knew had ever even heard of such a capitalist conspiracy, never imagined such a thing possible, and when the young man questioned those accused of having followed that line—party leaders at his own university, even Shanghai municipal leader Ma Tianshui—they, too, were baffled by the allegations of a capitalist road. The men now being accused of following the capitalist road had believed themselves to be the most loyal and devoted servants of the socialist cause. Repeatedly, too, Yuxian had observed, the people who had most loved Chairman Mao were the first and most viciously accused, and the more they protested their love for the man, the more unrelentingly they were attacked. Zhang Zhixin's tongue would be cut out before the young woman was led to her death, her executioners terrified that in her ardent adulation of the party line and its leader, she would call out "Long live Chairman Mao" just as the guns were fired.

• • •

As his doubts festered and the violence escalated, Ni received an urgent missive from the worker propaganda team at the Shanghai Maritime Academy: Return to the campus immediately to face investigation. If you refuse to return, you will be expelled.

The accusations against Ni were not yet formal. His case was still under investigation. He was suspected of having opposed the "three reds"—the red sun (Chairman Mao), the red People's Liberation Army, and red political authority. The evidence against him was rich indeed and included his reactionary big character poster attacking Zhang Chunqiao, his leadership of a counterrevolutionary organization opposed to Zhang Chunqiao (the Revolutionary Rebel Commune), and his publication of a book of Lenin's quotations that were clearly opposed to Chairman Mao's chosen successor and closest comrade-in-arms, Lin Biao. The fact that when incarcerated he had run away was further proof of his guilt. The innocent do not run away.

The young man was locked up again and assigned to a "study

class." The public adulation of Mao was reaching a frenzy. The morning began with the study class standing together, heads bowed, before a portrait of the party chairman and another of Minister of Defense Lin Biao, everyone in unison shouting their hopes for the party chairman's long life—ten thousand years—and wishing his closest associates—Lin Biao, Mao's wife, Jiang Qing, and her Shanghai confidant Zhang Chunqiao—good health. They sang songs in praise of Mao—the red, red sun in their hearts, the savior of China, and joined hands to dance together in a circle, step together, step together, kick, kick, as further proof of their devotion. They asked the party chairman for their day's instructions before they went off to class where everyone spent the day reading Chairman Mao's Little Red Book and writing his "self-confession." At the end of the day they returned, again to stand in front of the party chairman, to chant the rhythmic hope that he live ten thousand years, to call out for the good health of those closest to him, to sing and to dance again, and then to report on their day's activities—to confess, since they were political suspects and therefore guilty by definition, to their day's mistakes. Ni Yuxian was not accustomed to bowing before anyone. The party chairman's longevity was not a matter of great concern to him. He hated Lin Biao, and time had not erased his aversion to joining hands in the circle dance. He remained unrepentant.

Pressure was brought to bear. One morning, Ni Yuxian and others of his fellow suspects were boarded on the back of a truck under guard and taken through the gates of the Maritime Academy across the river to the huge Jiangwan rifle range in Shanghai. The bleachers in the rifle range were already filled to overflowing when they arrived, more than thirty thousand enthusiasts come to observe the spectacle. Most of the leadership of Shanghai, the new Revolutionary Committee, was there, too, seated at a long table on a platform facing the sports field.

Ni watched as some sixty people, all of them male and most of them young—in their teens and their twenties—were led out like dogs, hands tied behind their backs, thick rope around their necks, to the center of the field. He watched as the sixty youth were lined up and ordered to kneel. Hanging from the neck of each of the youths was a placard, and on the placard, in one or two lines, was written his name, his age, his hometown, and his crime— "counterrevolutionary," "wrote a letter to Chairman Mao criticizing the Cultural Revolution."

Beijing had recently amended the procedures for executions. Until 1968 the authorities in Beijing had to give final approval before the death penalty could be carried out. But as Zhang Chunqiao grew in favor, Mao Zedong himself had granted Zhang ultimate authority over the death penalty in Shanghai. Appeals to Beijing were no longer possible. The decision to invoke the death penalty was not made in court, through formal legal proceedings. Work units or the local police station each might recommend execution, the final decision resting in the hands of the Revolutionary Committee and Zhang Chunqiao's final stamp. The actual crime that provoked the death penalty was often amorphous, as simple as speech that did not conform to the prevailing orthodoxy or was critical of a leader in power. So long as the label "counterrevolutionary" was affixed to the behavior in question, even the most minor of transgressions was punishable by death. Executions in China were meant to be didactic. The chicken, the saying went, was killed to scare the monkey. Public executions of a few miscreants served to remind the vast majority of the price of deviance. Opposing Zhang Chunqiao had become an executionable crime.

The sixty youths kneeling before the crowd at the Jiangwan rifle range were the first to be executed under the new regulations. To mark the occasion, the new leadership in Shanghai had determined that the members of the Revolutionary Committee themselves would pull the trigger, with each member personally executing at least one criminal element. When the criminals had been properly positioned, the Revolutionary Committee rose collectively from their seats, each to be handed a gun. In a line, they walked to the waiting men, each taking his place behind a kneeling prisoner. One by one, they pointed at the base of the prisoner's neck. One by one, as the crowd stood, shouting revolutionary slogans, cheering its approval, wildly enthusiastic, they pulled the trigger. The prisoners toppled forward on the ground. It was a way for the leadership to demonstrate its revolutionary commitment and testify to the seriousness of class struggle.

One of the leaders who participated that day was a woman, Wang Xiuzhen. Wang had once been a worker, and as an activist in the Cultural Revolution, her promotions had been rapid, until finally she was selected to become a member of the municipal revolutionary committee. Wang Xiuzhen had never killed anyone before, had never even fired a gun, and Ni could see, even from a distance, that her hands were trembling as she stood behind her designated counterrevolutionary. She pulled the trigger. The bullet missed its mark, hitting the prisoner's ear. She tried again. The bullet grazed the top of the young man's head. On the third try, the bullet lodged in the young man's shoulder. He writhed in pain, but the wound was hardly lethal.

Zhang Baoling, once the commander in chief of the "attack with words, defend by force" revolutionary rebel organization and now with the Shanghai police, came to Wang Xiuzhen's assistance, taking the woman's gun and holding the barrel directly against the young man's neck. As the gun went off, the blood spurted out in a great gush, covering Wang Xiuzhen's white blouse in blood, bathing her arms in red. Zhang Baoling leaned down and plunged the cleaning rod of the gun deep into the bullet hole, rotating it inside the dead man's neck as the counterrevolutionary toppled to the ground.

When it was over, the sixty criminals lay in heaps like rocks. The stadium swam in their blood. The crowd that had been brought to watch was frightened on the one hand but fascinated with the spectacle. No one seemed to question the justice of executing so many young men for the words they had spoken or the letters they had written or the leaders with whom they had disagreed—or at least no one dared to say. Lu Xun, the great early twentieth-century writer, had written about the culture of executions in China. About the death of the hapless but innocent, would-be but failed revolutionary Ah Q, he wrote, "everyone agreed that the criminals were bad men, the proof being that they had been shot. For if they had not been bad, how could they have been shot?"

Lu Xun had written often about the Chinese love of spectacle, about the pleasure his fellow countrymen seemed to derive from watching executions. He cited the pleasure his countrymen took in watching such an execution at the hands of the Japanese as a reason for his leaving the study of medicine to become a writer. In China, Lu Xun often said, people eat people.

For Ni Yuxian, the horror of the executions he witnessed that day served as yet another turning point in his life. That people could be executed for the words they spoke and the letters they wrote was already egregiously injust. But those who were leading the Cultural Revolution were hypocritical in the extreme, touting the movement as a great democracy, encouraging people to speak out against injustice and against corruption, against party members who violated the socialist ideals, then drawing the line at criticisms against certain party members and the socialist system itself, of Mao and his wife, Lin Biao and Zhang Chunqiao, the inner circle most closely connected to the party chairman. The democracy of the Cultural Revolution was not democracy at all, he concluded, but fascism.

What was equally chilling was how Chinese citizens not only accepted but seemed to revel in the cruelty of the system, how tens of thousands could rise to their feet, apparently enraptured, cheering wildly, enthusiastically as they watched their fellow countrymen—young men full of vitality and youth—executed for speaking their minds. The whole system was corrupt, barbarian, black.

He was torn between a love for the Chinese people, for their simplicity and ingenuousness, on the one hand, and a recognition of a certain primitive propensity to cruelty, a willing complicity to serve the system, the knowledge that the citizenry was nearly as corrupt as its leaders on the other. The society was no different from the society Lu Xun had criticized in the thirties. China was not a society of humans. It was barbaric. Everywhere innocent blood was being spilled.

Then at the height of the red typhoon, in mid-1968, his father, Ni Jizhong, was arrested.

When the worker-peasant-soldier propaganda team had taken over Jizhong's clinic, the doctor was a natural target. Not only had he stood on the side of the rightists and spoken out against party abuse, he had continued to insist that the practice of medicine remain in the hands of doctors even as the fanaticism of the period declared that no task was too great for ordinary people armed with the thought of Mao. In hospitals and clinics throughout the country, doctors were reduced to carrying bedpans or were shipped away altogether as the demonstrably unqualified and incompetent were called upon to assume responsibilities for ministering to the sick. When the Cultural Revolution began in Jizhong's clinic, and its administrators were attacked and overthrown, Jizhong had taken over the administration himself, insuring thereby that patients continued to be seen by doctors and earning for himself the label of rebel. With Ni Jizhong's arrest, the family became distraught, fearing for his life, terrified that if the brutal treatment he was receiving at the hands of his captors did not kill him, his own despair would lead him to suicide. Yuxian was outraged at the injustice. He contemplated killing his father's captors with the BB gun the family kept to shoot birds but was dissuaded from his folly upon being convinced that the murder of his father's captors would result in the execution of his father and himself both.

For the Maritime Academy propaganda team gathering evidence of Ni Yuxian's guilt, the arrest of Ni Jizhong constituted further proof that the accusations against his son were correct. The "theory of the bloodline" was then in vogue, insisting that political proclivity is transmitted through the genes, that counterrevolutionaries beget counterrevolutionaries. "If the father is a hero," the saying went, "the son will be a hero, too. If the father is a reactionary, the son will be nothing but a rotten egg." The charges against Yuxian became formal. For the opposition he had demonstrated against Lin Biao in publishing the book of Lenin's quotations, for his challenge to Zhang Chunqiao while leading the counterrevolutionary Revolutionary Rebel Commune, for his entire spate of clearly counterrevolutionary thought, for being his father's son, he was charged with being a counterrevolutionary.

Ni Yuxian faced a dilemma. Injustice would not be righted until people spoke out against it. To speak out against injustice was to risk imprisonment—or death. But Ni Yuxian rarely chose to remain silent. He determined to write another letter to Chairman Mao.

The letter was constrained. The baby ox of the army had grown up to fear the tiger. Ni Yuxian pointed out that the dictatorship of the proletariat ought not to be the only goal of socialism, that Marx had seen dictatorship as merely an interim stage. Democracy— socialist democracy—was the goal.

He received no reply nor were there apparent repercussions. Later pronouncements from the party even seemed even to grant him his point. The dictatorship of the proletariat became only one of the goals of socialism, not its only one.

• • •

Ni Jizhong's imprisonment lasted only half a year, his release being secured with another political flip-flop and the revelation that the propaganda team that had arrested him had political problems, too, freedom or incarceration, guilt or innocence being decided then not by any abstract principles of justice but by which faction was politically ascendant. Jizhong was not fully exonerated, however. He was forced to spend his days in heavy manual labor on a farm outside the city.

Yuxian and Zhao Yuefang got married right after Jizhong's release, in February 1969. The family's future was precarious, and they needed to inject a little joy, a ray of hope, some indication that life and the family line would continue even if Ni Jizhong or Xu Fengzhen should soon depart the world. The young couple had anticipated their marriage. Within months, Zhao Yuefang delivered a son—the fourth generation in the line of eldest sons. Shortly thereafter, Ni Yuxian was sent to the countryside. In October 1969, following an order by Lin Biao that saw attack by the Soviet Union as imminent, staff and students of China's universities were moved to the countryside. Yuxian accompanied the Maritime Academy to a village in Jiangsu some four hours by train from his home, there to await his fate. He was allowed only monthly visits home.

• • •

It was only three days after one of those periodic visits that the ordinary afternoon quiet of his rural camp was broken with shouts for the whole team to report to an urgent meeting. As the Red Guards and representatives of the propaganda team rushed into his room and tied his hands behind him, Yuxian heard from the shouting outside that the meeting was about him and knew immediately that his fate was about to take a dramatic turn for the worse. The counterrevolutionary Ni Yuxian was being accused of rape and attempted arson and murder.

"You can't treat me like this," Yuxian protested as he was dragged outside and into the open courtyard where the struggle session against him was about to convene. "You're an old party member," he addressed the head of the propaganda team. "I'm a citizen."

"Citizen?" the team head mocked him. "You're no citizen. You're a rapist, you were going to commit murder, arson. Careful, comrades. This guy's crazy. He's some kind of mad dog. Watch out, he may bite."

"And who am I supposed to have raped?" Yuxian shot back in fury.

"Last Sunday, that girl you met. You do admit you met her?" the propaganda team head demanded.

"Yes. Yes, I did meet a girl. I found her purse and I returned it to her."

"You raped her."

Yuxian laughed a sharp, bitter laugh. "How could I have raped her? I was only with her for ten or fifteen minutes—in full public view."

"She says you raped her. She's already reported it."

"No. That can't be. She's not crazy. How could she have said I raped her? The place we drank tea—anyone could have come in. It was right on the street. Anyone in the street could have seen us. This isn't possible." Yuxian was aghast.

After the struggle session announcing his crimes to all assembled, Yuxian was dragged away to a dark, dank room on the outskirts of the village, adjacent to the silo where grain was stored. His captors tied his wrists together and managed to thread the rope through an iron loop in the rafters, suspending their prisoner, feet off the ground, from the ceiling. His captors waited, encouraging him, administering an occasional kick or hit. They knocked out one of his teeth. "Just confess, Ni Yuxian. That's all. Just confess that you're a rapist, that you were out to murder the members of the propaganda team, that you were going to burn down the propaganda team offices." His captors presented him with evidence of his alleged crimes. His bookbag had been found to contain a razor, the alleged murder weapon, and some matches and cotton, with which he had obviously intended to burn down the propaganda team offices. The books in his bag were marked with all manner of counterrevolutionary notes, including a question mark next to a quotation of Chairman Mao. No one but a counterrevolutionary would question Chairman Mao. "Confess, and we'll let you go. Confess and you can be free."

Yuxian would not be tricked. Any one of those crimes was a potentially capital offense. The best he could hope for if convicted was ten to fifteen years in jail. To confess was to write his own death warrant.

Still swinging by his wrists, his arms gradually began pulling loose from their sockets. The pain was first excruciating, then unbearable. "I have to go to the bathroom," he cried out to his captors.

"No."

"Damn you. You're fascists, nothing but a bunch of fascists!"

His guards freed him from the rafters, tying his wrists together behind his waist instead. With a knife at his back, they escorted him to the primitive, open-air shed that served as a latrine, unbuttoning his fly for him, his hands still behind his back, pointing his penis in the direction of the crockery jug submerged in the ground, later to be extracted, its contents used as fertilizer on the peasants' fields. His business done, the guards tucked back his penis, buttoned his fly, and escorted him back to the storage room. Again Ni Yuxian was suspended by his wrists from the rafters. All night he was alternately suspended from the rafters with his feet completely off the ground, or suspended with his feet just touching, on tiptoe, still in excruciating pain but able to bear enough of his own weight that his arms did not pull completely out of their sockets.

The next morning, the head of the Maritime Academy's propaganda team arrived to investigate the circumstances of Ni Yuxian's captivity and to urge the young man to confess. He ordered the guards to release him from the rafters. The prisoner was allowed to sit on the floor, his wrists tied tightly together behind his back.

That night, Yuxian managed to work the bindings loose. The rude hut in which he was being held was made of dirt, its walls of pressed mud and straw already cracked and weakened from too many rains. With his bare hands, he began digging a small hole in the wall, managing to extract chunks of pressed mud by the handful. As he reached through the hole expecting to touch thin air, his hand ran into an immovable obstacle. The water buffaloes' feeding trough ran the length of the hut.

In desperation, hearing the heavy breathing of his captors and knowing they were asleep, he decided to make a more direct break, to open the door and run. As the door opened, pushing outward, the pile of metal wash basins and bowls his captors had stacked in front came smashing down, earsplitting in the noiseless night. His guards were awake immediately, and people came running from all over the camp. Yuxian was kept awake all night from the curses of his captors. The next day, there was another struggle session against the counterrevolutionary rapist and attempted murderer and arsonist who had tried to escape.

Yuxian was moved to an even more miserable hut. No one but his captors knew where he was and no could hear his screams. A book by Marx and Mao Zedong's selected works were his only companions. He was fed irregularly and sporadically, never allowed to wash or change his clothes. He was permitted no exercise. He was allowed two sheets of rough brown toilet paper a day, and his visits to the latrine were infrequent and always took place accompanied by and under the close scrutiny of his guards.

For five months he remained thus in captivity, ever contemplating escape, ever attuned to potential opportunities to run away.

Once, during a visit by representatives of the propaganda team and investigators from the Public Security Bureau, he noticed with a start that a nail had accidentally dropped on the earthen floor. Ni recognized it at once as a potential escape tool, a means of burrowing a hole through the hut that served as his prison. Slowly he sidled over to the vicinity of the nail, all the while engaging the inspectors in lively conversation. His eyes still on the officials, his foot began feeling for the nail, closing over it, then covering it. As his interrogators moved this way and then that, Yuxian remained rooted in place, his foot hard against the nail, swiveling first in one direction and then another, always maintaining eye contact, his body becoming increasingly—and increasingly obviously—out of kilter with the natural distance human beings ordinarily maintain when standing in conversation. At first puzzled and then suspicious, the interrogators wondered out loud why their prisoner was not moving. They discovered the nail. Yuxian resigned himself to the impossibility of running away.

Early in 1970, with the Chinese lunar new year approaching, Ni's manipulations of his captors began moving in another direction. "Spring festival is coming," he implored them, "and I haven't taken a bath in almost five months. How about letting me bathe in honor of the new year? How about a little humanitarianism?"

He tore out the front, blank page of his book by Marx, and wrote a note to one of his father's closest friends. "I have lost my freedom," it read cryptically. "As soon as you receive this take it to your close friend. Tell him to take all necessary precautions." The letter was unsigned but the friend would have no trouble guessing its author. Knowing that the investigation of his case would surely eventuate in his house being searched and that his copious notes and unpublished articles would serve as additional damning evidence against him, Yuxian wanted to make certain his father had burned the incriminating evidence. Using the blank page at the back of the book to make an envelope, Ni used rice to seal the letter. Somehow, on the trip to and from the bathhouse, he would manage to find a way to send it. If all else failed, he would simply drop it on the ground and hope that some charitable soul would find and post it.

The letter was hidden in his sock when the guards who would accompany him to the bathhouse inspected every bit of his clothing, his soap dish, his toothbrush and toothpaste, and the bowl he would take with him. They inspected him again as he undressed before them in the bathhouse, delivering each item of clothing as it was removed, the whole bundle to be put under lock and key for the duration of the bath. Ni managed to secret the letter in his soapbox and extracted the five-cent piece he had hidden in the seam of his fly without his captors noticing. The captors—three of them—undressed, too, and together they entered the steaming baths.

Ten other men were already scrubbing and relaxing in the heated pools. Looking forward themselves to the chance to relax and bathe, certain beyond any shadow of a doubt that their prisoner could not escape—even Ni Yuxian, after all, would not be so bold as to run away in the cold without any clothes—the guards relaxed their vigilance, succumbing to the luxury of a long, slow bath. Ni inched out of earshot.

"Old master," he addressed an elderly worker, a particularly honest and ingenuous-looking man, as the old man was obviously preparing to leave the baths, "I just remembered an urgent letter I have to mail. Do you suppose you could mail it for me? Here's five cents for the stamp." The old man agreed.

Ni was allowing himself to relax luxuriantly in the bath when, minutes later, the voice of the old man came wafting anxiously through the steam. "Where is the comrade who asked me to mail the letter? Comrade, are you still here? I have your change from the stamp." The stamp had only cost four cents and the old man had returned to give Ni Yuxian his penny change.

Ni took a deep breath, and went under water, his back to the old man, praying that between the steam and his fishlike state he would remain invisible. The letter could easily be found were his act discovered, and the price of his defiance would be high. After a few more futile attempts to find his comrade, the old man gave up.

Ni Jizhong did get the message, and the distraught family mobilized all resources they could muster to secure their son's release, appealing one day to the authorities in the Public Security Bureau who were responsible for investigating the case and another day to the propaganda team at the Maritime Academy who insisted on pressing it, as Yuxian, still in captivity, steadfastly refused to admit guilt, his story unwavering.

The razor his captors alleged was the potential murder weapon was what he used to shave, Ni Yuxian argued, and the matches and cotton that were to serve as his means of arson were the natural contents of anyone's bookbag. Who does not carry matches, after all? The cotton had been grown in the production team of which he was a member. Why shouldn't he carry a bit of it around?

And the alleged rape? The story begins, as Ni tells it today, when he was returning by train to the countryside one Sunday morning after visiting his wife and infant son. On the train, he happened upon a purse containing both money and precious rice coupons. "Comrades," he addressed the assembled passengers. "Does this belong to anyone?" The purse was claimed by an exceedingly grateful young woman in her early twenties.

The two struck up a conversation, and when they discovered they were both getting off at the same station, the young woman invited Ni to join her for a cup of tea in her small dormitory room on the ground floor of the factory where she worked. The two chatted amicably for about fifteen minutes, in full view of passersby outside and of the comings and goings of the factory workers. Yuxian still had a long walk to his rural production brigade and arrived in time for the lunch that was served at noon. Back in his own rude quarters, he forgot the incident.

Ni Yuxian did not know as he chatted so pleasantly with the young woman that he had been followed. Such a thorn in the side of the leadership of the academy had he become that they had put him under surveillance, hoping to discover him in an overtly criminal or compromising act. They saw their opportunity in his brief dalliance over tea.

As Ni tells the story, representatives of the Maritime Academy propaganda team obtained a letter of introduction from the Shanghai Revolutionary Committee and used that letter to approach the revolutionary rebels in charge of the young woman's work unit, voicing a suspicion that the young girl had been raped. The young woman was confronted. She denied the charge. She was put in a small room, told that Ni had already confessed the rape, that if she did not recognize it herself she would not be allowed to work. The representatives insisted that she be examined by a doctor. Ni Yuxian, too, was insisting upon such an examination. It would exonerate him of guilt.

The young woman was not a virgin. Not only would disclosure of her fallen state render finding a willing mate nearly impossible, but the investigators assured her that her moral transgressions would be placed on public view. Unless she admitted to Ni

Yuxian's rape, she would lose her job, be accused of being an accomplice and illicit lover to a known counterrevolutionary. Her long plaited pigtail would be cut, and she would be given the *yinyang* haircut, one side shaved, the other cropped short like a boy's. She would be paraded on the streets in utter, abject humiliation, her immorality proclaimed to all the world, the public being invited to spit and to curse and to mock. The young girl was terrified. She had only a few years of primary school education, and her life had already been filled with tragedy. Her mother and all her siblings had died one horrible afternoon when the ferry on which they had been traveling collided with another and all the passengers drowned. As compensation, the government had found her this job, at a time when jobs were precious and exceedingly difficult to find. Exposed as a fallen woman, there would be no more jobs. From such public degradation, there was no coming back. Her life, her future, would be forever destroyed.

She accused Ni Yuxian of rape.

There are details of the story, though, that Ni Yuxian leaves out. His version of truth, like Xu Fengzhen's spinning of family lore, is less precise fact and historical detail than a protestation of his innocence, an avowal of his own worth, a demonstration of how perfidiously he, too, was wronged. Zhao Yuefang remembers—and Ni admits—that the propaganda team in the countryside found a set of condoms in his bookbag, too. Ni argues that he was a married man separated from his family and condoms were hard to find. He bought them when he could. Zhao Yuefang points out that condoms were freely dispensed at the time to all married men. Besides, she had just given birth and was still nursing her infant son. The couple had no need for birth control. Later she would find condoms hidden in the bill of the Lei Feng-style military cap he wore. Wives have a memory for such detail.

Yuxian's obvious flirtations, one must presume, were a source of no small vexation—and a certain perverse curiosity, too—to the rigidly conservative and self-righteous propaganda team. With privacy aggressively nonexistent, lifestyle was no less a matter of public concern than political thought, and the masses who might not find Ni Yuxian's political antics cause for punishment could more easily be convinced of the guilt of a man whose personal morality was so flagrantly in violation of traditional norms. Accusations of personal impropriety often accompany the charges of politically unacceptable thought in China, and allegations on both counts are frequently trumped up.

But rape?

Even the Public Security Bureau charged with investigating the case and prepared to be convinced of the young man's guilt found, after months of interrogation, that the evidence on all three counts was too circumstantial, too riddled with contradictions, to render a verdict of guilt. They washed their hands of the case. Ni was left to the mercy of the Maritime Academy, which continued to insist on his crimes.

The leader of the propaganda team came to visit him. "We all know you want your freedom," he began. "You want to go home. How about just cooperating with us?"

"How am I supposed to cooperate?" Yuxian demanded. "I didn't commit murder, I didn't commit arson, and I didn't commit rape. And never am I going to say that I did. So what do you want me to do?"

"We're going to have a big meeting," the representative replied, laying out his plan to the captive. "It will be a struggle meeting against you, to criticize you for all the things you've been accused of. If your attitude is good, if you recognize your faults, then we'll treat you generously. We can rehabilitate you. But if you argue with the masses when they criticize you, well, the masses will really be angry, you know. They'll demand that you receive a very strict punishment—the very strictest punishment. We can't go against the will of the masses."

"No," Yuxian responded. "I won't say that I did something that I didn't do."

"You don't have to say anything. We just don't want you to argue. When the masses criticize you, just remain silent. How about it? Afterward, when the meeting is over, you can talk to the Public Security Bureau. You can take your case to them. You can tell them that the accusations aren't true. But if you try to argue with the masses at the meeting, they'll be very angry, you know. They'll want to beat you, and we won't be able to intervene. We won't be able to protect you. Even if they beat you to death, we have no way to protect you. Think about it."

"So what do you want me to do?"

"We want you to guarantee that when the masses attack you at this meeting, you won't fight back, you won't respond. Later, you can state your case clearly. And afterward you can have your freedom. You do want your freedom, don't you?"

Ni Yuxian pondered his choice. If he were freed, he could search for sympathetic ears. He could defend himself before the authorities. He could bring his case to the Shanghai municipal revolutionary committee. Failing there he could go to Beijing to petition his case. He could make his case public. In captivity, there was no one to listen. Incarcerated, he stood not a chance. "Yes," he responded, "My freedom is most important. I agree."

The meeting was held the next day, on March 15, 1970. Ni Yuxian could hear the revolutionary music wafting from the auditorium as he was led from his months of solitary confinement to face the crowd. He heard the slogans—"Down with counterrevolutionary Ni Yuxian, down with counterrevolutionary Ni Yuxian"— and the enthusiastic cheering that followed. He stood silent on the stage as the crowd continued to chant in unison demanding his downfall. When the Red Guards who had brought him to the meeting pulled his hair in an effort to get him to bow his head and bend over from the waist, arms behind his back in the jet airplane, he did not, for once, fight back. When one after another of his fellow students and members of the propaganda team made speeches in accusation, declaring him a counterrevolutionary, a rapist, guilty of attempted murder and arson, still he did not respond.

The meeting was about to conclude. The head of the new Revolutionary Committee governing the Maritime Academy spoke. "We have all listened to Ni Yuxian's crimes," he said. The main crime of which Ni stood accused was counterrevolution. But he was also alleged to have made improper advances to women and to have improperly used school funds—some one hundred yuan— in printing the counterrevolutionary edition of Lenin. "We have today in our midst a counterrevolutionary, a man who has been involved in illicit relations with women, a man who improperly used school funds to print a counterrevolutionary book. He does not deserve to remain among us," the revolutionary leader asserted. "We have referred his case to the Shanghai municipal revolutionary committee, and they have reached their verdict. Ni Yuxian is hereby expelled from the Shanghai Maritime Academy."

As Ni's head shot up, the cheers had already begun rising from the crowd. This was the first time he had heard about his expulsion. The whole meeting, his agreement the day before, had all been a conspiracy against him. But he still had friends on the campus, friends who had to be in the audience then. If he were given a chance to speak, an opportunity to respond point by point to the accusations of his captors, his supporters would surely come forth in his defense. The mood of the crowd would turn. He could not be kicked out of the academy. However ostracized he had been in school, despite his dismissal from the military, even after months in captivity, he had never been fully excluded from the circle. He had always had a work unit. He had always had an income. To be expelled from the academy was to be set adrift with no means of survival. He would have no work. There would be no way to obtain work. He would be penniless, hungry. He would starve.

"I demand my right to speak," he began yelling above the din of the crowd. If he did not speak now, if he did not protest his innocence, even his friends might think him guilty. "This is a conspiracy. You deceived me. I am innocent. I didn't do it. Let me speak. I want to answer those accusations. I was tricked."

The rhythmic chanting continued, louder and louder. "Down with Ni Yuxian! Support the decision of the Shanghai municipal revolutionary committee! Down with the rapist! Murderer! Arsonist!" Yuxian was dragged away, still protesting.

"Where is your student I.D.?" one of the university administrators demanded once they were outside. Yuxian extracted his identification from his pocket. The official tore it to shreds. Yuxian was a man without identity.

Two cars escorted him, horns blaring all the way, the twenty minutes from the academy to the local police station just down the street from his home. Big character posters attacking him and announcing the decision of the Shanghai revolutionary committee began appearing along streets long before they actually arrived at the police station, and curious throngs, fellow villagers the young man knew well, had begun lining the streets to witness the counterrevolutionary being delivered to his home. That his case had actually been decided by the Shanghai municipal authorities meant that this was a really important counterrevolutionary, and the village gained a certain perverse honor in the notoriety of one of its members. The crowd grew larger as Ni entered the police station to be registered for the surveillance he would face the rest of his life. The chanting began again, echoing the slogans on the big character posters, the rhythmic cheers of the assembled community at the Maritime Academy: "Down with counterrevolutionary Ni

Yuxian! Support the decision of the Shanghai municipal revolutionary committee! Murderer! Arsonist! Rapist!'' The curious crowd still followed him, the chants continuing, when Ni was delivered to his home, his grim-faced family waiting in shame within.

"You can't imagine what it was like for my family then," his younger brother recalls. "You may say it was only words. But the pressure on us was almost unbearable. My father had already been jailed, was still doing hard labor in the countryside. He was depressed to begin with. We had worked so hard for Ni Yuxian's release. Those slogans, those big character posters were more than the family could bear."

That night while the village slept, Ni Yuxian went out and tore the posters down. The next morning he left early by ferry for the city of Shanghai. He wanted to bring his case to the Shanghai municipal authorities. He wanted to protest his innocence. He went to the offices of the revolutionary committee. No one would listen. Dejected, he returned home. He had no job and there was no chance of finding one. He had to find a way to live.

His life and his work were under the supervision of the local police station. He cleaned public toilets. Early in the morning, before the town was awake, he swept the deserted streets. For more than a year, he "dug tunnels deep." China was on war alert again, not from Taiwan or the United States but from the country's one-time big brother and ally, the Soviet Union. Throughout the country ordinary activities ceased as millions of urban Chinese were mobilized to build underground cities—air-raid shelters where life could be resumed, whole populations intact, in the event of nuclear attack. To this day, hidden from view, the major population centers of China are scored with these elaborate, useless subterranean mazes. The entire population of Beijing, keepers of the maze proudly assert, could disappear underground in three minutes flat.

Ni Yuxian's job was hauling the dirt that was being extracted in such enormous quantities that U.S. intelligence agencies were kept puzzled for months. Confronted with satellite photographs of the mounds of freshly dug earth that were popping up randomly throughout Chinese cities, the experts in interpreting aerial photography searched in vain for a theory that would explain the country's dramatic geological changes.

At night, because the money he received hauling earth was not sufficient to feed his family, and because he was relying heavily on Zhao Yuefang and his parents for mere subsistence, Yuxian offered his services to people arriving by ferry from Shanghai to Pudong too late to catch the last bus home. For ten or twenty cents, he would transport latecomers on the back of his bike.

His work—all of it—was loathsome, backbreaking, and miserably paid. What was most difficult was less the exhausting physical exertion than the public humiliation. To have descended from the exalted status of university student to mere beast of burden was a shame beyond the capacity of most Chinese intellectuals to bear. The whole family lost face, and for Ni Jizhong especially, in all his quiet dignity, that loss was particularly difficult to endure. Zhao Yuefang's parents, simple folk still guided by their blind and naive belief in the infallibility of the party, were also shamefully humiliated by the degradation of their son-in-law. The whole family waged a quiet campaign urging Yuefang to divorce and be done with her ne'er-do-well husband. Relations between the couple were strained.

Many of Ni's old friends refused to see him. Those who had yet to suffer political persecution avoided him because association with a counterrevolutionary might provoke political reprisal. Those already under a cloud of suspicion stayed away for fear of adding fuel to already incendiary political fires. Yuxian was excluded even from the relentless political meetings and study sessions the local residence committee continued to organize to bombard their charges with the latest messages from on high. He was an outcast, a thoroughgoing pariah.

For all its backbreaking tedium, his work was not without respite. As the country settled into a period of quiet political repression and the 1970 campaign to "clean up the class ranks" reached full swing, his frequent visits from the investigative staff of propaganda teams gathering evidence against the growing number of counterrevolutionaries became a major form of entertainment. Many of Ni's friends and acquaintances, and most of the revolutionary rebels who had once been his political allies, were being accused of being counterrevolutionary. Ni was one of the people to whom the propaganda teams naturally turned when gathering proof. Brought to the local police station for questioning, Ni would be urged to reveal the counterrevolutionary conversations and activities of his various friends and allies. "If you report to us fully," they encouraged him, "you'll receive leniency. If you refuse to cooperate, your life will be more difficult still." Ni had no reason to believe the promise of leniency, and threats of further deprivation were utterly without effect. He had already hit rock bottom. There was no lower place to sink. "My friends are all revolutionary," he insisted.

For a while, he found work—no less backbreaking but paying the relatively exalted sum of forty yuan a month—in a nearby factory. When the local constabularies found out, he was ordered back to hauling dirt. Factory work was too prestigious for a counterrevolutionary, forty yuan a month too much to pay. China, after all, was a dictatorship of the proletariat. For a counterrevolutionary to join the ranks of the working class was a travesty of proletarian justice.

Through the degradation and the ostracism, Yuxian's political antennae remained finely tuned. Expelled though he was from the circle, he never felt any guilt, never believed he had done anything wrong. His day of vindication would come.

The first sign of hope appeared on September 16, 1971, in the pages of *Reference News*—the daily compilation of foreign news that was circulated internally for the educated, loyal, and responsible and to which Zhao Yuefang as a middle-school teacher had access. A Soviet official traveling abroad, the newspaper reported, had suddenly been recalled. There had been a secret meeting, topic unspecified, at the airport immediately after the official had disembarked from the plane. Reading between the lines, Ni knew that something important had gone awry.

Suddenly all reference to Minister of Defense Lin Biao—Chairman Mao's closest comrade-in-arms and the party chairman's designated successor, the man who had claimed that one of Mao's words was worth ten thousand of anyone else's, the man to whom all China daily wished good health immediately after crying out their hope for Chairman Mao's long life—ceased. At the Ninth Congress of the Chinese Communist Party in April 1969, Mao had offered to relinquish his role as party chairman to his new political confidant. Lin Biao had graciously demurred, arguing that China could not do without the leadership of the greatest, most glorious, most correct Marxist-Leninist of his day, that even he, Lin Biao, owed his life to the great Chairman Mao.

After four days with nary a mention of Lin Biao's name, even the most casual of political observers surmised that something was amiss. The streets buzzed with rumor, but there were no hard facts. Yuxian was overcome with curiosity. Weeks went by. Autumn had come, and the weather was turning chilly. He had to go to Beijing.

Ni Jizhong loaned him a few yuan for food, but the cost of the one hundred-kuai round-trip train ticket was well beyond his reach. Yuxian took a bath and combed his hair and polished his only pair of black leather shoes. He washed the white artificial collar that fit neatly under the neck of his cadre's uniform. He borrowed the black plastic bag that was one of the distinguishing features of middle-ranking officials and covered his costume, despite the weather, with an army coat. Thus garbed, stomach puffed out and chin held up to just the right point of self-assurance, he arrived at the train station looking unmistakably like the Chinese bureaucrat he pretended to be.

Entry to the station was closely controlled. Friends and relatives of travelers were required to purchase a pass in order to bid farewell from the platform, and ticketholders were limited to two people sending them off. The comrade at the head of the line barely blinked when the young cadre so politely asked if he would kindly purchase an extra platform ticket for him. The line was long and even young cadres could not be expected to wait. The train attendants did not even think to check his ticket when the young cadre so officiously boarded the train.

They were beyond Suzhou, more than an hour outside Shanghai, when the three railway attendants entered the car, locked the bathroom doors, and demanded to inspect the passengers' tickets. As the train attendants worked their way down the aisle, Yuxian managed to stand with them and just to their rear. Garbed as they all were in army greatcoats, the passengers thought he was one of the train attendants and the absentminded attendants failed to notice the young man who was so cleverly managing to stay just out of line of their sight.

The train had reached Tianjin, only two hours outside of Beijing, before the attendants bothered to check the passengers' tickets again. Seeing them come, Yuxian walked forward through the cars teeming with cramped and dirty humanity until he came to a locked carriage. This car had curtains in the windows and gaudy artificial plastic flowers on the tables, and smokers were expected to use ashtrays instead of the floor. The seats were cushioned rather than hard and covered with white antimacassars, and the passengers would know better than to litter the floor with sunflower seeds and chicken bones. It was the carriage reserved for high officials and foreigners, and the car that day was empty. No high officials or foreigners were traveling from Shanghai to Beijing. Ni Yuxian easily picked open the lock. Sleep came quickly in the large soft seat.

Arriving in Beijing and facing the final check on his ticket, Yuxian searched for the personnel exit he knew would have to exist. He found the employee's cafeteria. ''I'm looking for Xiao Zhang,'' he explained to the attendant on duty, certain that among the hundreds of railway employees more than one would have to be named Zhang. The distinguishing feature of Chinese names is not the surname, of which there are few and Zhang is among the most frequent, but the given name. "He's already left for the day," the cafeteria worker replied without suspicion. Exiting by another door, Yuxian found himself suddenly, safely, on the streets of Beijing.

His luggage was still on the train. "Comrade," he implored the ticket inspector after he had worked his way back to the main entrance, "I left my bag on the train that just arrived from Shanghai. Is it possible to retrieve it?" Yuxian's bag was returned.

The streets of Beijing were still dotted with portraits of Lin Biao. Nothing about the city had changed. But the alleys were brimming with gossip. Lin Biao was dead.

Months would pass before the official story of Lin Biao's demise had been sufficiently perfected to present to the Chinese public. When Nixon and his entourage made their historic visit to China in February 1972, the word was still not out. The story that finally emerged alleges that Chairman Mao's closest comrade-in-arms, the man most trusted by the party chairman, the man who had proclaimed Mao the greatest Marxist-Leninist of his time and the indispensable leader of China, had turned against the man he had made a cult. Lin Biao had plotted the overthrow and assassination of Chairman Mao. The plot had been discovered on the very verge of its implementation. Lin Biao, realizing that he had been discovered, had commandeered a plane, his wife and son on board, and fled to the Soviet Union. The plane crashed (mysteriously, some have imagined) in Soviet-controlled Outer Mongolia. Everyone on board was killed.

Even on the Chinese political roller coaster, with all its loop-the-loops and heart-stopping, hair-raising surprises, Lin Biao's treachery was news of truly earth-shaking proportions. If Mao Zedong were really the great, the glorious, the infallibly correct leader of the Communist Party of China, then how could he have been so scandalously duped by his very closest comrade-in-arms? If the Communist Party itself was really so correct, why had it been riddled from the very beginning with so many traitors to the cause—Chen Duxiu, Qu Qiubai, Li Lisan, Wang Ming, Liu Shaoqi—and now Lin Biao? At best Mao was muddle-headed and stupid to have been blind to the perfidy engulfing him. At worst the Communist Party was not the party of the people at all but a tool for the power struggles among its elite. Whether Mao was a megalomaniac or merely muddle-headed, his prestige had suffered a cataclysmic blow.

With Lin Biao soon to be revealed as political criminal number one, Yuxian decided the time was ripe to test his own political waters. One of his crimes had been to oppose Lin Biao. With Lin gone, revealed as an arch criminal, perhaps Ni's time for vindication was finally at hand. He began joining the bedraggled and impoverished group of petitioners from all over the country who gathered each day before the office of the State Council on Beijing's Taiping Road to press their cases before the highest levels of government. Waiting by day with the petitioners, listening to endless stories of justice tragically miscarried, he earned a bit of pocket money helping the illiterates write out their tales of woe. By night, he slept in the teeming waiting room of the train station, having easily convinced one or another traveler to purchase the platform ticket that gained him entry. When the attendants came through each evening after eleven, sweeping the premises clean of miscreants who were using the waiting room in lieu of a hotel, Yuxian's cadre disguise was sufficiently convincing that his presence was never questioned.

When his money ran out after two weeks in the nation's capital, he sneaked aboard a train bound for home, in despair for his country's future and frustrated that his efforts at vindication had garnered only a letter to the municipal authorities in Shanghai passing responsibility for his case over to them. He was unperturbed when the train attendants finally discovered that he was traveling for free. There was no other choice but to send him back to Shanghai.

Once home, his efforts were concentrated on gathering the documentation that would finally convince the surly and sullen bureaucrats who reluctantly, belligerently, handled allegations of miscarriages of justice that his expulsion from the circle was unfair. He found the father of the young girl who had accused him of rape, and while the father would not permit his daughter to meet with Ni Yuxian, the young girl finally confessed the truth. Recognizing how grievously the young man had been wronged, the father wrote a letter on Ni's behalf, detailing the threats and the fears that had resulted in the false accusation. That letter and the book of Lenin's quotations were Ni Yuxian's most persuasive displays of innocence, for the quotations were proof of his political perspicacity, evidence that he had long been opposed to Lin Biao, having early seen through his false facade.

The Shanghai authorities were not kindly disposed to the case of Ni Yuxian, for while he had opposed Lin Biao, he had also opposed Zhang Chunqiao, and Zhang was then soaring to the very height of his political power. But Yuxian made an avocation of joining the hundreds of petitioners who came to press their cases each day. Meeting with others who had been no less grievously abused served to overcome his isolation and to fuel the fires of his anger. Righteous indignation had become a major source of meaning in his life. He enjoyed his fights with the arrogant bureaucrats in charge. Helping the aggrieved victims gather evidence and write their letters to the authorities also gave him small opportunities to use his gift of persuasion, to hone his writing skills, to make use of some of the prodigious intellectual talents the government had otherwise so wantonly ignored. His frequent visits to the authorities and the ensuing outburst of self-righteous anger were a way of maintaining his sanity in the face of a world that had lost all reason. Among the petitioners were many whose mental balance had disintegrated in the face of their tribulations.

One daily petitioner to the same office was a woman in her forties who continued to dress in the long but now tattered robes and black cloth Mary Jane shoes of prerevolutionary China and who had at first glance the look of a woman of considerable traditional upbringing and culture. But the woman stood too frequently before the portrait of Chairman Mao, eyes all aglow, her little red book held high, rapturously, repeatedly, wishing the party chairman long life. Even after Lin Biao died and everyone knew he was dead, she never forgot to include Lin Biao in her salutations of good health. As each new petitioner arrived, she greeted them individually with a rousing cheer of "Long Live Chairman Mao!" "The Best of Health to Vice-Chairman Lin Biao!" Even enveloped in their own personal miseries, the other petitioners still laughed at the behavior of this crazy woman who so loved Chairman Mao and continued to wish Lin Biao good health long after he was dead.

During the early stages of the Cultural Revolution, the woman's only son had been beaten to death during a struggle session against him. Then her husband had been executed, convicted of being a counterrevolutionary. It was after the death of her son and her husband, alone in the world, that her obsession with the longevity of the chairman and the good health of his closest comrade-in-arms had begun.

The male petitioners were additionally greeted by a young woman, still not yet twenty years old, her *yinyang* haircut, one side shaved and the other cut short, a visible symbol of her official pariah status. "Uncle," she would begin hopefully, imploring, "Give me one *kuai*, and I'll go to bed with you. One *kuai* and I'll go to bed." The girl laughed a lot but with vacant eyes when offering her body to men. Her mother, standing nearby, would tell the story to those who wanted to hear.

Her daughter had been a middle school student with excellent grades when the Cultural Revolution began, but at the age of sixteen, with Chairman Mao's call for educated youth to go to the countryside to learn from the poor and lower middle peasants, she had been sent to the rural northeast, accompanied en route by certain male members of the middle school's propaganda team. She had been raped by one member of the team and in terror and incomprehension had bolted, running away and staying alive by begging for food on the road. She had been captured and sent to her original rural destination where again she was the object of the cadres' repeated sexual abuse. They paid her one kuai to sleep with them. Then she began openly offering her services, one *kuai* a tryst. For selling her body she was accused by the same officials who had raped her of being a hooligan and a whore, was struggled against and given the *yinyang* haircut. It was then she ran away again, wending her way back to Shanghai.

Somewhere en route, the young girl's brain had first constricted and then shut down. The only words she could utter were, "Uncle, give me one *kuai* and I'll sleep with you." Her mother hoped there was medical treatment for such a case as her daughter's, and she wanted the Shanghai Revolutionary Committee to take responsibility for finding the young girl help. Ni Yuxian assisted the mother in writing letters on the young girl's behalf, but the Revolutionary Committee absolved itself of the obligation to help. "Take her home," they insisted. "There's nothing that can be done."

Yuxian mingled in fascination with the petitioners, learning their stories and writing them down. Someday, he thought, he would write a book.

One afternoon, coming out of the government building after a day with the petitioners, Yuxian reached the sidewalk just in time to meet an official limousine—clearly the car of a high-ranking official—pulling to a stop in front. He watched as the official got out. The recognition was mutual and instantaneous. "Xiao Ni, what are you doing here? What kind of work are you doing now?" It was Colonel Sheng, the ranking political instructor from the army, the man who had taken such an interest in the bright young soldier, the one who had betrayed him by reporting to his files. In the political fallout following the Lin Biao affair, Colonel Sheng had landed clean. He had just received a major promotion.

"I have no work," Yuxian responded.

"No work? You're in trouble, aren't you, Xiao Ni? You remember what I told you in the army? Yes, you do remember. I know you remember. I was right, wasn't I, when I told you that no matter how capable a person you might be, no matter how intelligent, if you leave the party you just don't have a chance in this society?

"Look, Xiao Ni, I want to help you. Here, here are some rice coupons. I can't talk to you right now, but come to see me. We can talk. I'll help you find a job."

Yuxian never did go to see Colonel Sheng. The self-congratulatory tone with which his one-time political instructor reminded Ni of how correctly his present plight had been predicted was more than he could stomach. But he did send his materials to the official. Within a month, the officious bureaucrat charged with holding petitioners at bay, the man whose intransigence had extended for well over a year, suddenly became solicitous. "We can solve your problem, Comrade Ni," he announced cheerfully one day. "We'll get you work. Where is your *hukou*—your household registration?"

The problem of Ni's household registration was intractible, even for so high-ranking an official as Sheng. Ni Yuxian would never work in the city of Shanghai. He was condemned forever to live and work in the rural county of which Yangsi was one of the towns. The Shanghai Revolutionary Committee did find him work, however—lowly work with miserable pay of only thirty-three yuan a month—in a factory only a half-hour bike ride from his home.

Fate had come full circle. When Yuxian had left the electrical parts factory some seven years before, celebrating his admission to the university by playing the harmonica as his bike was dragged down the street by a tractor, he thought he had tricked the gods, that he would never be forced to return to Yanggao Road. In October 1972 he returned to the spot he thought he had left forever.

The new factory to which he was assigned was also on Yanggao Road.

Ni Yuxian made a vow before he returned. This time, he promised himself, his behavior would be different. Uncomfortable though he was with the knowledge, Ni knew that Colonel Sheng was right. Ni was a misfit in his own society. He had been expelled from every institution with which he had ever been affiliated. He was grateful to Sheng for giving him one more chance. The work would be the lowliest of the low, and his talents and intelligence would continue to be tragically wasted, but at least he could reclaim a place, however humble, in Chinese society. He had a family to support and responsibility for their welfare. This time he would avoid the disturbances that invariably got him into trouble.

The vow had all the force of the ones Guansheng used to make when he had gambled and lost. The perennial conflict with authority that had begun the moment he walked through the gates of primary school quickly reasserted itself in the factory.

• • •

Hard work was not one of the virtues of the workers in Ni's new factory. One unintended consequence of Communist Party control of the Chinese factory has been the dissipation of the work ethic for which the country was once justly renowned. The collapse started at the top. The degree of authority exercised by the party over the factory and its workers was inversely correlated with the time and effort the leadership spent at work. Arriving each morning by car, ranking party members were in the habit of retiring immediately to their comfortable offices to peruse their newspapers, sip green tea served by carefully chosen pretty young secretaries, and place a few phone calls in peace. Lunch was ordinarily a social affair at factory expense, and in the afternoon, because official meetings were frequent and always elsewhere, the leadership often left the factory, not to return until the following morning.

The life of the four hundred workers was considerably less relaxed, but the hierarchy was complex, the struggles for advantage well fought. Office work, undemanding and high in status, ranked top on the list of workers' preferences, and the factory was therefore generously staffed with clerical help, further ensuring that the burdens of the clerical staff were light. The job of driver was also greatly prized, not only for the small number of hours actually worked but also for the sheer style of being in control of a motor vehicle and the freedom and mobility a car or truck afforded. For rides proffered to acquaintances and friends, drivers were kept generously supplied with the finest in cigarettes and liquor and partook of more banquets than anyone but the party elite.

The factory doctor also held a particularly exalted post. The Chinese worker spends six days a week on the job and vacations are limited to several national holidays a year. The factory doctor has power to grant or deny sick leave, and decisions can be made less for reasons of health than for gifts proffered or sexual favors granted. The factory doctor also determines whether a particular medical case is worthy of more specialized treatment and at which level of the decidedly hierarchical structure of the city's hospitals. No patient, however sick, receives further treatment without the doctor's recommendation. In the workaday life of colds and flus and chronic aches and pains, the doctor decides whether to prescribe modern antibiotics or traditional Chinese herbs, and a patient being treated traditionally faces the further disadvantage of a prescription of bitter rather than the preferred sweet herbal cures. The factory doctor is thus respected less for his medical skills than for the power he holds over his patients. The doctor in Ni's factory had long since been corrupted.

The factory's six workshops differed greatly in the demands made on the workers, and competition for position was intense. Because the supply of energy had yet to meet the demands of industrializing Pudong, the factory worked, ostensibly at least, in three shifts around the clock. Those on the morning shift, when the electricity was often turned off and workers were thereby permitted to emulate their leaders by reading newspapers, indulging in tea, and spreading the latest gossip, led considerably more leisurely lives than those who worked at night when the electricity was invariably on and workers were expected to work. With no supplemental pay bonus to compensate for the hours and the work, few people, had they been free to choose, would have opted for the shift that ran from eleven at night to eight the next morning.

It was the party secretary who assigned the shifts and made the work assignments, and merit was only incidental in his decisions. Competition for position took the form of cultivating a relationship with the party secretary and then currying favor with him. After a certain period of obsequious obedience, personal flattery, and a few well-timed gifts, the opportunity-seeker would present his request for a better position to the leader. The forthright and honest, those incapable of opportunism, were at a decided disadvantage. The good and sincere, no matter how skilled or appropriate to a particular position, often remained at the bottom of the heap. The authority of the party within the factory, as everywhere else in society, was absolute, arbitrary, and, Ni Yuxian was convinced, unjust.

• • •

Yuxian's first confrontation occurred after two of his fellow workers were docked in pay.

The sole advantage to the night shift rested with the fact that the party leaders preferred their own comfort to the possibly greater efficiency that might result were the efforts of their workers to be fully supervised around the clock, and hence ordinarily only appeared in the factory during the day. Sporadically, however, the workers were surprised with a nighttime inspection tour. On one such inspection tour, two men in Ni Yuxian's workshop were discovered sound asleep. When the two were reprimanded and told they would be docked in pay, they protested that because their assigned chores were already complete, production had not been harmed by their nocturnal snooze—a defense given credibility by the irrational allocation of labor in Chinese factories and the widespread featherbedding that results from the overloading of factories with workers.

Not long after the nocturnal inspection tour, in keeping with the allegedly democratic spirit the Cultural Revolution had wrought, the party leadership held an "opinion meeting," ostensibly to offer workers the opportunity to raise suggestions and speak their minds. Opinion meetings, in fact, were carefully orchestrated affairs, more on the order of well-rehearsed plays than spontaneous free-for-alls, the party leadership having designated the speakers and coached them in advance on acceptable criticisms and suggestions. The workers were well-socialized into the rules of the game. Opinion meetings were a time to remain silent.

At the end of this particular opinion meeting, when the script called for the party leader to ask whether anyone else had opinions to raise and the workers all knew to remain silent, the leader was naturally quite surprised and not a little irritated to confront an unforeseen departure from the plan. A hand had shot up. "Yes, I have something to say," he heard a voice call out. Ni Yuxian stood up.

"Good, that's fine," the party leader responded curtly. "Let's talk about it later, in private, after the meeting, huh?"

"No, I want to talk about it now, publicly," Yuxian insisted. "I want to talk about the two workers who were docked in pay. I think that docking their pay is unfair. It wasn't the workers' decision to turn off the electricity so we have to work at night. None of us have volunteered to come to work at night. If the workers want to work at night, if they're willing to sacrifice their own benefit for the good of the state, that's okay. But these workers who work so hard at night don't get any increase in wages, they get no better welfare benefits as a result of their sacrifice. And you cadres don't even bother to come to this shift. You cadres only come to work during the daytime, for all your meetings. You don't even see how hard the workers usually work. They get tired working at night. So it's not fair to reduce their wages. Our wages are already low enough. These men have families to raise. You reduce their wages and that's a pair of shoes their kids don't have. It's food their kids won't be able to eat. Their income is already so low, what do you think they're supposed to do? How are they supposed to live? You leaders are supposed to be concerned about the workers, you're supposed to help them overcome their difficulties, not add to them."

The workers listened rapt to the deviant in their midst as their leaders lost more and more face. Workers like Ni Yuxian were a genuine rarity in Chinese factories. Relations between workers and the party leadership were invariably strained, and workers cursed their leaders ruthlessly and callously and colorfully behind their backs, but their open greetings were invariably tendered with all due subservience, and outright rebellion was not only unheard of but close to unthinkable. No one had ever defended them like Ni.

Ni Yuxian could not be fired for his trangression. Another contribution to the decline of the work ethic was the near impossibility under Chinese socialism of dismissing even the most recalcitrant of employees. Instead, he was transferred to another workshop—the most undesirable and dangerous of them all, the one where the furnaces were housed, the heat intense, and the workers at the end of their shifts were dirty, sweaty, tired, and in need of nothing so much as a bath.

Yuxian's arrival at the workshop coincided with a change in the rules.

For years, the factory had provided the workers with a close approximation of a daily bath, supplying them each month with one bar of rationed, hard-to-find and therefore precious soap and allowing them in the last half hour of their shifts to fill their wash basins with hot water.

The new rules stipulated that every two workers would share one bar of soap a month and that the workers could not bathe until they were actually off duty.

There was an additional catch. The hot water would be turned off before the end of the shift. They would bathe in the cold.

The workers were furious at the decision, cursing the leadership vehemently behind their backs, silently obsequious in their presence. When a few workers privately, politely tried to raise the question with their superiors, they were rebuffed. "Workers aren't supposed to have demands of their own," was the response.

Yuxian set about organizing them.

Their demands were simple—one bar of soap per person per month and the right to hot water at the end of their shift. The workshop met and selected a twenty-year-old worker to represent their demands before the leadership.

"What is this, some kind of workers' rebellion?" the leadership exclaimed in exasperation when confronted with the workers' demands. "The Cultural Revolution is over. If you don't like not having soap and not getting to bathe, just transfer to some other workshop."

The workers reconvened. "This is supposed to be a socialist society," Yuxian educated them, "and in a socialist society, the factory is supposed to belong to the workers. The workers are supposed to be the masters. But look how much money we make. Our wages are as low as they can be, and we have no right to demand a raise. Look at our situation now. All we have done is to make the smallest of requests—a bar of soap, a bath. If they won't even listen to such a small request, what kind of masters are we, really? We have to unite. We have to take action. Let's ask our leaders for another meeting. If they don't agree to our demands, I suggest we just refuse to work."

"But that would be a strike," the lone party loyalist in the workshop protested. "That would be dangerous. Our socialist society doesn't allow us to go on strike." Word spread, too, that Ni Yuxian himself was dangerous, a reactionary, that the reason he had been sent to the factory was that he had been kicked out of his university for counterrevolutionary activity, for rape, for attempted murder and arson. The workers were warned to stay clear of this dangerous man.

The comrades gathered again. "They're trying to split us, can't you see?" Ni admonished them. "All we're asking for is a bar of soap and the right to take a bath. We shouldn't be afraid because they say so-and-so is bad. We have to stick together."

The majority of the workshop did support Ni, and the workers went out on strike. After three days, the leadership caved in—one bar of soap a month, hot water every day.

Ni Yuxian was transferred to another workshop.

For Ni Yuxian, the issue of the soap and hot water was symptomatic of much that was wrong with his country. Even the right to bathe was in the party's hands and hence a political question. Leaders within the factory stood at the lowest level of the party hierarchy, and their absolute authority, the resources they controlled, were small. But because of the all-encompassing nature of the Chinese work unit, because China is a society of scarcity, the power that leadership exercised over individual lives was enormous. With soap rationed, there was no way for the workers to obtain it on their own, and houses in Pudong had neither bathing facilities nor hot water. Without permission from the party, the workers could not bathe.

Yuxian believed he saw the issues more clearly than others. His fellow workers were frustrated and angry, and there was a pervasive underlying hostility to the leadership, but most workers were incapable of abstracting themselves from their personal situations and analyzing the system from an objective perspective. There was much that was baffling to Ni Yuxian, too, and his own anger and frustration often led him to rash and self-defeating behavior. The analytic tools he brought to the situation were limited indeed, but his analytic capacities far exceeded most of those around him. He wanted to make a political contribution, to provide his fellow countrymen with an analysis of the ills of their society, to suggest alternatives to their oppression. Ni Yuxian saw his role as that of teacher, educating young people in the basic principles of democracy, gradually spreading the democratic word in preparation for a massive democratic movement he knew some day would come.

For the systematic critique he intended to make, he first needed to educate himself, and to educate himself, he needed interaction with others to sharpen his still inchoate thoughts. The development of his ideas still depended on exchanges with other people to test and weigh his thoughts. But in the repressive atmosphere of China, sharing such unorthodox thoughts was dangerous, and the restrictions against expressing one's ideas, testing one's political opinions, was, for Ni Yuxian, the most difficult aspect of that repression.

Within the factory were a few young workers—bright and intelligent middle school graduates whose bourgeois class backgrounds had prevented them from going on to college—who shared many of Ni's political concerns and who were willing to risk meeting to exchange ideas. Periodically, they would gather together in a workshop under the pretense of studying the *People's Daily*, lock the door, and share their critiques of the socialist system. Ni was still most concerned with the lack of democracy in China. "When socialism exists without democracy," he would tell them, "that socialism is false. Socialism without democracy is even worse than capitalism, darker and more inhumane. The Communist Party criticizes the West for its 'bourgeois' rights but bourgeois rights are still better than no rights at all. Without human rights, this so-called 'socialism' just degenerates into socialist fascism. The power of the Communist Party under this so-called socialism is far greater, far more corrupt, than the power of the bourgeoisie under capitalism. They call their expropriation of private property 'ownership by the whole people' but this is just a joke, another mockery of reality. Who controls property? The Communist Party, not the 'people.' The Communist Party controls everything—factory and land, worker and peasant, everything and everybody. The oppression of the Chinese people today far exceeds the exploitation of workers under capitalism. Even under the most oppressive of capitalist systems workers still retain a realm of choice; some arenas of freedom continue to exist. But the realm of freedom has contracted under socialism to nearly nothing. 'Feudal fascist socialism' is what this political system is."

Over time, this small group of relatively educated workers shared their ideas with others, so many within the factory came to know something of Ni Yuxian's political thought.

• • •

Ni called, too, upon some of the contacts he had made during the Cultural Revolution, and three of those young men—Guang Ming, Huang Xixi, and Jin Renjun—became his closest, most trusted political allies. They were an unlikely assortment of comrades, united largely by a common political anger and their shared experience of political repression.

Tall, rough-hewn, and dashingly handsome, exuding the mystery and intrigue of a high-class gangster, Guang Ming had been a middle school student in Wusong when the Cultural Revolution began and a fanatic believer in Mao Zedong, becoming the head of one of the most militant of the Red Guard organizations. When the political tide turned and Guang Ming's organization was declared counterrevolutionary, the disillusioned teenager had spent half a year in jail, emerging skeptical about everything, cynical, and full of doubt. After meeting Ni Yuxian, Guang Ming was so taken with his new friend's interpretations of Chinese society that Ni became his new political hero, and Guang Ming hitched himself to that hero like a feudal knight to his lord. Whatever Ni Yuxian said was right.

Huang Xixi's thick-lensed, red, square-rimmed glasses hid perpetually swollen eyes, and his manner of quiet reticence lent him the look of an intellectual. His mother had been a Communist Party cadre and during the Japanese invasion had been a leader in the underground resistance. Huang Xixi, too, had been a believer in Mao Zedong. But during the Cultural Revolution, his mother came under attack and had committed suicide. Huang Xixi was irrevocably changed. When Lin Biao turned against Mao, Xixi lost all hope in the party chairman and came to rely on Ni Yuxian to analyze the world that had long filled him with frustration and anger.

Jin Renjun, intense and chain-smoking, his hands and teeth stained with years of nicotine, was more independent-minded and critical than the rest. His father, an intellectual, had been declared a counterrevolutionary in the early 1950s and had spent decades in the Chinese gulag. Jin, like Ni, had grown up excluded from the circle, disillusioned and restless. He wanted to do something big.

Together the four formed a political group with Ni Yuxian as their indisputable leader. Through these three friends, Ni Yuxian began sharing his ideas with other young workers in far-flung parts of the city. One member of the group would introduce him to a third new party, whom Ni would then meet one on one. With only two people participating, talk could be freer and more frank, the issues discussed more deeply with less fear of later betrayal.

Even in China, the rules of evidence required a third person to corroborate accusations. Later allegations could always be denied when it was one man's word against the next. They used false names or no names at all or surnames without given names, and they met in parks or small restaurants—only rarely in homes. Only Yuxian's three most trusted comrades knew his full name and address.

When Ni worked the afternoon shift that ran from two in the afternoon till eleven at night and thus had the mornings free, he often joined the petitioners at the Shanghai municipal government offices, mingling among them to hear their stories and to share his own political concerns and in the still undiminished hope that someday his own political vindication would come. If his opposition to Zhang Chunqiao prohibited him from being fully rehabilitated, he wanted at least nominal recognition that he had been wronged, and was attempting to sue the Maritime Academy for the years of back pay they continued to withhold.

It was there, among the petitioners, in 1974, that he met Kajia.

"Your father committed suicide," Yuxian heard the bureaucrat yelling the first time he noticed the young woman, her long plaited pigtail reaching all the way to her waist. "He's a counterrevolutionary. You're asking me to rehabilitate a counterrevolutionary. It's like trying to rehabilitate Liu Shaoqi. What do you think you're doing?"

"I don't know anything about Liu Shaoqi," the girl snapped back as Ni looked on in amazed admiration. "I don't know whether Liu Shaoqi was a counterrevolutionary or not, good or bad. Liu Shaoqi has nothing to do with my father. I do know my father. He was a good man. And you killed him. He was murdered and you have to take responsibility."

"Your father was a spy," the bureaucrat parried.

"No. He was a good man. You have to rehabilitate him. He was murdered."

"You're standing on the side of a reactionary, you know." The bureaucrat was becoming supercilious. "This is very dangerous, what you are doing."

"It's really no use talking to him like this," Yuxian interrupted the battle. The young woman was beautiful—not in the manner of fashion, for she was devoid of all adornment, dressed in the same shapeless, monocolor, padded jacket that was the only acceptable form of female dress in those revolutionary days, but rather in the perfection of her finely chiseled features, the way her separate parts came together to form a whole. The freckles that dotted her nose seemed to Yuxian more Western than Chinese and hence an additional attribute. It was the contrast between the gentle beauty of her youth—she was only twenty-three years old at the time—and her tough refusal to be intimidated that had caught the young man's eye.

"I could help you," he offered. "You have to gather documentation, get some materials together and then write letters to Beijing—to the Central Committee, to Zhou Enlai, Deng Xiaoping."

"I don't know how to write that kind of letter," the young woman replied in exasperation.

"Let me help," he responded. "What's your name?"

It was only then that Ni Yuxian realized that he had known the young woman's father, the man the Revolutionary Committee insisted was a counterrevolutionary and had committed suicide. Indeed, the general outlines of the case, though not the details, were known to Ni Yuxian, and to most of Shanghai, even before he heard Kajia argue on her father's behalf. Professor Ye had been well-known in the city, one of its leading scientists, a "returned student" with an advanced degree from M.I.T. Before the Cultural Revolution closed the universities, Yuxian's class had occasionally been brought into Shanghai to hear the distinguished scholar lecture. Yuxian had visited the family's house and been introduced to Mrs. Ye as well.

Professor Ye was another of those "natural" targets of the Cultural Revolution. His erudition, his academic prominence, and particularly the fact that in the 1940s—when the Guomindang was in power—he had been a student at a leading center of scientific research in the United States, conspired to insure the accusations against him. Like many with his past, he was accused of having served as a spy for the Guomindang and hence of being a traitor.

Professor Ye had remained immune from attack in previous political campaigns and did not respond well to the shock of his first bout with the accusations against him. Despondent, he took an overdose of sleeping pills, was discovered in time and resuscitated. The revolutionary rebels locked him in a room on campus, the better to protect and struggle against him. Attempted suicide was taken as an admission of guilt.

Professor Ye was badly beaten by his captors, escaped from captivity, and found refuge in the countryside. He was discovered, captured, and returned to solitary confinement on campus. Again he was beaten. Again he attempted suicide. Again he failed. Four young revolutionary rebels dragged him to an interrogation session, beating him ruthlessly.

Back in his room, Professor Ye died.

It was a suicide, the youths insisted when they brought Mrs. Ye to see the body—battered and covered with bloody gashes, swollen and bruised. The pitiful string they said he had used to hang himself could never have supported more than a very few pounds. He had died, she was certain, of the beatings.

The family was forced to scatter after Professor Ye's death. Mrs. Ye, as the wife of a counterrevolutionary, was sent to work the fields in her ancestral village and later was transferred to hard labor at a so-called May 7 Cadre school for intellectuals. Her two young sons were sent away, too.

So was Kajia. Seventeen years old when her father died, the young girl's beauty was inescapable. The state of disgrace that ordinarily extends to all relations of a counterrevolutionary did not deter the scouts sent by Lin Biao's son to build his sumptuous harem. In Shanghai Lin's son maintained an extravagant residence and had set up a room with one-way glass whereby he could inspect the bewildered and unknowing women brought before him without being seen himself. Kajia was chosen in secret to serve as one of his playthings, a modern-day concubine to the profligate, degenerate, high-living son of the then Minister of Defense. When the young girl discovered what fate the scouts had in store, she refused and was sent instead to one of the most remote and backward areas of Anhui Province—the same Anhui Province that Ni Yuxian had witnessed several years earlier in the throes of famine. At the time Kajia went, people were merely perpetually hungry without ever actually starving.

For six years, from 1968 to 1974, the young girl planted corn that steadfastly refused to grow, unable to eke out the barest of subsistence necessary for survival, surrounded by peasants with little sympathy for a city female with not even a rudimentary knowledge of farming and who was to them only one more mouth demanding to be fed. She stayed alive only through the financial contributions her mother was able to scrape together each month. Never before and never since had life been so brutally, relentlessly harsh. By the time she sneaked back to the city the year she met Ni, joining her mother who had also returned in order to "dig tunnels deep," Kajia had become hardened and tough, angry and fearless.

It was only after their return that witnesses to Professor Ye's beatings came, in fear and in secret, to tell Mrs. Ye of the brutality to which her husband had been subjected and to identify those responsible for his death—young activist party members, one of whom even today holds a responsible position on the same university campus. Mrs. Ye dared not confront her husband's murderers directly. She went instead to the party leaders in charge. "Your husband committed suicide," was the haughty reply. "He was a counterrevolutionary."

Mrs. Ye and her daughter wanted justice. They wanted the Shanghai Revolutionary Committee to investigate the case. They wanted Professor Ye exonerated of the accusations against him and they wanted his death to be recognized as murder. They demanded that his murderers be brought to justice.

Yuxian began going to the Yes' apartment to help Kajia and her mother put together a defense of Professor Ye. The meetings were useful to Ni Yuxian, too. Many of the students at Jiaotong University were the sons and daughters of high-ranking cadres in Beijing, and news from the center reached the campus quickly. Word of the latest change in political mood and reports of private conversations between the country's highest leaders traveled fast. No newspaper or magazine could match a visit to the university for news.

As they talked about political events in Beijing, Ni began sharing his own interpretation of politics with Kajia, holding forth for hours on his analyses and interpretations of what was wrong with China. "China's greatest failing," he would tell her, "is the absence of democracy. For more than one hundred years, our country has been struggling for democracy—just look at the Qing dynasty reformers—Liang Qichao, Kang Youwei, Tan Sitong—and their struggle for democracy under the Manchus. Look at the May Fourth Movement of 1919 and its slogans of science and democracy. Look even at Mao Zedong himself. Even Mao was once in favor of democracy. Instead the whole Communist Party has become completely undemocratic, nothing but a new, privileged elite class. The party has usurped the power of the people, gone against the will of the people, turning the people into mere tools." Ni Yuxian had read *The New Class* by Milovan Djilas, the one-time Yugoslavian Communist Party official become still Marxist dissident. The book had been translated in secret into Chinese and locked in a small room in the library of the Maritime Academy to which only a handful of party members had the key. Ni's librarian friend, the same one who had loaned him Lenin's collected works, was one of those with a key and had allowed Ni into the room at night to read. Ni thought that Djilas's argument about the Communist Party becoming a new class was true of China, too. "We're told that the people are masters of the country, but really we have no voice at all," he would argue. "No one has a right to express his opinions. We don't even have the right to have our own independent thoughts. Here we're supposed to have over-thrown the emperor but we got a new one instead. We have to find a way to establish a real democratic system." The young girl sympathized with Ni Yuxian's views. Their anger and indignation were shared. Under a democratic system her father would never have died. Under a democratic system, murderers could be brought to justice. Under a democratic system, the death of her father could be legally avenged.

As time went on and the two met more and more frequently, as Yuxian's viewpoint became Kajia's, too, Yuxian began sharing with Kajia the enormity of the dilemma confronting him. Some-time after his thirtieth birthday, Yuxian told Kajia the story of Tan Sitong, the late nineteenth-century Qing-dynasty reformer, exe-cuted at age thirty-three, who had become the young man's model. Tan Sitong had gone willingly to his death, warning that others would follow in his footsteps, knowing that more blood would have to be shed, more people would have to die, before China could be reformed. Yuxian was willing to be a modern-day Tan Sitong, but only if his death would make a difference, only if others knew and understood the ideals for which he was dying, only if those ideals sufficiently resonated with the ideals of his fellow countrymen that the living would carry on the work of the dead. "If I live, understanding our country's political plight, and yet die without ever having been able to share what I know with others, my life will have been meaningless," he confessed to her one day. "But how can I make my viewpoint known? I could try to make my analyses public but then what if I am executed without anyone ever seeing what I write? No one would ever know the ideals, the goals, for which I died.

"If I could be certain that my ideas would live after me," he confided, "I would be willing to sacrifice my life."

• • •

Zhao Yuefang, instinctively, had begun constructing a protective shell around her family. She had recently given birth to a baby daughter—one more mouth to feed, one more potential victim if Ni Yuxian's courtship with political disaster continued. Not only was her husband neglecting his family responsibilities, he seemed to be almost flagrantly inviting still further retribution. She knew that he continued to write articles and poems that were not merely at odds with the prevailing political orthodoxy but tempestuously critical of it. She saw his circle of political acquaintances expanding, even as such contact became more and more dangerous. She was aware of his secret meetings and heard him creep home late at night. She learned, when one or another fellow malcontent came to call, to lock herself in her room, refusing to offer even the minimal and necessary Chinese hospitality of tea. They no longer discussed his activities. The less she knew of her husband's private political life, the safer her family would be. In the face of her husband's flagrant disregard for the family's survival, she acted to protect them all.

In Yangsi Village, only blocks away from their house, one of their neighbors—an old man well into his seventies—had recently been executed for the counterrevolutionary slogans that once decorated his room. The man, everyone admitted, had long been a little bit daft, and for years he had jealously sealed his tiny room against all intruders, family members in whose courtyard his abode was located, included. It was only when he became ill and his daughter-in-law entered to minister to his health that the whole family was horrified to find his room plastered with slogans calling for the overthrow of Mao Zedong. The man had hated the party chairman in silence for years.

The extended family—sons and daughters, daughters-in-law and sons-in-law—convened a meeting. By government regulation, they were expected to report such counterrevolutionary behavior. They debated. Opinion was divided. Some of his relatives wanted to report the old man. But everyone knew that he would be punished. Family loyalty finally prevailed. They tore down the slogans, whitewashed the walls, and vowed never to tell.

But the vow of silence was broken. One of his own daughters reported her father's counterrevolutionary proclivities. The old man was arrested, convicted of being a counterrevolutionary, and shot.

Those members of the family who had tried to protect their father—the ones who had voted to destroy the evidence and never to tell—were sentenced to life in prison.

The old man was paraded through the streets on the way to the execution grounds as a lesson for others to learn. The truck passed in front of the Ni family home and everyone went out to look. It was after that that Zhao Yuefang began destroying all of Ni Yuxian's writings—his poems and critiques of the Communist Party—ripping them up and throwing them into the fire. That she knew her husband's misdeeds, was privy to his counterrevolutionary thought, and still did not report him was already dangerous enough. She and Yuxian continuously quarreled. Occasionally they talked about divorce. They became more and more estranged.

Ni Yuxian continued, impulsively, to write. He shared all that he wrote with Kajia. He began hiding his political tracts with her. He turned to her for solace and support. They spent more and more time together. Then they could not bear to be apart. They had fallen in love.

• • •

Not everyone with whom Ni Yuxian dared to share his political views agreed with the young man's ideas. Even the most profoundly disaffected were not always convinced that Ni Yuxian's interpretation of China's problems was correct. It was entirely possible to agree that the Chinese polity faced a serious crisis without at the same time concurring on the reasons for the crisis or the possible cures.

Beginning from time nearly immemorial, tracing at least to the fifth century B.C. and the age of Confucius, the greatest of all Chinese sages, governance in China had depended less on system or process than on moral leaders. If the leader is moral, Confucius taught and Chinese for centuries believed, government will be moral, the state will be well-ordered, and ordinary people will naturally behave according to the dictates of the good. Whatever changes the trappings of Marxism-Leninism Mao-Zedong thought had wrought, that earliest of all political beliefs was still deeply embedded in Chinese thinking. Even the philosophical underpinnings of the Cultural Revolution itself, however unorthodox the means, were rooted in that belief—throw out the handful of bad apples, change the leadership, get rid of the bad men, and government and society will become orderly and just again. The case of

Lin Biao was only one more particularly egregious example of the havoc a single bad leader could wreak. With Lin Biao gone, with a good man in his place, justice could reign once more.

Ni Yuxian believed that his country's problems inhered not in individual leaders but in the system of government itself. China needed democracy. The Chinese people, Ni insisted, must have the right to select their own leaders and to recall them if they abused their authority. The special privileges of the leadership must go. While the leadership might be permitted a higher standard of living than ordinary folk, the gap between leader and led must be reduced to reasonable proportions. China needed a system of justice where everyone, political leaders included, was equal before the law.

Ni Yuxian's views were unusual but not unique. In the culture of fear that had descended over China by 1975, merely to talk about such questions was dangerous. To agree with them was more dangerous still. Pockets of discontent were springing up throughout the country. But these dissidents remained isolated one from the other. Ni Yuxian did not know, even in the incorrigible optimism that gripped him each time he engaged in a political discussion and discovered that his opinions were shared, that the disaffection that engulfed him was becoming increasingly widespread, that other young men in other parts of China, similarly disillusioned, were writing similarly blunt and even more critical assessments of China's socialist system. In Canton, a foursome writing under the name of Li Yizhe posted a sixty-seven-page big character poster in November 1974 called "On Socialist Democracy and the Legal System," attacking Mao and China's "feudal-fascist" bureaucracy and advocating socialist democracy. Xu Shuiliang in Nanjing had talked of a new "revisionist privileged aristocracy." For their critiques of "feudal fascism," all had been arrested and sent to labor reform camps.

Those of Ni's political allies who did agree with his analysis were still divided about how widely and how publicly that analysis ought to be shared. Knowing the dangers, many advised him to follow the route of silence.

Over and over in his discussions, Ni Yuxian returned to his fundamental logic of political change. The Chinese people remain steeped in political ignorance. Only through education will they ever understand the fundamental injustice in which their society is mired. To attempt that education is to risk one's life. But if no one takes the risk, if no one speaks out against injustice, if the Chinese people remain in ignorance, society will never change, reform will never come. Yuxian determined to commit to paper the political thoughts that had been taking shape through his months of clandestine meetings. He wanted to present the Chinese public—as many people as could possibly be reached—a systematic critique of the Chinese political system.

For forty nights he wrote, trying to set out his fundamental views in a way that ordinary Chinese could understand. Entitling his essay, "How to Prevent People Like Lin Biao from Coming to Power Again," he argued that the rise to power of Lin Biao and his later betrayal of the man who had once been his closest comrade-in-arms was no mere accident but a natural, inevitable outgrowth of China's dictatorial system. Without legal limitations on the exercise of power, new dictators would always rise in an attempt to overthrow the old. If Lin Biao had not plotted to overthrow Mao, someone else would have. He made a plea for a system whereby the leadership was actually elected and subject to recall. He railed against the system of special privileges.

He chose the fifth day of the fifth month of 1975 to make his letter public, both for the numerical appeal of the date and because it was the birthday of Karl Marx. He sent a copy, registered mail, to Mao Zedong and to the party's theoretical journal, *Red Flag*. He shared copies with his friends in the factory and with his clandestine network of disaffected youths. Surreptitiously, he posted it on street corners and dropped copies along the sidewalk so people could pick them up. He gave copies to Kajia and to a handful of his closest political associates to hold in case of his arrest. "Save it," he urged them. "If anything happens to me, if they lock me up—if they execute me—keep it until the proper time. Then, when the situation has changed, make sure that my thoughts are published. Make sure people know why Ni Yuxian was arrested and why he died. That way, my life will not have been in vain."

He began dreaming the universal nightmare of the dissident. The police had come to arrest him. They searched his house, searched his locker in his factory. They found incriminating evidence—not just the article on the inevitability of Lin Biao but all the poems he had composed attacking Chairman Mao, all the notes he had written lashing out against the system, his fulminations against the Communist Party. He confessed his dreams to Xu Xingfa, his closest friend in the factory, a young woman his own age with whom he had maintained a long-term flirtation. "You must get rid of your papers, Yuxian," she urged.

He emptied his locker of the most flagrantly anti-Maoist of his writings, throwing them into the fire. There was little at home for him to destroy. Zhao Yuefang had burned everything she could find. Ni Yuxian's heart, and most of the incriminating evidence against him, remained with Kajia.

Xu Xingfa composed a letter to the Shanghai municipal party committee and convinced Ni to sign it, professing his loyalty to the party and Zhang Chunqiao, his fear of the return of capitalism to China and his willingness to sacrifice to prevent its restoration. This way, the young woman reasoned, Ni would be on record on the right side of the political fence. By the time Ni had time to think about this approach and to conclude that it was not such a good idea, the letter had already been sent. Later, when he came under attack, he would be accused of opportunism, his political integrity questioned for following letters of criticism with professions of loyalty.

He waited. No one came to arrest him. No one came to rifle through his locker or to search his house. While extolling the virtues of democracy, his letter of criticism had not actually called for the overthrow of the Communist Party and socialism, and at that very moment the campaign against "bourgeois rights" being led by Zhang Chunqiao was attacking party members who had claimed special privileges for themselves. Perhaps his point of view was not really so radical after all. Or perhaps his later profession of loyalty had been believed.

• • •

Then the noose began to tighten.

When his factory was honored by a day-long outing to learn from an advanced factory in another suburb, Ni Yuxian was told privately that he would not be allowed to accompany his fellow workers. "You're a counterrevolutionary," the party secretary explained. "We're afraid you might damage some of their advanced equipment."

When the day came, Ni Yuxian feigned ignorance and ignored the prohibition, attempting to board the bus together with his fellow workers. "You can't get on that bus," the party secretary intervened.

"Why aren't you letting me go?" Ni Yuxian demanded loudly, for other workers to hear. The party secretary stood in his path, preventing him from entering the bus.

Quickly, Ni Yuxian ran to his workshop, returning immediately with two steel pipes. Standing at the door to the bus, he announced his intention to kill anyone who came near him. No one dared board the bus. The factory leadership tried to call up the factory militia, but the militia were the same age as Ni Yuxian and just as frightened as the rest of the workers by the infuriated counterrevolutionary blocking the door to the bus.

"If I don't go, no one goes," Yuxian declared to the crowd that had assembled a comfortable distance away.

The outing was canceled.

A few days later, as Ni rode his bicycle through the factory gates, he was intercepted by the party secretary. "Why are you so late?" the leader demanded. "There are some people here to see you, a couple members of an outside inspection team, waiting in the office." Two members of the party committee followed Yuxian as he made his way toward the office.

Long before he reached the office, Yuxian spotted the red banners decorating the factory auditorium announcing a struggle session against him. "Struggle against the rightist trend of reversal of correct verdicts element Ni Yuxian," one of the signs read awkwardly. Ni Yuxian's name had been turned upside down to indicate that he was to be overthrown. There were other slogans, too. "Down with Deng Xiaoping," read one.

Tough, resilient, and outspoken, one-time general secretary of the party Deng Xiaoping had been purged by Mao at the beginning of the Cultural Revolution in 1966. In 1973, at the urging of Premier Zhou Enlai, he had been officially reinstated as deputy premier and had worked to combat the extremism of the time and to exonerate numerous party officials who had been purged along with him. By 1975, when Ni was accused of siding with the pragmatist, party extremists, Mao's wife and Shanghai's Zhang Chunqiao among them, were waging another campaign of vilification against Deng, accusing him of attempting to "reverse correct verdicts" and aimed at purging him once more.

"Wipe out the trend to reverse correct verdicts." "Down with Ni Yuxian." "Ni Yuxian refuses to surrender," the slogans read.

The factory had not had a struggle meeting in years. "What's going on here?" Yuxian demanded. "I thought you told me there were some outside investigators here."

"This is the decision of the municipal leadership. They organized it," the factory leadership responded.

Yuxian balked. "I'm not going in there," he informed his

guards as they approached the auditorium. "You deceived me. If you'd said openly there was a struggle session against me, that's one thing. But . . ."

"Look, it's not us. It's the decision of the municipal revolutionary committee. We can't go against the wishes of the revolutionary committee, can we?"

"This is political persecution. Out-and-out political persecution. I'm not going in."

"Comrade Ni, this is a question for the masses to decide. If you want to raise your own opinions, if you want to answer the charges at the meeting, that's okay. Let's see how the masses respond."

"Okay, you want me to go in there? I'll go in there. I'll go in there on one condition. You guarantee me the right to speak. I want the right to answer the charges, to speak on my own behalf."

"Okay, Comrade Ni. You have the right to speak."

The political cheerleaders were directing the audience in slogan-shouting as Ni entered the auditorium. "Down with Ni Yuxian." "Stop the rightist trend toward the reversal of correct verdicts." "Down with Liu Shaoqi." "Down with Deng Xiaoping."

One by one the party leaders got up to denounce him. "Ni Yuxian is a troublemaker who has opposed the rules and regulations of the factory," they pointed out. "He's written reactionary articles."

Demanding the floor, Ni Yuxian turned to the audience and summoned forth his prodigious powers of persuasion. "I'm being falsely accused," he lamented sadly. He began telling his story, describing his involvement in the Cultural Revolution, the persecutions that followed, playing to the sympathies of his fellow workers. "They are trying to trick me. Something funny is going on here and I'm going to find out what.

"You guys are going to be sorry," he yelled at the party committee. "You'll pay for this."

The audience was mesmerized. In all the struggle sessions they had witnessed, no one had ever fought back like this. No one had ever challenged the party leadership. Ordinarily the accused would be forced to do the jet airplane, bent over at the waist, hands held straight and up behind the back. His hair would be pulled. There might be a few kicks and punches. But no one dared to touch this counterrevolutionary who was brave enough to fight back.

"I'm leaving," Yuxian suddenly announced when his speech was finished.

"No you're not," the party secretary responded. "Not this afternoon. We've decided to detain you."

"That's ridiculous. It's illegal. How the hell can you detain me? What right do you have?" Yuxian yelled, heading for his bicycle with two party secretaries trailing behind.

Suddenly two of the factory militia soldiers appeared, guns at the ready, pointing in the general direction of Ni. He ignored them all, mounted his bike, rode out of the factory gates and kept pedaling, ferrying his bike across the river to the offices of the city revolutionary committee.

"How in the hell can the revolutionary committee just write an instruction to my factory telling them to hold a struggle session against me?" he demanded of the first responsible comrade willing to stop and listen.

"It wasn't a struggle session," the responsible comrade replied patiently. "We're just trying to help you. We want to educate you. It's for your own good."

Ni Yuxian returned to work the next day. No mention was made of the struggle session. The leaders behaved as though the event had never taken place. Many of the workers had supported Ni in the debate, and the party leader was fearful of losing his authority and face if the accusations were pressed.

• • •

The political situation was changing rapidly, with the country's radical leadership careening further and further to the left and popular malaise growing more and more palpable. Rumors began circulating that Zhou Enlai, premier of China since the inception of the People's Republic in 1949, the one Communist Party leader genuinely, fulsomely, beloved of the Chinese people, the only man besides Mao who was virtually immune from attack, was dying of cancer.

Sophisticated and urbane, handsome and cosmopolitan, brilliant of intellect and dazzling in conversation, Zhou Enlai had come to stand as the symbol of everything that had been lost in China during the decade of the Cultural Revolution—for all that is cultured and orderly, literate and refined, good and kind—a symbol of what the Chinese describe as *wen*. History, and the Chinese people, too, will judge Zhou more harshly than he was judged at that time. He was, after all, complicitous in the politics of hate so deliberately fostered by the highest party elite, the hate that had torn his country apart. But his countrymen then attributed to Zhou a special, almost preternatural grace. As the Cultural Revolution degenerated deeper and deeper into violence, as more and more of the innocent, the good, and the merely ordinary were tossed willy-nilly into its maelstrom, and Zhou Enlai did not speak out, refusing to challenge either Mao or the radicals closest to him, his silence was explained by the importance of his maneuverings behind the scenes. Bad as the Cultural Revolution was, the argument went, without Zhou Enlai it would have been worse. The premier had not supported the Cultural Revolution, the Chinese people believed, but had he ever directly challenged either the movement or the man who led it, he, too, would have been overthrown, losing thereby his control over the apparatus of state and with it his power to protect the innocent. Zhou had used his office to work quietly, patiently, to protect the innocent, defending the integrity and revolutionary contributions of those who might otherwise have been labeled enemies of the people, securing safe havens for others whose fall from grace he could not prevent. Intellectuals in particular came under the premier's special protection.

Intellectuals saw much of themselves in Zhou Enlai. Like the premier they so respected, they, too, had wished and worked for the modernization of their country, had stood faithfully and loyally by the party chairman, slavishly sacrificing the integrity of their own beliefs in order to remain loyal to the chairman's cause. And just as many believed that Zhou had been betrayed by Mao, so many Chinese believed that they, too, indeed all of China, had been betrayed by the party chairman. Mao had let everyone down. Many felt that so long as Zhou Enlai was alive and in power, there was still hope for their country.

He died on January 8, 1976.

The country was struck by a collective pain, an incandescent grief, a surge of anger almost transcendental in effect. With Zhou Enlai gone, many people lost hope.

And when he died, the Chinese people believed, their beloved premier had not been properly mourned. Mao Zedong, to whom Zhou had remained loyal for more than forty years, steadfastly refusing to challenge his leadership, had not even attended the funeral. In the newspapers, tributes to the premier were sparse, their pages filled instead with attacks on Deng Xiaoping, regarded by many as thinly veiled attacks on Zhou Enlai as well. True, millions of people spontaneously braved the winter chill to line the streets of Beijing as Zhou's body was borne to Babaoshan cemetery where his remains were cremated, then to be scattered, according to his wishes, across the rivers and the earth of the land he had loved and served so long and so well. The people of Beijing had wept bitterly and openly as the funeral coach passed by.

But China is a country that believes in mourning its dead. The officially sanctioned, highly controlled and muted ceremonies were not enough. The grief-stricken Chineses people would find a way to pay proper homage to their dead premier.

In the privacy of their homes and behind the closed doors of their work units, on buses and in the narrow alleys of the nation's capital, the word quietly spread. The Qing Ming festival was approaching, the day the Chinese had traditionally honored the dead by sweeping their ancestral graves and placing upon them various profferings of food. Since 1949 attacks against superstitious practices had ended the sweeping of the ancestral graves, the day having been set aside instead for honoring the heroes of the revolution, of whom Zhou Enlai was unquestionably one. In 1976 the Qing Ming festival would fall on Sunday, April 4.

On March 23, 1976, a single wreath of white paper flowers, China's traditional symbol of mourning, was placed at the foot of the Monument to the Revolutionary Heroes in the center of Beijing's Tiananmen Square. Two broad ribbons streaming from the wreath bore an inscription in commemoration of Zhou Enlai. When the wreath was removed, another took its place.

A modest and unprepossessing obelisk carved with scenes from China's recent century of rebellion and revolution and inscribed with the calligraphy of both Mao and Zhou, the Monument to the Revolutionary Heroes stands in the midst of the vast open space that is Tiananmen Square and capable of holding upward of half a million people. It was fitting that memorial wreaths to Zhou Enlai should be placed before this, the most modest, most honest of China's monuments—not only because a monument to the dead was a proper place to mourn, or because the monument was dedicated to revolutionary heroes, or because it was inscribed with Zhou's own calligraphy, but also because part of Zhou Enlai's own monument, in the eyes of his countrymen, lay in the fact that he had seemed to behave as a man among men, no bigger than life, unprepossessing, even modest.

It was fitting, too, that the wreaths should be placed in Tiananmen Square, in the very heart of China, redolent in history, the point where all the country's great twentieth-century protests had either begun or had ended. It was to Tiananmen Square that Beijing intellectuals, led by the faculty and students of Peking University—the same Peking University (albeit in a different location) where nearly half a century later Nie Yuanzi had hung the big character poster that started the Cultural Revolution—marched on May 4, 1919, to protest the terms of the Versailles Treaty and to begin a movement devoted to the introduction of science and democracy, and hence, many believed, to the salvation of their country.

It was in Tiananmen Square, too, that the Communist Party brought its twenty-five-year struggle for power to its successful conclusion. On October 1, 1949, Mao Zedong and those closest to him had stood on the podium of Tiananmen—the Gate of Heavenly Peace and the outer entrance to the Forbidden City where the emperors of the Ming and Qing dynasties once had ruled—to declare the establishment of the People's Republic of China. Many who had stood with Mao were dead by 1976, and many more were in disgrace, Mao himself having turned against his one-time closest comrades-in-arms. Liu Shaoqi, one-time president of the People's Republic who had been singled out as the number-one target of the Cultural Revolution, had died in 1969 of the lingering wounds and lack of medical care his public humiliation had wrought. None of his one-time closest colleagues—neither Mao Zedong nor Zhou Enlai—had come to the dying man's aid.

Tiananmen Square had also been the site, early in the Cultural Revolution, of the massive, meticulously staged demonstrations by the country's Red Guards, a million strong each time, in support of the party chairman and the tumultuous movement he had unleashed.

The citizens of Beijing who brought their wreaths to the Monument to the Revolutionary Heroes as the Qing Ming festival of 1976 approached were well-versed in the history of Tiananmen Square. They were the children and the grandchildren of those who had come during the May Fourth Movement of 1919. They were the once-fanatic Red Guards who had come a decade earlier to sing their praises of Mao.

In April of 1976, for the first time since Mao had stood on the podium some twenty-seven years before, they came not because the Communist Party had organized them to come but spontaneously, to pour out their hearts. They came not to praise Mao but to defy him, not to support the Cultural Revolution but to oppose it, not in struggle but in harmony, shouting not slogans but reading their poems. There were poems in commemoration of their dead premier, simple and almost childlike in their innocence;

> The people loved their premier.
> The people's premier loved the people.
> The premier and people shared weal and woe.
> Their hearts were always linked.

There were poems, brilliant and biting, attacking the radical leadership of the Cultural Revolution:

> In our grief we hear the devils shrieking;
> We weep while wolves and jackals laugh.
> Shedding tears, we come to mourn our hero;
> Heads raised we unsheathe our swords.

There were poems in support of Deng Xiaoping, and poems of odium against the radical leaders of the Cultural Revolution, Mao's wife, Jiang Qing, and her close colleague Zhang Chunqiao, the Shanghai leader Ni Yuxian most despised, among them.

The most famous poem of all was an attack on Mao Zedong himself. "China is no longer the China of yore," it read. "Its people are no longer wrapped in ignorance. Gone for good is the feudal society of Qin Shi Huangdi." No one could doubt that the reference to Qin Shi Huangdi, the first emperor of the Qin dynasty more than two thousand years before, was to Mao himself. Qin Shi Huangdi had begun the dynastic tradition that was to continue almost uninterrupted for more than two thousand years. He was the founding father of imperial, unified China. But for ordering the burning of the books and sentencing the country's intellectuals to death, Qin Shi Huangdi was remembered in history as despotic, brutal, and cruel. Mao had enjoyed being compared to the first emperor of the Qin dynasty. "Yes, we are Qin Shi Huangdi," he once said. "We are Qing Shi Huangdi. But Qin Shi Huangdi only killed several hundred intellectuals. We have killed four hundred thousand."

As March turned to April and the Qing Ming festival approached, the crowds in the square began to grow—from the hundreds to the thousands, from the thousands to the tens of thousands, from the tens of thousands to the hundreds of thousands. On Sunday, April 4, the day of Qing Ming festival itself, the square was full from morning to night, the wreaths encircling the monument piled higher and higher, reaching up to touch the sky, as the mourners—and protesters—came and went by the hundreds of thousands. It was the largest spontaneous demonstration in the history of China—in the history, indeed, of humankind. Not for thirteen more years, in May 1989, when the people of Beijing rose up in protest once more, would the crowds in Tiananmen Square ever rival those of the Qing Ming festival of 1976.

The movement was widespread. When, in early March, Shanghai's *Wen Hui Bao* had written about one capitalist roader who had been responsible for the rehabilitation of another capitalist roader, the readership correctly inferred a criticism of the role of recently deceased Zhou Enlai in the rehabilitation of one-time Party Secretary General Deng Xiaoping. Nor did anyone seem to doubt that the source of the veiled accusations was Mao's wife, Jiang Qing, and Shanghai's Zhang Chunqiao. Even before the wreaths began to appear in Tiananmen Square, the people of Nanjing, university students especially, had begun taking to the streets in protest. When the arrests began, Li Yonglin, one of Ni Yuxian's clandestine political contacts, was among those imprisoned.

In Shanghai Ni Yuxian was active, too, writing poems and stenciling them, then dropping copies along the sidewalk for passersby to read and share with others—or to toss away in fear:

> A man has died but his soul cannot depart
> A terrible injustice has been done
> Blood must be shed
> People want revenge
> For those who have died.

He and his friends were still meeting about what action to take next when, more suddenly than it began, Tiananmen of 1976 was over.

Deep in the night of April 4, as the citizens of Beijing slept, dozens of trucks had converged on the square, carting away the thousands of wreaths that had covered the Monument to the Revolutionary Heroes. The next morning, outraged, thousands of the city's residents, mostly young and largely male, began converging on the square in protest, demanding that the wreaths be returned, the culprits who stole them punished, and that people be given the right to mourn their dead premier.

Negotiations with the Public Security Bureau proved fruitless. The crowd grew angrier. the violence escalated. A small group of militants, young people of middle-school age, broke through the police lines and into the public security barracks on the eastern edge of the square, smashing and looting the interior, then setting the barracks on fire. Smoke filled the square.

At six thirty in the evening, in the gathering darkness, the voice of the mayor of Beijing, Wu De, came over the hundreds of loud-speakers attached to the darkened lightposts along the perimeter of the square, loudspeakers ordinarily reserved for announcing to officially approved crowds yet another amazing victory in China's glorious march through socialism. From inside the Great Hall of the People overlooking the square, Zhang Chunqiao, Yao Wenyuan, and other top leaders had been surveying the situation all day. Over and over their message was repeated, broadcast on Beijing radio and television as well.

In the past few days while we were studying our great leader Chairman Mao's important instructions . . . a handful of bad elements, out of ulterior motives, made use of the Qing Ming festival to deliberately create a political incident, directing their spearhead at Chairman Mao and the party central committee in a vain attempt to change the general orientation of the struggle to criticize the unrepentant capitalist roader Deng Xiaoping's revisionist line and beat back the right deviationist attempt . . .

Today, there are bad elements carrying out disruptions and engaging in counterrevolutionary sabotage at Tiananmen Square. Revolutionary masses must leave the square at once and not be duped by them.

The crowd in the square thinned considerably, but thousands of the boldest remained.

Sometime after nine o'clock, the elaborate bulbous lights around Tiananmen Square flashed on, lighting the massive area like a playing field at night. From staging areas on the grounds of the Workers' Cultural Palace and Sun Yatsen Park, north of Changan Avenue and to the east and west of the Gate of Heavenly Peace, some ten thousand worker-militiamen, people's policemen, and soldiers of the People's Liberation Army rushed south across Changan Avenue, clubs ready, and encircled the square. In a divide-and-conquer tactic as old as the ancient military strategist Sun Tzu and reminiscent of nothing so much as Chinese chess, the guardians of social order quickly formed one grid of police lines running north and south, across the length of the square, and another running east and west across its width, their bodies tracing the lines of a gigantic checkerboard, tens of small, discrete squares within the massive square of Tiananmen. Within the squares, surrounded and isolated, were small groups of demonstrators, overwhelmed in numbers by the guardians of social order, the prisoners being led back to the staging areas from whence the protectors of law and order had come.

How many were arrested, how many were injured, how many died, has never been revealed. There were parents in Beijing who went for several years before hearing again from the children to whom they had bid good-bye on the morning of April 5. Some never heard from their children again. Many who were arrested and released after serving their time went on to participate in the protest movements that followed. Wang Juntao and Chen Ziming were among them—both having participated actively in the Democracy Wall movement of 1979 and later during the democracy movement of 1989. The two were sentenced to thirteen years in jail for their activities in 1989.

When the crackdown began, the people of Shanghai, like those in the nation's capital, were forced to the streets in staged celebrations of the suppression of the counterrevolutionary rebellion in Tiananmen, joyously—the press enthusiastically reported—welcoming the second overthrow in a decade of party pragmatist Deng Xiaoping. The turmoil was blamed, as it always was and would be again, on a "small handful of people," counterrevolutionaries of course, bent on creating a disturbance.

Word of the events in Beijing filtered quickly by word of mouth to Shanghai. Kajia's mother had been in the nation's capital at the time and reported what she had heard. Ni Yuxian went to wait outside the Shanghai railway station, accosting passengers from Beijing to hear their descriptions of the event. Ni Yuxian knew, as everyone in urban China knew, that millions of ordinary Chinese had been involved, people who had once genuinely loved Chairman Mao and the Communist Party, socialism and the Cultural Revolution and who had believed in all those promises of a better future for them and their country. Something fundamental, Ni Yuxian believed, had changed. For so many to have risked so much by coming to the square, the seeds of dissatisfaction must be very deep indeed. In nearly thirty years of Communist Party rule, nothing like this had ever happened. The Chinese people had stood up at last—together and against the Communist Party itself. True, many were barely conscious politically. They really had gone to mourn their beloved premier. But the poems they read bespoke a deeper, more profound, dissatisfaction.

That the party had so flagrantly flown in the face of the Chinese people, first removing the wreaths and then turning violently against the protesters, testified to how deep the chasm between leader and led, what a ridiculous, sorry sham the party's pretensions to "serve the people," had become.

For Ni Yuxian, as for millions of other Chinese, the Tiananmen incident of 1976 was the decisive turning point. The difference between Ni and his countrymen was merely that his level of dissatisfaction had already reached its limit. Until April of 1976, Ni had still harbored some small hope that Mao Zedong and the Communist Party might somehow be reformed, that they might become, as the ethics of Confucius would have it, "good," actually listening to the popular will and acting upon it. With the suppression of the Tiananmen demonstrations of 1976, Ni concluded that Mao Zedong, the Communist Party, the socialist system, were hopeless.

"We must resist," he urged his friends, meeting again in secret. "We have to use our own voices to make the Chinese people understand how repressive this fascist system really is. We have to oppose this system with all our might. We have to do something really big."

CHAPTER

9

The year of the dragon comes, according to a regular cycle, once in every twelve, and Chinese have learned to be wary when the dragon year arrives. They expect the unexpected. The dragon is the symbol of the emperor and hence of power, which is often unpredictable and frequently abused. The dragon is the only animal attached to the twelve-year cycle that is not real but a figment of man's imagination.

1976 was a year of the dragon, and the year was true to its reputation, rich in omen and full of portent, a turning point in the history of modern China. It was the year the dragon died.

Zhu De went first, six months after Zhou. The general who had joined with Mao to found the People's Liberation Army and then to lead the communist revolution to victory died on July 6 at the age of ninety. Symbolizing the military and force, what the Chinese describe as *wu*, Zhu De was the cultural counterpoint to Zhou Enlai. With the death of the symbols of both *wen* and *wu*, so some people reasoned, the death of the emperor himself could not be far behind.

But the death of Marshal Zhu De was immediately followed not by the death of Mao but by yet another portent, a portent that the transition to power would not be entirely smooth, that a certain amount of disorder was at hand.

As millions slept in the early morning hours of July 28, a massive earthquake, registering 7.5 on the Richter scale, leveled the entire city of Tangshan in a matter of seconds, its tremors causing major damage to Beijing and Tianjin as well. A quarter of a million people in Tangshan died at the moment of the quake; half a million more died later of the wounds they received in that instant. More people died in less time in the city of Tangshan on July 28, 1976, than have ever died in any disaster, natural or man-made, in the history of humankind. More people died in that single instant than died in the bombings of Hiroshima and Nagasaki combined.

In imperial China, the weather reports received by the emperor were among the state's most carefully guarded secrets, for the emperor ruled by mandate from the same heaven that also dictated the weather. Natural disasters stood as a signal that the emperor's mandate was slipping. If the citizens of China had the obligation to be loyal and obedient subjects when the emperor's mandate was intact, they had the right to rebel when the mandate came into question. Leaders of traditional Chinese rebellions, and emperors, too, had often read their future from signs that nature gave. The earthquake in Tangshan, officially downplayed, the magnitude of its devastation not publicly reported for years, stood as further mute but provocative testimony that the contemporary emperor's mandate was on the wane, that heaven was siding with the rebels of Tiananmen.

It was on September 9, 1976, just as life in the earthquake areas was regaining a semblance of order, that chairman of the Chinese Communist Party Mao Zedong, architect of both the party's greatest victories and its worst defeats, the man who had led a revolution designed to eradicate forever the hold of China's feudalist past only to install himself in the role of emperor, met the inevitable fate of emperors and men.

For many his death was a deliverance.

In less than a month, the Maoist era came to a sudden end. In the dark of night between October 6 and 7, some thirty high-ranking party and government officials, close adherents of Mao's most radical tenets, were arrested and imprisoned. Among them were the four ranking members of the Chinese politburo who came then to be known as the Gang of Four—Mao's widow, Jiang Qing; Shanghai party boss Zhang Chunqiao; Shanghai ideologue Yao Wenyuan; and Wang Hongwen, the young Shanghai worker risen like a helicopter to the most exalted reaches of power. China took its first small step in the slow and painful ascent from an abyss of darkness, ignorance, terror, and fear.

The changes, for Ni Yuxian, did not go far enough. Mao had died and the Gang of Four had been overthrown, his archenemy Zhang Chunqiao was in jail, but the new leadership was only marginally better than the old. The Tiananmen incident was still officially designated as counterrevolutionary, the protestors in jail, the dead unmourned. Ni no longer harbored illusions that his country's problems could be solved by substituting one set of Communist Party leaders for another, but he still believed that some leaders were better than others. Purged with the suppression of the Tiananmen incident, the pragmatic and reform-minded Deng Xiaoping, bent on modernizing his country and ending the divisive ideological struggles that had brought China to the brink of collapse, was not yet returned to power. Convinced that Deng was at least better than the immediate successors to Mao, Ni began composing a poem, written in the cadence and meter of ancient traditional poets, calling for the reinstatement of Deng, sharing the poem with friends, refining and expanding it as the months wore on. He continued, too, to write poems in commemoration of Zhou Enlai and of Tiananmen, and for the people who had fought and been imprisoned and died in April of 1976.

The first anniversary of Zhou Enlai's death would be the occasion to present his poetry to the people of Shanghai, and, he hoped, the world.

Kajia, of course, would help. The two were inseparable now. Together they would post two poems—the one in praise of Deng Xiaoping, the other in commemoration of Zhou—on the facade of the Donghu Hotel on busy Huaihai Road, one of the three main boulevards that intersect central Shanghai east to west.

The couple met near the Bund late in the evening of January 7 to go together, Kajia riding illegally on the back of Ni Yuxian's bike, to the hotel. They were nervous. Posting such decisively critical messages at one of the city's busiest locations was risky and dangerous business.

En route, cycling through crowded streets, Ni heard a policeman's voice. "What do you think your'e doing, riding her around on the back of that bike?" The voice was coming through a microphone from inside one of the round traffic control boxes that dot the major intersections of Shanghai. "Come over here."

"What is it?" Ni asked innocently, sauntering up to the policeman. "Is something the matter?"

"Park your bike over there," the policeman instructed rudely. "What's in that bag?" he asked Kajia. "Let me see the bag." The big character posters were rolled up inside. The whole plot would collapse if the policeman saw.

"Start walking," Yuxian directed Kajia. "Wait for me over there."

"Comrade Policeman, I'm from the countryside. I really don't know the traffice regulations in the city. I'm really sorry. I made a mistake, I admit it. I apologize." Yuxian was obsequious.

"This isn't something you can just apologize for and forget about, 'I'm sorry Comrade Policeman, I made a mistake, let's forget about it,' " the policeman responded sarcastically. "Are you going to obey me and put your bike over there or not?"

"Sure, sure," Yuxian responded obediently "I'll give you my bike." Yuxian began wheeling the bicycle in the direction of the policeman.

"Fuck you, you son of a turtle's egg," Ni suddenly shouted, hurling the foulest of all Chinese obscenities at the guardian of Shanghai's order, hopping on his bike and pedaling away at breakneck speed, continuing to shout obscenities over his shoulder as the policeman continued to shout after him to come back. "I didn't have any other choice," he argues. "The situation was too dangerous. If he had ever seen those big character posters, everything would have been over. That guy was stupid. He was bored. He didn't have anything else to do. He saw a young couple on a bicycle and just wanted to give us trouble. That's the way Chinese policemen are."

Yuxian caught up with Kajia and together the couple walked to the Donghu Hotel, the street in front still bustling with activity even so late at night, the crowds too thick to risk hanging their message. The intervention by the police was a bad omen. But Ni wanted to go ahead. He wanted to hang his poems. The two loitered among the crowd, waiting for the appropriate time.

At eleven o'clock, they decided to take the risk. Carrying the brush and powder that, mixed with water, would become glue, Ni Yuxian went to a nearby public lavatory to make the paste while Kajia waited in front of the hotel. Yuxian was also carrying a decoy—an announcement, common in those days, by a fictitious worker whose assigned apartment was too far from his factory and who wanted to exchange his designated apartment for one closer by. In front of the hotel, Yuxian quickly brushed the paste on the back of the decoy, prepared to display it to the police should suspicions be aroused. Then, one by one, Kajia handed him the poems and he covered their backs with the sticky paste. Feigning casualness, chatting and smiling, their eyes searched the darkness for signs of the police. The crowd seemed unconcerned. Turning their backs to the street, still smiling and talking, Kajia began leisurely pasting up the fake announcement as Ni Yuxian hurriedly plastered up the two poems, signed for the occasion by "Old Dong" and "Old Zhu," not only giving the impression that the authors were advanced in age but carrying the hint that the poems may have been composed by ranking revolutionary cadres—Dong Biwu and the deceased Zhu De. The bureaucracy that worked to assure that only politically orthodox thoughts were publicly expressed would be slowed by the signatures. No ordinary policeman would risk removing poems by ranking officials without first receiving instructions from higher levels. If the two did not immediately get caught, the slow motion of the bureaucratic machinery would gain time for the poems. The longer they stayed up, the more people would read them.

Their task complete, the two turned quickly and walked away, evaporating anonymously into the crowd. They continued walking, walked for blocks, glancing frequently over their shoulders to see whether they were being followed.

They were safe. They circled back and returned to the scene of their crime.

A crowd had already gathered, intently reading the poems, openly wondering who indeed had composed them. Surely they had been written by some old revolutionary cadres. The style and the language were old, and the signatures, too, were the signatures of senior party officials. Maybe the poems had even been written by members of the party's Central Committee.

Pleased with their work, and with the reception the poems were receiving, Yuxian and Kajia returned to their separate homes.

They met again early the next morning, Yuxian with his young daughter in tow. Even from a distance they could see the crowd, several hundred people in all, still gathered around the poems. The foreigners had turned out, too, just as Yuxian had hoped, and several of them were busily snapping the photographs that might carry his message west. Many of the people were copying the poems, often copying from others' copies. Some were crying, so moved they were by the ancient language and the emotions expressed. Mingling shoulder to shoulder, feeling the sentiments of the Shanghai people, Yuxian knew he had expressed what had been locked by fear in the hearts of his countrymen. They, too, wanted Deng Xiaoping to be rehabilitated and returned to lead the country. They, too, agreed that the Tiananmen incident was not counterrevolutionary at all but an historic event of great popular significance. The word would quickly spread. Yuxian was well pleased, his heroic instincts whetted.

That afternoon, the crowd was still there, but the people were milling around in barely subdued anger. "The police tore down the poems," he heard people explaining to the newcomers. "The first time they came, late in the morning, so many people protested that they had to hang them back up. But they came back later with new instructions and tore them down for good. Lots of people were crying."

•   •   •

Emboldened, Ni prepared to make a more radical statement still. The first anniversary of the Tiananmen demonstrations cried out for commemoration. "We must have a movement," Yuxian urged his friends. "We must do something important."

Yes, they all agreed. But what?

•   •   •

For months Ni had been secretly, feverishly, refining the text, expanding the contents of the poem he had composed for the hundred day anniversary of the Tiananmen incident. "I Do Not Believe" was the title he had given the poem. It was histrionic, full of anger and blood and revenge, the pleas for democracy gone, devoid of reason and balance. It was a reversion to the doctrine that government is determined not by process but by men, but without the search for the mean that had governed Confucian thought. He called it a poem, but the poetic language, the rhythm, the resonance with traditional poetry, was gone.

—"I do not believe," he wrote, "that the blood of my countrymen is so cheap and life so light, that one hundred days have passed and the martyred heroes of Tiananmen are still labeled thugs while their murderers are decorated with medals. Today, in the twentieth century, in the decade of the seventies, the actions of those murderers are a hundred, a thousand, ten thousand times more cruel than those we labeled enemies fifty years ago.

—"I do not believe that our brothers are so indifferent, that our sisters still sleep. Are we really mere cattle, the slaves of ten thousand years ago, at the mercy of murderers? Does not our constitution grant the right of free speech, of publication, the right to demonstrate? We have placed a few simple wreaths, written a few pages of honest commemoration. Nothing more. Never did we imagine that there in Tiananmen Square under the Monument to the Revolutionary Heroes, in the heart of the nation's capital, would animals eat our people, madly, wantonly committing atrocities, smashing our brothers' brains with clubs, thrusting bayonets through our brothers' hearts, attacking the unarmed with lethal weapons.

—"You lords who sing about socialism, your achievements in putting down the students rank higher than those of Hitler.

—"You believers in Marxism-Leninism, you who murdered women and children, you are wiser than Mussolini."

—"I do not believe that the fires of justice which light the world have been extinguished. I do not believe that the tree of truth is bare. But where are those protectors of our human rights? Where are our revolutionary writers? Are they deaf or blind? Why are they so unconcerned? Why don't they care about these barbaric atrocities? Have you no conscience, you living corpses, you worms? Where are the angry waves, the thunderings of revenge?

—"How sad I am to see my silent, miserable, suffering, motherland, like a child watching the rape of its mother, like a son forced to watch his father crawl on hands and knees. I do not believe this ugly land is my motherland. I do not believe these are the people I love. I do not believe those murderers are wandering peacefully at large.

—"If we tolerate these evil and ugly murderers, silently accept these atrocities, our motherland will never have freedom and light, our offspring will never escape the fate of slavery.

—"Stand up, my suffering countrymen, stand up, you who refuse to be slaves! Wake up! Wake up! Blood must be avenged by blood, life for life! Let us unite to struggle against fascism, sweeping away all the poisonous snakes and evil animals who drink of our blood and eat of our flesh. Let us hang those heroes of murder, nail them to the post. Let them know the people's revenge. I do not believe the 800 million sons and daughters of China will long tolerate this socialist fascism. If we do not speak out, we will die in silence."

• • •

Yuxian wanted to seize the occasion of the first anniversary of the Tiananmen incident to post the poem at some central, focal place. He shared the poem with his friends—with Guang Ming and Jin Renjun, with Huang Xixi and Xu Xingfa, with Kajia. Above all with Kajia.

"I know it will be torn down as soon as the police discover it," he argued, "but if it could stay up even an hour, just long enough for a few people to read, then that would still be a great victory." He knew, too, that imprisonment was certain if the author of the poem were ever discovered, that those who had conspired with him would be arrested, too.

Jin Renjun was dubious. "I thought the language was much too strong," Jin remembers. "He made the leadership into monsters. I thought the point could have been made without having been so extreme. If he had used milder language, he could still have said what he wanted to say, and there would not have been so much trouble. Oppressive, yes, but fascist? I didn't really think the Chinese leadership could be considered fascist.

"I thought, too, that the dangers probably were greater than whatever benefits might come.

"But Ni Yuxian was always too impatient," Jin continued. "When he wants to do something, he wants it done immediately, on his terms, when in fact it could be done much better if he waited and did it right. In retrospect, it seems that he wasn't always honest with us, which is one of the reasons he will always have a hard time developing support.

"But he was so much better educated than the rest of us. His thinking really was clearer and more advanced than ours, and for those reasons we really did respect him."

"I'll be the one to hang the poem," Yuxian had assured the doubters. "If we get caught, I'll take full responsibility for the contents."

In the end, Jin Renjun agreed to go along with Ni Yuxian, less because he was convinced he was right than because Ni was their acknowledged leader. The group tied themselves to him as much by bonds of feudal loyalty as by the high-flown democratic principles they all rhetorically espoused.

Kajia, too, had serious doubts. She, too, knew the language was excessively harsh. But encapsulated in the anger of the poem was all the pain and anger and all the anguish and the tears she had harbored for the murder of her father. She had no other way to avenge his death. For years she and her mother and her brothers had tried. Only a government of the most odious criminals could have murdered her father and then insisted he had killed himself. Only her hate relieved the pain. If justice could not be done, if the authorities persisted in ascribing his death to suicide, she had no other recourse. The big character poster was a token of revenge. Besides, she knew that if she and the others did not help, Ni would insist on hanging the big character poster himself. "I couldn't let him risk so much alone," she recalls.

Infatuated with Ni Yuxian and lacking in critical capacity, Xu Xingfa was the least reluctant of the potential participants. She was willing to follow Ni, even to jail, to demonstrate her loyalty.

Several expeditions into downtown Shanghai were necessary before the conspirators agreed on the most appropriate spot. The Donghu Hotel was too dangerous. This poem was long and Ni intended to write it big. When finally copied, it would stand three feet high and thirty feet long. At least fifteen minutes would be required just to paste it up, and the crowd around the Donghu Hotel was too thick even at night for such an activity to go unnoticed. Besides, there were likely to be extra policemen stationed nearby on the chance that the original culprits might strike once more at the scene of their crime.

The lumbering old Peace Hotel, just at the intersection of east Nanjing and Zhongshan Roads, right across from the Bund, had much to commend it as a site. Catering almost exclusively to foreigners, a major happening there would surely be reported widely abroad. So close to the Bund, the crowds were always thick, the local Shanghaiese mingling with Chinese and foreign tourists alike. Word of a poem pasted at the Peace Hotel would surely spread not only throughout the city but to the far parts of China and the world as well.

But the very factors that made the Peace Hotel such an appealing site had also led the city authorities to saturate the area with police. No matter what the time, the security presence was pervasive. If their first venture went well, the group decided, they would convene on the following night at the Peace Hotel to post a second copy of the poem.

They chose the Park Hotel—the same Park Hotel where half a century earlier Guansheng had celebrated his lucky streak by becoming the only man in Cao Family Village ever to eat Western food. Located on Nanjing Road about a mile from the Bund and just across from People's Park, the Park Hotel was still the tallest building in Shanghai. The area was heavily traveled without being overly crowded, and the hotel was certain to have foreign guests.

Paper was still expensive and in critically short supply, and a poem three feet high and thirty feet long required a suspiciously large number of sheets. Frequenting the stationery stores of Pudong and Shanghai proper, Yuxian bought a few sheets in one store, a few more in another, a few more in a third. Then he shut himself alone in the upstairs room where his entire unhappy and unsettled family was housed and began the arduous task of copying the poem. Zhao Yuefang spent most of her time at her middle school and remained ignorant to the end of her husband's plot. When eight-year-old Caocao stumbled unwittingly into the room one morning, walking unknowingly across the paper set out on the floor for the brushwork to dry, Yuxian exploded in anger. "Get out of here," he yelled at his startled son. "Get out and leave me alone. Don't you dare to come back!" Confused and frightened, Caocao had quickly retreated.

On the evening of March 31, from disparate parts of the city— from Pudong and Wusong and the old international concession— the group began assembling at a small restaurant in People's Park to share a nervous meal. It was the first time Huang Xixi, Guang Ming, and Jin Renjun had ever seen Kajia. It would be two years before they learned her name.

Waiting to meet Xu Xingfa at the bus stop on Fuzhou Road facing People's Square and just across from the rear entrance to People's Park, Yuxian was startled to find himself face to face with an older woman, a complete stranger, who seemed nonetheless to look him directly in the eye and say with a booming voice he was sure was intended for him, "At age thirty-three, life is cut to shreds." Yuxian was reminded with a start that he had just entered his thirty-third year, the year the fortune-teller had predicted would be the most dangerous of his life, the major turning point, the period he might not pass through. It was the year Tan Sitong had died.

Overcome by the superstitions of childhood, Yuxian was suddenly struck by fear. Xu Xingfa was already a mother. She had a daughter Lingling's age. If anything were to go wrong, if the group were to be arrested, what would happen to the child? What would happen to the mother? Yuxian could not allow Xingfa to participate. "Go back," he instructed her. "You can't participate. It's just too dangerous. We must think of your daughter."

Xingfa protested. Willingly she would go to jail.

Yuxian insisted. Xingfa returned home.

At dinner, quietly, tensely, they discussed their assignments. Guang Ming and Jin Renjun would be posted at the intersection of Changjiang Street and Nanjing Road, chatting like old friends, their eyes peeled for the police. Kajia would carry the big character poster while she and Huang Xixi stood across the street, pretending to be amorous, similarly on guard. Yuxian would make the necessary preparations to paste up the poem, first mixing the glue and then spreading it over the shiny black marble facade of the Park Hotel. At the signal the paste was ready, Kajia would quickly step forward with the big character poster, and the two would then work together as a team to get it up. If any of the lookouts spotted a policeman, he would quickly light a cigarette, and the glowing ember would be the signal to Ni Yuxian to cease his work immediately. If any of the men got caught, they would deny all knowledge of Ni Yuxian and the big character poster. There was no evidence to link them together. If Kajia got caught in the act of helping Ni, she would play dumb, denying knowledge of the contents of the poster, coyly admitting only that she knew it to be a criticism of the already officially fallen Gang of Four. Ni Yuxian alone would admit responsibility. "Don't worry," he had promised his followers. "I'll never implicate you."

At eleven o'clock, the five emerged from the small restaurant, walked out the gates of the park, and took their posts. Ni Yuxian worked quickly spreading the paste across the facade, aware of the curious stares of the pedestrians who were stopping to look, pausing in their homeward journeys to wonder whether the drama about to unfold would be worth the wait.

The paste was up. Ni gave the signal to Kajia. She had already seen and was trotting up the entrance steps, feigning nonchalance. Quickly, one by one, she began handing Ni the sheets of numbered paper. The crowd was growing curious. People were beginning to stop to take in the show. The street was filling with workers just coming off the two to eleven o'clock shift.

The work went quickly, smoothly. The two made a good team. The seventh sheet went up, then the eighth. There were only two more sheets to go.

"The cigarette. He lit the cigarette," Kajia said sharply. Absorbed in her task, and with the growing crowd obscuring her view, she was not positive she had spotted the flame immediately. Perhaps a few seconds had already elapsed.

"It's okay, we have time," Yuxian responded. Their calculations had been based on a policeman on foot. No one had ever thought that the police would arrive on bikes.

The last sheet of paper went up.

"Let's split," Yuxian commanded.

From the corner of his eye, he saw the two policemen dismount their bikes, and as he quickly scanned the crowd, he failed to detect his friends. Looking straight ahead, never pausing or looking back, he headed for his bicycle, parked next to the entrance to the park just across the street. Unlocking it, mounting it, still never pausing to look, nervous, frightened, he began cycling rapidly east on Nanjing Road, in the direction of the Bund. He was nearly to the Bund before he was certain he was not being followed, before the fear of being caught had lifted sufficiently for a new fear to strike.

Kajia. "Where was Kajia?"

"I shouldn't have left her," his mind suddenly screamed in panic. "What should I do? Should I go back? Maybe she's okay. Maybe she just walked away. Maybe they didn't get her.

"Maybe they did. Maybe she's been arrested." He was immobilized by fear. Should he turn around? Go back? What if they had captured her? His heart was pounding, his head was bursting, his stomach a concrete knot. "She is so young, so delicate, so fragile. What if they interrogate her? She'll never be able to take it. What to do? Oh, God, what should I do?"

Ni Yuxian turned and cycled back to the hotel.

The street in front was nearly deserted. The big character poster was gone. Kajia was nowhere to be seen. He cycled back and forth along the side streets, looking for her, returned to the hotel, rode his bicycle up and down Nanjing Road, scouring the area for the young woman he then so desperately loved.

Kajia. Kajia. Kajia.

It was two in the morning before he gave up and returned home, still not knowing whether the young woman was arrested or safe.

• • •

At five the next morning, he was up again, crossing the Huangpu River by ferry, rushing by bike to Kajia's apartment.

He knocked, waiting.

Kajia opened the door.

"Thank God, you're safe. What happened?"

"They caught me," the young woman responded. "They took me to the police station. They questioned me."

"What did you say?"

"Just what you told me to, just like we agreed. I admitted that I had pasted it up. I told them that you'd asked me to help you, that I didn't know the contents, that I just knew it was opposed to the Gang of Four and I thought that was okay."

"Did you tell them my name?"

"Yes, your name, the name of your factory. I had to. They opened my bag and found the other big character poster. I couldn't pretend I didn't know anything about it. I had to tell them about you."

"We have to talk. We have to figure out what to do. This is a big thing, Kajia. They're going to come after us. We're both going to be arrested. Your house isn't safe. We have to find some place to talk. Meet me at the little alleyway behind your house in a couple minutes."

The couple walked the narrow streets and public thoroughfares around Kajia's house, discussing what to do.

"All you have to do is stick to your story," Yuxian urged. "Just tell them it was something I asked you to do. Tell them you don't know what it said. But, Kajia, we may still have time. We still have that other big character poster to put up. We could do that tonight. We're going to be arrested anyway. It's too late to change that. The poem was up for such a short time. We have to give more people a chance to read it. I'm going to talk to the others."

Kajia did not challenge her lover. She would do whatever he asked. Yuxian went to Wusong, changing buses frequently to make certain he was not being followed, to talk to Guang Ming and Huang Xixi.

"It's for certain I'll be arrested," he explained. "The girl, too. They caught her." Ni did not yet realize that Guang and Huang had followed Kajia to the police station, waiting outside until they had seen her leave. "You can be sure I'll never expose you," Ni continued. "They'll never know and you must never tell anyone that you cooperated. If they come to ask you, don't ever admit to it. No matter what they do to me, I'll never confess.

"But I want you to continue my work, the Charter seventy-seven especially. That's the most important thing now." Word of Charter 77, the human rights declaration by scores of Czechoslovakia's leading, most-respected intellectuals had filtered into China. Inspired by the courage of their comrades in repression, Ni had composed a Chinese Charter 77. It was to be published on the seventh day of the seventh month, 1977, and would have seven points, reduced to seven easy-to-remember, rhymed words—

xuan, huan, pi, bao, ji, gao, di. Point number one, *xuan*, meaning to elect, demanded the right of the people of China to elect their own leaders; and point number two, *huan*, to change, would guarantee the right to change those elected officials if their performance proved unacceptable to the public. *Pi*, to criticize, granted the populace the right to public criticism of the officials they had elected and *bao*, to guarantee, granted basic human rights and the fundamental assurance that individuals who exercised their rights of free speech and open criticism would be free of any interference and would suffer no punishment. *Ji*, to take over, granted children the right to take over their parent's job upon the parent's retirement—a practice common in China in those days, a form of guaranteed employment and job security and an encouragement to early retirement as a means of preventing the ranks of the employed from swelling too large. *Gao*, or high, would set a high ceiling on wages, limiting even the most exalted officials to salaries two or three times that of ordinary workers and would abolish all the special privileges of Communist Party cadres. *Di*, or low, would set a minimum wage for workers, promoting a genuine egalitarianism the present, ostensibly socialist and egalitarian, system lacked.

"And tonight I want to hang up the other big character poster, tonight before they arrest me," Ni continued.

"That's crazy, Yuxian," his friends were adamant. "Don't do it. It's too dangerous."

"I have to."

"No, you don't. Wait, Yuxian, wait to see how the situation develops. We can't do it now."

Yuxian returned to the city and met with Jin Renjun. He, too, was adamant. Yuxian agreed not to put up the second copy of the poem. "I won't expose you," Yuxian promised again, "and don't go to the Public Security Bureau asking about me either. Don't try to do anything to help me. If you do, you might expose yourselves. You could be arrested, too. Relax. They won't catch you. You're not going to be arrested."

It was already early afternoon. Yuxian was expected at work.

• • •

The police were waiting.

"Come into the office, Ni," the party secretary directed him gruffly as he cycled through the factory gates. "You're in real trouble. They've already told me."

There were ten blue-trousered, black-leather-shoed policemen, and their pockets were the pockets of officials. They wore no insignia. The atmosphere was tense.

"What is your name?" the leader began the usual questioning. "How old are you? Where do you live?" Two secretaries started taking notes.

"You already know the answers to those questions. If you have business with me, just tell me what it is. Who are you, may I ask?"

"Don't bother who we are. We have the right to ask you questions."

"If you don't tell me where you're from and who you are, you can ask all the questions you want but I won't answer them," Yuxian shot back.

The two in charge exchanged glances.

"We're from the Public Security Bureau."

"Let me see your identification."

The leader took out his identification card and showed it to Ni Yuxian. "Public Security Bureau. Huangpu District. Qiu Linting." He was a man of about fifty, tough, and the set of his face, the eyes behind his glasses, suggested he was not inclined to believe the suspect's responses.

"What were you doing yesterday?" Qiu asked.

"I was at home," Yuxian responded.

"That's a lie. You put up a big character poster, didn't you?"

"Yes, I pasted up a big character poster." A look of surprise crossed Qiu's face.

"Who wrote it?"

"I did."

"Do you know you've committed a crime?"

"I know I haven't committed a crime. Putting up a big character poster is our citizens' right. I was only taking advantage of the rights that are guaranteed by our constitution. The constitution says we have four big rights—the freedom to speak out freely, to air our views fully, to hold great debates, and to write big character posters. Remember?"

"Sure. You think you're so smart, don't you, you arrogant little . . . You think you've so brave, so tough. Well let me tell you something. You're a criminal. You committed a crime. You're a counterrevolutionary. Do you know that the Tiananmen incident was a counterrevolutionary incident?"

"I don't agree with that viewpoint."

"You don't agree, huh? Okay, we'll read the document to you. Listen." The female secretary handed Qiu a sheet of paper. "This is a decision of the Communist Party central committee, Chairman Hua Guofeng's speech. 'The Qing Ming incident is a counterrevolutionary incident that used the pretext of commemorating Premier Zhou Enlai's death to oppose our great leader Chairman Mao Zedong, the Central Committee of the Chinese Communist Party, and the dictatorship of the proletariat. It is absolutely necessary that those counterrevolutionary elements should be completely suppressed. After the overthrow of the Gang of Four, some counterrevolutionary elements are trying to use the Tiananmen incident to create further disturbances. This kind of counterrevolutionary element must also be dealt with very strictly.' Do you understand?"

"I understand. I think Comrade Hua Guofeng is mistaken. The Tiananmen incident is revolutionary." The female secretary snickered behind her hand. Criticism of Hua Guofeng, the lackluster leader who had been designated to replace Mao Zedong, was heresy. "I'm not a counterrevolutionary. What I did was revolutionary. I put up a big character poster opposed to the judgment on the Tiananmen incident—that was fascist oppression arresting so many people, killing our own people. It was completely wrong, and I have the right to put up a big character poster saying so."

"God are you ever arrogant. Such a rotten counterrevolutionary, and still you're arrogant. What you've done is a very serious counterrevolutionary act. But we want to be good to you. We want to be lenient. If you honestly admit to your crimes, and tell us the full circumstances in which they occurred, if you can introduce us to other counterrevolutionaries, then you have hope of a lighter sentence. If you continue with today's attitude, you're walking the road to your death."

"From the time I wrote the poem, I have been preparing myself for whatever you might do to me. Do what you want. Arrest me. Arrest me now, and I'll go with you. But just you wait. History and the Chinese people are on my side. I'll be proven right. What happens to me right now doesn't matter."

A collective flash of doubt crossed the faces of Ni Yuxian's interrogators, the party secretary of the factory included. The police above all were aware of the widespread popular sentiment in support of the demonstrators at Tiananmen. They knew, too, that millions of their countrymen, many in the Public Security Bureau included, favored the reinstatement of Deng Xiaoping. The Public

Security Bureau itself was deeply divided internally. The political situation was in flux. Everything could change. Ni Yuxian might in the end be proved right.

But the flash of doubt was replaced immediately by a look of smug satisfaction. The party secretary, in particular, was well pleased. The troublemaker who had brought nothing but headache since the moment he had joined the factory was about to get his come-uppance. Ni Yuxian was no mere troublemaker. He was counterrevolutionary through and through.

"I'm hungry," Ni announced. "If you have nothing else, I'd like to go eat."

"Okay, go eat."

Yuxian went immediately to his workshop, locking the door behind him. Opening his locker, he took out the notebook that contained all the names, addresses, and phone numbers of his friends and political acquaintances. He removed the few remaining notes and articles still stored there—all the physical evidence of his counterrevolutionary thought. He threw everything into the fire.

No one came to arrest him.

Returning home after his eleven o'clock shift, still no one had come for him. He was still free. He went out.

"The Public Security Bureau questioned me today at the factory," he told Kajia on the phone.

"Me, too,' she replied.

"They're going to arrest us. I know they are. Meet me tomorrow morning at nine o'clock at the bus station," he said. "We have to talk some more."

The public security representative he spotted en route was wearing different clothes and had made herself up, but Yuxian had no trouble recognizing her as one of those who had questioned him at the factory. He led her on a wild goose chase, jumping off the bus just as it started pulling away, changing buses frequently, taking a roundabout route, quickly outwitting her. By the time he arrived at the bus terminal, he was quite certain he was no longer being followed.

Kajia was still waiting. Again, they hopped on and off buses, shaking their unseen tail, arriving finally in Jasmine Park.

"It's already been two days, Yuyu," Kajia began optimistically. "Maybe they're not really going to arrest us."

"No, they're just waiting to see if we expose the others."

"What are we going to do?"

Yuxian's head was swimming. He could not think clearly. "We only have two choices. We could run away or we could not run away. We could just wait until they come to arrest us.

"Kajia," he said, "you're still young. You're just a middle school graduate. They'll never believe you were capable of thinking for yourself. All you have to do is tell them I asked you to do it, you didn't know what the big character poster was all about, you just thought it was some kind of criticism of the Gang of Four. Blame me. Tell them I tricked you if you like. Above all, most important of all, you must never mention the other three. This was just the two of us, you and me, okay? If you talk like this, they'll just question you for awhile and let you go. It will be over for you quickly, Kajia. And for me, maybe they'll keep me there for a few years, but I'm strong. I can take it. I won't confess. They'll let me go eventually."

"No, Yuyu. Let's run away together. I could take the interrogation. I would never say anything but what you've told me, I promise. But still, I want to go away with you. Let's go away together."

"But if we run away, Kajia, that's the same as admitting our guilt. It's like saying they're right, that we really are counterrevolutionaries. But we're right. They're the ones who are wrong. We haven't done anything illegal. Let them catch us. Let them try us.

"Besides, how can we hide in this society? What about our rice coupons? How would we eat? How would we live? We could run away and hide for a while maybe, but still, eventually they'd find us. There's no place to hide in this country."

"My mother has some money. She could give us money and we could borrow rice coupons. We could manage, Yuyu. Please."

Yuxian's mind flashed to his family and to what would happen to them if he were to run away. The police would go every day to question them, to find out if they knew where he was hiding. They would become a counterrevolutionary family. His father had never recovered from the psychic wounds of his imprisonment; his health was not good. How could he bear being humiliated further still? And his mother? Xu Fengzhen had been so strong, the rock of the family. But the strains on her as helpmate would surely begin to show. And his children—Lingling and Caocao. The face of his son—wounded and hurt when he had yelled at him for disturbing his writing—flashed in his mind's eye. He had not seen Caocao since. Did he want his son to have a counterrevolutionary, runaway father? And he could not bear leaving beautiful little Lingling, the pride and joy and love of his heart.

"Wait for me, Kajia," he replied. "It won't be that long. A few years at most. And when I'm free again, we'll get married. We can be together forever then. I'll get divorced and we can get married."

"Okay, Yuyu, let them arrest us then. I'll wait."

It was close to midnight by the time he arrived home. The place was locked. Yuxian knocked. His little brother opened the door.

"They've been looking for you all day, Yuyu. What did you do?" he demanded. "The residence committee keeps coming to look for you. The police are waiting for you. Go see mother immediately. She and father are upstairs."

"What have you done?" his father asked.

"I put up a big character poster."

"What kind of big character poster? What did it say? Quick, Yuyu, tell us quickly. They'll be here soon. What did it say?"

"It was about the Tiananmen incident."

"Yuyu, be more specific. What about the Tiananmen incident?"

"It was a poem opposed to the suppression of the Tiananmen incident. I accused the government of fascist atrocities. It's serious. The public security bureau already knows. They've questioned me. At the factory. I'm going to be arrested."

The knocking on the door began. "Don't be afraid," Yuxian cautioned his parents.

"Who is it?" his younger brother called.

Silence. More knocking.

"Yuyu, please tell us more," his mother pleaded. "What exactly did the big character poster say? Quickly, tell us clearly what you did, what you said. Quickly, Yuxyu, time is running out."

"There isn't time, mother. Maybe it's better you don't know."

The knocking continued.

Ni Yuxian went downstairs to open the door.

CHAPTER

10

"Where were you today, Ni? Why didn't you go to work?" one of the policemen mocked sarcastically when he opened the door. "Trying to run away, weren't you?" There were at least ten of them standing there in the night, several of whom Ni already recognized. They had questioned him at the factory.

Ni became serene, suffused with a sudden calm. The dream he had dreamt for so many months had finally come to pass. The nightmare was upon him. He no longer had to run.

Two of the policemen drew their guns just as two others grabbed him from behind and another read from an official document. "Ni Yuxian is a counterrevolutionary in action. Today, on orders of the Shanghai municipal court, he is to be arrested." They forced down his head, clamping cold handcuffs around his wrists. "Be honest. Tell the truth. Do what we tell you or we'll bash your head in." It was not hard to believe that the two holding him down were capable of bashing heads—and that they frequently had.

"It's just one of me against ten of you," Yuxian protested. "You don't have to be so rough."

They grabbed him by the hair and half pulling, half shoving dragged him through the Ni family courtyard and into the narrow, dark, deserted street outside. Ni was aware of footsteps going up the stairs and from the corner of his eye saw a light flash on just as he was being led through the gate. They were about to search his room. Zhao Yuefang and the two children were still asleep. This was the first they realized that anything was amiss.

Qiu Linting, the public security official who had been in charge of questioning him at the factory, was waiting at the local police station. He laughed as Ni was delivered before him. Ni laughed back. "Why did you send so many people to get me?" he asked. "That's not your problem," Qiu responded as Ni's body was searched, his pockets emptied, the police roughly probing his every nook and cranny. Ni was locked in a small holding cell.

The cell door opened half an hour later. The house search was over. Zhao Yuefang had protected her family well. The police found nothing incriminating.

In the paddy wagon that was to transport Ni to the Huangpu District Detention Center in the heart of Shanghai, Qiu sat with the driver in front, separated from the prisoner and the police who were guarding him by a window of steel wire mesh. The driver was confused. They had crossed the Huangpu River by ferry but at this time of night the boats to the city no longer ran. "Take the tunnel," Yuxian instructed from the back. "It's really fast right now. Just keep going straight till the next big intersection, then turn left."

"Shut up," commanded his guards. "Who gave you permission to speak? Keep it up like this, Ni, and we'll beat you."

"Well, you needed to know how to go, so I told you. Isn't that good?" Ni insisted.

"Shut up, Ni," Qiu commanded.

Suddenly, the paddy wagon sped up and its siren sounded, joined by the sirens and the whirling red lights of a police car in front and another behind, the motorcade of three speeding rapidly through the tunnel and into the Shanghai night. In half an hour, they had reached their destination.

Built by the French in the declining years of the Qing dynasty, sometime around the turn of the century, the Huangpu District Detention Center is a fairly tall building, some eleven stories high, with little to distinguish it from other Western built edifices that give the city of Shanghai its character. Pedestrians passing in front are drawn by a lurid curiosity to the photographs of the latest captured criminals and the descriptions of their crimes and punishments posted outside, but the thousands of tourists who yearly peruse the adjoining museum, the finest in all of China, filled with priceless treasures of ancient bronzes and of Buddhist art, Ming and Qing landscapes, celadon and porcelain, a whole panoply of the best representations of Chinese civilization, may gaze for minutes from the museum's windows at the brownstone next door and never suspect the dramas within.

Ni was led for interrogation to a fourth-floor office, a comfortable room, where Qiu and two of his colleagues were waiting, together with two notetakers and two prison guards. More interrogators arrived as the session dragged on. "Where did you go today? Why weren't you at work? Who did you meet? Who did you talk to?" Qiu wanted to know. It was nearly two thirty in the morning, and Ni's adrenalin was running out. "Where were you at two o'clock this afternoon? Where were you from three to four?" The questions were fast in coming, the interrogators never pausing to give Ni time to think.

They had to know of his morning meeting with Kajia, of that Ni was certain, but they must never find out that he had also gone to Wusong, that he had spent the afternoon and evening conferring again with Guang Ming, Huang Xixi, and Jin Renjun. He decided to account for the hours between two in the afternoon and eleven at night by saying he had wanted to hang a second big character poster and was scouting an appropriate place. They began questioning him specifically. "What time did you leave Kajia? How did you get from her house to the Bund? What bus did you take? What number? How long did it take? How long did you spend on the Bund? What did you see? Who did you see? How did you get to Huaihai Road? From Huaihai to Nanjing Road? How long did it take you to walk from Zhongshan Road to the department store?" He was confused. They found a soda bottle in his bag. "Where did you buy the soda? Where did you eat lunch? What time?" He was tired, too tired to think. He was afraid of contradicting himself.

There was a sudden commotion, and Qiu left the room. Ni heard talking. Someone else was being brought down the hall. He heard Kajia's voice. So Kajia had been arrested, too. She was put in an adjoining room.

"What did you talk about with Kajia?" the interrogators wanted to know.

"She has absolutely no responsibility for this," Ni insisted. "You're making this thing too serious. I want her case to be settled quickly. She really has nothing to do with it. I did it all by myself." Suddenly he was overcome with fatigue, and with the fatigue a gnawing fear. His story and Kajia's would have to coincide completely or the police would be suspicious, press to know more about whom else he had seen, what else he had done that day.

But they were already suspicious. Qiu knew he had not acted alone. They stopped asking about Kajia. They asked what he had done the rest of the day, after he had left her. They wanted him to account for every minute. In concocting the story he would tell the police, he had never counted on this type of questioning, on having to say where he had been at exactly what time, how long it had taken him to get from one place to another, how he had gone from one place to the next, where he had eaten, when, what, how much it had cost, whom he had seen, with whom he had talked, what they had said.

He had not counted on an interrogator like Qiu either—he seemed to be a mind reader. He could sense what was going through Ni's mind and immediately direct his questions right to the weakest point. Somewhere in the middle of his story about spending the afternoon looking for a suitable place to hang another big character poster Ni realized, and Qiu clearly knew, that the description he was giving could not possibly contain enough hours to account for all the time he had spent between leaving Kajia and arriving home at night. But he could not let them know that there were others involved, that he had spent the afternoon and well into the night meeting with his political accomplices. He could not be positive that Kajia would not crack under questioning, but until the night they had put up the big character poster, the young woman had never been directly involved with his political allies. She did not know even their names. Her ignorance was a form of protection.

But his political accomplices could not be trusted. The police would play the four of them off against each other, say that one had talked, that one had betrayed the other. They could tell his friends that Ni had betrayed them, and his friends in their anger and spite and hate could betray him and implicate all sorts of others as well. His friends knew too much. If any one were questioned and cracked, he could implicate the whole clandestine network they had established. Tens of people could be brought in for questioning, detained, imprisoned, sentenced for counterrevolutionary activity. People were always cracking under questioning, confessing to more than they had done, implicating friends, acquaintances, the innocent and not so innocent alike. Just recently one of Ni's friends had been arrested for a minor remark—an outburst of simple anger against one of his superiors. He was locked up and interrogated and not allowed to sleep.

That was it. It was not being allowed sleep that led so many to crack. They had promised the man leniency, promised him sleep, if only he would confess to his crime of counterrevolution, if only he would say who the other counterrevolutionaries were. Then his friend had cracked, confessed to being a counterrevolutionary, and he began implicating all sorts of others, the usual malcontents and innocent people as well, and then they became a counterrevolutionary clique and everyone was arrested, and the people who were arrested, in order to sleep, in order to get leniency, also cracked and also confessed and also implicated others, and the whole thing kept getting bigger and more serious, and no one knew yet where it would stop. But really, it started with nothing. Just a chance remark in anger.

He had to stop the interrogation. He could go no further. He had to have sleep. It must be four o'clock in the morning.

"I'm too tired," he said. "I can't remember anything anymore. I have to get some sleep."

Remarkably, his interrogators relented.

Ni was led out, down the corridor, and into another dimly lit room, the door locking behind him as two guards accompanied him in. "Take off your clothes," a fierce, thin, middle-aged woman commanded. Ni stripped down to his undershorts.

"Why are you still wearing those?" the woman snapped.

"You want me to take these off too?" Ni asked. The female guard took the opportunity of his apparent recalcitrance to slap the new prisoner twice, hard across the face.

"You see that sign on the wall?" one of the male guards demanded. "Read it. Out loud."

Ni read the prison regulations: Obey the prison guards. Honestly accept their education. Don't move or talk without permission. Conscientiously study Mao Zedong's thought. Reform your thought.

Ni was given a set of black cotton prison pajamas, devoid of buttons or snaps. A drawstring held up the trousers, and the shirt was meant to stay closed by a series of ties. Thus garbed in his new prison attire, he was led out of the room, down the stairs, through two more doors and into a darkened corridor.

• • •

It was the stench that hit him first, the stench of some four hundred filthy men and their unwashed *matongs*—the wooden buckets that serve in Shanghai as toilets—and overlaid with that the smell of the harsh disinfectant that was sprayed weekly as a precaution against infectious disease. The light was dim, and his guards continued to force his head down in an effort to prevent him from seeing, but Ni was aware of being led through a long corridor, lined on each side by cells—ten to each side—where the prisoners were now asleep. They stopped in front of one of the cells. "From now on, you have no name. You're number 824. Remember your number," the guard commanded as he opened the door and shoved the new prisoner in. "Don't talk."

The door slammed locked behind him.

Ni stumbled. He had stepped on someone's leg. "Fuck your mother's cunt," a voice at his foot snarled. This was not a cell for intellectuals become political prisoners. The voice and the language were of the criminal underclass.

He tried moving his foot. "Fuck you," another voice hissed as he stepped on another body. There was no place to stand. As his eyes adjusted to the darkness he began to be aware that there were bodies everywhere, lined in a row, body sandwiched between body, alternating head-foot, head-foot, head-foot. "There's no place for me to sit," Ni lamented out loud.

"Hey, new *hutou*, new account," a voice rasped from a corner, beginning the new prisoner's initiation into the prison jargon. Ni was a full-fledged prisoner now, registered, a number, an account, one of them, with no way out. "Over here. What are you in for?"

"I put up a big character poster about the Tiananmen incident."

"Oh, a counterrevolutionary head. Some kind of big counterrevolutionary fish, huh? Here, I'll give you a place. Sit on my leg."

Why was this guy being so polite?

The whole cell woke, filling with the vilest of curses, as Ni struggled his way across the bodies to the corner. "Come on, sit down, on my leg, like that, yea." Ni sat down on the prisoner's leg.

"You just arrived. You don't understand the rules yet. Sit here tonight. I'll help you out. Tomorrow you give me your breakfast."

As Ni's eyes gradually adjusted to the darkness, he began to grasp the dimensions of his new surroundings—about six feet long, four feet wide, and six feet high. The French had once used the cell for solitary confinement. There had been windows then, and there were bars over what had once been the windows, but steel plating now covered the opening that would have allowed the prisoners a view of the outside world. The room was sealed, the walls black. The fifteen-watt overhead bulb burned night and day, the light in the cell never changing. The signals that would tell the prisoner whether it was night or day would come not from nature but from the daily routine. The floor was concrete, covered with a movable raised wooden plank platform, wide spaces between the planks, bodily liquids, shedding hair, and sundry detritus from unwashed bodies dropping through the slats and onto the floor beneath. In one corner was the *matong*, hard now to discern. Someone was on it, asleep.

Ni counted nineteen men in his cell.

The steel door that served as the entrance was covered with open gridwork, and through the mesh, Ni could make out the mirror image of his own situation, the shadows of his fellow inmates across the way.

His mind raced in turmoil, unable to comprehend his circumstances or what the coming days might bring. Even in his exhaustion, there was no way to sleep. As he sat on the prisoner's leg, enveloped in his own confusion, his new cellmates settled back to sleep.

Then suddenly, after how many hours it was impossible to say, he heard running in the corridor, and people were yelling, "Get up, get up, get up!" Immediately the cell was awake with frenzied, silent activity. His first day in jail had begun.

The door opened and Ni watched as two of his cellmates deftly picked up the *matong* and handed it to two prisoners waiting in the corridor. While the prisoners in the corridor ran to the latrine to dump its contents and to rinse the wooden bucket quickly with water, the prisoners in the cell rapidly folded their quilts, one for every two persons, and piled them in syncopated motion one on top of the other in the corner opposite the *matong*. In another swift movement, the prisoners flipped over the wooden platform. Then the whole cell lined up in two rows, ten to each row, facing the door, two enamel wash basins placed just before the door. The working prisoners returned with the *matong*, carrying basins of water, too, and used a small aluminum lunch box to pass precious water through the small window in the door of the cell to the "convener"—the prisoner in charge of the cell. The convener, in turn, poured the water into the basins that sat before the door, passed the lunch box back to receive another ladle of water, until the basins were filled with a presumed teacup full of water for each prisoner in the cell. Then the convener used a teacup to distribute the water to the prisoners. Some of the prisoners used wash basins to receive their water, some their teacups, using half the water to wash their faces and run a wet washcloth over their bodies, half to brush their teeth. Then each person dumped his water back into the two wash basins, and the convener used a teacup to ladle the water back into the lunch box and passed the lunch box through the small window to the waiting working prisoner, the process repeated until the two basins were empty. The morning toilet was accomplished in minutes.

The convener made the daily assignments. Two people were ordered to clean the concrete floor, using a small tattered cloth and crawling on hands and knees to scrape the fallen debris onto a piece of toilet paper and dump it into the *matong*. Someone else was assigned to distribute the one large piece of rough brown toilet paper each prisoner was allotted daily. Then the convener made the seating assignments. The choicest spots were closest to the door, where there was a possibility of occasional ventilation, or along the walls. The worst seats were in the middle. Ni was assigned a seat in the middle.

The prisoners took their places, sitting with legs crossed, backs straight, hands in their laps, in the pose of meditation, waiting the half hour before breakfast. They were not allowed to talk or to close their eyes or to lean against the wall. With now twenty prisoners in the cell, they were crowded one on top of the other, body rubbing against body. Prisoners were not meant to be comfortable.

Breakfast arrived on carts, the blackened aluminum boxes in which the food had been steamed piled one on top of the other, delivered again by the privileged working prisoners.

It consisted of three ounces of sandy rice, some pickled vegetable, and a radish. From the corridor, the working prisoners handed the food boxes one by one through the window to the convener, whose job it was to distribute the meal. The working prisoners took little care to divide the food equally, so the convener had to make certain, before distributing the boxes, that his contained the most. He was skilled at making the selection, quickly distributing the boxes containing meager amounts of food, holding the fuller box for himself until one still fuller came along. He allocated the boxes according to whom among the prisoners he wanted to reward and whom he wanted to punish. Ni gladly donated his box to the cellmate who had given him a place to sit. The boxes were still steaming when they arrived, too hot to touch, and the prisoners took them with their daily allotment of toilet paper. Every box had a pair of chopsticks.

It took less than a minute for the prisoners to down their food, but they lingered much longer over the meal. The aluminum food boxes were battered and bent, and a grain of rice here, a tiny bit of vegetable there might be lodged somewhere in the many crevices. The prisoners worked intently, using their tongues to dislodge every minute morsel of food, every grain of rice. The men were perpetually hungry.

At the end of the distribution, a few extra food boxes were always left in the cart. Newly arrived prisoners, women especially, almost invariably refused to eat the first day, and sometimes several days went by before the new accounts became sufficiently hungry to swallow the miserable fare. Accompanying the working prisoners, strutting puffed with arrogance before them, were two police guards vested with the awesome authority of determining how to distribute the extras. One of the boxes went to the convener, for the spirit of cooperation he had displayed, and another to a particularly malleable account. The extra food was a way of eliciting cooperation between the prisoners and the guards, of sowing dissension among the prisoners, of getting prisoners to betray each other. No matter how small one's appetite outside, a month in jail left every prisoner in a perpetual state of hunger. They would do anything for food.

The lingering over, the food boxes returned, the prisoners sat motionless in their required places. They were offered weekly education sessions, one of the wardens lecturing as he paced the corridor, or sat smoking on a soft comfortable easy chair placed for his benefit at one end, while the prisoners sat silent and straight in their cells. The theme on Ni Yuxian's first day was one with which he was already familiar—the theme of gratitude to the government for its boundless generosity. "You prisoners are really lucky," the prison warden began. "You are not people. You are enemies of the people, wild beasts, not men. We can't let you loose on the streets of Shanghai, can we? We have no choice but to lock you up. But look how lucky you are. People have to work for their living. You don't work and still you are fed. The wind doesn't blow on you to make you cold. The sun doesn't shine on you to make you sweat. Somebody even changes your *matong* for you every day. The government is so merciful to you, and still you are ungrateful. The government feeds you, and all you can do is shit. You're nothing but fertilizer factories."

The main function of the warden's education was to persuade

the prisoners to confess to their crimes. "If you admit to your crimes," the warden would explain, "you will be given mercy. Not to recognize your crimes is an even bigger crime."

The prisoners were taught that whether their crime was large or small was not the basic question. The basic question was one of attitude. "If your crime is great but your attitude is good, your punishment will be lenient," the prisoners were assured. "If your crime is minor but your attitude is bad, your punishment will be heavy." Prisoners were provided with living examples of how the principle worked.

A murderer lacking the proper attitude, for instance, could naturally expect the death penalty. But the prisoners were told of the murderer who, after being incarcerated and receiving the education of the Public Security Bureau, not only confessed to his own crime but implicated many other of his criminal friends as well. The government, in its mercy, sentenced him to only twenty years in prison. The murderer became such a model prisoner, obedient and faithful, hard working and grateful, that he was released after serving only ten years of his original sentence. Naturally, he was eternally and vociferously grateful for the generosity of the government. The warden frequently read letters from former inmates of the detention center now serving their ten or twenty years in labor reform, thanking the prison officials for the generosity and understanding they had displayed.

On the other hand, there was the famous case of the two-bit gambler who thought his crime so minor as to be of hardly any consequence and scoffed at the reform that prison offered. He was labeled a counterrevolutionary and sentenced to life in prison. The prisoners were frequently warned of the possibility of transforming themselves from ordinary petty criminals into active counterrevolutionaries. Naturally, it was worse to be a counterrevolutionary than to be an ordinary criminal, and ordinary criminals were encouraged to keep the counterrevolutionaries in line, reporting on what they said in conversation and any other suspicious activity.

Prisoners with experience all knew of instances of petty criminals become life long prisoners and of leniency granted to prisoners who had both confessed to their own crimes and implicated others as well. But they also provided their own whispered corrections to the education the warden gave. Prisoners who confessed to a capital offense without implicating others were often executed in a matter of days.

• • •

Opportunities to confess were liberally granted. After two days in his cell, Ni was called to the interrogation room once more.

"Why did you put up the big character poster?" Qiu wanted to know.

"To oppose the government's suppression of the Tiananmen demonstrations."

"That's counterrevolutionary."

"No, it's not. I was opposing the Gang of Four."

"You were opposing China's present-day leaders. The Gang of Four has already been overthrown. Why should you have to sneak out in the middle of the night to hang up a big character poster attacking the Gang of Four? You were trying to provoke the masses into rising up against our country's leaders. You're not being honest. Recognize your guilt and we'll be merciful."

"The Tiananmen incident was a fascist atrocity. I am opposed to the suppression of Tiananmen. I have committed no crime."

Yuxian was escorted back to his cell.

Ni demanded to see the superintendent. "I am innocent," he asserted.

"No, you're guilty," the superintendent had responded. "Otherwise, what would you be doing here? If you keep insisting you are innocent, we'll get you for opposing the government. You're just making your case more serious."

A few days later, Ni was again brought face to face with Qiu.

"Are you ready to confess?" Qiu asked.

"I have committed no crime," Ni responded.

"You like it here, huh? Prison life agrees with you?"

"I'm used to it now."

• • •

"You won't be here long," his cellmates had assured him during those moments when the guard was occupied elsewhere and the prisoners could exchange whispered thoughts among themselves. "Your face is not the face of a man who is going to be executed. When the first anniversary of Tiananmen is over—if there are no major incidents—they'll let you go."

The government was in the habit of rounding up people in anticipation of trouble, releasing them sometime after the potential happening had passed. Anniversaries of significant events were potential precipitators of dissent. So certain was Ni of the justice of his cause, so convinced that most of Chinese society shared his views, so vast the differences between himself and the common criminals with whom he shared his cell, so deeply held the superstition that his face was the face of a hero, that he could almost persuade himself that his cellmates were right, that his time in jail would be fleeting. There was even empirical evidence for believing his sojourn would be brief. The other prisoners' heads were shaved. Ni's was not.

• • •

The system of incarceration in China is complex, providing those labeled as criminals with several forms of involuntary confinement and with several ways of determining which criminals will be incarcerated where and for how long.

Prisons are generally reserved for those who have actually been tried and sentenced, and in Shanghai, the largest and most famous of the jails is Tilanqiao. Only officials charged with singing the praises of the country's prison system would suggest that conditions in Tilanqiao are comfortable, but, comparatively speaking at least, the food can be considered adequate, crowding merely moderate, and opportunities for its inmates not bad. Many imprisoned in Tilanqiao are allowed to labor in one of its several prison workshops and thus to earn a small amount of pocket money with which to buy cigarettes and other incidentals.

Labor reform camps are another variety of incarceration, the preferred form of punishment for political prisoners—landlords and rightists and others alleged to oppose the socialist system—and for minor crimes committed by minors, juveniles under eighteen years of age. No trial is necessary to send a prisoner to two to three years of labor reform. The decision can be made administratively, by public security officials themselves, without the bother of courts.

To be dispatched to a labor reform camp is greatly to be feared. However light the initial sentence, most offenders stay for years. Once one's household registration is changed from the city of Shanghai to a rural labor reform camp, regaining an urban registration is a nearly impossible task. A convict who completes his two-to three-year sentence and has no job waiting in the city and no way to find one may simply be assigned to remain on the farm, working "in freedom" as one "staying after completion of sentence." Many, and particularly those without immediate family, stay for decades, lost and forgotten in the Chinese gulag. Most, in fact, never return.

In addition to several labor reform farms in the Shanghai suburbs, the municipality maintains several large, more distant labor reform camps—one in Anhui Province, another in remote and desolate Chinghai, another in Shaanxi. All the prisoners, and all the guards, too, are from Shanghai.

Shanghai also sentences some of its petty and younger criminals to labor reform factories run by the public security bureau. In 1977 the city and its suburbs had seven or eight such factories where all the workers were prisoners. Only a simple sign identifying them as "labor" factories provides a clue to the unwitting passerby of the situation within.

During the Cultural Revolution, when the places of incarceration overflowed and the system of dispensing justice was decentralized to the level of the work unit, another form of detention was established—the *niupeng*, or ox pen, the name deriving from the individuals who occupied them, known collectively as *niugui sheshen*—ox ghosts and snake spirits. Any place might serve as a *niupeng*—a dormitory room, an office, a tiny closet under a stairway, a basement storage space. The quality of the *niupeng* was a measure of the status of the criminal and of the crime he was alleged to have committed—the more objectionable the *niupeng*, the greater the crime.

Everyone confined by the Public Security Bureau passes through the final (but actually the first) form of incarceration—the detention center. The distinguishing feature of the detention center is that the fate of the prisoner there has yet to be determined. He is still awaiting sentence. Indeed, many prisoners in detention centers have yet to be formally arrested, for preventive detention is not uncommon, and the law allows suspects to be held for three months without formal charge. Suspects are often incarcerated before all the evidence against them is gathered.

Most prisoners do not remain in detention centers for long. The primary function of the detention center is to force the prisoner to confess, and so many factors conspire to force that confession that usually it is only a matter of time before most prisoners capitulate and declare themselves guilty of whatever is necessary to be moved on to prison or to labor reform. But sometimes it can take years for a prisoner's fate to be decided, years of waiting before evidence is gathered and the case is "clarified," years before the prisoner himself is moved to recognize his guilt. Once the prisoner proceeds from the condition of being detained to the condition of being under arrest, there is no guarantee of a speedy trial. Without sufficient evidence, or a confession from the prisoner, the courts are reluctant to pass final judgment on the accused. A recalcitrant case may take two years to settle—or four or five. Particularly recalcitrant prisoners, it is said, have stayed for ten and even twenty years. In the early 1980s, one accomplishment of prison reform was the release of long-term prisoners for whom the evidence was insufficient and who had still refused to confess.

In China's system of justice, the punishment often does not fit the crime, and the death penalty is liberally dispensed and for offenses—crimes against property, for instance—that might not be minor but are hardly so serious as to justify depriving the accused of his life. Appeals appear to be granted or denied at whim, and executions are often carried out immediately upon sentence without even the possibility of appeal. The criminal is expected to confess to his guilt, and torture is often used to extract those confessions. Forms of expression which in the West are assumed as basic human rights are regarded by the Chinese government as counterrevolutionary and hence as criminal, and counterrevolutionaries have regularly been shot.

Among the most odious aspects of the Chinese system of justice is the degree of dehumanization and degradation to which the prisoner is subjected, the success with which the prisoner is stripped of all that makes him human. Prisoners who have confessed to their crimes and moved on to spend the rest of their lives in labor reform camps may well regret having succumbed so soon, wishing in retrospect that they had held out a little longer in the worst of circumstances in order to avoid a lifetime—decades, at least—at labor reform. But in the short run, Chinese who have themselves passed through the system of incarceration agree that the detention centers are the most dehumanizing of all. Life in the detention centers is what the prisoners describe as *men*—long, slow braising over a hot, hot fire. "One month in a detention center," the prisoners say, "is equal to a year of labor reform."

Shanghai has more detention centers than prisons—some twenty-two in 1977, one for each of the ten districts in the city, one for each of the ten counties that make up the greater metropolitan area, and another two that were added because the twenty were not enough. Later, in Pudong, still another would open.

Prisoners held in detention exist in complete isolation from the outside world, no matter how long they might be detained. They are not allowed to write letters or to receive them, and they are permitted no visitors, even from members of their families. The prisoner's family is required to provide him with the basic necessities of prison life—soap, toothpaste and toothbrush, toilet paper, teacup, blanket, and winter clothing—and the family will receive periodic requests, written on a rough postcard with the detention center as the return address, suggesting that those supplies be replenished. But those requests are written not by the prisoner himself but by one of the privileged "worker prisoners" on behalf of the detainee.

In 1977 prisoners in Huangpu Detention Center were not allowed to read newspapers or books, except of course for Chairman Mao's Little Red Book, which they were encouraged, indeed required, to read for an hour or two each day. What occasional word they received of events beyond the prison walls was dispensed by the prison guards and through the internal public announcement system.

In one of the crueler ironies of the crowded Huangpu District Detention Center, prisoners who lived day and night one on top of the other in the most intimate physical contact remained isolated not only from the outside world but from each other as well. Little camaraderie grew up among the prisoners at the Huangpu Detention Center, little shared sense of a common fate or of a collective struggle against their common oppressors. The prisoners were not allowed to talk to each other—a ban, like all prison regulations, that was presented as a protection for the prisoners, necessary for their own good. "If we let you talk," the guards would say, "you might say something wrong. You might break the prison regulations or talk about your own case. Maybe you would say something counterrevolutionary, and your crime and your punishment would become worse. In fact, initially it was the prisoners themselves who raised the request that they not be allowed to talk. So you should be grateful. You should thank us for not allowing you to talk."

For Ni Yuxian, whose very existence depended on sharing his ideas with others, the restrictions against talking were as close to death as he had ever been—like being deprived of food, or sleep, or air to breathe. During the course of his confinement, he would devise a means of overcoming the strictures against speech,

assigning numbers, from one to ten, to each part of the facial anatomy—forehead, eyebrows, cheeks, nose, nostrils, mouth, and
chin—and then going through a series of steps to locate in
Chairman Mao's Little Red Book the word to be communicated—
the first set of numbers identifying the page, the second the line,
and the third the place of the word on the line. But the system
was inefficient and cumbersome—a single sentence took hours to
communicate—and was difficult to teach when communication
was so constrained from the start. Never was his sign language
particularly successful.

The isolation was compounded by the extreme sensory deprivation to which the prisoners were subjected. Locked in darkened,
windowless, putrid cells without ever seeing the sun or breathing
fresh air, prohibited from talking or moving or exercising the body,
the prisoners existed in an enforced state of suspended animation.

Of all the tortures devised by man to use against man, isolation
is the worst—worse even than most forms of brutal physical abuse.
Psychiatrists argue that the pathways to madness are ordinarily
complex, but the one psychic punishment that alone is capable of
producing mental breakdown is isolation—to isolate the individual
and treat him as an enemy. Used as a weapon to force a prisoner
to crack—to admit to his guilt and confess to his crimes—the isolation of Huangpu Detention Center was effective indeed.

But isolation was not the only means used by the authorities
to force their will upon prisoners. Deprivation of food was another.

The prison served three meals a day, three ounces of food per
meal, and the food was inevitably the same—sandy, gritty rice,
dotted with tiny black stones that viciously attacked both stomach
and teeth, and leftover, bitter, often rotten, bug-infested vegetables
that the state stores had been unable to sell. Once a month they
were treated to a bit of meat; rarely was there oil or salt. On nine
ounces of rice a day, the adult male is reduced eventually to a state
of nearly perpetual hunger. Except for the forty-five minutes or
hour after each meal until the food is fully digested, the prisoner's
entire waking life is devoted to thoughts of hunger and to fantasies
of food. No matter how he tries to concentrate on other matters—
on his own case, on his family, poetry, sex, any source of meaning
beyond his own stomach, he returns inevitably, almost immediately, to food. He elaborately calculates the hours, the minutes until
the next meal will come, his entire body attuned to any clue that
food is on its way. Awake or asleep, he dreams of food. The sim-

plest noodles, the most humble dumpling, the unadorned bowl of pure white rice is transformed into a coveted delicacy, and ordinary family fare, with meat and fish and eggs, is imagined as the most opulent of banquets.

After three months on such a meager diet, his health begins to suffer. In prolonged immobility, his muscles atrophy, become useless, and the lack of food leaves him weak. After several months at the Huangpu Detention Center, the prisoner has difficulty standing, can not walk without stumbling, must hold on to something stable. His body swells. His skin becomes diseased, a condition that is exacerbated as the sweat pours out in the heat of summer, since the crowded bodies rub against each other and prisoners are forced to sit all day without moving and they have no way to keep themselves clean. Once a month the prisoner's heads are shaved to cut down on the incidence of lice, but the lice still manage to thrive. Once every two or three months, the time determined by the whim of the guards, the hot water is turned on and the prisoners are given an opportunity, cell by cell, to bathe. Early in the morning, the order comes to strip, and the prisoners wait naked, locked in their cells, for their time to come. Then the cell door is opened, and the prisoners run out in single file, coaxed by billy clubs swatted against their bare behinds, guards yelling at them to hurry, to the bath room—seven pools some three by eight feet each, filled with water not merely black with dirt but sticky with oily filth. Soap is not permitted, and the prisoner is given one minute flat to luxuriate in the dark and tepid liquid.

The prisoner's skin is marked by sores, his bottom covered with pimples, and the pimples are filled with blood and with pus, and when the pimples burst open the pus and the blood stick to his bottom like glue, so that when he has to remove his cotton trousers to use the *matong* the sores pull painfully open and frequently become infected, and every trip to the *matong* becomes a matter of dread.

But the prisoner does not often have to use the matong. The warden was wrong to accuse the prisoners of being fertilizer factories. In their condition of semistarvation, with no oil, no salt, and meat only once a month, virtually all food that enters the stomach is quickly digested, and the bowels do not move with any great frequency—once a week at most and sometimes only once or twice a month. The stools of the prisoner are small pellets, rock hard and odorless, that often lodge painfully in the bowel, refusing to move, causing the prisoner to double over in pain and tears to run down the cheeks of even the most stoic of the lot. Faced with such a case, the guards will dispense a vial of soapy water to cleanse the intestines. But if soapy water does not work—and often it does not—the guard will call for help from other prisoners—an extra box of food in return for reaching inside the suffering man's rectum with a soap-coated finger to extract the hardened pellets.

In his perpetual state of hunger, the prisoner will go to almost any lengths to obtain extra food. He will gamble, a zero-sum game, winner take all, for an extra box of food, the challenge being to guess whether the page to which Chairman Mao's Little Red Book is turned is even or odd, the loser sacrificing his evening meal. It is the prisoner's perpetual hunger that renders so effective the system of prisoner managing prisoner, prisoner reporting on prisoner. Hunger is also the main reason the job of convener is so ruthlessly sought. The convener eats more than other prisoners. Charged with distributing the food, he naturally chooses the fullest box for himself and works to ingratiate himself with the guards and thus to secure one of the extra boxes that are available every day. The convener not only gets more food, he also gets the best place to sit and to sleep—next to the door. Occasionally, he can leave the cell to get some exercise, scrubbing the corridor floor or carrying the prisoners' blankets to air, where he can see the sun and look at the sky and the clouds and breathe fresh air. When the prisoners' families deliver the toothpaste and toothbrushes and toilet paper, it is the convener who goes to the office to pick up the necessities and distribute them to the prisoners.

Competition to become convener is intense and prisoners go to great lengths to prove their worthiness to serve. Success in the role depends in no small measure on the prisoner's willingness to report on his fellow accounts. The convener reports twice daily on his cellmates' misdemeanors. He is often the cruelest and most hardened of the prisoners, and often he has been there the longest or returned the most frequently—long enough and frequently enough to have learned the rules and to have forsaken his hesitations about playing them.

But no convener serves for long, because the longer the convener serves the greater the possibility of collusion between the convener and the prisoners, the greater the possibility of an outbreak of prison violence, and it is the possibility of riots that gives the prison officials greatest cause for fear. So the convener was chosen weekly, when the working prisoners would carry the warden's easy chair into the corridor, and the warden would proceed cell by cell, perched comfortably on his chair before each door, to hear the weekly report and make the weekly assignments. Conveners were changed and prisoners moved, too, for to allow prisoners to stay too long together in the same cell was also to risk the possibility of collusion and hence of untoward disturbance. It was during these weekly sessions with the warden that all the prisoners were given the competitive opportunity to rat. Prisoners competing for the position of convener, or those seeking to ingratiate themselves with the authorities and thus win an extra box of food or a more favorable reading of their case, regularly rose to report who had violated the rules against talking and what the violator had said, who slept while he was supposed to be sitting eyes opened wide, and who tried to curl up comfortably at night. Because so many accounts wanted to work as conveners and most accounts wanted to ingratiate themselves with the authorities, most lost any compunction about reporting—true or false—on their fellow cellmates. Attack first, the philosophy went, before being attacked yourself.

Prisoners were regularly punished for their misdemeanors, and punishment took many forms. With his authority over the details of everyday life, the convener's authority could make or break a prisoner's life. He could turn a blind eye when others stole your food or make sure your food box was always less than full. He could assign you the worst place to sit—in the middle of the cell without even the possibility of a place to rest your back—or have you sleep next to the dirtiest and smelliest of the accounts or the one with the most rancid and putrified skin. If you were slight, he could sandwich you in between two of the huskiest, destined to spend sleepless nights in a struggle against being crushed. He could humiliate you by refusing your request to use the *matong*, taunting to test how long your bladder or bowels would hold. Good relations with the convener were vital to surviving life in detention.

The more overtly brutal forms of punishment were the preserve of the prison guards.

One favorite form of torture simply required the prisoner to stand in the cell, unsupported, for an entire day. When the muscles have atrophied and the body has cried out for months in hunger, standing is an act of will the body often refuses to perform. The punishment for the body's refusal to obey is another day—maybe two—of standing.

Or the guards might grab the prisoner from behind, force his wrists together at the back, and yank his arms back and up toward the head, so that the prisoner falls down on his knees (which was why the punishment was known in prison jargon as "pressing the feet to the floor"), crying out in pain, as the arms nearly break loose from their sockets. Alternatively, for variation, the wrists could be forced together in front, the arms jerked up over the head and then back, in the torture known as "chicken claws," again to excruciating pain.

Or the guards might take the huge steel master key that opened the cell doors, the key as round as a thumb, and pound the tip into the prisoner's breastbone.

Suspension was another form of punishment, the prisoner being suspended by the wrists just inside the door of his cell, feet off the floor. Suspended by his wrists, which were variously tied together or spread out in the manner of a crucifixion, the prisoner could only be left dangling for an hour or so. After two hours, the arms would come permanently out of their sockets, leaving the prisoner crippled for life.

But handcuffing—the handcuffs having been imported during the days of the Guomindang from France, Germany, and even the United States—was the most convenient and therefore the most frequently employed form of punishment in Huangpu District Detention Center, the torture for which Shanghai is justly infamous. Every day, several people were taken out of their cells and placed in the corridor or an empty cell on the same floor to be handcuffed, and the handcuffs, once locked on the wrists, would be closed more and more tightly, cutting off circulation, digging into the skin, tearing the flesh, sometimes even breaking the bones. The very young and the very old were most likely to suffer from broken bones.

If the bones do not break there is little pain at first. After a few minutes the pain begins. At six minutes, the hands turn black and lose all feeling, becoming like wood, and the pain is concentrated in the arms, running gradually up the arms and into the head. When the pain hits the head it concentrates there, sending smaller waves of pain out to every part of the body. Then the pain fills the head and the head beings to feel as though it will burst, and when the head does not burst the pain again travels through the rest of the body, picking up and gathering strength. At fifteen minutes, the pain is so intense the prisoner breaks out in sweat, is covered, soaked, in sweat. Twenty minutes is the turning point. The pain becomes unbearable. The prisoner will topple over and begin writhing on the floor. If he is lucky, he will faint. But most prisoners do not faint. They begin sobbing, begging, pleading, crying like babies, calling to the prison guard, promising profusely never to misbehave again. Prisoners with weak hearts or high blood pressure have been known to die at this stage.

It is at this point, with the prisoner sobbing and writhing on the floor, in the depths of his pain and humiliation, that the guards will usually unlock the handcuffs.

The pain does not stop when the handcuffs are off. The body fills with a new type of pain, as though the whole interior is being stabbed by thousands and thousands of needles.

When, after five or six minutes, the pain of the needles has subsided and the prisoner begins to grow calm, the whole process begins again. The guard snaps on the handcuffs once more, the hands grow numb, the arms feel pain, the head begins to ache, the body is suffused with pain, the head seems about to burst, the prisoner sweats and writhes and cries, the whole torture being repeated over and over for half a day.

The prisoner who cries out—and nearly all of them do—is looked down upon as a coward when he returns to his cell, and for days thereafter his cellmates take advantage of his cowardice by attempting to steal his food.

Applied often enough or long enough, the handcuffs can cripple a prisoner for life. After only one session, the mere threat of being handcuffed again is sufficient to cause even the most stoic of prisoners to cry again like a baby, to plead with the prison guards, to promise repeatedly never to misbehave again.

•   •   •

Prisoners learn, often the hard way, after they have been betrayed, not to trust anyone in jail, not even the people who assure you they can be trusted. To be a prisoner, the saying goes, you have to be able to be a prisoner. And to be able to be a prisoner, you learn whom to flatter—the convener and the guards—and how to fend for yourself and how to betray the men with whom you share every minute of your every day.

Some never learn to cope, and manage by a variety of stealthy and ingenious means to commit suicide. Occasionally a prisoner would manage to kill himself by beating his head against the wall while his cellmates slept. Other swallowed the handle of their tea-cups or ate light bulbs. Ni Yuxian woke one night covered with a sticky moisture he knew could not be urine or sweat. His sleeping partner had managed to obtain a small nail meant for the sole of a leather shoe, had punctured the veins of his wrists and bled to death.

It was a daily war of all against all, brutal and nasty, and most prisoners did all they could to make certain their stay was short. The quickest, surest route out was simply to confess to the crime—the crimes—of which one was accused, even when the accusations exceeded, as they often did, the actual crime itself. Whatever the faults of the Chinese system of criminal justice, it is probably not often that the truly innocent find themselves under arrest. The Public Security Bureau usually gets the right man. Huangpu Detention Center really was brimming with the unsocialized dregs of Chinese society—the thieves, the rapists, the murderers. The mere fact that the criminal is caught, however, suggests to the Public Security Bureau that the criminal is guilty of other breaches of the law as well, and the criminal is thus encouraged to confess to far more than the evidence in hand might warrant.

Having caught a thief stealing a purse, for instance, the guardians of public order naturally find it difficult to believe that this is the only purse the thief has ever stolen. They want the thief to confess to having stolen others as well—say an average of one a month over a two-year period, for a total of twenty-four. If the thief refuses to confess, his verdict might be delayed—one year, two, three, or four—until he does. But if the prisoner confesses to his crime, if he says he stole twenty-four—better yet, thirty—purses, then he can be sentenced. He can go to prison. He can see the sunshine and breathe fresh air. He can have a pallet to sleep on. Once a month, he can write a letter to his family and once a month he can receive a letter, too. Occasionally, his relatives might be allowed a visit. If he is lucky enough to be sentenced to labor reform—to work in a prison factory or a farm—he will earn a little spending money each month—five or ten kuai, and he can buy some cigarettes or a pencil or a washcloth. At Chinese new year, he can buy a little something extra to eat—some sweets, maybe, or some dumplings. And he can talk. In prison, in the factories, on the farms, the prisoners are allowed to talk.

But most of all, the prisoner in jail or in the factories or on the farms can eat. Not well, to be sure, but the condition of perpetual hunger is over.

Most prisoners in Huangpu District Detention Center eventually confessed to whatever the authorities requested, even to crimes they had never committed. Confession was the best route out.

• • •

After three and a half months in confinement, Ni Yuxian still had not confessed. No amount of degradation, no amount of interrogation had shaken him from his conviction that he had done nothing wrong. More importantly, he knew from the whispered exchanges with his fellow prisoners what the price of his confession might be. Confessed counterrevolutionaries faced the possibility of death by a firing squad. At best, he would face decades of labor reform. It was not merely out of heroism that he refused to recognize his crimes but the raw instinct of self preservation.

• • •

Summer came to Shanghai. The city is always hot in the summer, miserably, ruthlessly, aggressively hot, and the summer of 1977 was the hottest the elders could remember. For the prisoners in Huangpu District Detention Center, the summer of 1977 was unbearable. The iron sheeting over the windows remained tightly in place; there were no electric fans and no ventilation, and the lights that had once seemed so dim became unbearably bright, the heat that emanated from them intense. The men stripped down to their undershorts and sweated and stank and sweated. The sweat was everywhere. When it dried, it dried on bodies in a sticky, smelly paste, and when it dripped, it dripped down bodies and through the wooden planking and onto the concrete floors where it sat in foul, dank puddles. When body rubbed against body, the sticky skin clung. The prison authorities bought huge blocks of ice and put them at the front of each cell, but the ice simply melted without cooling the prisoners at all. The guards took a basin of water and put it inside each cell in front of the door, and prisoners were allowed, when they could bear it no longer, to dip their washcloths in the water and sponge their bodies and place the wet washcloth over their heads. The water turned black, rancid, sticky. Twice a week, the heat was relieved when the guards used fire hoses to spray the prisoners with cool water, the force of the spray knocking the prisoners off their perches, throwing them willy-nilly on top of each other. The relief was short lived. The discomfort began again immediately after the water had evaporated. The prisoners began fainting. Every day, tens of prisoners would faint, and some, in their misery, would cry out begging for the opportunity to die. By August, several had died.

Sleeping was the worst. It was always the worst. Lying together like crowded sardines, body on top of body, made it impossible to move, and the more impossible it was to move the more the body and soul cried out to move. When the urge became irresistible, the result was inevitably a sharp hard jab from a neighbor's elbow or a quick deep bite in the flesh. Sometimes a single movement began a chain reaction, and the whole cell awoke cursing and fighting, and sometimes violence broke out and the guards came running, and the offenders were put into handcuffs. In the summer, with the sweat pouring off and body stretched against body, sticking together, the skin putrefied, air unbreathable, nose inevitably pressed against another prisoner's nauseatingly smelly feet, sleep was nearly impossible.

• • •

One afternoon in mid-July, Ni was called into the superintendent's office, and invited to sit on the sofa. The superintendent offered him tea and turned on the electric fan. Deng Xiaoping, purged immediately after the suppression of the Tiananmen demonstrations and accused of instigating the protests, the party leader Ni's poetry had praised, the man he hoped would return to lead the Chinese people, had been restored to power. China, at last, was on the brink of change.

"You've already been here for several months," the superintendent said. "But now that Comrade Deng Xiaoping has been restored to office, your case can be resolved quickly. We'll be able to release you very soon. Our law isn't like capitalist law or Guomindang law. We don't have any law code. We act under orders of the communist party, according to communist party policy. Your case was a mistake. Now that Comrade Deng is back, you'll be going home soon."

Ni was delighted, properly grateful to the Public Security Bureau for recognizing its mistake. He returned to his cell to await the release that the superintendent had assured would come in a matter of days.

A month later, he was still waiting.

Then one afternoon, the cell door opened and Ni was ordered to gather his few possessions. He was confused. He should be going home, but the surliness with which the guard delivered the order was not the attitude ordinarily displayed to prisoners on the verge of freedom.

He was escorted up two flights of stairs, to the third floor. The corridor was a duplicate of the one he had just left, but it was eerily silent. On the first floor, discipline was lax, the place fairly buzzing with whispering prisoners defying the regulations. One knew on entering the passageway that the cells were filled with living, breathing men. But the third floor was silent as death. It was the floor reserved for those who had moved from the stage of investigation to the stage of being under arrest, and the cases held there were the most serious in all the prison.

Ni Yuxian had been placed under arrest.

The order, he would learn later, had come from Su Zhenhua, the highest-ranking government official in Shanghai. In the official order charging him with counterrevolution, Su had added some of his own thoughts in hand. "This man is a reactionary through and through. If he is not executed, the indignation of the masses will never cease."

Ni was placed in cell number thirteen, a special cell, heavily guarded. Many of its inhabitants were scheduled to die.

There were more regulations—some thirty-six altogether—for third floor prisoners, and the regulations were strictly enforced: When sleeping, do not curl your legs. When sitting, do not close your eyes for more than three seconds at a time. Do not change places. Do not pretend to use the *matong*. No talking. No whispering in each other's ears. No talking about your own case. Do not tell anyone why you are here.

The guards were different on the third floor, too, took special delight in torturing their charges, seemed to have been chosen especially for their cruelty. Prisoners charged with violating the regulations were regularly handcuffed, their cries of pain and pleas for mercy piercing the otherwise eerie silence of the block.

An ignorant lout named Shan, aggressively contemptuous of intellectuals, the cruelest and most feared of the guards, served as bad cop to Wang Zhong's good. Red face–white face the prisoners described the relationship, referring to the red faced villains of Beijing opera. Wang Zhong would never handcuff a prisoner, but

Shan swaggered into the corridor each day with six sets of handcuffs clanging from his waist, revelled at the opportunity to force a prisoner into handcuffs, tried to find an excuse to use the whole panoply of his collection each day. He was skilled in their application, managing, by bracing himself with a foot in the prisoner's stomach, to surpass all others in the tightness with which the manacles were closed. Out of their hate and their fear, the prisoners alternated between cringing in silent terror and gushing in lavish obsequiousness, extravagant praise, before him, as Shan received their manifestations of subservience with bravado, fancying himself a hero.

The hatred between Ni and Shan was mutual, instantaneous and unceasing.

Ni could not sleep that first night, or for many nights thereafter. The heat alone was sufficient cause for insomnia, but Ni was kept awake, too, by the brutality of his new circumstances and because he could not understand—does not understand to this day—why he had been catapulted from the promise of imminent freedom to imprisonment on death row. He began dreaming the dream that would haunt him the rest of his life in prison. He was locked in a darkened jail cell. Each of the four walls had a door through which prisoners could enter but from which there was no escape. He lay on a narrow ledge that traced a rectangle around the cell, and on the ledge other prisoners, too, the dregs of humankind, lay lounging. In the middle was a huge, deep, open black pit, and at the bottom of the pit, he knew, were all the prisoners who had fallen off the ledge. Periodically one of the other prisoners would lose his balance and fall screaming from the ledge and into the pit, and as he was falling the pit would momentarily light up as if by fire to reveal the blood and the exposed red flesh of the fallen prisoners. Ni's life on the ledge was a constant struggle to maintain his balance, a fight against the temptation of looking down. He knew that if he fell asleep, he would lose his balance and fall into the pit. He struggled constantly against sleep, his eyes closing, his body relaxing, his body tottering, his eyes opening, regaining his balance, succumbing again to exhaustion, tottering, slipping. Just as he fell forward, plunging into the pit, he would awake with a sudden start.

• • •

The second morning, when the convener gave his morning report, Ni was surprised to hear him say, "There's a terrible person in here. He did a terrible thing last night, an obscene thing. Those guys will tell you.''

Two other prisoners stood up. "It was the counterrevolutionary, number 824. He's a homosexual. He raped us last night when we were trying to sleep."

Ni was astounded. Homosexual behavior was a criminal offense. Surely there could be nothing worse than a homosexual counterrevolutionary.

"That's outrageous. I've never heard of such a thing," Ni responded, dumbstruck.

Shan did not believe him. He clamped handcuffs around Ni's wrists and shoved his foot in the prisoner's stomach, turning the handcuffs as tight as he could. Twenty minutes on, twenty minutes off, the hands turning black, the body breaking out in sweat, the head bursting with pain, the whole body convulsing in pain, writhing in pain, Shan kept up the torture for the entire morning, waiting for the prisoner to confess.

The pain was unbearable, and Ni was already weak from hunger and heat. He would have done anything for respite. But if he confessed, his sentence would be harsher still, his reputation would suffer. He would be seen as a homosexual.

When good cop Wang came on duty that night and the convener made his nightly report, Ni called out from his place on the platform. "I have something to report," he said. His hands were still limp and swollen. "They said today that I did something obscene. So they handcuffed me and wouldn't let me eat. This is inhumane. You shouldn't behave this way to people."

"What? You're opposing the government? You're saying the government is wrong?" Wang responded.

"No, I'm saying the guard is wrong. I'm saying the prisoners were wrong to accuse me. This is not opposing the government. I'm innocent. I did absolutely nothing."

"Who can give evidence against 824? Who accused him?" Wang wanted to know.

The two prisoners stood up. "We were sleeping next to him. He raped us," they avowed.

"Take off your pants," Wang commanded the two prisoners. The two men stripped. "Take off 824's pants," the guard commanded the working prisoner who stood beside him. The men stood there naked, their rear ends covered with the usual blood and pus from the sores that never healed. Wang examined Ni's penis, looked carefully at the two prisoners front and behind. There was no evidence of rape.

The prisoners who had accused him were required to stand the entire next day.

• • •

September 1, 1977, was a brilliantly beautiful day—one of those rare Shanghai days when the sun actually shines and the sky is utterly blue and dotted by a few fluffy white clouds, when the air has lost its pollution and the temperature is pleasantly warm, the oppression of the heat temporarily lifted. Ni Yuxian left the Huangpu District Detention Center in much the same manner he had come, sitting in the back of a paddy wagon, sirens blaring, red lights whirling, with police cars accompanying him ahead and behind. He was still wearing his prison garb, the black pajamas with the name of the detention center stamped in yellow across the front and the back, and his head had long since been shaved. They had manacled his wrists again, though not too tightly, and tied a long rope around his neck, winding it several times around his body. Traveling through the streets, passing by the Bund, everywhere Ni looked were people, more people than he remembered from a few months before, when he had last seen the streets of his city, and the atmosphere, he thought, had changed. The people of Shanghai seemed freer, somehow, and more relaxed, smiling, even, and unconcerned. They wore brighter colors, and for the first time that he could remember China seemed a land of the free. He thought fleetingly of attempting to bolt to freedom himself.

They went by ferry this time, arriving in Pudong to a profusion of colored flags and streets lined with all manner of police. Surely they had not gone to so much extravagance for his execution? But no, there were slogans everywhere, too, "Warmly welcome Yugoslavia's President Tito," the head of the communist nation from which China had so long been estranged. The rift finally mended, Tito had passed in cavalcade only moments before on a visit to a commune in rural Pudong.

Ni was back once more on Yanggao Road, returning to his factory. The entire workforce was assembled to shout slogans demanding his execution, the slogans calling for his death greeting him along Yanggao Road well before the factory gates. His name was written upside down, crossed out with thick red Xs. They led him, tied like a package, two police standing on either side, supporting and propelling him forward, into the familiar auditorium and onto the stage. He was weak from lack of food and the degeneration of his muscles. The police let go, and he began swaying. His legs buckled. He could not stand. He had to be held for the duration of the meeting.

Weak though he was, his head was clear as he looked out across the sea of familiar faces—his friends, his workmates, his political allies and confidants. He read sympathy on many of those faces, even as they joined in the slogan shouting against him. Xu Xingfa was there, with her husband. She had tears in her eyes and cried for most of the meeting. The police knew of Xu Xingfa and had come to question her and her husband about their relationship to the counterrevolutionary Ni. All Ni's friends in the factory had been questioned.

But as he looked out at all the faces staring at him so openly, so curiously, suddenly Ni felt another feeling emanate from the crowd. He was no longer one of them, no longer even human. They were staring not at a man but at an animal, a beast.

He was silent for most of the proceedings. His strength to resist had dissipated. But as the meeting drew to a close, he turned to Qiu Linting and tried to summon a voice that the audience could hear. "I have been falsely accused," he said. "Execute me if you like, but in the end, the Chinese people will settle accounts."

Still tied with rope, they put him in a small room, its door still open and windows facing onto the corridor. One by one, the factory workers came to look at him there, as though he as a human being, Ni Yuxian, the man with whom they had once worked, the man they all had known, no longer existed. "I'm hungry," he would plead with each one. "Can you find me something to eat?" It was as though he had never spoken.

The man who had served for years as the factory equivalent of the village idiot, the mentally incapacitated lowest figure on the factory totem pole, came to stare and to strike out in power against the only man he had ever encountered who stood lower on the social hierarchy than he.

A neighbor came, keeping a proper distance, a young man who had gone with Ni to Yangsi Middle School, who had been together with him in the army, who had also been at the Maritime Academy, who lived only doors away from the Ni family. Yuxian hoped the young man might communicate some word of his current state to his parents. But as Ni gestured, the young man fled in incomprehension and in terror.

They had taken a vote that day in the factory workshops, and there had been only one dissenter, the foreman of Ni's own workshop, one of the oldest and most experienced of the workers. "He wasn't such a bad worker," the old man had said. "Maybe he should be given more of a chance to reform. Why not sentence him to life imprisonment instead of having him killed?" But the foreman got in trouble for his compassion, and the rest of the factory voted for Ni's immediate execution. The materials sent by the Public Security Bureau for them to consider left no doubt what course the government had chosen, what decision the masses were expected to make. "Ten thousand deaths are not enough for this man," Qiu Linting's report had concluded. "Even his death is not sufficient to avenge his crimes."

When the paddy wagon left the factory and sped, sirens screaming and red lights flashing, back down Yanggao Road, Yuxian did not expect to return to the detention center. Most prisoners who returned to their factories to be sentenced to death by the masses were executed immediately thereafter. Ni expected to be delivered to the execution grounds.

But the motorcade retraced the familiar route, delivering Ni alive back to the Huangpu District Detention Center, third floor, cell thirteen, from whence he had come only a few hours before. His life, temporarily at least, had been spared.

No one ever formally notified Ni that he was on the list to be shot. The notification would be made just preceding the execution itself. But from that day forward, he knew what the decision had been. Ni was a *qiangbi gui*, an "execution ghost." He had been sentenced to death.

Back in the detention center, Ni demanded paper and pen to write an appeal. "We still haven't chopped off your head," the guard responded. "Why do you want to appeal?"

"When you've chopped off my head, I won't be able to appeal," Ni responded. "I want to write it now."

They gave him paper and pen and put him in a small room where he composed his letter to the Chinese supreme court. He included excerpts from "I Do Not Believe." "Do you really think this poem is an attack on Chairman Mao?" he asked. "Is it really counterrevolutionary? It is an attack on the Gang of Four and how they handled the Tiananmen demonstrations."

• • •

On September 5 they came for Gao Fei. A guard yelled his number. "What's your name?" they asked after the skinny little man with the sunken cheeks and puckered mouth, not three ounces of flesh on his monkeylike face, stood up.

"Gao Fei."

"Where are you from?"

"Shanghai."

"How old are you?"

"Sixty-three."

"Get your things together."

The whole cell watched as Gao Fei put a few pitiful belongings—some worn-out shoes and some tattered clothes, his toothbrush and toothpaste, his washcloth and teacup—into his little bag. After more than fifteen years in the hands of the Public Security Bureau, all of Gao Fei's possessions were contained in that little bag. He had been arrested for writing a letter critical of the Communist Party and mailing it without signing his name. Most of the counterrevolutionaries in Huangpu District Detention Center were there for writing letters, or because a relative or colleague had read their diaries and discovered antiparty thoughts, or because of certain words they had spoken, even in private. To send a letter critical of the Communist Party without having signed one's name was considered a particularly counterrevolutionary form of counterrevolutionary activity, and particularly dangerous, too. Some critics seeking anonymity would compose letters by gluing ideographs cut from newspapers onto blank pages. Compositions cut from the pages of newspapers were hard to trace. But handwriting, even without a signature, could be traced, as Gao Fei's finally was.

He was sentenced to fifteen years at labor reform and when his time was up, because he had no job waiting, he was assigned to continue at labor reform, working as "one who had completed his sentence." After a while, though, Gao Fei had run away, back to the city of Shanghai, managing to stay alive by helping peasants who came to the city to sell their produce and because he had a brother who looked out for him. Gao Fei's mistake was to write another letter critical of the Communist Party and to send it to Chairman Mao.

Gao Fei did not want to die. He never thought he would be executed. His will to live—and the extent to which the guards were willing to go to deceive him—was witnessed in the fact that he actually served as convener in cell thirteen—a position he had won through the enthusiasm and frequency with which he reported on his fellow prisoners. Having survived so many years of labor reform and prison, he was as hardened as they came and thought that after all those years, he really knew how to be a prisoner.

As he was led away, the prison broadcast the news that the final decision on Gao Fei's fate would be made that very day.

His cellmates always knew that Gao Fei would be shot. After all, his monkeylike face without three ounces of flesh was the face of a man whose fate was doomed. Besides, Gao Fei was just too bad to live. His cellmates hated the man for the insistence and enthusiasm with which he reported every minor transgression of the rules. And a man who would still dare to write a letter to Chairman Mao after fifteen years of labor reform was a man beyond reform.

The announcement came only a few hours later. "Today, the Shanghai municipal court held a large meeting to decide the cases of a small group of counterrevolutionaries. Several tens of counter-revolutionaries have been executed. Gao Fei, because he twice wrote letters attacking Chairman Mao and the Chinese Communist Party, was executed."

The prison doctor, the man who accompanied the prisoners to the execution grounds to verify that they were dead, the man who had just accompanied Gao Fei to his death, who had certified that Gao Fei was no more, came to visit cell thirteen soon after. "Hey, 824," he addressed Ni, "Gao Fei was executed today. How do you feel about that?" Ni had slept next to Gao, back to back, ever since being moved to the cell. "See you at the execution ground," the prison doctor said in taking his leave. "Give 824 a little more rice tonight," the guard instructed the working prisoners ladling out the evening meal. "Pretty soon we won't be seeing him anymore."

Ni knew his death was imminent. On the rare occasions when the prisoners actually spoke, he was now referred to unsparingly as the "execution ghost," and his fellow prisoners often used pantomime to make the point, directing a finger like a gun at their heads, pulling the would-be trigger with their thumbs.

China's National Day—the twenty-eighth anniversary of the establishment of the People's Republic of China—was on October 1. The government would want to use the occasion, as it always did, for a few more public executions, warning the citizenry of the price of deviance. Ni was sure he was scheduled to die.

September 15 was another sleepless night. He lay awake with the same words repeating in his mind like a broken, inescapable record, "crossing the Rubicon, crossing the Rubicon, crossing the Rubicon." He knew that if he did not do something immediately—something very dramatic—his life would soon be over. This was his Rubicon, his last chance to fight.

Suddenly, in the darkened, crowded, stultifying jail cell, crowded now with the prone bodies of the sleeping prisoners, Ni Yuxian stood up. "I want to protest," he yelled as loudly as his voice would allow. "I want to protest the unfair judgment of the Shanghai municipal government. I am innocent. I want to appeal to the central government."

The prison was waking up. "Are you crazy?" some of the prisoners were asking.

"Everyone listen," Ni continued. "All of you listen carefully. My name is Ni Yuxian. Ni Yuxian, from Pudong, Yangsi Village. I am locked in here because of the Tiananmen demonstrations. Because I wrote a big character poster opposing the fascist atrocities of the Gang of Four. The leaders of Shanghai want to execute me. But I am innocent. The new leaders are as bad as the Gang of Four. They're fascists. This is my appeal. Listen. If any of you friends here have the opportunity to leave jail, please tell the others about my case. Let the Chinese people, Chinese society, know that Ni Yuxian is innocent."

The guards were in front of the cell. "What are you doing?" they demanded.

"I want to write an appeal. I want you to take my appeal to the highest court. If you don't let me write, if you don't make certain that my appeal is delivered to the highest court, my death will be on your hands. You will be responsible."

"Okay, okay. You can write. But if you say another word, you're going to get a wad of cloth stuffed in your mouth." The cell door opened and Ni was taken to another small cell set aside especially for prisoners writing their confessions.

The next day, he received a visit from the public security official in charge of his case. "I hear you created some kind of ruckus last night," he said. "I'm handling your case right now, and you should know that your case has already been decided. There's no way to overturn the decision. It's gone all the way up to Chairman Hua

Guofeng, so no matter what kind of appeal you write, there is no way to change it. We'll let you write your appeal, but you're on the road to death. Your last day will be upon you sooner rather than later. Don't get any false hopes."

"I'm not afraid to die," Ni responded. "When I hung up the big character poster, I was prepared to die. But I still believe that the judgment on the Tiananmen incident will be reversed, that history will prove me right, and you have responsibility for making sure my appeal reaches the court. I want the chance to write out my entire viewpoint, the whole circumstances that led to my arrest."

"Okay, write, But don't hold out any hope."

For five days he wrote, protesting his innocence, until finally they would let him write no more.

The country celebrated the twenty-eighth anniversary of the founding of new China, and Ni was still alive. His letter must have reached the court.

Still, the pressure was on to confess.

Qiu Linting, in particular, seemed to lose face over Ni's stubborn refusal to recognize his guilt. "We know you oppose socialism. We know you are against the Communist Party," Qiu would reiterate each time Ni was called in for an interrogation. "There is no doubt about it." Qiu had a way looking directly into Ni Yuxian's heart. "But you have to say so more clearly. The reason you wrote the big character poster was to get the masses to rise up and oppose socialism, right? You want to overthrow the government, don't you? You're trying to get the people to rise up in a second Cultural Revolution, aren't you? Confess, Ni. Recognize your guilt, and we'll give you a way out. We won't execute you. The more you admit, the more merciful we'll be. We'll let you go home. We'll find work for you, good work. But if you don't confess, if you don't recognize your guilt, it will be worse for you. Just admit that you really are a counterrevolutionary, that you really were trying to create *luan*—turmoil."

They wanted, too, for Ni to implicate others, to admit that he had not acted alone. They wanted him to identify his co-conspirators.

But he knew, as everyone in prison knew, that to admit his guilt was to sign his own death warrant, that there would be no leniency, no release, no return to his family or work. However close his execution might be without an admission of guilt, it would be immediate once the confession was signed.

Bad cop Shan was another of the representatives of public order who tried, by tricks, to wrest a confession.

Once a week, the prisoners were stripped and ordered out of their own cell and into another while the cell was sprayed with a disinfectant. As the naked prisoners passed before him, Shan was in the habit of requiring them to state their crimes. "I am innocent," Ni had responded the first time Shan asked. "I have committed no crime." Shan put Ni in handcuffs, vowing to handcuff him whenever he refused to admit to his crime. Thereafter, Yuxian simply remained silent.

His mental balance suffered. One afternoon, assigned a position in the very inside of the cell, suffocating from the heat and the lack of air, suddenly he could stand it no more. He stood up and stumbled for the door, gasping for breath. The convener called for the guard. "824 violated the regulations," he yelled. "He ran to the door."

"Why are you so disobedient?" the guard yelled in exasperation. "You're the worst kind of criminal. You're a counterrevolutionary."

"I'm not a counterrevolutionary," Ni snapped back.

They took him to a separate cell and handcuffed him again.

His hands turned black and numb. His arms began to ache. The pain hit his head. He broke out in a sweat. He could bear it no more.

"What crime have I committed?" Ni suddenly yelled at his captors, yelled at his cellmates, yelled at the top of his lungs for the whole prison to hear. "What have I done wrong? I wrote a big character poster opposing the Gang of Four, opposing their suppression of the Tiananmen demonstrators. I only wrote what should have been written, what everyone feels. And for that, I have suffered so much." Suddenly he was sobbing like a baby, uncontrollably. He could not stop. His captors misunderstood. They thought he was crying in pain, from the handcuffs that were cutting his wrists. But he was crying in anger and in hate. He hated Shan; he hated the guards, hated everyone in the prison. They are not human, he thought. They are animals, worse than wild beasts. How did they become like this? What is wrong with this country? Why was I born here?

When he stopped crying, he felt toughened by the depth of his hate. He vowed never again to talk to Shan, never to give the guard another excuse to handcuff him. He vowed that if he ever left the prison alive, he would devote his entire life, every last measure of his energy, to fighting against the system that sent men like him to prison, the system that produced prisons like the one he was in.

. . .

With the threat of execution ever present, with the constant, unrelenting pressure to confess, after so many months of hunger, without exercise, with his muscles atrophied, his skin constantly bursting with blood and with pus, his health deteriorated. His whole body swelled with edema, his face puffed up like a balloon, he was so weak that he could no longer stand or walk. Finally, when the guards knew from experience that the prisoner was close to death, would die without medical care, they took him handcuffed in the paddy wagon, through the streets of Shanghai, to the prison hospital at Tilanqiao. Again Ni looked out at the city, at all the people who seemed so free, and thought of escape, but again it was a fleeting, passing thought. He was too weak to run, and surely they would shoot him if he tried.

"Take off your clothes," the nurse commanded when Ni was brought before her. She took his blood pressure, then began massaging his penis, fondling it, Ni thought. "Why are you doing that?" he demanded. "For your illness," she responded, but Ni saw her massaging other prisoners' penises and thought the nurse perverted.

In the hospital, they gave him a bun of steamed flour for breakfast, and rice porridge—white rice porridge, and the rice was free of sand. There were no bugs. The breakfast was the most delicious he had ever eaten. Three times a week there was meat. He slept in a real bed, soundly and long, turning over on his back, tossing and turning, curling up his legs. There were only two other prisoners in the hospital room, and they could talk to each other, get up, and walk around.

And he could write. He wrote another letter of protest to the Shanghai municipal government, another declaration of his innocence. "I have been jailed because I protested the Gang of Four's fascist atrocities at Tiananmen," he wrote. "I know that someday the Tiananmen demonstrators will be recognized as revolutionary. My resistance to the Gang of Four, to the handling of Tiananmen, someday will be recognized as right."

Again, he thought of trying, somehow, to run away. Two prisoners had recently escaped from Tilanqiao by hiding themselves in the underbelly of a truck that had been making a delivery to the prison. But the pair had been captured within a matter of days and executed immediately. Ni dismissed the thought. There was no way out.

His health recovered quickly in the luxury of the prison hospital. After a week, they were ready to send him back to the detention center.

He returned to prison toughened by health. He vowed to learn how to be a prisoner, when to flatter and when to remain silent. As months had gone by without his sentence being carried out, he came to believe that either he would be executed or he would be freed. There would be no middle path. He wanted to be free.

He tried to train his mind. In the few hours every day when his thoughts were not overtaken by hunger, sitting still and straight, his eyes always open as required, he would stare, transfixed, at the wall or the ceiling. Then, somewhere in his mind's eye, flowers would begin to appear on the wall, all manner of flowers in rich profusions of colors and scents, and suddenly the cell would be filled with spring. He pictured a boat, a gentle junk like the ones Guansheng used to own, and then the cool waters of the canals and the paddy fields that lined their banks would begin to appear, and the water buffalo with their plows, and then he was slowly poling the junk through the lush green countryside of his youth. He pictured the sun and a blue, blue sky and fluffy white clouds, and the air clean and fresh, and suddenly he was outside and it was spring again and he was running through the fields with his friends in laughter and in play. Or he saw a tree, a tall, green tree, its leaves spread wide, reaching for the sky, and he was sitting under the tree, reading, thinking, his mind wandering through a thousand pleasant thoughts.

He lost his sense of time. Sometimes months passed in a matter of what seemed like days. Sometimes a single day could last a month.

He recited Tang poetry to himself, and he made up his own poems and tried to memorize them. Every week he would write a new poem, and then every two months or so, when he was taken out of the cell to write again his version of the events that led to his arrest, he would carry his little red book of Chairman Mao's quotations, and along the margins, between the lines, he would write his own poems so they would never be forgotten.

And he thought of Kajia. Always, obsessively, when he did not have to think of food, he thought of Kajia. He wrote her letters, letter after letter. And poems. Many of the poems were to Kajia.

When they transferred Ni Yuxian from the first to the third floor and put him under formal arrest, they had finally let Kajia go. The young woman had never cracked, never deviated from the story of her innocence and naïveté, the story that Ni Yuxian had duped her into putting up a big character poster whose contents she had not understood. When the police became convinced of her political innocence, they had begun to attack her morals, trying to force her to admit that her alliance with Ni was, if not political, then sexual. Most of the women with whom she shared her cell were charged with illicit sexual relations of one form or another, and her cellmates all assumed that Kajia shared their crime. But the young woman never admitted to anything more than friendship with the young man who she said had once been her father's student.

When they tried to cut the long plaited pigtail that reached all the way down to her waist, she had protested so vehemently that she left the jail with her braid intact. The young woman passed her time in jail without great complaint, because prison for her was still better than the time she had spent hungry and frightened, alone in the countryside of Anhui. The nine ounces of rice she was served every day was better than what she had eaten there, and it was served with predictable regularity.

Only once in her three months in prison did Kajia ever cry. Her cellmates told her about it the next morning. She had dreamed about her mother that night. Mrs. Ye had not known of her daughter's political activities, learned that something was amiss only at the moment of her daughter's arrest, when the police came to take her away. By then it was too late to talk. The woman had already suffered so much, with her husband's murder, her own period of exile, the disintegration of her family, and now the additional humiliation of her daughter's arrest. In her dream, Kajia had cried out in loneliness and in pain and loss for all that her mother, her family, she herself, had endured.

When Ni learned, through one of the guards, of Kajia's release, he was desperate to send her a message. One night, in a conversation whispered ear to ear, he learned that his sleepmate was soon to be released.

"Will you do me a favor?" Ni asked. "I'll share my food with you if you agree. Will you take a message to one of my friends?"

In return for a portion of Ni's food until the time of his release, the soon-to-be-free prisoner agreed. Ni gave him Kajia's name and address. It was winter then, and every Sunday, in order to give them a little exercise and as a small antidote to the cold and damp of their cells, the men were allowed to exercise in one of the nearby cells. The window was not completely sealed, and from a small crack one could look out at the rear exit of the museum.

"Tell her to stand just in front of the museum door on Sunday morning," Ni instructed. "If everything is okay, tell her to carry a copy of Chairman Mao's Little Red Book. If there is a problem, tell her to carry a white book."

Ni's great concern was whether any of the others had been arrested. One day, when a new prisoner had been delivered to an adjoining cell, he had heard him called Guang Ming, and spent days of anxiety until a chance glimpse of the man assured him that the new prisoner was not in fact his friend.

But above all he wanted some sign from Kajia, some indication of her concern, some message of her love. Week after week, every Sunday during exercise, he looked through the crack in the window expecting, hoping, to see her standing there. The weeks went by and the weeks turned to months, and still Kajia had not appeared.

He looked for some other sign of her concern, searching the deliveries of toothpaste and soap for evidence she had visited his family, left some visible, tangible display of her love—like the green-labeled, expensive brand of toothpaste rather than the ordinary brand his family invariably sent.

And when the months went by and no sign came his heart began to harden. If Kajia loved him, he reasoned, if she really were concerned, she would have found some way to provide him with a sign. She would have come to stand weekly before the door to the museum. She would have sent him the expensive, green-labeled toothpaste. Obviously, she no longer cared.

What Ni could not have known, did not know until much later, when his heart had already turned hard, was that the soon-to-be-freed prisoner never was set free. But as evidence of how badly he wanted to be free, as evidence of the degree to which he was willing to cooperate with his captors, he had informed the police of Ni's request. Kajia's political naïveté had been thrown into question once more. She had been brought back to the police station for questioning, forced to undergo repeated interrogations about the "problem" to which Ni referred.

The young woman remained indomitable. Her story never changed. But she never knew she was supposed to appear on Sundays at the door to the museum. To have visited the Nis, to have tried to provide a sign that she still cared, would have been dangerous in the extreme. The young girl pined and waited, still in love and deeply concerned, in solitude.

• • •

The jail grew more and more crowded, filled to overflowing. Government policy was changing, and judgments against prisoners were no longer so intrinsically obvious. More and more prisoners awaited their final verdicts.

Summer was approaching, and the experts were predicting that again it would be wickedly hot. The authorities were loathe to preside over a repeat of the previous year's deaths. When Ni was selected as one of several hundred prisoners to be transferred to a temporary, makeshift jail, a building that had once housed a middle school, he knew that his most dangerous period had passed. He would not be executed. But neither were the authorities ready to let him go free.

In the makeshift jail, Ni's circumstances seemed to improve. The summer was wickedly hot, and the new prison was only marginally more comfortable than the detention center had been. In the new jail, the prisoners had to contend with mosquitoes as well as the heat. But after more than a year in captivity, Ni was finally learning how to be a prisoner. The prisoners had begun to treat him with the deference reserved for accounts who have endured without ever having cracked.

Ni had come to know the guards, too, had studied their character, learned whom and how to flatter. He knew that good cop Wang, for instance, fancied himself an intellectual and that he saw in Ni Yuxian something of a kindred spirit. Wang was fond of reading the newspaper out loud to the prisoners, of sharing his own viewpoints with the men behind the bars. Yuxian had learned to flatter him. "You're so smart," he would say, "such an intellectual. You shouldn't be doing this kind of work."

"Do you know where thought comes from?" Wang asked Ni one day.

"Sure, from the brain," Ni had replied.

"No, you're wrong," good cop Wang had responded. "It comes from the heart."

"So you've made a new discovery," Ni flattered him. "That's amazing. You're really smart."

Good cop Wang would make certain that Ni often got an extra box of food.

In the makeshift prison, each cell was allowed a collective newspaper, the *People's Daily*, of course, in addition to Chairman Mao's Little Red Book, and Ni was frequently assigned to read the magazine articles out loud to his cellmates. The national organ of the Communist Party was speaking with a new voice now, new because there were several different voices, and some of them were openly demanding a reconsideration of the Tiananmen incident. The poetry people had brought to the square—poetry once taken as evidence of the counterrevolutionary intentions of the demonstrators—was being openly reprinted, the poets—and the demonstrators—lauded as heroes. Critiques of China's system of justice began to appear, and gradually it became clear that a massive reconsideration of the millions upon millions of people who had been accused over the whole decade of the Cultural Revolution was finally underway.

The prisoners were encouraged, during their newspaper study sessions, to comment on the government's changing policy. Good cop Wang, recognizing a fellow intellectual, was particularly solicitous of what Ni had to say. Ni hesitated, fearing a trap. Wang would prod. "Well, if I'm not mistaken," Ni Yuxian said, "and maybe I am mistaken, but if I am not, our country is in the midst of some pretty significant changes. From what we've been reading lately, it seems as though lots of things are going to have to be judged anew. What is now called right will be labeled wrong, what is now deemed wrong may be seen to be correct."

Yuxian dared not continue, but the guard nodded. "What 824 says is reasonable."

One day, after another newspaper reading, one of the guards took Ni Yuxian aside. "I'm well acquainted with your case," he said. "I know you have committed no crime. I have reason to believe—you must not tell anyone this, never tell that I told you—but I have reason to believe that your case is going to be reconsidered from the very beginning. I believe that in time, you'll be proven right. But what is most important right now is that you not create any more disturbances. Don't make any more trouble here. And don't tell I told.''

But Ni Yuxian did not easily stay out of trouble. The guards really had no authority over the prisoners' cases. Only the Public Security Bureau officials themselves really knew; and the officials in charge of his case had long since given up on Ni. They no longer called him in to try yet again to coax a confession. Ni needed to create an excuse to see them. He waited for a chance to create a disturbance.

''I know you're really good at writing articles,'' good cop Wang said to him one day. ''Can you write poetry, too?''

''Of course I can write poems,'' Yuxian responded confidently.

''Yea, but I'll bet you can't write a poem in the space of time it takes to walk seven steps,'' the guard came back, referring to the challenge thrown to Caocao, one of the villains in the *Romance of the Three Kingdoms.*

''I don't need seven steps,'' Ni responded. ''I can write one right now.''

''Let's see.''

Ni took out a piece of chalk he had hidden in his trousers, removed from a cell where he had been sent to write one of his many appeals. He wrote in big letters across the wall of the cell.

For speaking out on behalf of Xiaoping, I have been punished
For defending Tiananmen I am in jail
Chop off my head; execute me if you like
The people are the real masters of the country
The feudalism of 1000 years ago is still with us
In the form of the Gang of Four
Arresting me is no use
I am willing to shed my blood to cleanse the world.

Good cop Wang was terrified at what the prisoner had written. ''It's counterrevolutionary,'' he gasped.

''No, it just says I'm falsely accused,'' Ni retorted.

Ni was handcuffed. The police came to take pictures of his latest counterrevolutionary activity. But still there was no word on the disposition of his case.

No one seriously believed the new poem was counterrevolutionary, but Ni was kept in handcuffs, loosely applied, for months, as protection against himself. When he ate, when he urinated, he was still in handcuffs, assisted by his fellow prisoners. Prison regulations in the makeshift jail had been considerably relaxed, and in the new, less troublesome atmosphere the fighting among the prisoners had quieted. A certain camaraderie was developing. Ni was respected.

• • •

In mid-November 1978, the verdict on Tiananmen was finally reversed. The people of Beijing who had brought their poetry to the square, the youths who had protested when the wreaths of mourning were surreptitiously removed, the young men who had struck out in anger and in violence at the refusal of the government to accommodate their demands, were not counterrevolutionary. They were good revolutionaries after all. And if the poets and protestors of Beijing were innocent after all, then so were those who had spoken out on their behalf, who had railed against their punishments, who had insisted on a reversal of the verdict. If the poets and protestors of Tiananmen were innocent, Ni Yuxian was innocent, too.

He waited.

Nothing happened.

On the morning of December 16, 1978, the prisoners were still in the makeshift jail when they were told to prepare for a major announcement. They listened to the news over the prison broadcasting system.

"The United States of America and the People's Republic of China have agreed to recognize each other and to establish diplomatic relations as of January 1, 1979," the announcement began.

No announcement in Ni Yuxian's lifetime had been more important. China would change rapidly now, he thought, and so would his fate.

Still, nothing happened.

The end of the year was upon them, time once more for the Public Security Bureau to settle accounts, to dispose of the undetermined cases. Surely there would be new word on his case.

But the new year of 1979 came and went and still Ni sat, handcuffed and without an indication of his fate, in his crowded cell.

The morning announcements of January 10, 1979, started earlier than usual. "Get ready," the loudspeaker warned. "Lots of prisoners will be sentenced today. Many of you will be leaving for labor reform camp."

One by one, throughout the day, names were called and prisoners left as Ni sat handcuffed in his cell. A third of the jail had been evacuated, half his cellmates gone before Ni's name was called. After two years in jail and so many false hopes, he no longer really dared to believe that his fate had finally changed. Most of the other inmates, he knew from the commotion around him, were being sentenced to labor reform. Their sentences had been light. They were pleased with their fates.

"Gather your things together," the guard directed him politely.

His handcuffs were removed just as the cell door opened. The guard put his hand on Ni's shoulder, directing him gently left down the corridor. The other prisoners had all turned right.

The door to the office opened, and the guard motioned him in. Yuxian stood dazed, staring at his father, his younger sister, and Zhao Yuefang.

"You're free," the superintendent informed him. "The party has just held the Third Plenum of the Eleventh Congress. It's a turning point in our history. The Shanghai municipal leaders have decided that you are innocent. You can go home. We'll have a big rehabilitation meeting for you in a few weeks. In the meantime, go to the police station to get your *hukou* changed and pick up your rice coupons. We'll talk about the rest—your work and all, soon. Now, go home." It was the same man who months before had assured Ni that his case was ironclad, irreversible, that Hua Guofeng himself had made the decision.

His family had brought a change of clothes—civilian clothes— and a hat to cover his barren head. Ni refused to change. He wanted all the city to see the injustice to which he had been subjected. Ni Jizhong insisted.

A car was waiting to escort them back in honor and in style, the only time in his life that Ni Jizhong ever rode in a car, and the head of the Shanghai municipal court came personally to see Ni Yuxian off.

"Be careful next time," the head of the court warned, his arm around Ni's shoulder. "Never in all my years have I seen anyone with your luck. You'll never know how close you were to being shot. Just this far. This far."

Waiting at home, Xu Fengzhen burst into tears when she saw her son. In all his time in jail, not a word, not a sign had passed between Ni and his family, and he had come to conceive of himself as deserted, fighting his battle alone. He did not know, does not appreciate to this day, how many pleas the family had written on his behalf, how many times they had visited the court to petition for his release, how much effort had been devoted to saving his life. The message from the factory had reached them after all. They knew of the struggle session against him and that he had been sentenced to death.

Six-year-old Lingling did not recognize the man with the head that was shaved. "He's your father," Xu Fengzhen prompted. Ten-year-old Caocao opened his schoolbag and showed his father his grades. It was the first time the two had met since that morning more than two years before when Ni Yuxian had lost his temper when his little son burst into the room to disturb his writing.

They were grades to make any father proud.

He slept that night on the carved wooden bed, Lingling on one side, Caocao on the other, the two children teasing their father for his silly bald head, giggling as they took turns massaging his glistening scalp.

At the local bathhouse early the next morning, he washed away months of grime and sweat and dirt, donned clean clothes, put on a cap to hide his barren head, and crossed the Huangpu River to the city of Shanghai. He had to see Kajia.

"I escaped," he teased the young woman when she answered the unexpected knock on the door. Torn between the joy of seeing him again and her fear that the police were close behind, Kajia pulled her boyfriend inside. "I'm going to need some money. Can you lend me some?" Ni continued in mock alarm.

The young woman was dumbstruck.

"I'm just teasing," Yuxian finally relented. "I'm free. They let me go."

"I thought you might be home soon," Kajia replied. "With all the political changes, the rehabilitation of the Tiananmen incident."

All that morning and until late in the afternoon, they walked the streets together, bundled against the January cold, Kajia reliving her months in prison and detailing her life thereafter, Ni recounting the horrors of his own two years behind bars.

"Have you found a boyfriend yet?" Yuxian finally asked. The isolation of prison had sown too many doubts. He was afraid to ask directly whether she had had kept her promise to wait.

"No, not yet," Kajia answered, leaving nonetheless the impression that she had been looking.

He was puzzled, disturbed. "Maybe you should find one," he responded, not wanting to lose face.

It would be months before Kajia dared to confess how much she had wanted him then to protest his continuing love, to renew his promise to marry.

• • •

Zhao Yuefang did not have to be told that her husband had visited Kajia on his first morning home. His absence could mean nothing else. She intercepted the letter that Kajia sent to Yuxian several days later. The quarreling, the bitterness, the recriminations began again.

Ni Jizhong accompanied his son on a visit to Kajia's home. There were apologies to be made that properly required Jizhong's participation. During the early stages of Ni's incarceration, while Kajia was still in jail, the Public Security Bureau had frequently brought Mrs. Ye in for questioning, attempting to establish a link between the woman's trip to Beijing during the time of the Tiananmen incident and Ni's decision to write the big character poster. They wanted Mrs. Ye to admit that it was upon her encouragement and urging that Ni had begun composing his poems of protest. To implicate the wife of a counterrevolutionary and spy would have served as powerful public proof that the conspiracy theories upon which the police based so much of their work were justified. Besides, to implicate Mrs. Ye would free them from her allegations that her husband had been murdered.

As an inducement to confess, the police assured Mrs. Ye that she had already been implicated by Ni himself, that in the confessions he was giving in jail he had accused her of encouraging him to write the reactionary big character poster. Mrs. Ye was not completely persuaded that the police were telling the truth, but knowing nothing of the political activities of Ni and her daughter, neither could she fully trust the young man. Upon his release from jail, Ni had demanded—and received—all the statements he had written while there. He needed his father to accompany him to show those statements to Mrs. Ye to prove to her that not only had she not been implicated but that he had vociferously denied that she knew anything of his political activities.

He also wanted his father to meet Kajia.

Ni Jizhong could not deny the obvious. His son was in love with the young woman. Jizhong knew, too, that Yuxian's relations with his wife were tense. Their quarrels already were frequent and loud, staged so even the neighbors could hear.

Returning from the visit by ferry, Ni Jizhong suddenly paled and clutched at his heart, complaining of sudden weakness and a feeling of dizziness. His legs gave way underneath him, Yuxian barely catching his father as he fell.

Yuxian attributed his father's attack to the tension of the visit, to his fear that his son might have gained his freedom and been absolved of his crime only to plunge the family into yet another public scandal and the humiliation of a divorce. How much more loss of face could one family endure?

Ni's determination to divorce Zhao Yuefang and marry Kajia, already wavering after the months of isolation and his fears that she no longer cared, was further undermined. Perhaps his father's heart could not bear the loss of face.

Days later, the entire Ni family had an opportunity to meet the young woman about whom they had wondered for so long.

Yuxian's freedom had thrown his superiors at the factory into a quandary that finally proved impossible to resolve. After having lobbied so assiduously and so openly for the execution of their most noisome worker, his rehabilitation came as a major embarrassment. To permit Ni back could undermine their own control. Instead, the factory continued to pay Ni a salary, not in return for work but in return for staying away. As compensation for having been wronged, the former prisoner was awarded eight hundred yuan in back pay, which he used to buy a black-and-white television set—one of the first in his neighborhood—and to repay his parents for the support they had provided through all the difficult years.

But the factory leaders were, reluctantly, forced to hold a rehabilitation meeting to proclaim that Ni was innocent after all. Kajia was rehabilitated with him, and the minibus that took the entire Ni family to the meeting stopped first in Shanghai to pick up the young woman and her mother. Xu Fengzhen sat next to Kajia on the way, and wife and lover were introduced for the first time. The whole factory got a glimpse of the young woman whose alliance with Ni had sent her to jail. Held in the same auditorium that had been the scene of the earlier struggle meetings against him, the rehabilitation ceremony was brief, perfunctory, and grudging. "After investigation by the supreme municipal court of the city of Shanghai," the document read, "it has been determined that the poem 'I Do Not Believe,' hung by Ni Yuxian at the Park Hotel on the night of March 31, 1977, is in accord with the citizens' rights as outlined in the constitution. Ni Yuxian is therefore innocent." A similar statement was read on behalf of Kajia.

Kajia and Yuxian continued frequently to meet in the months that followed and just as frequently to quarrel. Kajia, wanting to hold Ni Yuxian to his promise, insisted that the time had come for him to divorce his wife and marry her. When he did not, local matchmakers began to intervene on Kajia's behalf, insisting that she be introduced first to this potential husband and then to that. Kajia was in her late twenties by then, and Chinese custom dictated that the time had come for her to marry.

Yuxian and Zhao Yuefang, too, continued to fight ferociously and often talked about divorce. Zhao Yuefang had sensed instinctively that her husband had made a pact with Kajia, though she would date his promise to marry the young woman earlier than it was actually given. No woman would have taken the political risks, allowed herself to go to jail, Zhao Yuefang reasoned, unless the man for whom she had made such sacrifices had promised to marry her in return. Once, after a particularly bitter quarrel, Ni Yuxian and Zhao Yuefang actually went together by bus to the Shanghai municipal court where they filled out the papers requesting a dissolution of their marriage. When the time came to sign, however, the couple balked. Ni Yuxian says that Zhao Yuefang refused to sign. Zhao Yuefang says that at the last minute Yuxian inexplicably relented.

• • •

Ni bided his time. In the early weeks after his release, still weak from prolonged hunger and lack of exercise, he worked to regain his strength. His friends—Guang Ming, Huang Xixi, and Jin Renjun—came frequently to visit, bearing traditional herbal nourishments designed to restore his weakened health. They treated him to numerous dinners in the city's restaurants, delighted that their leader had been safely released, grateful to him for having protected them, filled with respect for the strength with which Ni had been able to resist. The three had spent a nervous several months following Ni's incarceration preparing for the possibility of their own arrests. Not until the autumn of 1977 had come and gone, knowing that prisoners who crack usually do so within the first few months of their incarceration, did they allow their vigilance to relax. Dictated ever after by caution, their Chinese Charter 77 had never reached the public eye.

Ni's friends helped, too, in overcoming his months of isolation, bringing him news of the world around him, giving him a feel for the city's new mood, helping him to grasp what the transformations really meant.

The changes he had sensed through the windows of the paddy wagon were real. Shanghai was shedding the radical conservatism of the Cultural Revolution and becoming a livelier, looser, more colorful place. The city that had once been the most cosmopolitan in all of China was being stimulated anew by a fresh influx of foreign influence, a burgeoning of foreign movies, books, and commercial contacts. The citizenry was exhilarated, giddy with hope and expectation.

A new upsurge of political activity had started, too. The reevaluation of the Tiananmen incident and the decision that the protests had been revolutionary after all had loosened the bonds on freedom of expression, sparking a new outpouring of demands for democratization, a revival of the big character poster, and the introduction of numerous small, hand-stenciled, privately produced publications. The movement began in Beijing, where the big character posters were centered on a hundred-yard-long wall located about a mile to the west of Tiananmen Square, just at the busy shopping area where Changan Boulevard intersects with Xidan Road. Xidan Democracy Wall, the place came to be known, and the movement was quickly labeled the Democracy Wall movement. Never in the history of post-1949 China had the country seemed so free.

Many of the Democracy Wall activists, like Ni Yuxian himself, had received their political baptism during the Cultural Revolution, often as enthusiastic Red Guards or revolutionary rebels responding to Mao Zedong's call that proclaimed rebellion as just. Chastened by their own later victimization and the revelations of the unbridled power struggles within the party and of Lin Biao's attempted coup d'état, they had emerged from the crucible with a healthy skepticism for all authority, often believing only in their own independent thought. Angry and outspoken, many were nonetheless cautiously positive toward Deng Xiaoping and his proposed reforms. That Deng had inaugurated the policy of the "four modernizations," committing the country to the modernization of industry, agriculture, science and technology, and the military by the year 2000, that he was calling for far-reaching economic reforms and had asked for a reevaluation of the Cultural Revolution and restitutions to the millions who had been made its victims, provided reason to believe that the emerging leader would welcome political reform as well. The democracy envisioned by the Democracy Wall activists was not democracy American style, nor did their democracy necessarily entail the wholesale destruction of the Chinese political system. But the activists did call uncompromisingly for free and open local elections at the grass roots levels—in factories, universities, and basic work units. They labeled their brand of democracy variously "socialist democracy" or "humanistic socialism." Remarkably, beginning in 1980, numerous local level units throughout the country did begin conducting elections—elections that ran the whole spectrum from party monopolized and controlled to remarkably open and free. In units where elections were genuinely free, nonparty candidates often won. In Peking University, nonparty student advocate of freedom of expression Hu Ping, later to become a student at Harvard and still later to assume the leadership of the Chinese Alliance for Democracy in New York, won the majority of votes. When the party central committee annulled Hu Ping's election, kindred spirit Wang Juntao, now imprisoned with a thirteen-year sentence for his role as a "black hand" in the later Tiananmen democracy movement of 1989, received nearly half the votes.

The movement that had begun in Beijing spread quickly to other parts of China, too, and Shanghai soon was abuzz with political ferment. Ni was cautious about participating. Still shaken from his experiences in prison and sobered by the months of degradation, he was not willing to risk a return to jail. But as soon as his legs would carry him, he began going daily to the city parks to read the big character posters and to exchange his views with the democracy activists there.

He was skittish. Some of the big character posters were extreme, far more extreme than his had been, calling as they did for the overthrow of the Communist Party and demanding the removal of the opportunistic followers of Mao Zedong. There were criticisms, too, of Chinese involvement in Vietnam and attacks against the leadership's enthusiastic support for Cambodia's murderous Pol Pot. It was first time since the establishment of the People's Republic in 1949 that the citizenry had dared to speak out so boldly.

The secret police, not so secretly, were everywhere, taking pictures and recording the proceedings, and Yuxian even suspected that some of the most extreme statements might have been prompted by agents provocateur. Having spent nearly two years on death row for a big character poster that was angry and indignant but still milder than the ones that were appearing now, he feared that the government was delaying the clampdown simply to trick the malcontents into revealing themselves. The situation was too tumultuous, too unpredictable for any government to countenance for long.

Cautious though he was, he still established contact with several of the leading dissidents from other cities—with Wang Xizhe in Guangdong, only recently released from labor reform after he and three colleagues identifying themselves as Li Yizhe had been arrested for the huge big character poster they had posted in 1974; with Xu Wenli in Beijing, the editor of the unofficial journal *April Five Forum*, so named in commemoration of the Tiananmen incident of April 5, 1976; and with Xu Shuiliang in Nanjing, also recently released from jail and now tempting fate again. Ni even traveled to Nanjing to meet with Xu Shuiliang.

Ni did not always agree with the other dissidents. Some, he claims, were too radical for his taste. Some had begun to talk about the possibility of armed struggle if the government refused to reform. Some of the younger dissidents in Shanghai made him particularly nervous. "You're still young," he claims to have admonished them. "You haven't yet spent time in jail, haven't really experienced political struggle. What you're saying isn't appropriate now. We need to think of a way to use peaceful means, reasonable methods, to promote democracy. You have to be careful."

The Public Security Bureau was observing Ni closely, and Ni was aware of being watched. They knew he went frequently to the parks, reading the big character posters and talking with the democracy activists. They knew that some of the most outspoken of the activists had visited him and that one of the underground publications had even written an article about him. Representatives of the police paid a visit to Ni Jizhong. "Your son has just gotten out of jail," they warned him. "Don't let him participate in this movement."

Representatives from the Public Security Bureau ordered Yuxian to meet with them. "We know you have contact with the activists," they said. "If you keep up your involvement, you'll find yourself back in jail." They showed him numerous photographs of the participants. "Do you know these people?" they asked. Ni did know many of them, was wary of them and their extremism, had warned them frequently against going too far, cautioned them about the risks they were taking, about what imprisonment really meant.

• • •

In the meantime, continuing to draw a salary from his factory but denied the right to work, Ni had pressed his case with the Maritime Academy, demanding that he be fully reinstated as a graduate in good standing and given employment commensurate with that status.

It is the nature of the totalitarian state that power over individual lives is exercised not by a distant central government but at the grass roots, by people who stand at the lowest level of the political hierarchy. While the grass roots levels necessarily owe allegiance to those that stand higher in the hierarchy, their powers to impede and to delay are considerable indeed. The Maritime Academy balked at reinstating Ni Yuxian, delaying until Ni had petitioned the Shanghai municipal supreme court and the Academy was actually ordered to take him back.

It is also the nature of totalitarian systems that the grass roots can misinterpret and twist the orders that come to it from on high, drawing on a whole panoply of devices to make life miserable for those over whom it exercises control. When Ni was finally reinstated in September 1979, he was not exonerated. His expulsion was retracted, but he still stood as a man who had "made mistakes."

Of the variety of punishments the Chinese work unit can inflict on those over whom it has control, expulsion is the most severe, but four other punishments can also be invoked—the warning, the least serious of the labels, the serious warning, the demerit, and the serious demerit. Ni was reinstated with a "demerit." The accusations that he had been a counterrevolutionary during the Cultural Revolution because he had opposed Lin Biao and Zhang Chunqiao were retracted, but suspicions about his political proclivities clearly remained. He was not formally labeled a counterrevolutionary but was still regarded as one. Allegations concerning his personal morality—his improper relations with women—were not dismissed. Ni's integrity remained in doubt.

His request to work in the academy's library, where he could feast on the reading of books, was approved at the university level over the strong objections of both the library director and its party secretary—the latter an uneducated and not very talented revolutionary whose party membership dated back to 1938. In preparing for the impending arrival of Ni, the director announced to the staff assembled for their weekly political study session that Ni was a young man with problems to whom the party had, magnanimously, granted another opportunity. "We must all work together to help him, to educate him," the party secretary encouraged the staff. "If the party could reform the last emperor, Pu Yi, then surely we can also reform Ni Yuxian." Ni was still the bad guy, the class enemy.

But Ni insisted on regarding himself as the equal of those who claimed to be his superiors, refusing to think of himself as in need of education, continuing to scorn the hypocrisy of those who on the one hand claimed to serve the people and who on the other insisted on subservience and flattery. Ni's insistence on treating the party bureaucrats as equals, withholding the fawning they had come to expect and receive, was seen in fact as rudeness, an uncalled for slap in the face.

Working in the library reading room, Ni's opportunities to meet students were numerous, and he immediately set forth to make friends with the university youth, propagating his views.

He began receiving oblique warnings about his behavior, polite admonitions that he should make self investigations, self criticisms, that he should focus on reforming himself. He was reminded that he was a man "under supervision." The staff was called upon to help educate the wayward son. Yuxian bristled. "What do you mean investigate myself? Reform myself? This is talk for the four bad elements. Why are you still treating me like a class enemy?

"Do you really still think I'm a class enemy?" he demanded one day of the party secretary in the library. "Tell me. I want to know."

"You know whether you're counterrevolutionary," the party secretary responded superciliously. "You know in your heart, when you make your self investigations, whether you're a four bad element."

Ni lost his temper, demanded that the party secretary accompany him to the personnel department to clarify his case, grabbed hold of his arm and began pulling, struggling. "The government rehabilitated me. I'm not a class enemy. I'm not a bad element," he cried. "I'm a university graduate sent here to work. I'm not a thing. I'm not an animal. I'm a human being."

"You're trying to hurt me," the party secretary complained when Ni refused to let go of his arm.

"I'm not going to hit you, but we are going together to talk to the personnel department. I want my case clarified," Ni responded. The staff who had gathered around to watch stepped in to separate the two. Ni had committed yet another egregious affront. Party secretaries, however low on the totem pole, were not to be challenged and certainly not to be physically molested.

But the two did go together to the personnel office where Ni registered his complaint. "You can't just push me this way one day and that way another," he argued. "You can't say you want me one day and don't want me the next. You have to stop treating me like the class enemy. I'm a human being."

• • •

The crackdown against the Democracy Wall dissidents began in October 1979, only weeks after Ni's return to work. Beijing's Wei Jingsheng, the young worker who had irreverently castigated Deng Xiaoping, warning him against becoming a new dictator and calling for a "fifth modernization" in the form of democracy, was arrested then and sentenced eventually to fifteen years in jail. Shortly thereafter, the Democracy Wall itself was moved from bustling Xidan to a quiet park still further west. In January 1980 the right of Chinese citizens to post big character posters was taken away. The movement, in its most radical form, began to peter out.

But it would be more than a year before the movement was fully squelched, and in the meantime demands for democratization at the basic levels of Chinese life continued.

The trade union elections at the Maritime Academy library provided Ni his first major opportunity to demand democracy within the university and to remind the leadership of the gap between the party's description of the country as a dictatorship of the proletariat and the reality of party control. The elections were held on a day when Yuxian was not at work. Controversial political activities were often held, spontaneously and unannounced, on Ni's days off. Openly to prevent him from participating in political events would have risked raising his public ire. The risk was reduced by arranging political activities to take place while he was away.

The union had never been imbued with great power. Employees paid one percent of their salary to the organization, and the funds were used to help people in economic difficulty, to buy occasional tickets to a play or a movie, or for periodic sightseeing excursions. Sometimes the union offered its opinion about how housing ought to be distributed. But the organization was tightly controlled, managed in the interests of the party rather than serving the demands of the workers. Strikes were explicitly forbidden, and workers were expected never to demand a raise. Elections to the library's trade union had always been pro forma. The party secretary was in the habit of simply putting forth a few names, knowing the staff would automatically raise their hands in agreement. Yuxian knew that a real labor union elected its own leaders.

Informed on the day of his return of how the election had been held, Ni naturally protested. "But it was perfectly fair," the party representative parried, "Everyone agreed."

"What do you mean everyone agreed? You're supposed to have elections. People are supposed to cast ballots. Secret ballots. Didn't Comrade Deng Xiaoping say we have to have democracy? This absolutely isn't democracy. Democracy isn't decision by the party. It's decision by the people. We have to have an election."

At the next session of the Friday political study session, Ni rose to speak. With attendance at the sessions mandatory, Ni could not easily be prevented from participating, nor, without considerable embarrassment, could he be refused the right to speak. "With respect to the labor union," he said, "your elections were not democratic. We pay one percent of our salary to the labor union every month, and we have the right to elect our own representatives. This isn't for the party secretary to decide. If it is the party secretary's decision, there is no point in having a trade union." He began reading from the *People's Daily*—a speech by Deng Xiaoping to the national trade union leadership calling for direct elections at local levels.

The leadership was pushed into a corner. Comrade Deng Xiaoping really was paying lip service then to democracy, and many parts of the country were holding elections at the grass roots levels. In Shanghai, the city's most outspoken and notorious young democracy activist, Fu Shenqi, had stood for, and nearly won, election in his generator factory—even after party officials had threatened that those who voted for him would not receive their raises.

The chairman relented. "Okay," he said, convinced still that he had the support of the staff. "We'll take a vote. How many people agree that we should start the elections all over again? How many are satisfied with the results as they stand now?"

Eighty percent of the participants agreed they wanted to hold new elections. The only dissenters were the members of the party.

The election was held by secret ballot, and the result, like the results of similarly real elections in other parts of the country, was that no party members were chosen. The masses really did elect their own representative. The staff of the university library really did have its own labor union.

Yuxian was well pleased. The authority of the labor union was small to be sure but democracy, he was now convinced, had to start small. Moreover, it was a way of educating the young people and students. Why had there been a Cultural Revolution? Why had the masses so enthusiastically and vociferously attacked the party? Because the country was lacking in democracy.

Some people, though, were suspicious of this democracy. Some people thought that what Ni Yuxian really wanted was not socialist democracy but capitalist democracy. Rumors began to circulate that he was a bourgeois liberal. The political climate was changing again. Deng Xiaoping was about to prove that he was not so liberal after all.

The crackdown against the Democracy Wall activists that had begun with the arrest of Wei Jingsheng was continuing. In April of 1981, some twenty-five democracy activists were rounded up and sent to jail. Xu Wenli and Ren Wanding in Beijing, Wang Xizhe in Guangzhou and Xu Shuiliang in Nanjing were arrested then, as was Shanghai's own Fu Shenqi.

Ni was called privately into the office of the director of the library. "The Shanghai municipal party committee has decided to arrest certain counterrevolutionary elements," he began. "Fu Shenqi has already been arrested. Those who participated in the movement, those who had connections with these counterrevolutionaries, are going to have to confess their mistakes. If they don't confess, they'll be arrested."

"Why are you telling me this?" Ni demanded.

"Because you were associated with them."

"I was not associated with them."

"Fu Shenqi came to see you once. You talked to him. Others came to see you, too. You wrote letters to them. What did you say? What did you talk about?"

"I've talked to lots of people since I got out of jail. Lots of people came to see me. What are you trying to say?"

Ni knew that the Public Security Bureau had been keeping close track of him since the time he had been released from jail. The lesson he learned from the director was how well they had tracked his moves, how faithfully they had conveyed that information to his superiors at the academy. Ni had distanced himself from the radicalism of some of the youth who had been arrested and had little faith in the ability of some of the younger dissidents to withstand the treatment he had undergone in jail without confessing. But he still had common cause with most of the democracy activists and there were those among the arrested whom he particularly admired. Wang Xizhe, sentenced in May 1982 to fourteen years in jail, was one.

"Wang Xizhe's arrest is absolutely unfair," he blurted out during the meeting. "He was a hero in criticizing the Gang of Four. He criticized Jiang Qing. All he did was to demand socialist democracy. This is not a crime. It's reasonable."

The party secretary was delighted. Ni was so openly counterrevolutionary. He had been taking notes on Ni's responses, wanted the counterrevolutionary to sign a statement admitting to what he had said. Ni refused. He had no reason to trust the party leadership, was worried about the possibility of being arrested again.

The subject of Ni's involvement in the movement was dropped. Ni was not questioned again. The Public Security Bureau continued to watch him closely.

• • •

Ni continued to focus his political efforts on the university itself. The allocation of university housing provided his next opportunity for conflict.

In the early years after Shanghai's opening to the West, American visitors to the city were inevitably and proudly invited to the "new socialist villages" that had been built shortly after "liberation" to replace the rude lean-tos of straw matting or the primitive mud and water walled huts that had once sheltered the city's most desperately poor. But in the years following the Great Leap Forward and throughout the decade of the Cultural Revolution, construction of new housing had ground to a standstill even as the population of Shanghai continued to grow. By the early 1980s, in Shanghai as in cities everywhere in China, the problem of housing had reached startling proportions, and crowding had become endemic. American academics doing research in China and living on university campuses were dismayed at the living standards of their Chinese colleagues. Whole families—two and some-times three generations—often lived together in a single, crowded dormitory room, cooking on propane stoves in corridors danger-ously filled with the cooking equipment of tens of other families, too, the same tens of families sharing filthy lavatories where toilets were often broken, the contents spilling over the floor. Showers were generally located in another building and hot water was infre-quent, rendering bathing at best a weekly event.

Deng Xiaoping's reforms included the promise to construct new and more modern housing for the masses, and by the early 1980s, the skyline of Chinese cities had begun to change as new apartment buildings began springing up, as the Chinese say, like mushrooms after a spring rain. But construction of new housing was not fast enough. Apartments were still scarce, and with living space so hard to come by, decisions about how new housing was to be allocated provided fertile opportunity for corruption. Newspapers, emboldened by the more relaxed political atmosphere, were filled with stories of new apartments being assigned not to the working staff for whom they were intended but to greedy party cadres and their relatives.

The Maritime Academy was no exception. The state had allo-cated substantial sums to solve the housing problem of the univer-sity faculty. But when the assignments were made, the newly built apartments were allocated according to a complicated point system that guaranteed that party cadres would inevitably win out over the faculty. The entire party leadership of the university, whose housing was already substantially better than the faculty's, was to be assigned new housing, while the bulk of the teaching staff would continue muddling along in their overcrowded, dilapidated, and often downright dangerous quarters.

The weekly political study sessions were Ni's opportunity to persist as thorn in the side of the university leadership. As the implications of the housing allocations became clear and everyone gradually realized that the party leadership had claimed all the new housing for itself, Ni naturally delighted in standing up to castigate the leadership. "The distribution of housing has been completely unfair," he argued. "The reason the state allocated so much money was in order to solve the housing problem of the ordinary people and the intellectuals. Instead, the party has taken it all. This is special privilege."

He solicited opinions from his fellow staff members and had no trouble winning support for the statement of concern he had composed. Many were eager to sign a letter of protest to the university leadership. No other issue was as likely to arouse such support, no other special party privilege likely to raise such ire. Years later, in 1989, when the citizens of Beijing—and Shanghai—took to the streets to rail once more against party corruption, the issue of housing, still unresolved, stood at the top of their list of concerns.

Ni's efforts on behalf of the equitable distribution of housing were viewed by the party as rebellion. "Ni Yuxian is trying to start another Cultural Revolution," the party secretary reported. "He even wrote another big character poster, solicited signatures and tried to get people to rebel." But Yuxian's action had widespread support. The leadership could not hide from the criticism. In the end, the criteria for allocating the apartments had to be changed, and the distribution was made on the basis of a formula which included age and seniority, level of education, size of family and size of current housing. Ni had won a major victory.

But the leadership of the Maritime Academy detested him all the more. Living still in his parents' house, with his wife and two children of different sexes all in a single crowded room, Ni's own score under the new formula guaranteed him a university apartment. When the housing was actually distributed, his request was denied.

Then Ni was transferred from the reading room to the acquisitions department. The library leadership wanted to minimize his contact with students. He was stirring up too much trouble.

Ni had little but contempt for the party leadership within his new department. The responsibility of the acquisitions department was to provide students and faculty with the latest and best books on maritime affairs, but the leaders were uneducated and ill-informed and stood on the fundamentalist side of party ideology. Their acquisitions were a mockery of the university's intellectual needs. Substantial sums were expended on picture books for the leaders' children, while Western classics were scorned as bourgeois and pornographic. One month the department spent more than one hundred U.S. dollars of scarce and hard-to-come-by foreign exchange to buy a book called *Crows*, which described in pictures and in words the entire crow population of the world, detailing the varieties of crows country by country, providing more information about the bird than all but a small handful of the world's crow experts could possibly want to know. Scant attention was paid to acquiring books on maritime affairs.

In keeping with the democratic spirit then bubbling up from China's basic level units, Ni demanded that the leadership be replaced. The acquisitions department held elections. All but one person voted for the young graduate of Fudan University's library school who had recently joined the staff, one of only two trained professionals among them. The only vote for the reigning party head was cast by the party head himself.

The election was declared invalid. The young man was not a party member, and—according to regulations—even the acquisitions department had to be under the control of the party. The staff ignored the party leader, behaving as if their elections had been valid and the party director was no longer in charge. The party leadership was infuriated.

In 1983, when the central leadership launched a new, conservative campaign based on China's century-old fear that Western culture and Western technology are inseparable and that renewed economic exchanges were necessarily being accompanied by the introduction of bourgeois and Western values, Ni was identified to the Shanghai municipal committee as a bourgeois liberal, a man who had been polluted spiritually by Western bourgeois thought. The conservative leadership at the Shanghai Maritime Academy attempted to mobilize the faculty and students in a campaign against Ni. The movement fizzled and died. No one was willing to criticize. Ni remained immune from popular attack. The movement fizzled in others parts of China, too. The campaign against spiritual pollution stood as the first of China's post-1949 efforts at political mobilization to fail. Exhausted and disillusioned from the endless campaigns of the previous three decades, exhilarated that China's doors were finally opening outward, all but a few opportunists simply clamped silent when the party called for attack.

The leadership at the Maritime Academy concluded that Ni would make trouble wherever he went. Put the man in a room with other people, and Ni would soon begin to organize them against the party's interests. The leadership hit upon a solution. Ni Yuxian would be promoted. They would make him a cadre.

The decision was announced at the weekly political study meeting. "We have some comrades," the director began, "who are very capable. They have lots of knowledge, lots of talent. But as yet we haven't found a good way to let them really develop their talents. For example, Ni Yuxian reads lots of books, has a deep understanding of many matters. He is very good at writing articles. But we haven't given him a chance yet to develop those talents. So we're going to promote him. We're going to make him a department chief. From now on, Comrade Ni will be chief of the library's propaganda department. His department will be responsible for reading new books as the library acquires them, and then reporting their contents, in writing, to the library staff, making certain to point out which new books are particularly worthy of note."

It was a job that many might envy. As department chief, Ni had his own office, a rare privilege in overpopulated Shanghai, even for relatively high ranking cadres. He was given complete freedom. He could come and go as he pleased, arrive late and leave early or even not show up at all. He could decide which of the new books to read and which to review for the library staff. Beyond reading and writing reports, he had no other responsibilities. It was quite a comfortable position. In China, his job was downright plush.

But whereas other departments had several staff members and the chief had a pretty secretary to serve him tea, Ni Yuxian was a department of one. The real purpose of his promotion had been to separate him from the rest of the library staff, to deny him contact with others, to prevent him from meeting with students or organizing his fellow workers against the party leadership. He was, again, completely isolated.

Ni was becoming aware of how closely he was being watched. Frequently, he knew that he was followed. The phone calls he made from his office were monitored. His mail was opened.

Then he was accused of theft.

It happened, as Ni tells the story, late one Saturday afternoon toward the end of the year in 1983, when two students came to him with a key they had found in a bicycle parked in front of the library. The key to the unobtrusive circular locks that fit around the back wheel of Chinese bicycles can be removed only when the device is actually locked, a key still in place therefore signifying that the bicycle is unlocked. With bicycles both expensive and in very short supply, theft was not uncommon. An unlocked bicycle stood as an invitation to steal.

Ni claims that when the students gave him the key, he went to the parking lot and wrote a message in chalk on the pavement next to the bicycle, informing the owner that the key was in his office, room 203. That evening at closing time, when no one had claimed the bike, Ni rode it home himself. He and Zhao Yuefang were staying then at Zhao Yuefang's family place nearby.

The stories related today by Ni Yuxian and by his wife are different. Zhao Yuefang remembers how nervous she was to see her husband with someone else's bike, and credits him with the intention of claiming it for himself. "If I don't take it, someone else will," she reports him as having said. She insists he delivered the vehicle to the local police station a week later only after repeated entreaties on her part. Ni claims though that he continued to ride the bike back and forth to school because he was afraid someone else would take it and wanted to make certain the bike was there should its proper owner come to claim it. He credits the decision to deliver the bicycle to the police to his own unfailing honesty.

The leadership of the library naturally stood on the side of suspicion. "Why didn't you take the bike immediately to the campus police?" they wanted to know.

"Because it was late Saturday afternoon and the office was closed," Ni responded.

"Why didn't you hand it over much sooner?" they insisted.

"I just kept thinking the owner would come back to get it. Besides, I did hand it over to the police."

"You were trying to steal it."

"Why would I want to steal a bicycle? I already have my own."

The leadership of the library continued to insist that Ni had intended to steal the bike, just as Ni continued to insist on his essential, unfailing honesty. The campus security department ultimately ruled in Ni's favor—or at least decided not to press the case. He had, after all, eventually turned the bike over to them.

Ni was refused a salary increase when everyone else received a raise. His continued presence in the library was making everyone uncomfortable. Even Ni himself was coming to realize there was no way for him to stay at the academy.

The head of the library called Ni into his office one day. "I know your work here isn't peaceful," he began. "There's a school nearby that needs a teacher of Chinese. How about going there to work? Your salary will still come from the Maritime Academy. You'll still be considered one of our employees."

Ni thought about the offer. His relationship with the party leadership had been irreparably damaged. Without a dramatic change at the academy, there would never be any way for him to coexist in peace. Perhaps it would be best to try a new milieu. He accepted the offer.

His new responsibilities were light, and he got along well with his students. He had plenty of time to meet with his political allies, to write articles on the need for democracy, to share his views and his writings with others. Chastened still by his experience in prison, wanting to avoid a return, and despairing of the possibility of major political reform, he turned his efforts to more modest pursuits, drawing upon his own experience with the prison and police systems to help other individuals and their families in their attempts to redress their personal political grievances.

But peace, stability, and predictability remained elusive. The economic reforms that the Chinese peasants had so enthusiastically accepted, reforms that were returning collective land to individual families and opening up a whole range of new opportunities for economic well-being, had no great effect on life in Yangsi Village, and the central leadership seemed reluctant to expand the reforms from the countryside to the cities, from the economic to the political. Chinese political life continued to proceed in ebbs and flows of liberalization followed by clampdown, relaxation of the political strings followed by a tightening—a campaign against spiritual pollution followed by a time of relative quiescence, a campaign against bourgeois liberalism followed by a renewed invitation to investments from abroad. Never did the campaigns approach the hyperbole of the Cultural Revolution, but with each new clampdown, a few more people, people whose crimes could hardly have exceeded Ni's, were rounded up, seemingly at whim, to suffer for a few weeks or a few months or a few years in detention centers or jails or in labor reform. Ni lived in a state of constant fear, never knowing when—or whether—his time might come. He knew he never wanted to go to jail again.

• • •

He decided to try to leave. He wanted go to the United States. The United States was already democratic. People there had freedom. It was the richest, most powerful nation in the world.

• • •

The Chinese government does not make it easy for its citizens to leave. Nor does the American government make it easy for people to enter. Finding a purpose that satisfies the demands of both the Chinese and the American governments is a complex and arduous process. The Chinese government, for instance, will readily issue passports for its citizens to visit relatives abroad, but the United States is reluctant to issue visas for such a purpose. Anxious to keep the number of immigrants at a manageable low, the United States routinely refuses visas to those they suspect might immigrate. Relatives, they reason, may want to stay. In the early 1980s the Chinese government would permit individuals without government sponsorship or university fellowships to go abroad to study if an overseas relative was able to offer financial backing. The United States, on the other hand, was more likely to grant student visas to Chinese who had been accepted for graduate work at a major university and who had been given a university fellowship—or financial backing from the Chinese government. But American government regulations are vague, perhaps deliberately so, fostering thereby in the Chinese mind the belief that the final decision rests really on luck—on one's own inexorable fate.

Ni Yuxian had no chance of going to the United States in any government-sponsored capacity. His only possibility was to find a relative in the United States willing to back him financially and a school that was willing to accept him. That he had no relatives in the United States was only a minor deterrent. The major hurdle was the leadership at the Shanghai Maritime Academy.

If Ni were to go abroad, the Maritime Academy would first have to agree. Obtaining a passport is the first step in the process of leaving, and the process begins at the level of the work unit. If the work unit does not agree, for whatever reason and however arbitrarily, the passport is nearly impossible to obtain. With the opening up to the outside world, the granting of passports provided new opportunities for corruption and control and bureaucratic red tape, with each constituent unit demanding its right to grant or deny, and each therefore receiving its share of flattery and gifts.

Early in 1984 Ni Yuxian approached the party committee at the Maritime Academy to inquire whether they would approve his application to study abroad. "Of course we will," was the glib reply. "We will treat your case as we would treat any other. All you need is economic sponsorship from a relative in the United States and an I-20 form from an American school showing that you have been accepted to study there."

Ni assumes the reason for their quick approval was their certainty that he would find fulfilling the requirements impossible. Ni, they all knew, had no relatives abroad. During the Cultural Revolution, having contact with anyone overseas was considered a crime, and individuals with relatives abroad often came under vicious attack. In all the attacks against Ni, no one had ever accused him of having relations overseas, and the party committee knew there was nothing in his file to suggest that any such relatives existed. How much easier to agree to Ni's request, knowing that he could never fulfill the conditions, than to say no at the outset and have the troublemaker accuse them of unfairness and begin yet another round of recriminations against them.

But when relatives do not exist, it is possible to invent them. China is one big family.

One of the people Ni had helped after temporarily reducing his sights from saving all of China to helping a few who had been wrongly accused was an elderly gentleman—the father of a friend—who had been horribly abused during the Cultural Revolution, accused, because he had a distant cousin in Los Angeles, of being a spy for the United States. The man had yet to be rehabilitated and was living in misery on only thirty yuan a month. Frightened and weakened and beaten down by the continuing oppression and by the frequent struggle sessions against him, the man was incapable of acting on his own behalf. Ni began helping the old man compose letters to the government and arranged for Ni Jizhong to treat the aches and pains that continued to plague him after all the beatings to which he had been subjected. Gradually, the man began to regain his health, and finally the government admitted that an injustice had been done. The old man, at last, was rehabilitated, his salary restored.

He was profusely grateful to Ni. He wondered if there was anything he could do to repay him.

There was. Would it be possible, Ni wondered, for the old man's cousin to claim him, Ni, as a relative, to serve as his economic sponsor, to help him find a school that might accept him as a student?

The old man agreed to try.

Distant relative wrote distant relative of the dilemma Ni faced. It was all explained in the cryptic language dictated by the fact the letter was likely to be read by the Public Security Bureau. The distant relative was invited to add another member to his family, asked if something might be worked out whereby the Los Angeles branch of the family would take on the economic sponsorship for the young man still in Shanghai, a responsibility that would never actually be assumed because the young man naturally would find work immediately upon arriving in the States and take responsibility for himself.

Ni wrote a letter, too. "Dear Uncle," he began, "I really would like the opportunity to study in the United States. I wonder whether you would be willing to help." He enclosed a copy of his graduation certificate—the one he had received after being reinstated into the Maritime Academy and which retroactively granted him a degree—to present to the American school.

Within ten days, Ni had received a reply. "Dear Nephew," the letter began.

Yuxian had found an uncle. The arrangements had been made. The man in Los Angeles agreed to serve as his economic sponsor—provided, of course, that Ni never held him to his promise. He was investigating an English-language training school that might be willing to accept him. He was optimistic that a school could be found.

Ni took the letter to the party committee.

"What's this about an uncle in the United States?" they wanted to know. They knew of Xu Fengzhen's brother still living, as he had all his life, in Three Forest Village, but the files mentioned no one else. "There's nothing in your file that says you have an uncle in the United States."

Ni had already thought about that problem. He had even come up with the proof.

There had been another uncle—an uncle the party committee never had cause to know. Remember Xu Fengzhen's other brother? The youth who had quarreled with his father and had run away to join the Guomindang forces and fight the Japanese? The one who had died fighting the Japanese and whose body had never been recovered, who had become a hungry ghost because he had died away from home, the hungry ghost who had come that night when Yuxian was but a tiny infant, carrying his baby sister away, taking her with him to the netherland? There had never been any proof that that uncle had died, no documents to attest to his fate. After all these years, the family agreed, he had suddenly—miraculously—turned up alive. Alive and living in the United States—Los Angeles, no less.

And why was it, the officials at the Maritime Academy wanted to know, that the family's surname was Xu and the surname of this newly rediscovered uncle was Huang? The answer to that question was simple, too. Is it not a tradition in China that when a man from a family where there is more than one son marries into a family that has no son, the man will take his wife's surname so the male offspring of the couple can continue the family line? The uncle had married into such a family, had taken the surname of his wife. The uncle had originally been named Xu Ahe. He had changed his name to Huang Baihe. But you could tell from his given name "He" that Huang Baihe and Xu Ahe were one and the same, that only the surname had changed.

The story, in fact, was not entirely preposterous. In the aftermath of the communist takeover in 1949, millions of families had been separated, as some fled with the Nationalist government to Taiwan, others migrated to Hong Kong, and others managed to settle in the United States. In the thirty years that had passed before Deng Xiaoping opened China's doors, communications between families were rare. To have communicated would have been to invite trouble for the relatives left on the mainland—accusations that they had overseas connections, even that they were spies. Many families, both in China and abroad, had undergone deliberate metamorphoses.

But with Deng's open door, the government began encouraging lost families to reunite, hoping, among other things, that prosperous overseas relatives might invest a bit in China's economic development. As overseas relations began returning to the mainland in droves, rediscovering their lost families, anomalies abounded. Some found themselves with two spouses—the one they had left behind and the one they had married overseas. Names had been changed for protection. Ni's story was no more unbelievable than any of the others. Party officials at the Maritime Academy found no other choice but to accept his story as true. Ni Yuxian had an uncle in the United States.

The I-20 form arrived. Ni now had all the materials he needed to get his passport. He needed only final agreement from the academy's party committee.

The Maritime Academy refused. They had never really meant to let him go. Ni Yuxian was still a person with problems. They could not permit a man like Ni to leave.

Ni was furious. Without the academy's permission, without a passport, he could never get out of China.

He had no intention of giving up. There was still hope. If the Maritime Academy refused, he could still go to Beijing to present a formal petition to the central government there.

Thus he traveled once more to his nation's capital, joining the wretched masses who congregated each morning in front of the government offices on Taiping Road, the bedraggled, unwashed, uneducated, country people who begged by day and slept on the ground by night, who cooked their meager food on outdoor fires, who could not read or write but who still hoped somehow to convince the central government that they had been wronged by their local officials, who trusted in the central government that justice after all would be done. Rarely, either historically or under communist rule, did the central government override the decisions of local officials, and in 1984, the security forces in Beijing were in the habit of periodically rounding up the wretched petitioners by force and sending them unwillingly home. But cases of redress at the national level were known by all to exist, and for the desperate with nowhere else to turn, for those who had come to the end of the line, the petition was worth a try.

Ni had several demands. He wanted his administrative demerit expunged from his record. He wanted the Maritime Academy to pay him the difference in the salary he would have made had he not been expelled and the salary he did in fact receive. He wanted the academy to treat him as a man who had been genuinely exonerated rather than as one who still had problems. He wanted the Maritime Academy party committee to assign him housing. He wanted permission to study abroad.

He tangled for days with the Beijing bureaucracy, pleading first with this bureaucrat and then with another, joining the petitioners at night. But he was unable to convince anyone in the central government that the decisions of the Maritime Academy ought to be overturned. Ni's case, the Beijing bureaucrats argued, was a local matter. He was advised to return to Shanghai.

Ni still refused to give up. There was one faint hope. There was Liu Binyan.

•   •   •

Liu Binyan is the most famous, most highly respected, most widely read of all of China's journalists, his prestige among the Chinese reading public surpassing that of Edward R. Murrow and Walter Cronkite combined. Born in 1925 in China's northeast, he joined the Communist Party as an idealistic young man believing that the hope for China's future lay in socialism and the leadership of the party. Confronted in the early years of party rule with a bureaucracy that made a mockery of its own ideal of serving the people, but believing still in the capacity of the party and the system for reform, he began publishing articles critical of the party's abuse of power. In 1957, when the party cracked down on those who had spoken out in criticism of it, Liu Binyan was labeled a rightist and exiled to several years of labor reform. Briefly rehabilitated in the early 1960s, he was attacked again with the opening salvoes of the Cultural Revolution in 1966, and sent once more to the countryside. For twenty-one years, the prime of his life, he was not allowed to write.

In the more relaxed political atmosphere and the wave of rehabilitations of 1979, Liu Binyan was exonerated, reappointed to the staff of the *People's Daily*, and allowed to write again. His articles became overnight sensations.

A man of awesome integrity, Liu Binyan had come by the early 1980s to serve as the social conscience of his nation, daring—as no other writer after 1949 had dared—to write about two kinds of truth—the rosy, optimistic truth that filled the pages of the party press even in the worst of times and the truth to be found in the nitty-gritty reality of everyday Chinese life. Digging here and investigating there to uncover and write about instances of party corruption and injustice, Liu's most famous early post-Cultural Revolution piece, the one that catapulted him overnight to nationwide fame, was titled "People or Monsters?" and exposed the sweeping bribery, corruption and abuse of power of a female cadre in a small county in the northeast province of Heilongjiang.

Ni was convinced that his own case would provide fertile opportunity for Liu Binyan's investigative skills. He wanted to convince the reporter to write about the injustice to which he had been subjected, to expose the continuing abuses of power of the leadership of the Maritime Academy.

Ni was not alone. The lines in front of the *People's Daily* formed early, and by five o'clock in the morning, well before dawn, they were already long. The party newspaper claimed to be the eyes and the ears of the people, the lifeline between the people and the government. Several hundred petitioners from all over the country came each day hoping that someone at the newspaper might give their private complaints a public voice, find a way to right their particular injustice.

Not all of the petitioners were there to see Liu Binyan, but so many wanted to meet him that the journalist found it impossible to see them all. His visitors were carefully screened. Those who came early enough were given a number which entitled them to the opportunity to present their case to a representative of the newspaper. Ni went three times before even receiving a number.

"What is it?" the representative asked when his turn finally came.

"I want to see Liu Binyan," Ni responded.

"Liu Binyan is very busy," the representative replied. "He doesn't have time to see so many people. What is it you want to discuss with him?"

"There are lots of things. I was persecuted because I criticized the Gang of Four. I went to jail and then was declared innocent and released but I am still being made a victim."

"He really doesn't have time to see you."

"I have lots of materials about my case with me. What if I leave the materials with you so you can give them to him?"

"That won't work either. He gets hundreds of pages of materials every day. There's no way for him to read it all."

Ni decided to try anyway. He wrote a note. "Comrade Liu Binyan," he wrote, "I've come all the way from Shanghai to see you. I never thought it would be so difficult. If it's so hard for an ordinary person to meet with you, whose whole purpose is to represent the ordinary people, then our country has lost all reason." Ni enclosed the materials he had gathered in support of his case and left the packet with the representative of the *People's Daily*.

He returned to Shanghai.

•   •   •

Three months later, he had nearly forgotten the matter. He had only dreamed but never really dared to hope that any good would come from his efforts.

At the end of 1984, when Ni went to pick up his monthly salary, the cadre handling his pay informed him that a registered letter was being held for him in the party secretary's office.

The letter had obviously been opened—and read—by the time Ni Yuxian was able to claim it.

It was from Liu Binyan.

"Comrade Ni Yuxian," Liu wrote, "I was very excited to receive your letter and read your materials. The struggles you have waged on behalf of our country are really amazing. I would like very much to meet you and to write an article about you." Liu Binyan planned to be in Shanghai in just a few days. He told Ni how to find him.

The party committee at the Maritime Academy did not want Liu to write, began mobilizing to insure that Ni's story was never publicly told. Ni was called in for a meeting.

He was offered two choices. They would give him permission to go abroad. He could get his passport. But he would have to give up his demands for redress.

Or he could wait six months for them to reinvestigate his case. If, after investigation, the committee decided his record in fact was clear, they would make certain that he got back pay, proper work, proper housing. But the committee might also decide that he was guilty of unspecified crimes.

Ni chose to go abroad.

Within a week, he had received his passport.

But he still wanted housing. His family, initially at least, would not accompany him to the States. They needed a proper place to live.

And contrary to the Academy's understanding of the agreement, Ni never had any thought of suggesting to Liu Binyan that his story not be told. In China or abroad, Ni wanted his story known.

Liu Binyan arrived in Shanghai in January 1985, just as Chinese new year was approaching. His arrival was a great event for the intellectuals of the city, and when he spoke at a local auditorium that held some fifty thousand people, every seat was full. In the mind of the educated public, Liu Binyan was imbued with special powers. He was believed to serve at the behest and under the protection of the newly appointed general secretary of the party, Hu Yaobang. It was said, though falsely so, that he had been given a special pass that granted him access to information that no other journalist was given. To those with secrets to protect, Liu Binyan was a man to be feared.

"I took something of a risk in writing about Ni Yuxian," Liu Binyan recalled at one of our meetings. "I had still not met him when I began writing the article. I relied on the written materials he had supplied me. But after so many years of experience, I thought I had developed the ability to distinguish what was true from what was false. Memory for details might differ and people have a tendency to exaggerate the extent of their persecution and suffering, but rarely—only two or three times—have I been outright deceived." Liu had already written the bulk of "A Second Kind of Loyalty" by the time he met Ni in Shanghai.

Liu met Ni at his hotel. He needed to interview Ni and the leadership at the Maritime Academy in order to fill in some details of the story he had already written—and as a necessary check against the story Ni had told.

• • •

When the leadership at the Maritime Academy read in an article in the Shanghai *Liberation Daily* that Liu was visiting in order to investigate the situation of an anonymous university student who had barely escaped execution after writing a poem of protest against the Tiananmen incident, who had been exonerated of his alleged crimes only to suffer continuing persecution by his own university, they knew that their efforts to prevent Liu from writing had failed.

Ni was brought before them again. The party committee offered to solve his problems. His family would be given an apartment. They would help him to leave the country. In return, he was to encourage Liu Binyan not to write the article.

They called Liu Binyan. "Ni Yuxian is a man with problems," they explained. "He's not a good person. You really shouldn't be writing an article about this type of person." They called the *Liberation Daily*, invited two of its reporters to the Maritime Academy to see their materials on Ni—materials relating to his activities during the Cultural Revolution that Ni had been told had been burned. In fact the materials had been very well preserved. The *Liberation Daily* reporters were chastened by what they read. Perhaps the matter of Ni was not so simple after all. Liu Binyan would have to be careful. They agreed to talk to Liu.

Ni went to pick up the key to the apartment he had been assigned, prepared to move in immediately. The apartment had been taken away. The leadership was confident that the *Liberation Daily* reporters had convinced Liu Binyan not to write.

Liu Binyan invited Ni to meet with him again. "The Maritime Academy says you have lots of problems," he informed Ni.

"Of course they think I have lots of problems. The question is which of those problems are true and which are false."

"Are you willing to talk about these problems directly with them?" Liu asked.

"Of course."

"Okay, tomorrow when I go to the Maritime Academy, you

go, too. Be available so that when I am meeting with the leaders you can come and present your viewpoint."

Three other reporters, including the two from the *Liberation Daily*, accompanied Liu that day, and most of the party committee of the academy was there to meet with him. Liu was presented with considerable argumentation that Ni's character was wanting. Ni had been a rebel during the Cultural Revolution and had participated in struggle sessions against the teachers and the cadres, the party committee alleged. And he had lied about having written a letter to Mao Zedong in 1963. Nowhere was there any evidence of such a letter. They accused him of having tried to steal a bicycle and made numerous allusions to the flaws in his personal morality. They argued, moreover, that they had been perfectly fair to Ni, were treating him properly and in accordance with the party's policies of rehabilitation. It was just that it was impossible to satisfy a man like Ni. He kept threatening to sue.

Liu Binyan was puzzled. "I thought," he says, "that there might be some truth to the allegations of the party committee." There was much to be clarified. Liu suggested that Ni be brought before them to answer the charges directly. "If he were here, of course we could meet with him," a party representative responded benignly. "But Ni is not at school today. We have no way of contacting him."

To the surprise and consternation of the party committee, Liu Binyan went and found Ni Yuxian, inviting him into the room. Question by question they proceeded. "Yes, I participated in the Cultural Revolution," Ni responded. "But I did not write a single attack against a teacher nor did I ever participate in a struggle session against a teacher. Never did I participate in any of the house searches or in any of the beatings. In fact, I tried to help the intellectuals avoid the attacks against them. You were all there during the Cultural Revolution. Which one of you can say that Ni Yuxian struggled against anyone, beat anyone? Who can say I wrote a big character poster attacking any intellectual?"

The participants remained silent.

"Well, it seems as though this attacking of intellectuals did not actually occur," one of the party representatives finally assented.

"Not 'it seems as if,' " Ni responded. "Either it was or it wasn't, and it wasn't. If it was, then say so. Tell me, Teacher Wang, you were struggled against lots of times then. Did I ever participate in any of those struggle sessions against you? Did I ever beat you? Did I ever write a big character poster against you?"

"No," the teacher responded.

They turned to the question of the bicycle.

"I took the bicycle to the police station. So what did I do wrong? The public security people said this absolutely was not a problem. So why are you still insisting that I stole a bicycle?"

Again, the party leadership had no response.

Liu Binyan raised another question. "One night you did not return home," he said. "You borrowed a key to sleep in the library's dormitory. They say that the next morning a female's hair was found on the pillow. I am afraid I must ask you about this. Is what they say true?" The accusation was designed to demonstrate Ni's involvement in yet another romantic affair.

"Who told you this?" Ni wanted to know.

"The head of the library," Liu Binyan replied.

"If anyone else had told you that, I could have believed it was a misunderstanding. But he's the head of the library. I was on the two to eleven shift and had no way of going home so late at night. I had to sleep in the dormitory. This is how we have always arranged things. I already had a key. It was my right to have a key according to the regulations. And besides, the room is for four people, not just one. Why do you say it was just me? Why do you say I borrowed the key? What you're saying is completely false," Ni insisted.

Liu Binyan intervened. "Did he borrow the key from you, or did you give it to him?" he asked the administrator.

"I gave it to him," the head of the library admitted.

Ni began his own litany of allegations, beginning with the recent rescinding of his apartment.

"Just a few minutes ago, when we were meeting, you said you had assigned housing to Ni," Liu Binyan turned to the party leaders. "Now he says you've taken it away. How do you account for that?"

"I don't know," the party secretary replied hesitantly.

"What do you mean you don't know?" Ni intervened. "What do you mean trying to deceive the *People's Daily*?"

The meeting continued for nearly four hours. At the end, Liu Binyan remained convinced that truth rested largely on the side of Ni.

"That he wrote a poem attacking the Gang of Four and their

handling of the Tiananmen demonstrations, accusing them of fascist socialism, that he went to jail and was nearly executed for this poem, that he published a book of Lenin's quotations in order to oppose Lin Biao, all of this he did," Liu Binyan summed up, "and none of it was easy. But you're still attacking him, still treating him like the enemy, you're still unfair to him. This isn't right. And while he does have problems, basically he's still a good man."

The leadership urged Liu not to write the piece. Ni's activities during the Cultural Revolution really had been counterrevolutionary. He was, to this day, a counterrevolutionary. He had tried to steal the bicycle. He was a philanderer.

Liu insisted that he would write the article.

They tried to persuade him to compromise, not to use names, not to write about the mistakes of the party committee.

Liu could not be budged. He would call the article "A Second Kind of Loyalty," and it would be published in the inaugural issue of *Kaituo*, the new nationwide journal founded under the auspices of the *Workers' Daily*. "If you have any criticisms after it's published," Liu informed the academy leaders, "you should let the *People's Daily* know."

But a number of questions, Liu remembers, did remain unclear. Ni's personal morality was still a matter of concern. "I decided that the questions of his relations with women were personal matters, and besides, they had taken place before he was married," Liu recalls, though incorrect about Ni's marital status at the time of his alleged philandering. "Since these were private matters, I decided not to pursue them. I was most concerned about the allegations that he had not actually written the letter to Chairman Mao."

Both Liu and the Maritime Academy launched separate investigations, attempting to determine whether the letter had in fact been written.

The Maritime Academy had good reason not to believe Ni's story. The mere fact that Ni was at the academy was powerful evidence that his political past was clean. Academy students had all been thoroughly, carefully screened. The sensitivity of the jobs they would be assigned upon graduation demanded purity of political heart, unswerving loyalty to the party and its cause. Ni's personnel file was now thick with his misdemeanors, every conceivable transgression, large and small, having been duly and properly recorded there. But no matter how many times and how many people went through the file, there was simply no mention of a letter to Mao. If the incident was not recorded in his file, it could not have happened. A letter of protest to Chairman Mao is the type of matter any party member anywhere would surely have recorded. They could not have known that Ni had earlier destroyed his files.

Just to make certain, the Maritime Academy contacted men who had served as Ni's leaders in the army and soldiers who had worked alongside him. No one could remember such a letter.

The Maritime Academy wrote to the central government asking that they check their own files to determine whether such a letter had been sent, warning them of Liu's impending article and of the false allegations it would contain, suggesting that a way be found to dissuade Liu from writing it. All letters from ordinary citizens to the party chairman were on file. The word came back. There was no record of a letter from Ni to Mao in the files.

Liu Binyan, too, talked with soldiers and officers who had worked alongside Ni. They pointed out that the alleged letter had been written such a long time ago, more than a decade earlier, that so much had happened in the meantime, that they really could not be expected to remember clearly. Liu suspected that it was in their political interests not to remember clearly. Then he met a soldier who did remember. He had loaned Ni the money to buy the stamps.

Liu contacted his friends in the central government, asking them to check their records for a letter from Ni to Mao in 1963. There was no such record.

It was only later that Liu Binyan realized his own mistake. Ni had sent the letter in 1962, not in 1963, and the search of the files had been for a letter sometime in 1963. The files were searched again. The records were found. Ni Yuxian had sent a registered letter to Mao in 1962.

In February 1985, excerpts from "A Second Kind of Loyalty" began appearing unofficially in newspapers and magazines throughout the country, printed each time in tens and hundreds of thousands of copies. The article itself was published in the first edition of *Kaituo* in March.

The attacks against Liu Binyan began immediately. The article, it was said, was opposed to Chairman Mao, opposed to the spirit of Lei Feng, sympathetic to known counterrevolutionaries. His facts were wrong.

The Shanghai municipal party committee, in concert with the

Maritime Academy, appointed a special investigative group to look into the matter, to gather the evidence against Ni that would be necessary to counter the assertions that Liu Binyan had made. Ironmouth Zhen, the political instructor with whom Ni had clashed in his first weeks at the university, took a particularly active role in undermining both Liu and Ni, even traveling to Beijing to gather evidence and to present the academy's case.

The investigative committee expended considerable effort attempting to demonstrate that Ni Yuxian had lied. They still insisted that he had never written that early letter to Chairman Mao. They argued that he had only written one big character poster—the one called "I Do Not Believe"—and that the big character posters in praise of Deng Xiaoping and in commemoration of Zhou Enlai that he claimed to have hung on Huaihai Road were sheer fabrication. He had not only opposed the now discredited Lin Biao and Zhang Chunqiao but Mao Zedong as well. He really was a counterrevolutionary. He had tried to steal a bike. His personal morality was questionable.

When the investigation was complete, the Maritime Academy sent its report to the Shanghai municipal party committee. The Shanghai municipal party committee sent the report to the central committee. The central committee, in turn, sent the report to the chief editors of both *Kaituo* magazine and the *People's Daily*. The chief editor of the *People's Daily* showed the report to Liu Binyan. Liu Binyan showed it to Ni.

Kaituo magazine folded after only two editions. The criticisms were crippling to the editor and his staff.

But Liu Binyan decided to strike back. For some time, the journalist had ruminated about the possibility of writing a piece of exposure literature about the Cultural Revolution in one of China's universities. He had concluded that the Shanghai Maritime Academy was a perfect case study of the factionalism and violence, the political strains, the wrongs that had yet to be righted. He called upon Ni to help.

Liu returned to Shanghai in May of 1985 and stayed for over a month, meeting then with numerous of the Maritime Academy professors who had suffered during the Cultural Revolution, recording his impressions of the city and the academy in a daily notebook, which was published serially as "My Diary" in a leading, nationwide magazine that emanated from Shanghai. The leadership of the Maritime Academy again intervened, writing its own response. The party committee of Shanghai joined in the attacks, accusing Liu of writing irresponsibly, of failing to distinguish between fiction and fact. After several installments of Liu Binyan's diary, the editor capitulated. Publication of Liu's notes suddenly ceased.

Liu Binyan returned to Beijing at the end of May. He was under attack. His situation was serious. One magazine had already been forced to close down because of his article, and another was no longer allowed to publish his diary. The issue of *Kaituo* containing "A Second Kind of Loyalty" had been withdrawn from circulation. Rumor had it that he had described the party as a cancer. He was under investigation. Everything he had written since returning from exile would be put under scrutiny. No newspaper or magazine was willing to publish him.

Liu Binyan preempted his accusers. He announced that he was withdrawing from the world of literature. He would no longer even attempt to write.

• • •

In Shanghai, Ni Yuxian was also under attack.

All work at the Maritime Academy ceased as the party committee turned its efforts to discrediting both Liu Binyan and Ni Yuxian. Meetings were held in every department to present the case against Ni and to argue that Liu Binyan was a rightist, not to be believed, that he refused to listen to the party and had deliberately engaged in falsity.

Liu had sent thousands of copies of the banned *Kaituo* to Ni, and Ni arranged to have the magazine containing "A Second Kind of Loyalty" sold at the gates of the academy. University officials chased the vendors away.

Ni struck back, posting an announcement in the student cafeteria that he would speak in the university auditorium at two o'clock in the afternoon to answer the charges against him. He welcomed everyone to come.

Nearly a thousand people showed up. One by one Ni answered the points against him, taking care to criticize the leadership of the Maritime Academy, his voice reeking with sarcasm, calling the intelligence of the party committee into question, receiving enthusiastic applause with every point he made. The Maritime Academy had accused Ni of establishing a revolutionary rebel organization in cooperation with the notorious Zhang Baoling—the young radical become city leader whom Ni had once witnessed helping municipal committee member Wang Xiuzhen fulfill her task in executing a counterrevolutionary. The Maritime Academy got the name wrong, however. It was with Zhou Baoling, not Zhang Baoling that Ni had cooperated. Ni was convinced that the mistake was deliberate.

They said he had not written a book and sent it to Mao in 1962—the proof being that a number of his colleagues in the army did not know of such a book. "But it was a letter I wrote, not a book" Ni protested. Of course the soldiers did not remember a book. But the letter? They all remembered the letter. Ni held aloft letters from seventeen of his military comrades who remembered.

"The Maritime Academy says that I am deceiving the party and government, that Liu Binyan is deceiving the party and the government. But who really is deceiving whom? The Maritime Academy is deceiving the people," he argued, again to resounding applause. Students asked for his autograph afterward, promised to do all in their power to protect him.

The party posted an announcement that Ni's meeting had been illegal and that Ni was responsible for the results. "But we have freedom of speech," Ni protested. "How could the meeting be illegal?" He ripped the announcement off the wall.

Ni left Shanghai and went to Beijing, accompanied by Zhao Yuefang, to confer with Liu Binyan and do what he could to help. Ironmouth Zhen and the team from the academy were in the nation's capital, too, continuing to press their case against Liu. Their paths crisscrossed and overlapped as the group from the Maritime Academy visited an office only to be followed later by Ni, or Ni presented his case to another office only to be followed by Zhen.

Knowing that Ni would never work with the Maritime Academy again, Liu Binyan tried to help him find a job, hoping at first that Deng Pufang, the son of Deng Xiaoping who had been paralyzed when he had fled from Red Guard attack during the early stages of the Cultural Revolution, might be willing to take him on as a reporter for his newly founded journal. After an initial expression of interest, Deng backed out, knowing that Liu and his protégé were under attack.

Failing in the endeavor to find useful work for Ni, Liu hoped to help him to leave the country, thinking he might call upon Betty Bao Lord, the Chinese-born writer wife of Winston Lord, then the American ambassador to China, to help Ni obtain a visa. Ni's application for a visa had already been refused three times. The money from his American sponsor was not enough. The American government did not permit Chinese to go to the United States to study English. The consulate suspected he was going not to study but to stay—"suspicion of immigration" was how they phrased it.

He had thought that if only he could meet one of the American consuls privately and tell him his story, the consul would give him permission to go. But the Chinese employees who screened the applicants for visas already knew his story, and part of their job was to prevent such a meeting from occurring. Twice they had turned him away. When he finally did get to meet with an American, there were so many Chinese within earshot that he dared not tell his tale. The last time he had been to the Shanghai consulate was February 2, 1985, just as news of "A Second Kind of Loyalty" was hitting the stands. Any effort to try again would be pointless. Special intervention was needed. But Liu's connections came to naught.

Ni returned to Shanghai. The Maritime Academy continued to pay his salary, but he no longer had work. The leading Hong Kong magazines had all published excerpts from "A Second Kind of Loyalty," and both Liu Binyan and Ni were much in the Hong Kong news. The story was creating a sensation. Ni was interviewed by one of the Hong Kong magazines. He wrote an article for the magazine, arguing that unless China also introduced political reform, the economic reforms then underway would be meaningless. He attacked the cadre system, arguing that Chinese cadres had to be supervised by the populace. He raised the question of democracy.

The attacks against Ni escalated. To write an article for a foreign magazine was to have "foreign connections," and foreign magazines were all reactionary. The Shanghai municipal party committee called him in for questioning, again raising concern about the accuracy of "A Second Kind of Loyalty."

He was warned against leaving China, informed that the consent of the municipal party committee would be necessary for him to go.

Ni knew that if he did not find a way to leave China, his situation would only worsen. He was trapped. He believed his arrest was imminent.

• • •

In mid-November, he fled from Shanghai to Guangdong, the province that borders the British colony of Hong Kong, to see if he could escape from there. "If I'm not back by the turn of the new year," he had told Zhao Yuefang, "then you'll know I have gotten out." He stayed on the run for weeks. He went to Shenzhen, the new city close to the border that owes its existence to foreign investments. He called a few of the leading news journals in Hong Kong. The reporters knew his name. His story was big news, his picture on the cover of that month's *Zhengming*, one of the city's leading magazines. They came to Shenzhen to meet him. They were sympathetic. They wanted to help. But there was no legal way to get him to Hong Kong.

He went to the resort city of Zhuhai. The only way out from there was to swim. Too dangerous. Too cold.

He went back to Shenzhen. He obtained false papers easily, cheaply. His friends had helped. One of his friends accompanied him to the border. He looked across to Hong Kong. He could use the false papers to get across.

But he would still be there illegally, and if he were caught the British government would send him back to Shanghai. He would wind up in jail for sure. Or in a labor reform camp. He balked. He dared not take the risk.

He returned to Canton, the capital city of Guangdong Province, disappointed—bitterly disappointed—prepared, reluctantly, to return to Shanghai.

There was an American consulate in Canton, in the Dongfang Hotel. It was a long shot to be sure, a real long shot, but if he did not try, if he did not exhaust every possibility, he would never know for sure.

He was stopped at the front desk. "You're from Shanghai," the Chinese gatekeeper had said. "We can't give you a visa here. You have to go back to Shanghai."

He turned to leave, noticed a bank of elevators, saw that the elevators were guarded by Chinese attendants. He was on the ground level, in the visa section of the American consulate. The consulate offices were on the eleventh floor. The job of the attendants was to keep people from getting there. He was denied entry into the elevator. It was then that he bolted, getting on the elevator and pressing the button that brought him to the consular offices and the meeting with John Lundeen, the cultural affairs officer who finally set in motion the series of connections that led to Ni's escape.

• • •

Ni finally received his American visa in Shanghai on Thursday, January 16, 1986. He went the next day to buy his airplane ticket.

The Chinese bureaucracy does not make buying an airplane ticket simple. There was first the problem of money. The thousand-yuan ticket represented more than a year of Ni's salary, and he had to borrow most of that amount.

He went to Kajia. The young woman loaned him all the money she had that night—some three hundred yuan. It had been several months since the two had met. The matchmakers had finally prevailed. Kajia was married—to a man she could not claim to love. She was pregnant when Ni saw her that one last time.

Yuxian offers numerous reasons why he never married Kajia— his father's sudden attack and the additional scandal a divorce would cause his family; the irresolvable contradiction between Kajia's decision, after her time in jail, forever to eschew political involvement and Ni's determination to devote his life to political change; the fact that Kajia did not particularly like his daughter Lingling; the diminution of love when Kajia did not communicate with him in jail.

But Kajia still does not understand, and flatly rejects the reasons he has offered. Divorce is not so uncommon or so scandalous in China today, she says, especially in sophisticated, cosmopolitan Shanghai. Zhao Yuefang, far more forcefully than she, not only avoids political involvement herself but is actively opposed to Yuxian's continuing activities. Lingling would have continued to live with Zhao Yuefang, not with them, so her feelings toward the daughter were a matter of no great consequence. That she could have found a way to communicate with Ni while he was still incarcerated is a possibility she dismisses as preposterous. The danger of detection—and of being arrested again—was far too great. That his love for her should have diminished because she could not communicate is simply inconceivable.

Ni made her another promise that day. "I'll help you get to America," he said. Kajia believed him.

Other friends loaned him the rest of the funds. Ni took the money to the airlines. More than money was needed. "You have to go to the bank to get a statement from them," the airline representative said. The airline wanted the money in the exchange certificates, purchased in foreign currency, that foreigners use in

China. Bank permission was needed to buy an international ticket in ordinary Chinese currency.

Ni went to the bank. "We can't sign the statement until your household registration office gives you permission to leave," the bank representative pointed out.

The household registration office was under the auspices of his local police station. "We can't give you permission until your work unit agrees," the police woman in charge said. "The Maritime Academy will have to write a letter giving you permission to go to the United States."

Ni knew that the Maritime Academy would never give him permission to leave. "But I can't get there until tomorrow and tomorrow is Saturday. No one will be on duty. I'll come back and give you their letter Monday. But I need your permission so I can buy my ticket today."

"Come on, give him permission," another policeman chided the woman.

"Oh, all right." The local police agreed.

Ni returned immediately to the bank, obtained the required official stamps, and raced to the airline office.

"Tomorrow's flight goes to New York, not Los Angeles," the representative informed Ni.

"Fine, I'll go to New York," Ni responded.

"No, you can't go to New York. Your permission is to go to Los Angeles."

"That's okay. I have relatives in New York. I can visit them," he lied.

"You'll have to go back to the bank and get them to change the destination then," the airline representative responded.

Yuxian returned to the bank. "Why do you want to change this?" the teller wanted to know.

"I have relatives in New York. I want to visit them."

The official relented. Ni got permission to go to New York.

He returned to the airline office shortly before five, just in time to purchase his ticket for the plane that left at noon the next day, Saturday, January 18.

Only his parents and his wife knew that he was leaving. Ni carried little luggage, packing a few clothes into a small suitcase and putting a few papers into a plastic briefcase. If anyone were to discover his plans to leave, and he were reported, he could still be picked up at the airport.

Zhao Yuefang, his two children, and Yuxian's younger brother saw him off. They took a few pictures, and Ni passed through the passport and security checks without difficulty. He sat down to wait in the passenger lounge.

"Where are you going?" a policeman asked suddenly as Ni gobbled down a bowl of noodles he had just purchased from one of the vendors.

"To the United States." Ni was terrified. He thought he had been discovered.

"Let me see your passport," the policeman demanded.

The policeman inspected Ni's passport and left him alone. Without the piles of luggage that Chinese usually carry overseas, the guardian of the law had thought that Ni was a domestic passenger who had managed to slip through to the international section.

An announcement came that the flight was delayed by three hours. Ni was certain that the flight was changed because of him, that the police were making the final check, that the bureaucratic wheels that would prevent his departure had already begun to turn.

Time dragged on, and people waiting with him began talking, trying to draw Ni into their conversations. He remained silent, afraid to speak a word, terrified that anything he might say would give him away. If he were asked his name, they would know him immediately as the character in Liu Binyan's "A Second Kind of Loyalty."

For hours, the clock seemed not to move as Ni remained tense and on edge, alert for the security forces he feared would take him away.

Finally, the announcement came. The Civil Aviation Administration of China flight to New York was ready to board. Ni stood in line with the other passengers. They let him on the plane.

He found his assigned seat and buckled himself in. All the passengers were on board. The time had come to take off.

Still nothing happened. Something had gone wrong. The plane was delayed again. For another hour the passengers sat as final checks were made. Ni sat wordless, immobile, certain that his escape had been discovered, his arrest imminent. Then the doors swung shut, and the jet engines roared. The plane began taxiing down the runway. Ni was bound for New York.

E P I L O G U E

The sky was dark when the plane landed in New York some eigh-teen hours later, and he had only forty-five dollars in his pocket. Hoping to go to Los Angeles, but having no idea where it was or how to get there, he decided to spend the night in the airport, waiting until the airline offices opened the next morning. He barely noticed the magazine the youth shoved into his hand at the bottom of the escalator near the baggage claim area.

He found a seat in the terminal. Hours passed. The airport emp-tied. He began to doze.

"You want a place to sleep?" the black man standing in front of him asked.

Ni's English was limited, but he understood "sleep," and nod-ded his assent.

"Follow me," the man instructed.

Ni found himself in a taxi and noticed as they left the airport grounds that the driver removed from the dashboard the license that displayed his picture and permit number. The meter was not turned on.

The ride seemed to last for hours, and Ni did not know where they were going. "Friends, lots of friends," he kept repeating to the driver, in an effort to convince the man that he was not alone in the city, that there were those who would come to his aid if the driver tried anything untoward. Finally Ni remembered the word that would save him. "Chinatown," he kept repeating. "Chinatown, go Chinatown."

The driver dropped him finally in Chinatown, demanding fifty dollars for his services. When Ni gave him forty, the driver grabbed him, angrily insisting on more. Ni showed him his empty wallet, then opened his bag and offered the man some Chinese ginseng, the precious root tonic Chinese use to preserve their youth and vigor. He had planned to present the ginseng to his false uncle in Los Angeles as thanks. The driver did not appreciate the gift. Thwarted in his efforts to extract more money, recognizing the impossibility of the situation, the driver left Ni in a sleeping Chinatown.

He found an all-night Chinese restaurant and explained his plight to the manager, who fed him a hot meal and found a man willing, if Ni would pay the two-dollar round-trip subway fare, to escort Ni to the Port Authority Bus Terminal where he could find a bus to Los Angeles. Ni arrived, after paying his own subway fare, too, and hence with only two dollars left, to discover that Los Angeles was days away by bus, the ticket far more than he could afford. It was now two or three in the morning, and the terminal itself was terrifying, filled with strange black men he later learned were homeless. The terminal denizens played games, taunting him. One man would shove another in front of him, so Ni was forced either to hold on to the man to prevent him from falling on top of him, or step aside and risk the man tumbling to the ground. He thought they were trying to pick a fight, forcing him into bodily contact so they could accuse him of attack. Ni had never seen black men before and was not inclined to view them sympathetically. He thought his situation might be better on the street.

The section of Forty-second Street just outside the New York Port Authority Bus Terminal fairly teems with the city's lowlife and at three in the morning was still pulsating with drug pushers and prostitutes, all-night pornographic movies and sex shops. Still carrying his plastic overnight bag and his plastic briefcase, dressed in the dull gray suit that is unmistakably mainland Chinese, speaking no English and still reeling from residual fear and lack of sleep and culture shock, Ni was an easy target and knew it. He found an all-night coffee shop, sat down and ordered a fifty-cent glass of milk, hoping to wait out the night.

A Chinese couple from Hong Kong came in. He asked for their help. Were there Chinese newspapers in New York? Surely the Chinese newspapers would have heard of him. Maybe the newspapers could help. The Hong Kong couple called the *China News*. There was no answer. They called the Chinese *World Journal*. Again no answer.

Ni Yuxian picked up the magazine that had been handed him as he stepped off the plane and began thumbing through it. *China*

Spring it was called. Suddenly he was staring at a picture of himself. Two of the articles in the magazine were about him. "If you are an overseas student and are having problems, call us," read an announcement at the back, listing a phone number in Queens.

Ni called again upon the assistance of the Hong Kong couple. They dialed the number. A man named Wang Bingzhang answered the phone. Ni got on the line.

"Hello, my name is Ni Yuxian," he began. "I am in New York."

"You mean the Ni Yuxian of 'A Second Kind of Loyalty'?" the voice on the other end asked.

"Yes."

"Where are you?" the voice continued to probe.

"At a coffee shop on Forty-second Street," Ni answered.

"But that place is too dangerous," Wang replied. Suddenly, he seemed seized by doubt, began questioning Ni in detail, probing to make certain the voice on the other end of the line really did belong to Shanghai's Ni Yuxian, the hero of Liu Binyan's "A Second Kind of Loyalty." Ni passed the test.

"Wait there. Don't move," Wang instructed. "I'll be there in half an hour."

• • •

Wang Bingzhang had graduated from medical school in Beijing in 1971 and was in the first wave of students to be sent abroad after Deng Xiaoping opened China's doors, receiving a Ph.D. in medical research from Canada's McGill University in 1982. In November of that year, at a press conference in New York, he announced his intention, after a long period of introspection, to give up the practice of medicine and devote himself to the cause of democracy. If he were to return to China, Wang said later, the moral compromises required to survive in such an unjust and corrupt society would make it impossible for him to live with his conscience clear. He recalled Lu Xun's decision early in this century to give up medicine in order to write because medicine could only cure a few patients but could not cure the disease of the Chinese nation.

Another tradition was at work in Wang Bingzhang's decision— the tradition of Sun Yat-sen and the dissident in exile. From his safe haven in the West, Sun Yat-sen had established the Guomindang—the Nationalist Party—raising the funds and leading the movement that Chinese history has credited with causing the collapse of the Qing dynasty in 1911 and the establishment of the

fragile new Chinese republic. Wang Bingzhang, too, would organize from exile. He formed the Chinese Alliance for Democracy and
established the magazine *China Spring*, serving as its chief editor.
Following in the tradition of Beijing's Wei Jingsheng, still imprisoned after calling for a fifth modernization in the form of democracy, *China Spring* also focused on the fifth modernization,
publishing articles on democracy and human rights, freedom of
speech and the rule of law, a pluralist society. Hu Ping, the student
at Peking University who had won the election in 1980 after calling
for freedom of speech only to have the election declared invalid,
later became a student at Harvard and one of the more active and
visible members of China Spring.

The Chinese government had responded to the formation of the
new dissident exile organization by declaring Wang Bingzhang, his
colleagues, and the organization itself reactionary. The label gained
considerable credibility both in China and in the West with rumors
that Wang's organization was financed largely by contributions
from the Guomindang in Taiwan. Even Chinese students who
believed deeply in the democratic ideals espoused by Wang and
China Spring avoided association with them. The price of being
labeled reactionary was too high. Others joined the organization
precisely because it was labeled reactionary, for more self-interested
reasons. Association with China Spring was a stepping stone to
political asylum and hence the right to permanent residence in the
United States.

Within hours of his landing in the United States, Ni had thus
managed unwittingly to become involved with the exile organization most vigorously denounced by the communist government, an
organization whose reputation was well-known even in Shanghai.

Wang and his colleagues took Ni to Queens and put him up in
a cheap Chinese-run hotel, returning the next afternoon to invite
him to speak at a public meeting about "A Second Kind of
Loyalty," about himself, and about Liu Binyan. They would publish his remarks in *China Spring* and pay him $200. Ni agreed. His
new colleagues found him a cheap room, $150 a month, in a
basement in Queens, loaning him the money as an advance against
his article. Ni moved in.

He called Liu Binyan to let him know that he had arrived.
The call went through immediately, and Liu remembers that the
connection was clear, far better than a phone call from Shanghai
to Beijing. Liu was delighted to learn that Ni had been able to

leave and was safely in New York. He had, though, several bits of advice. He thought it best for Ni not to participate in politics in the United States, arguing that he should devote his energies to study. China's problems had to be settled domestically, by those who remained behind. It was wrong for a Chinese publicly to criticize his country while in exile abroad. Above all, Liu admonished, Ni should avoid involvement with China Spring.

Ni was too embarrassed, and too afraid, to admit to Liu that he was calling at the expense of China Spring—or that the meeting he would be participating in the next day had been organized by them. Long distance phone calls to Liu Binyan were likely to be monitored.

The meeting was a big success. Suddenly the whole overseas Chinese community knew that the hero of "A Second Kind of Loyalty" was in the United States. Journalists began calling him, inviting him out for meals, interviewing him. His story and the interviews were in all the Chinese newspapers.

• • •

Liu had also warned Ni to stay away from Lin Xiling—the fiery, outspoken female student leader at Beijing's People's University during the blooming phase of the hundred flowers movement in 1956. For her blistering criticisms of socialism in China, Lin had been branded a rightist and punished with twenty years in jail, emerging from the experience equally fiery, irritatingly tough and outspoken, and, some suspected, not entirely balanced. She had already phoned Ni. He was expecting her visit soon.

Lin Xiling, too, urged Ni to sever his ties with China Spring, and the colleague who accompanied her gave Ni $200 to repay the loan from China Spring and end his dependence on the organization. They urged him to contact the Chinese consulate in New York. "The Communist Party today isn't like what it was before," they argued. "It's good now. Don't let yourself get involved with an organization like China Spring."

One of the consul officials obtained Ni's phone number and began calling him, inviting him to meet. Finally, Ni agreed.

The consul was polite, excessively so. No representative of the Chinese government had ever been so polite to Ni. "I know you suffered a lot in China," the official lamented. "I sympathize with you. We all sympathize with you. But you should look to the future now. Don't hate us. And don't allow yourself to be used by others. You've come to the United States to study. You should devote yourself to your studies. Study hard. If you have any problems, let us know. We want to help. We're here to help you."

Ni was skeptical. "If the Communist Party were so concerned about all the Chinese people, our country wouldn't have so many problems," he replied.

Others came to meet him. The political situation in New York is too complicated, some said. You don't know what you are getting yourself into. Los Angeles is better. Maybe you should go to Los Angeles.

Ni is reluctant to discuss the details of his move to Los Angeles. Word of his association with China Spring had already reached China, where the attacks against Liu Binyan were escalating. Many of those attacks had to do with the fact that Liu had written about Ni Yuxian, who had been a revolutionary rebel during the Cultural Revolution, who had escaped to the United States, who was a counterrevolutionary now involved with China Spring. Ni wanted to protect Liu Binyan. He had to sever his ties with China Spring.

A new friend bought him a plane ticket for Los Angeles, gave him five hundred dollars to set himself up there. "Don't tell anyone I've done this," the man warned.

The Chinese government, Ni is convinced, also wanted him out of New York.

He left. He met his false uncle and began attending classes at the school which had accepted him to study English, living in a church-run dormitory room that cost seventy dollars a week, meals included.

The Communist Party found Ni in Los Angeles, too. "Don't talk," he was instructed. "Forget who you are. Change your name. Call yourself Michael. Start a new life."

Ni responded by writing an article for a Chinese magazine in California and was paid a thousand dollars, enough to pay his room and board for several months.

Wang Bingzhang found him in Los Angeles, too. Ni says that Wang wanted China Spring to do more stories on Ni and needed materials—the articles he had written in China, court documents, copies of his sentence. Ni had not cooperated, and two representatives of China Spring had gone to Ni's family in Shanghai, requesting that his father give them the documents. Ni Jizhong, angry that representatives from an organization the Communist Party accused of being reactionary should visit his house uninvited, refused to comply. Wang invited Ni to join some friends for dinner, but Ni arrived only to discover that the dinner was a meeting of the Los Angeles branch of China Spring. When Ni was introduced as a new member, he protested, "No, I was invited here to meet some friends, not to participate in your meeting. If you're going to have a meeting, I'll go."

He was invited to speak at the University of California, Berkeley. Asked what he thought of China Spring, he responded, "I support their goal of democracy, but I am not one of their people." Asked what he thought of Wang Bingzhang, he said that he respected him but did not like how he operated.

Wang Bingzhang heard about Ni's remarks and was furious. The rumor persisted, both in the United States and China, that Ni Yuxian really was a member of China Spring.

• • •

Liu Binyan's article about Ni Yuxian described a man who put principle above politics and was loyal to his country, willing to sacrifice—to go to jail, perhaps even to die—for the good of China. But Liu Binyan believed then and believes now that the Communist Party, under pressure, is capable of reform, that the ideals which initially attracted him to the party might eventually become reality. He places his hopes in Ni's generation, which had participated so enthusiastically in the Cultural Revolution. The suffering they had endured when their education was disrupted, when they were sent to serve as peasants in the countryside or as workers in factories, when their rebellion earned them sentences in jail or labor reform, was tragic and difficult but ultimately edifying, Liu Binyan believes. Forced to confront directly the realities of Chinese society in a way no city intellectual, safe in his ivory tower, ever could, they understand China's problems and know the necessity of reform. Far from being the "lost generation," as so many had described them at the end of the Cultural Revolution, they are the hope for China's future, the generation who will ultimately bring reform.

Ni Yuxian had said little in his meetings with Liu to suggest that he did not share the writer's faith. Ni's escape from China— for he did not leave legally—his immediate connection with China Spring, the public meeting where Ni made it known that the hero of "A Second Kind of Loyalty" was now in the United States, that Liu Binyan was being persecuted and his position in China was precarious, placed Liu in an exceedingly difficult position. Ni's behavior seemed only to confirm the party's allegations against both Ni and Liu.

Thus in March 1986, some six weeks after Ni's arrival, Liu published a statement dissociating himself from the man he had made a hero, stating that the relationship between the two was that between writer and subject and that Ni had no right to speak on his behalf. What was particularly distressing, Liu asserted, was Ni's allegation that he had lost the right to publish, an allegation Liu argued—disingenuously—was false. Ni was speaking irresponsibly. In China, Ni Yuxian had claimed he wanted the country to improve and society to progress, Liu said, but his speech and his behavior since arriving in America belied his earlier words.

Ni, in turn, wrote a response to Liu Binyan, lamenting the fact that even after coming to the United States, he still had no freedom to say and to publish what he liked. He remembered that once, at a dinner with Liu Binyan after drinking a little wine, the journalist had said that he hoped his tombstone would read, "Here lies a man who dared to tell the truth." Those who knew Liu well had claimed that the man was incapable of uttering a falsehood. Ni, too, knew that Liu was a man of truth and honor.

But, Ni argued, China is a country where power outweighs justice. That Liu had attacked Ni and testified to his own freedom could only mean that Liu was not in fact free, that he had been placed in an impossible position, forced to write what he did not believe. Ni renewed his criticisms of Chinese intellectuals, attacking them for their cowardice, their lips that trembled in fear, their failure to speak out. He reminded his readers why Liu Binyan had written "A Second Kind of Loyalty." It was a story about two men who were not afraid to tell the truth, who were not afraid to die. The Liu Binyan who had dissociated himself from Ni was not the real Liu Binyan. The real Liu Binyan, Ni knew, would want Ni to continue to speak the truth.

When his money ran out, Ni returned to New York. The opportunities were better there, he thought. Still speaking no English, he had been unable to find work in Los Angeles. In New York, he worked for several months as a common laborer in a printing factory, then left to serve as a research assistant at Columbia University. He applied for political asylum, and his lawyer assured him that he had never seen such an irontight case.

• • •

In December 1986 the university students of Beijing and Shanghai took to the streets in protest, demanding democracy. At the height of the movement, Ni called his old colleagues in the library at the Shanghai Maritime Academy. "Come home," they urged. "We have democracy now. We have freedom of speech. We can say whatever we want. We can openly criticize the party. You could say what you want if you were to come back. You could do important things."

Ni was more skeptical, certain that the crackdown would inevitably come, knowing that he would be arrested were he to try to return. He did not go home.

Ni was right. The democracy movement was short-lived. In Janurary 1987, Hu Yaobang, the liberal-minded general secretary of the Communist Party, the man many had credited with protecting Liu Binyan, was purged. Days later, Liu Binyan himself, together with two other leading and outspokenly reformist intellectuals, astrophysicist Fang Lizhi and Shanghai writer Wang Ruowang, a friend of Ni Yuxian's, were expelled from the party. The student movement was suppressed.

The party launched a campaign against what it called "bourgeois liberalization," those infectious ideas from the West, ideas like democracy, the rule of law and human rights, that were finding their way into China through Deng Xiaoping's open door. Liu Binyan, Fang Lizhi, and Wang Ruowang were the leading targets, their writings removed from circulation even as excerpts from their allegedly most noxious articles were sent to work units everywhere for Chinese citizens to study as "negative examples." People who had barely heard of the three bourgeois liberals and had certainly never read their works were suddenly enamored of their words, introduced to compelling criticisms of Communist Party corruption and persuasive arguments on the need for democratic reform. Private entrepreneurs, in defiance of government regulations, began selling their works on the street for double and more the original price. The favorite joke was that the surest route to becoming a best selling author was to be criticized and expelled by the party.

Students in the United States, Ni Yuxian among them, were galvanized into action with the dismissal of Hu Yaobang and the expulsion from the party of Liu, Fang, and Wang. Ni was one of the organizers of a meeting at Columbia University in late January where students took the unprecedented move of drafting a letter of protest to the Chinese government. More than a thousand students eventually signed, and a network of democratically minded, politically active Chinese students in the United States was thus established. The Chinese government never responded to their politely worded letter, but the network was easily mobilized into action in the spring of 1989, when the students of Beijing took to the streets in protest once more, joined this time by citizens from all walks of life.

•   •   •

Ni Yuxian's request for political asylum was granted in April 1987. His status as a political refugee allows him to receive federal welfare support, thus freeing him from work to devote his energies to the democracy movement in exile, to writing occasional political tracts and to organizing the overseas Chinese.

Politics continue to dominate Ni's life. There has been much to occupy a Chinese democrat in exile.

•   •   •

The situation in China deteriorated in 1987 and 1988. People became angry. Much of that anger, ironically, grew directly from the reforms that Deng Xiaoping had begun instituting in the late 1970s in order to modernize and revitalize the country after the disastrous final decade of Mao Zedong's rule. In placing economic development above ideological purity, promising that China would become a modern industrialized nation by the year 2000, the austere and egalitarian ethos of the Maoist era was gradually supplanted by the pursuit of wealth and a new money-grubbing, and often crass, materialism. People who under Mao had been proud to be poor were becoming consummate consumers.

But the new materialism gave rise in turn to a new disaffection, a perception that the distribution of rewards was patently unfair.

That sleazy young entrepreneurs were making fortunes hawking their wares in the open-air free markets springing up all over the country seemed, to many, unjust. The greed associated with the pursuit of profit has always had a slightly immoral tinge to Chinese, and the new entrepreneurs who emerged with Deng Xiaoping's reforms were often the most marginal members of Chinese society—largely uneducated, often undisciplined, sometimes only recently released from prison, and unable or unwilling to work in state-controlled jobs. Yet by buying cheap and selling dear, the profiteers were able to take in ten times what an educated professional, employed by the state, could earn. Workers and intellectuals on state-controlled salaries often saw the hard-working entrepreneurs as crooks.

More than that, they saw the party itself as increasingly, blatantly, corrupt. The loosening of political controls under Deng Xiaoping had been accompanied by a growing abuse of power, a burgeoning of special privileges, and the outright corruption of many members of the Communist Party.

Chinese everywhere, from the old retired workers who spent their days reminiscing together in the parks to the young and aggressive entrepreneurs, from students and intellectuals to peasants in the villages, agreed that the opportunities afforded by the decentralization and reform of the Chinese economy had been unequally distributed and that party officials and their children were both getting more than their fair share and becoming increasingly corrupt in the process. Graft, bribery, tax evasion, misappropriation of public funds, speculation, and profiteering were rampant. Nepotism was widespread as the children of the highest party officials reaped money and power. Zhao Ziyang, the man who had replaced Hu Yaobang as the secretary general of the Communist Party, had a son who was the vice-president of a profitable business on Hainan island, where opportunities for fortune were abundant and official corruption had reached new heights, and a daughter who was a vice-general manager at the glitzy Great Wall Sheraton joint venture hotel in Beijing—the hotel where Ronald Reagan had served turkey dinner to Deng Xiaoping and where Fang Lizhi would later be denied entrance to the banquet being hosted by President Bush. One son of the elderly conservative Bo Yibo headed the National Tourism Administration while another was the mayor of the northern port city of Dalian. Deng Xiaoping's most famous child, Deng Pufang—crippled while trying to escape from his Red Guard captors—was simultaneously head of the charitable Fund for the Handicapped and general manager of the much more profitable Kanghua Corporation. As ordinary educated Chinese struggled for the opportunity to study abroad, the children of the very party leaders who inveighed so self-righteously against the "bourgeois liberalism" of the West were already living in the United States, and their younger siblings were lining up outside the American consulate to request—and receive—their visas.

In the countryside, too, tales of flagrant corruption were every-where. When the state had allocated one hundred thousand yuan to construct a new road in a picturesque county that skirts the Yangtze River, local party officials scraped twenty thousand into their own pockets, and the road could not be built. Everywhere stories circulated of rural officials selling state-distributed fertilizer to friends at below-market state prices, then sharing the profits when the fertilizer was resold at higher prices the peasants had to pay but could ill afford. For those individuals with control over cheaper state-controlled goods, the opportunities for scams were virtually limitless—persuasive evidence that a country cannot have socialism, capitalism and honest administration, too. At the same time, the state was running out of money and could not afford to pay the peasants for the grain it requisitioned, giving them white slips—IOUs—instead.

By the fall of 1988, a new and even more pressing grievance had been added to the undercurrent of disaffection. On park benches and in the streets, in taxis and buses, in every conversation with acquaintances and friends, the most insistent, pervasive com-plaint was inflation. Prices had remained stable under the highly centralized economy of the Maoist years, but with Deng Xiaoping's reforms, the decentralization of the economy, the introduction of a free market into an economy of perpetual shortages, and initial attempts at price reform, inflation was inevitable. Official estimates of the rate steadily increased as the year proceeded, reaching about 30 percent by early 1989. But ordinary Chinese were mystified as to how those rates were calculated, indignantly pointing out that prices for key items in their daily shopping baskets—such as eggs and vegetables and meat—had more than doubled. Prices on such luxury items as televisions, refrigerators, tape recorders and videos, minimal aspirations for the newly materialist young urban Chinese, had skyrocketed. An imported Japanese television set cost some 5,000 yuan or nearly $1,400 U.S.—about three-and-a-half-years' salary for a middle-income Chinese lawyer or teacher.

• • •

Nowhere was the sense of anomie and moral crisis more palpable than on the university campuses—where the decay of the spirit was matched by a decay of the physical plant.

"You talk of the alienation and depression of the victims of the Cultural Revolution," a young man had challenged me at the end of a talk I gave at Peking University in the fall of 1988, "but I hadn't even been born when the Cultural Revolution began. Yet I—and my schoolmates, too—feel depressed, alienated, hopeless. How do you explain that? We are victims, too." The response of his fellow students, and the conversations that ensued, left no doubt that his alienation was widely shared.

My own alma mater, Beijing Normal University, typified the demoralization and decay. The interiors of the dormitories and classrooms seemed not to have been painted in decades, and the walls were blotched with layers of filth. The smell of unclean toilets pervaded the halls, and sometimes water from the lavatories seeped into the corridors. Six to eight students were jammed into dormitory rooms that would have comfortably fit two. The dining hall where I had once reluctantly taken my food lacked even a nod in the direction of sanitation and cleanliness. Old Wang still eschewed soap as she rinsed bowls and glasses and chopsticks under cold water. A young student recounted his experience of waking up one night to find two rats fighting on the railing of his bed and of discovering dead flies in the sandy rice he bought from the student canteen.

Despite the much touted opening to the West and a sporadic flourishing of intellectual ferment, intellectual apathy, if not actual atrophy, had set in among many of the university faculty. So beaten down by forty years of party intrusion, so wounded by their experiences in the series of political campaigns of which the Cultural Revolution was merely the worst, so cut off from world academic trends, their teaching had become outmoded, hackneyed, and above all, safe. "In class," one student complained, "all the teacher does is read from a book. An approved book. But I already know how to read. What we really want is to be able to think for ourselves—and then to say what we think. School is a waste."

Students had thus retreated from serious study into cynicism, hedonism, and sometimes outright nihilism, ruefully joking about the four "factions" on campus, each a sarcastic play on words. The *tuo* (Trotskyite) faction devoted all its energies to studying for the English-language TOEFL (*tuo*) exams in an effort to go abroad. The *ma* (Marxist) faction spent all its time gambling at *ma jiang*, eating, drinking, smoking, chasing girls and otherwise making merry. The *you* (rightist) faction spent all its time traveling (*you*), while the *qian* (progressive) faction was engaged in the hot pursuit of money (*qian*).

But underneath the haughty veneer of adolescent cynicism was still a strain of youthful idealism. "Young Chinese intellectuals are very idealistic and really devoted to helping the country, despite their own corruption," one student explained. "At night, we get together in our rooms and talk about our country's problems, about what we can do and what our responsibilities are. We are very political." Small groups of students at Peking University, led by history student Wang Dan and with the cooperation of Fang Lizhi's wife Li Shuxian, herself a professor of physics at Peking University, even met together periodically in what they called "democracy salons."

Popular grievances festered, waiting only for the moment when anger could be given voice.

•   •   •

1989 was a particularly appropriate year for the people of China publicly to vent their grievances. The year marked the two-hundredth anniversary of the French Revolution, the fortieth anniversary of the establishment of the Chinese People's Republic, and the seventieth anniversary of the May Fourth incident of 1919—the day when several thousand Chinese intellectuals, led by the students and faculty of Peking University, took to the streets in protest against the acquiescence of their government to the terms of the Versailles treaty.

The May Fourth incident became part of a much wider movement, one of the rare episodes in Chinese history during which intellectuals really did fight for basic human rights and democratic ideals. An intellectual renaissance, the May Fourth Movement called for the destruction of China's traditional political culture and the inculcation of democracy instead. Its participants believed in science, too, and hoped that science could be absorbed into the culture and then be used to solve pressing social problems. China thus might be made modern and come once more to occupy its proper place in the new world order.

In the winter of 1988–1989, with the seventieth anniversary of the May Fourth incident approaching, Chinese intellectuals began talking about a new May Fourth, arguing that sometime after the establishment of the Chinese Communist Party in 1921, the ideals of democracy and science had somehow gone awry. The country had yet to accept the scientific method of solving social problems, and a democratic system of government was still a distant dream.

Pointing to the dazzling, creative, iconoclastic minds of the faculty who had been gathered on the staff of Peking University during May Fourth—men like the president, Cai Yuanpei; Hu Shih, who led the literary renaissance; and Chen Duxiu, who would become one of the founders of the Chinese Communist Party—students called for a new intellectual awakening and argued that Peking University should again take the lead. The legacy of May Fourth was powerful, the students' historic sense of responsibility strong. "We want a new May Fourth movement," they said, "only more significant still."

Fang Lizhi took the lead. Dismissed from his post as vice-president of Anhui's University of Science and Technology of China at the time of his expulsion from the party, Fang had moved to Beijing to join his wife and to serve as a researcher with the Beijing Astronomical Observatory. On January 6 he wrote an open letter calling upon Deng Xiaoping to seize the occasion of the seventieth anniversary of the May Fourth Movement, the fortieth anniversary of the founding of the People's Republic of China, and the two hundredth anniversary of the French Revolution to release China's political prisoners, including Wei Jingsheng. Chen Jun, a daring young activist cum businessman who ran a popular pub in Beijing and had an English wife and a flair for the limelight, followed suit, organizing thirty-three of China's leading and most respected intellectuals to sign a similar letter. Chen Jun found himself expelled from China for his efforts and returned to New York to link up with other exiled democracy activists, including Hu Ping of China Spring—and Ni Yuxian.

In Beijing, forty-two leading scientists joined the thirty-three intellectuals, calling for the release of "youth imprisoned or sent to labor reform for ideological problems." In March another forty-three intellectuals published a similar plea.

In New York the Chinese intellectual community was abuzz. The time was ripe, Ni thought, for a new organization, led by distinguished Chinese intellectuals in the United States, Hong Kong and Taiwan, to work together with compatriots on the mainland for the promotion of democracy. He called his proposed organization the Committee for the Promotion of Democracy in China, and its goal would be to solicit 100,000 signatures over a two-year period in support of its five-point declaration calling for the right to publish independent periodicals without government interference, the right to free association, popular election of leaders at the district and county levels, the immediate release of all political prisoners, and the separation of the party and government.

Ni's efforts to elicit support were remarkably successful. Such leading scholars as Princeton's Yu Ying-shi, Harvard's Tu Wei-ming, Columbia's C. T. Hsia, University of Chicago's Leo Ou-fan Li, and Hong Kong journalists from *Nineties* and *Zhengming* were among those who lent their names as initiators of the effort.

Ni wanted Fang Lizhi to head the new organization. He telephoned Fang in Beijing. Fang wanted to see the documents Ni had drafted and to know who else had signed. Ni sent the materials through the mails. They never reached Fang. I delivered the materials to him personally at his home in Beijing in mid-February. Fang agreed to serve as the organization's head.

Both in China and among liberal-minded Chinese in the United States, the focus of political activity for 1989 was on May Fourth. Everyone knew that something would happen then.

In Bolinas, California, leading China specialist and writer Orville Schell and his Chinese-born wife Liu Baifang organized a major meeting of China's most respected dissident intellectuals and a few American sympathizers for a discussion of China's future. The meeting was to convene at the end of April, leaving time for those who wished to return to China to witness the events of May 4.

When the meeting opened, several chairs stood vacant. Fang Lizhi and Wang Ruowang had not been permitted to leave China. Liu Binyan was there, having left in April 1988 to spend several months at the University of California Los Angeles before going to serve as a fellow of journalism at Harvard's Nieman Foundation. So was Ge Yang, the exuberantly feisty seventy-year-old female editor of *New Observer* magazine in Beijing, who was later to be labeled a leading behind-the-scenes manipulator of the uprising that ensued while she remained in the United States, everyone's favorite co-conspirator. Liu Xiaobo, the controversially outspoken angry young literary critic and lecturer from Beijing Normal University did not attend the meeting, having left New York, where he held an honorary position at Columbia, the day before the conference began to return to Beijing and seize his role in history.

Thus it was that several of those whose own writings and publications served as the intellectual inspiration for what transpired in Beijing in the spring of 1989 were safely out of reach of the Chinese Public Security Bureau when the crackdown began, and others who might well have been safe were not. When the army moved into Beijing, Fang Lizhi and his wife Li Shuxian fled to safety in the American Embassy in Beijing while Wang Ruowang, who had marched at the head of a Shanghai parade with a banner across his chest declaring his support for the student demands, was imprisoned incommunicado for more than a year. Liu Xiaobo, who had negotiated with the army for the safe exit of the students from Tiananmen Square, was finally released from jail in February 1991.

• • •

The death of Hu Yaobang on April 15, 1989, had been unexpected, precipitating weeks earlier than planned the protests that had already become inevitable and most believed would begin on May Fourth. Like Zhou Enlai some thirteen years before, Hu Yaobang could not be properly mourned. He had been purged as general secretary of the party in January 1987 for his "bourgeois liberal" views and his support of the student protesters. The outpouring of public mourning for Hu provided the opportunity for an expression of political grievances as well, just as in 1976 the public outpouring of grief over the death of Zhou Enlai had provided the backdrop for a massive protest against the radical politics of the Cultural Revolution and the leadership of the Gang of Four. The occasion of his death prompted a delegation of students to demand that his case be reopened and publicly reevaluated.

Like the lotus blossom that springs from muddy waters fresh, clean and pure, the Chinese student movement of the spring of 1989 rose unexpectedly from a morass of cynicism, materialism, and moral decay. The youthful idealism of the students and the real material grievances of the ordinary citizenry suddenly were joined. "Man is born good," an older Beijing man argued, trying to explain how a movement apparently so innocent and good emerged from a society so corrupt. "It is society that corrupts him. The students were still too young to have been really corrupted, so it was possible for them to lead."

• • •

From exile in New York, Ni Yuxian followed the evolution of the movement day by day and hour by hour, organizing Chinese students and scholars in the area to demonstrate on May Fourth in sympathy with the march for democracy their compatriots in Beijing would be holding that day, too. The occasion is an historic one, the advertisement calling the march argued, and their fellow students in Beijing were in danger. Students safely ensconced in the United States could not standly idly by with arms crossed as their fellows in Beijing took to the streets to call for democracy.

A thousand Chinese students joined the march in New York on May 4, the largest demonstration of Chinese in the United States to date. And Ni's signature campaign in support of the declaration of the Committee for the Promotion of Democracy began to take off. Ni had received two thousand signatures in the first few months after the committee was formed and the declaration published, before the death of Hu Yaobang and the onset of the student demonstrations. In the months after Hu's death, the number grew to sixty thousand. Indeed, the committee's manifesto, calling for freedom to publish and associate, the release of political prisoners and the election of local officials, figured prominently among the big character posters at Beijing Normal University when I visited there on May 5, having arrived the day before to witness the historic march in Beijing.

As the democracy movement in Beijing progressed, money began pouring into Ni's fledgling organization—from Chinese students and participants in the May Fourth march and from ordinarily apathetic overseas Chinese businessmen. The Committee for the Promotion of Democracy in China was able to open an office with telephones and a fax machine. Ni, together with Chen Jun, stayed in constant contact with friends and acquaintances in the United States and China. He began calling me daily in Beijing.

I was spending every waking moment following the expanding movement, visiting the university campuses to read the big character posters and talk to the student participants. I was in endless conversation with faculty and friends and marched alongside the students, humming the "Internationale," when they left their campuses and took to the streets, headed ultimately to Tiananmen Square.

In the square, the students began organizing impromptu democracy salons as a way of providing an education on the meaning of democracy to themselves and the tens of thousands of Beijing citizens who were coming to show their support.

As a Chinese-speaking American writer, and hence both an assumed expert on the meaning of democracy and someone they believed could convey their hopes and ideals to the entire Western world, the students invariably welcomed me to the square. Whenever conversation would spring up between me and one or two students, a crowd would begin to gather, and sometimes the sessions would go on for hours, organized in something of the style of an old town meeting. A handful of students and particularly interested citizens would sit with me on the pavement with the crowd clustered around us in a series of concentric circles. Together we discussed the meaning of democracy, the failure of the Chinese leadership, the goals of the student movement, and the frustrations of ordinary Chinese citizens. Cameras clicked and tape recorders whirled as secret police and citizens alike recorded the event for posterity.

"We've had ten years of opening to the West," said a well-groomed, articulate Qinghua University student at one such typical democracy session. "So we can see the strong points of the Western political system. We followed your presidential election very carefully. If you don't like your leaders, you just vote them out of office. Reagan at most gets to serve eight years. But look at us. Deng Xiaoping is eighty-five years old. Do you think his head is still clear? Of course not. So why hasn't he stepped down and retired? He still wants to stay. The Chinese political system doesn't work."

When the students began their hunger strike on Saturday, May 13, I was visiting a friend at Peking University and watched as the students left the campus. "A revolution is not a dinner party," read one banner, quoting from Mao Zedong's classic 1927 definition of revolution. "Have you eaten, Deng Xiaoping?" read another, in ironic imitation of the traditional Chinese greeting. "Mother, I don't want to die," read another.

I was there, too, when the students arrived in the square, the waiting crowd cheering as the students first hoisted the huge black flag proclaiming their hunger strike and then, one by one, raised the twenty-four red flags of each participating school atop the sixteen flagpoles that stand at the foot of the Monument to the Revolutionary Heroes.

A collective gasp rose from the city. Support for the student hunger strike was instantaneous and universal. The students had seized the moral upper hand.

I was welcomed into the circle of students from my alma mater.

The next day, Sunday, rumors persisted that the police would move in that night. Mikhail Gorbachev would arrive that Monday for the first Soviet-Chinese summit meeting in some thirty years. For China's leadership, the presence in Tiananmen Square of tens of thousands of protesting students would be an unbearable loss of face.

At midnight the atmosphere was still festive and noisy, the crowd by no means diminished. Somewhere near the middle of the square, the music students were holding an impromptu and raucous jamboree, with choruses competing to see who could sing Beethoven's "Ode to Joy" the loudest.

Then word came, from the elected student representative of Beijing Normal University and delivered in the form of a chant, that negotiations between the students and the government had broken down. "There is some indication," the student representative chanted. "There is some indication," the students echoed back. "That the government will take action tonight." "That the government will take action tonight." "Probably at about three in the morning." "Probably at about three in the morning." "Probably the signal for action." "Probably the signal for action." "Will be to turn off the lights in the square." "Will be to turn off the lights in the square." "Probably it won't be peaceful." "Probably it won't be peaceful."

The student representative paused for discussion. Perhaps the students should leave the square now, voluntarily. He was afraid the police would use force. He wanted to avoid bloodshed and feared his comrades could be hurt. "Should we leave?" he asked his fellow students. "No, we'll stay," they yelled back in unison.

"Okay, then let's keep the hunger strikers in the middle, with the girl students in a circle surrounding them. The boy students should form a circle around the girls." The haphazard rearrangements resulted in only a rough approximation of the proposed concentric circles. But the male students did occupy the outermost positions in the amoebalike configuration, locking arms to keep out intruders. Around the tens of thousands of students who now occupied the square, divided into clusters by school, another huge series of concentric circles had formed. Thousands of young Beijing citizens, mostly male, were staying. They would serve as the last line of defense protecting the students from the police.

"Please don't be nervous," the student representative chanted, as the rearrangements settled in. "We are not nervous," the students sang back. "Keep order," he yelled. "We will keep order." "Sit hand in hand, facing the center." "Hand in hand, facing the center." "Struggle to the end." "STRUGGLE TO THE END!" they yelled. "Thank you." "THANK YOU."

"Will you stay with us?" the students asked me. I was trembling with cold and with fright. If the police did come to the square, violence was certain. I could not help but remember how they had cleared the area during the Tiananmen Incident of 1976, the militia moving in and isolating the protesters in the checkerboard squares, beating and bloodying them with their clubs.

"But these students are the best and the brightest of China, the hope for the country's future," I thought. "How can they turn against their own children?"

I left my friends to have time alone to think, the sound of the singing and chanting growing ever fainter as I walked north through Tiananmen, the Gate of Heavenly Peace, under the huge portrait of Chairman Mao Zedong that overlooks the square, heading toward the Meridien Gate that serves as the southern entrance to the Forbidden City, grandiose and awesome home to the emperors of the last two of China's dynasties. Within seconds, I had arrived in another century, the thick vermilion walls of the Forbidden City, Chinese history congealed in stone, oblivious to the revolution outside. Somewhere nearby, just to the west, behind the same walls in the area known as Zhongnan Hai, was the Chinese leadership of today. "The last emperor," the people of Beijing had begun calling Deng Xiaoping. Was he as sealed off and oblivious to the hopes in the square as earlier emperors must have been?

It was in this spot just north of the Gate of Heavenly Peace and in the two parks that flank the Forbidden City east and west that the militia had gathered in April of 1976 to launch their assault on the protesters in the square. Indeed, there were police there tonight, but only about fifty of them, pants legs rolled up, smoking cigarettes and playing cards. Attack hardly seemed imminent.

As I walked in solitude along the moat that surrounds the Forbidden City, I made the same decision that many other Westerners in Beijing, I later learned, were making that night. I decided to stay with the students. If the police did move in and I died, my life had been worth living, I concluded, and if I lived to be a hundred, I would never be given another opportunity to witness an event such as this. However dangerous, it was still my duty to bear witness.

I returned to the students from Beijing Normal University.

"I'll stay," I told them.

"Are you frightened?" one asked. "No," I lied. "Have you ever done anything like this before?" someone asked. "Yes, something like this, in the 1960s, during the black civil rights movement."

"Did the police ever come?"

"Sometimes."

"What did you do?"

"We were peaceful, like you. Usually, we joined hands and sang a song so we wouldn't be afraid."

"Will you teach us?"

We crossed one arm over the other, joined hands, and I taught them "We Shall Overcome."

I left the square finally sometime after dawn. The police had not come. But the decision to stay to bear witness was one I made night after night for the next several weeks, returning home each morning around dawn for a few hours' sleep—and my daily call from Ni Yuxian.

• • •

That so large a movement should be evolving without his direct participation was agonizing to Ni. The mass movement he had dreamed of for years, the Chinese people rising up at last to demand democracy, was expanding day by day, and he was irrelevant. He believed he had contributions to make. Above all, he was frustrated at the lack of leadership in the square and disturbed that the movement remained in the hands of the students—that no middle-aged intellectuals had come forth to lead. He was angry in particular that Fang Lizhi, the head of his own Committee for the Promotion of Democracy in China, whose spiritual presence dominated the movement, was remaining silent, had never even appeared on the square. Ni decided to return to China. He and two of his political allies—Hu Ping, now the new leader of China Spring and a man whose intellect, political viewpoint, and integrity Ni greatly respected, and Chen Jun, the young human rights activist who had been expelled from China months earlier for organizing the petition calling for the release of political prisoners—booked plane tickets for Beijing. Neither Ni nor Chen Jun were officially members of China Spring, but the diverse democratic Chinese activists resident in New York had always maintained close contact, and the politics of the student movement were making strange Chinese bedfellows, too.

The trio was dissuaded, finally, from going, convinced that the Chinese authorities would either deny them entry or arrest them immediately. Wang Bingzhang had tried to go back a few weeks earlier, and had not been allowed to board the plane. Ni Yuxian turned his efforts to organizing Chinese in the United States instead, urging upon me the difficult, and ultimately impossible, task of distributing the Committee's funds in service of the students' needs. The students wanted an expensive printing press to publish their views, but the movement was badly disorganized and deeply divided, and the distinction between the various student groups leading the movement and the individuals within those groups was often unclear. In the turbulence of the times, there seemed no guarantee that the money would actually be used for its intended purpose, no way to be certain that the funds would not simply be used by whichever individual happened to receive them.

• • •

By twist of fate, I was not in Beijing on the night of June 3 when the tanks rolled down Changan Boulevard and the army finally moved in. I was in Chongqing, responsible for a group of tourists from the American Museum of Natural History, and it became my task to get the group safely from Chongqing to Guilin and then on to Hong Kong. Students and workers, hearing of a massacre in Beijing, were blocking all the main roads in Chongqing, and in the terror of the moment it seemed possible that the revolution was upon us, that the government of China was on the verge of collapse. No official news was coming from Beijing, and after getting a couple of calls through, phone and fax lines in Chongqing were cut off. My sources in Beijing had relayed graphic stories of a massacre in Tiananmen Square, saying that the army had come in and mercilessly slaughtered thousands of innocent students. It was several weeks before a different truth began to emerge—that most of the deaths had occurred in others parts of the city, when the army and tanks and armored personnel carriers were moving in and the people of Beijing took to the streets, as they had every night for several weeks, to prevent the military from entering, and that most of the dead were ordinary citizens. Few students in fact had been killed.

• • •

Ni Yuxian came to Hong Kong just after the massacre. The ordinarily politically quiescent Hong Kongese had suddenly been activated by the movement on the mainland, and the whole city went

413

into mourning when they heard the news of June 4. Ni wanted to establish links between the democratic activists in Hong Kong and the United States—and to find people with ties to the underground railroad that was spiriting people out of the mainland so he could give them names of activists he knew who were in danger of arrest and needed to be rescued. We met there.

Ni was not greatly surprised by the violence in Beijing. Several months earlier, in an article noting the rising level of popular discontent in China and predicting a period of *luan*, he had raised the possibility that the government might use violence to quell a popular disturbance. He saw the use of violence as a sign of the government's weakness. And a government that could not allow for popular expression, that relied on force to suppress the popular will was, he felt, worthy of being labeled fascist. "Now are you willing to admit that they are just a bunch of fascists?" he pressed me, knowing my discomfiture at applying the fascist label to any but the regimes the Allies had fought in the Second World War. "No, I still think they are communists," I retorted, "and what they have done is quite bad enough."

"And nonviolence? Do you still believe in that?" he demanded. Ni believed that the citizenry had the right to use violence to oppose the military's use of force. "Yes, I still believe in nonviolence," I answered. The nonviolence of the students had been tactical rather than strategic, political expedient rather than political principle. Nonviolence as a philosophy had never been put to the test. The young males of Beijing had used every means at their disposal to stop the military from entering the city. The specter of underdeveloped China at war once more with itself was too horrifying for me to contemplate.

We parted unhappily, Ni Yuxian and I—he to return to the United States and I to Beijing, where I stayed for another year and much of this book was written, witness myself to the various forms of inhumanity that Ni had encountered over the years of his growing up—executions, arrests, intimidation and persecution, ideological indoctrination and the government's lies. I watched as my friends were forced to speak in support of the government they had come to oppose and listened as the government repeatedly urged its citizens to serve as informers on relatives, colleagues, and friends. The repression following the massacre was so medieval in its methods and its goals that life often seemed surreal.

Through imprisonment, intimidation, death, and by means of

the grinding power of everyday petty control, the voices of protest were silenced, and the people of China were quickly cowed into submission. The same people who had carried banners reading "give me liberty or give me death" bowed once more before the superior force of authority. Terror, even in small doses, is a highly effective means of social control, more so in political cultures habituated to submit to authority. The emperor, while a bad emperor, is nonetheless the emperor, and fundamental political change must necessarily await his death. The legitimacy of the Chinese system was profoundly undermined by the use of the military to quash the popular revolt in Beijing, but it was not fully destroyed.

Chinese withdrew from public, political life, into private familial concerns, living, as Timothy Garton Ash would say, in a "sort of 'inner emigration' from the totalitarian demands of the Party-state." Passivity and withdrawal are the tradition-honored means of the honest Chinese intellectual faced with a corrupt government that refuses to reform. The Chinese state has always defined the terms of acceptable political debate. When government refuses to reform, the only way to remain free from corruption oneself, according to the Buddhist and Daoist conceptions, is to retreat, biding one's time in research and writing, in calligraphy and art, in nurturing and preserving one's body, until the time when one can re-emerge to participate again with integrity in the political realm. The apparent passivity of the Chinese intellectual is not always an indication of indifference but rather a commitment to remain pure.

As the Chinese withdrew to their private pursuits, we waited for the Ni Yuxians of Beijing, for the rare individual willing to live publicly in truth, to stand up and shout out in anger against injustice. Occasionally an individual did cry out in lonely protest—a big character poster hung surreptitiously at night, a commemorative visit to the square. He was inevitably arrested. Sometimes we heard shots in the night.

• • •

Ni returned to the United States to face a new set of accusations against him—that he had misused the funds that had poured into the Committee for the Promotion of Democracy in China. The leading professors who had served as the backbone of the organization withdrew their support, openly dissociating themselves from him and demanding that he give a public accounting of how the funds had been used. Others, who claimed their organizations as cosponsors to the several demonstrations the Chinese activists had held in New York, claimed that Ni never gave them their fair share of the money. The allegations of financial malfeasance have damaged Ni's reputation, especially within the overseas Chinese community.

Objective judgment of the allegations against him and of Ni's own defense is vexingly difficult. That Ni should have been accused of financial malfeasance is no surprise. Having never had money to spend, he has always been careless with it, and accounting is foreign to his nature. While Ni had assembled an impressive group of members, day-to-day affairs on the Committee for the Promotion for Democracy were his responsibility. The man who solicited the money for the Committee and the man who spent it were one and the same; Ni acted as president, treasurer, and the board of directors. He is arrogant in the manner of kings. *"L'état, c'est moi,"* is an apt description of Ni's conception of his relationship to the Committee he founded. The money was his to spend, so long as the cause was democratic and not for his own personal benefit. Because his whole life is devoted to the cause of democracy in China, Ni can reason, everything he does supports that cause. That there might have been a board of some sort to oversee expenditures, that individuals might share his belief in democracy yet disagree on how the Committee's money might appropriately be spent, seems never to have occurred to him. Besides, he argues, events were proceeding with such alacrity and the money started pouring in so suddenly that there was no time to establish procedures. The accusations were upon him before the first bank statement had been mailed.

A number of democracy-minded activists, men like Fang Lizhi and Liu Binyan, lead lives of political integrity above public reproach, and some organizations, such as Human Rights in China, have so structured their finances, supervised by a board, as to remain immune from attack. But Ni is not alone among China's democratic activists to be accused of financial misdealings. Nor is his organization alone in having failed to develop agreed-upon procedures for receiving and spending money. China Spring was split in two when Wang Bingzhang was accused of financial misdealings, and Hu Ping, who took over the leadership, later faced similar accusations himself. Wuer Kaixi, the brash, to some charismatic, and certainly controversial young leader of the Tiananmen democracy movement in 1989 was eased out of the leadership of the

Federation for a Democratic China for his political and financial irresponsibility. He is alleged to dress in Italian designer suits and was once ensconced by Pacific Rim CEOs in a $3,500-a-night hotel. Rumors persist of financial misdealings by a host of Chinese democracy activists recently arrived in the United States.

There are those who would argue that the failure of so many of China's would-be democratic organizations to institute proper financial procedures is a function of the communist political culture from which they come. Not only are public accounting and accountability absent in the communist system but it has become commonplace for everyone within the party-dominated work unit to milk their own unit for everything it is worth. Leading cadres and their associates literally feed off the work unit, freely spending their unit's funds to indulge in banquets at local restaurants, eating, drinking, and generally making merry at work unit expense. Less privileged members of the unit thus do not hesitate to extract from the organization whatever can be extracted, whether by pilfering from the coal pile used to heat the building, stealing bricks from the local construction site, or simply taking liberal helpings of a whole range of office supplies. What else can ownership by the people mean than consigning for one's own use what everyone owns jointly anyway?

But just as cadre behavior within the Chinese work unit makes a mockery of the governing principle "to serve the people" and pilfering from the work unit transforms the meaning of socialism, so failure by China's would-be democrats to devise acceptable accounting procedures undermines the goals around which they have ostensibly been organized. China's democracy movement in exile is composed of a dizzying variety of organizations, many locked in battle with each other. Petty squabbling between organizations, accusations and counteraccusations flying, is endemic. Often such organizations owe their formation and continued existence to a single individual, and the problem of organizational succession remains unsettled, provoking internal power struggles when the need to choose a new leader arises. In other cases, internal power struggles are present at the outset and rarely settled. The result is that these organizations, and the democracy movement itself, are too often deflected from their original goals of promoting democracy, human freedom, and individual rights.

Ni Yuxian did finally give a written accounting. It is possible that much of the money he gathered into suitcases never found its way to the ledger, though Ni claims that the cash collected at public rallies was counted in the presence of several checkers who also accompanied him to the bank to deposit the money. Ni himself admits that he kept all the publicly collected money for his own organization. ("I did all the work," he claims, "and besides, no one ever asked me for the money. Tell them to ask.") The fax machine and the tape recorder, the telephone and the answering machine, all the equipment bought in the name of the Committee, remain now with Ni. "What else was I supposed to do with it?" he wonders. Of the more than $30,000 collected, Ni has publicly accounted for some $20,000, and while some might disagree about his interpretation of democracy-related activities, nothing in his accounting seems seriously awry. The $10,000 remaining Ni claims to have used in the year following July 1989 for other democracy-related activities.

Ni thinks that people are out to get him, that anyone who devotes himself to the cause of democracy will necessarily suffer the slings and arrows of those opposed to liberal democratic ideals. Indeed, Ni's enemies are many, and several are so vociferous in their invective that it is easy to believe they may deliberately be trying to destroy him. Ni's single-minded activism, his disregard for those who would be his allies, his insistence on doing things his own way render him difficult to like and an easy target for attack. But there is as yet no real evidence to prove major financial malfeasance and a great deal to suggest that he is not unlike many other democracy activists.

• • •

Ni's activism and commitment to political change remain undiminished. He vehemently disagrees with those who still argue that the party will reform itself from within or who believe that with the passing of Deng Xiaoping and the rest of the senior leadership a new, more reform-minded generation of party elite will finally gain control. He is contemptuous of those who call for major reforms, like the introduction of a multiparty system and a separation of powers, without first calling for the overthrow of the Communist Party. He is impatient with those who insist that the absence in Chinese culture of a democratic tradition will necessarily slow the course to democracy. The downfall of the Communist Party has become for Ni the *sine qua non* of any major and meaningful reform. He thus became one of the founding members of the new

Liberal Democratic Party devoted to ridding China of the Communist Party—and taking control itself.

Founded by a group of dissident Chinese students in exile in the wake of the military occupation of Beijing, the Liberal Democratic Party is still in its formative stage, its goals and organizational structure in a stage of flux. Based on the assumption that the communist party has lost its legitimacy, the Liberal Democratic Party believes that the death of Deng Xiaoping and the octogenarians still in power will plunge China into a state of disorder during which numerous new parties and numerous competitors for power will emerge. The time to prepare, they believe, is now. The Liberal Democratic Party wants to be in a position to lead when China's plunge into disintegration begins.

The basic principles of the new Liberal Democratic Party are comfortably democratic, familiar to the Western ear, calling as they do for free elections and a multiparty system, the separation of party, state, and army, freedom of speech and basic human rights, a rule of law and the end of the household registration system, private property and a free market economy.

But just as the Communist Party once took as its goal the overthrow of the Guomindang and its own ascension to power, so the Liberal Democratic Party has as its goal the demise of the Communist Party. The structure of the party is disturbingly Leninist, duplicating in many respects the structure of the Communist Party itself, and the language of its organization carries an all-too-familiar ring—from its top to bottom hierarchy with a chairman and party branch cells, to its division of responsibilities between those whose job it is to prepare for the revolution and those charged with constructing a new society on the remains of the old; from its secret, underground members to its right to discipline recalcitrants. The organizational structure suggests that it is less democracy the new party is seeking than power.

It is the great tragedy of those who work for a more democratic China that they are as yet incapable of transcending the system against which they so vehemently protest. In their outrage against the injustices of the Communist Party and their desire to extract revenge, they become mired in the same anger and hate that inheres in Mao's own rhetoric of unrelenting class struggle.

While righteous anger is a necessary motivating force in the pursuit of political reform, and we might wish that more of Ni's countrymen were as angry and motivated as he, there is a sense in which his articulation of democratic ideals serves more as a cloak to legitimize his anger than principles truly held. That Ni Yuxian is engaged in a ceaseless struggle for his own personal freedom there is no doubt, but democracy and freedom are different. Democracy for Ni is more a way of overthrowing the Communist Party than an end in itself, and to achieve the end of ridding China of communism, and to pursue his own immediate political ends, Ni is often inclined to use fundamentally nondemocratic means, thus calling into doubt the depth and authenticity of his democratic ideals.

Impatient to find alternatives, he returns to the same organizational structures that produced the unworkable dictatorship against which he so vociferously inveighs. Struggling for personal freedom, he forgets the lessons of responsibility. The opportunistic pursuit of political power sometimes takes precedence over larger political principles.

This is true not only of Ni Yuxian and his Liberal Democratic Party but also many of the students who led the would-be democracy movement in Tiananmen Square and who later became heroes to the democracy-loving American public. As the movement progressed, the self-appointed leaders of the naive students who filled the square began reproducing—because they knew of no other alternative—the structure and organization of the Communist Party itself, complete with internal struggles for power. They often behaved callously and irresponsibly toward the people they claimed to lead, histrionically promising to die for democracy, the hunger-strikers and China all the while using the drama for their own self-aggrandizement and creating in turn their own internal, ultimately tragic contradictions.

China has no democratic political culture, no tradition of democratic institutions to guide those who would lead the country to a more democratic future. Without obvious alternative institutional arrangements, the stated democratic goals and the organizational arrangments designed to achieve them remain sadly at odds.

Ridding China of rule by the Communist Party is no guarantee of the establishment of a new republic, and an organizational structure based, however unwittingly, on the Communist Party itself is not likely to lead to the institution of democracy. If the communist world has taught us anything in the last seventy years it is that organizational structures develop their own imperatives, that secrecy and subterfuge in pursuit of a better tomorrow are antithetical to a free and open society, and that revenge is no basis for a government that is just and good.

China's dissidents will need to turn to their country's own past for guidance on how to build a more democratic, more humanitarian future, for the legitimacy of the democracy movement at home demands that its roots be genuinely Chinese. But they will have to turn to the Western experience for instruction and inspiration, too, because only the West can provide them with a model of success. The ultimate dilemma of the Chinese democrat is how to introduce Western political ideals and Western organizational structures without violating China's own sense of cultural identity, a dilemma that is all the more painful for dissidents living abroad. For just as Chinese dissidents have much to learn from the West, so, in the eyes of their countrymen, is much of their legitimacy to lead lost by flight. To escape from suffering China, as Liu Binyan pointed out to Yuxian in his first phone call back, and as Liu was later to learn from his own bitter experience, is also somehow to be denied the right to speak on its behalf. To leave is to be rendered irrelevant.

But the Communist Party has failed in China, and that failure alone ensures that the search for a democratic way, however fumbling, will continue. The inversion of truth will someday have to be righted.

The process of political change will be slow. During the Cultural Revolution, one of the most frequently read tracts was Mao Zedong's retelling of an ancient Chinese fable. In front of an old peasant's home were two huge mountains that the old man wanted removed. After digging away at the mountains all his life, ridiculed by his neighbors and friends, the old man passed the task over to his sons, who in turn spent all their lives shoveling away at the mountains. When they died, their sons took over, and when their sons died the next generation continued to dig at the mountains, until finally, after generations, God took mercy on those who would remove the mountains and carried them away himself. To Mao Zedong, the two mountains stood as symbols of feudalism and imperialism, weighing China down, while the old man and his descendants he depicted as the Communist Party, intent on saving the country. The God who was ultimately victorious was the people of China.

To many Chinese, the meaning of those mountains has changed. It is the Communist Party and the political system that Mao himself erected that must now be dug away.

The digging will continue. Ni would tell you that it is his destiny to be at the vanguard. He has recently been elected vice chairman of the new Liberal Democratic Party. His one-time political rival, Wang Bingzhang, will serve as the chairman.

Ni epitomizes the dilemmas and the contradictions—eating away at the country on the one hand, propelling it forward on the other—that have been part of China since its defeat by Great Britain in the Opium War of 1839 when the country's doors were first forcibly opened by the West. Thoroughly and incorrigibly Chinese, irrevocably rooted in its culture, Ni turns to the West to change and reform and democratize China, caught in an endless tug of war between being Chinese and the desire to be free. The answers to China's problems, Ni believes, lie in the West—in its democratic traditions, its freedoms, its human rights and respect for the individual. But the pull of China is ever there.

• • •

When I took my leave of Ni Jizhong that hot and sultry night late in the month of June 1988, I did not know that it would be our last good-bye. I was to return in only a couple of months and had thought his health would hold.

Just before leaving, sitting with him on the carved wooden bed and clasping his hands in mine, I asked whether his son's political activities had really been worth the price. The dying man burst into tears, sobbing, holding my hands even tighter. It had been worth the price, he said.

"You don't think the big character poster was a bit extreme?" I asked.

"No," he insisted.

"And two years in jail, was that too long to spend?"

"No," he answered.

"And all the pain inflicted on the family?"

"He had to do it," Jizhong insisted.

He let go of my hands and pulled down the sheet that covered him, lifting up his pajama top to reveal his sunken, already emaciated chest. He reached down and pulled up the legs to his pajamas. "Do you see?" he asked.

Fifty years later, the scars from the wounds he had suffered when the dogs attacked him while he was incarcerated by the Japanese still covered his body.

"When I was a young man, I was put in jail by the Japanese," he said, "and I nearly died from being attacked by those dogs. But those were Japanese, invaders, the foreign devils. We expected it of them. Then in 1968, during the Cultural Revolution, I was put in jail again. And again I nearly died. I was nearly beaten to death. But those were my own people, Chinese. Yuxian had to do what he did."

I was still not sure I understood. "You mean, he had to do it for you?" I asked.

He nodded. "For me," he said.

In Shanghai the summer of 1988 was the hottest on record, like living in warm soup, the temperature and humidity shooting sky-high and staying there without respite for forty days and nights. Air-conditioning is unknown in Pudong. The elderly and infirm were the hardest hit.

Ni Jizhong died on July 30, just before the heat wave broke.

• • •

May he rest in peace.

ENDNOTES

Preface

Page ix. Both Lloyd Neighbors and Ni himself reported the story of his meeting with John Lundeen and his visits to the Shanghai consulate.

Chapter One

Page 1. Ni Jizhong and Xu Fengzhen themselves told the story of their courtship and marriage, of Guansheng, village life, and the Japanese invasion. Ni Jizhong's sister, who had been with Xu Fengzhen when she left home to marry, provided additional details. Numerous other family members—Ni Jizhong's children and grandchildren, his sister's children and their spouses, plus several unidentified members of Jizhong's generation listened to parts of the story. Ni Yuxian knew the stories well, as did his siblings.

Page 4. Ni Yuxian's younger brother showed me around Three Forest Village, introducing me in particular to Xu Fengzhen's brother and his wife and to the then aged wife of the brother who had run away because he did not want to marry her. Again, numerous relatives and village folk participated.

Page 9. Harold Isaacs, *Re-Encounters in China: Notes from a Journey in a Time Capsule* (Armonk, N.Y.: M.E. Sharpe, 1985), p. 6. See also Betty Peh-T'i Wei, *Shanghai: Crucible of Modern China* (Hong Kong: Oxford University Press, 1987).

Page 24. *Water Margin* has been translated into English by Pearl Buck as *All Men Are Brothers*. For an abridged version of *Romance of the Three Kingdoms*, see Lo Kuan-chung, *Three Kingdoms: China's Epic Drama*, translated by Moss Roberts (New York: Pantheon Books, 1976).

Page 27. Lynn T. White III, in explaining the depth of violence during the Cultural Revolution, focuses on the evolution of socialism in Shanghai from 1949-1976, telling more abstractly the same story described here by Ni. See his *Politics of Chaos: The Organizational Causes of Violence during the Cultural Revolution* (Princeton, New Jersey: Princeton University Press, 1989).

Page 29. For the early years of communist rule, see A. Doak Barnett, *Communist China: The Early Years, 1949-1955* (New York: 1955)

Page 32. For Lu Xun's story about the culture of executions, see "Medicine," in *Selected Stories of Lu Hsun* (Peking: Foreign Language Press, 1972), pp. 25–35.

Chapter Two

Page 37. This chapter is based largely on interviews with Ni Yuxian and on visits to the places mentioned, including a visit to Yangsi Middle School and talks with two teachers there.

Page 46. For an overview of the hundred flowers movement, see Roderick MacFarquhar, ed., with an epilogue by G.F. Hudson, *The Hundred Flowers* (London: Stevens & Sons Limited Atlantic Books, 1960), Roderick MacFarquhar, *The Origins of the Cultural Revolution*, vol. 1, *Contradictions among the People, 1956-1957* (New York: Columbia University Press, 1974), Merle Goldman, *Literary Dissent in Communist China* (Cambridge: Harvard University Press, 1967), and Mu Fu-sheng, *The Wilting of the Hundred Flowers: The Chinese Intelligentsia under Mao* (New York: Praeger, 1963).

Page 55. For Mao's statement in Moscow, see Roderick MacFarquhar, *Origins of the Cultural Revolution*, vol. 2, *The Great Leap Forward, 1958-60* (New York: Columbia University Press, 1983), pp. 18-19.

Page 59. For examples of these fantastic claims, see MacFarquhar, *Origins*, vol. 2; and Tao Zhu, "Refutation of the 'Theory of Limited Increase in Food Production,'" *Red Flag*, (August 1, 1958), translated in Joint Publications Research Service, no. 7837, pp. 39-51.

Page 60. For analyses of the famine of 1958-1961, see Basil Ashton, Kenneth Hill, Alan Piazza, and Robin Zeitz, "Famine in China, 1958-61," *Population Development Review*, Vol. 10, no. 4 (December 1984), pp. 613-644, and Ansley J. Coale, *Rapid Population Change in China, 1952-1982*, Committee on Population and Demography, Report 27, National Research Council (Washington, D.C.: National Academy Press, 1984). See also Thomas P. Bernstein, "Stalinism, Famine, and Chinese Peasants: Grain Procurement during the Great Leap Forward," *Theory and Society*, vol. 13, no. 3 (May 1984), pp. 339-377.

Page 69. For an excellent analysis of competition within schools, see Susan L. Shirk, *Competitive Comrades: Career Incentives and Student Strategies in China* (Berkeley and Los Angeles: University of California Press, 1980).

Chapter Three

Page 73. For the story of Qu Yuan, see Laurence A. Schneider, *A Madman of Ch'u: The Chinese Myth of Loyalty and Dissent* (Berkeley: University of California Press, 1980).

Page 74. For Peng Dehaui's criticisms, see *The Case of P'eng Teh-huai, 1959-1968* (Kowloon, Hong Kong: Union Research Institute, 1968), and Roderick MacFarquhar, *Origins*, vol. 2, *op. cit.*, pp. 187-255.

Page 75. For a translation of Wang Meng's writings from the period, see Wang Meng, "The Young Man Who Has Just Arrived at the Organization Department," in *Literature of the People's Republic of China*, ed. Kai-yu Hsu (Bloomington: Indiana University Press, 1980), pp. 229-242. Fei Xiaotong's writings from this period have been translated in *Fei Hsiao-t'ung: The Dilemma of a Chinese Intellectual*, translated by James P. McGough (White Plains, N.Y.: M.E. Sharpe, 1979). For the story of Fei, see David Arkush, *Fei Xiaotong and Sociology in China* (Cambridge: Harvard University Council on East Asian Studies, 1981).

Page 91. Vaclav Havel, "Politics and Conscience," in his *Living in Truth* (London: Faber and Faber, 1987), p. 140.

Page 92. For a description of land reform in a single village, see William Hinton, *Fanshen: A Documentary of Revolution in a Chinese Village* (New York: Vintage, 1966).

Page 93. R.H. Tawney, *Land and Labor in China* (London: 1932).

Page 94. Recent evidence suggests that Mao did know about the extent of famine in the countryside.

Chapter Four

Page 107. This chapter is based on interviews with both Ni Yuxian and Zhao Yuefang. The two do not always remember the same events, or they remember the same events differently. When those differences are significant, and have bearing on Ni's character, I have introduced them into the text. Otherwise, I record those differences in the notes. Zhao Yuefang does not remember Ni's visit to her at the university, remembering that she wrote Yuxian to tell him of the regulations prohibiting students from romantic involvement. Yuxian remembers the incident vividly and insists it happened as described here.

Page 122. For Mao's argument on class and class struggle, see Richard Baum, *Prelude to Revolution: Mao, the Party, and the Peasant Question, 1962-1966* (New York: Columbia University Press, 1975).

Page 130. *Dream of the Red Chamber: A Chinese Novel of the Early Ching Period* (New York: Grosset & Dunlap, 1958).

Chapter Five

Page 143. See Richard Baum and Frederick C. Teiwes, *Ssu-Ch'ing: The Socialist Education Movement of 1962-1966* (Berkeley: Center for Chinese Studies, 1968).

Page 150. For the story of Hou Yi and the ten suns, see Qi Xing and Ren Jiazhen, *Folk Customs at Traditional Chinese Festivities* (Beijing: Foreign Languages Press, 1988), pp. 51–52.

Page 168. For an overview of Wu Han and Hai Rui, see James R. Pusey, *Wu Han: Attacking the Present Through the Past* (Cambridge: Harvard University East Asian Research Center, 1969).

Page 168. For Wu Han's death, see *Huiyi yu Daonian* (Reminiscences and Memorials), vol. 1 (Kowloon, Hong Kong: Chunhui Publishers, 1979), pp. 38-42.

Page 170. Nie Yuanzi's big character poster was translated in Survey of the Chinese Mainland Press, No. 3719.

Page 171. For the story of Liu Shaoqi's death, see the articles written by his children, Liu Pingping, Liu Yun, and Liu Tingting, *"Shengli de Shenghua Xian Gei Nin: Huainian Women de Baba Liu Shaoqi"* ("Presenting You the Flowers of Victory: Remembering Our Father, Liu Shaoqi"), *Gongren Ribao* (*Workers' Daily*), December 5, 8, & 12, 1980. For the death of Tao Zhu, see the article written by his daughter, Tao Siliang, *"Yifeng Zhongyu Fachu de Xin: Gei Wo de Baba Tao Zhu"* ("A Letter Posted at Last: To My Father, Tao Zhu"), *Renmin Ribao* (*People's Daily*), December 11, 1978.

Page 172. For the story of Lin Biao, see Michael Ying-mao Gao, *The Lin Piao Affair: Power Politics and Military Coup* (White Plains, N.Y.: International Arts and Sciences Press, 1975).

There are a number of useful books on the Cultural Revolution. See, for instance, Richard Baum, with Louise B. Bennett, eds., *China in Ferment* (Englewood Cliffs, N.J.: Prentice-Hall, 1971), Stanley Karnow, *Mao and China: From Revolution to Revolution* (New York: Viking, 1972), Edward E. Rice, *Mao's Way* (Berkeley: University of California Press, 1972), Lowell Dittmer, *Liu Shao-ch'i and the Chinese Cultural Revolution: The Politics of Mass Criticism* (Berkeley: University of California Press, 1978), Robert Jay Lifton, *Revolutionary Immortality: Mao Tse-tung and the Chinese Cultural Revolution* (New York: Vintage, 1968), Hong Yung Lee, *The Politics of the Chinese Cultural Revolution: A Case Study* (Berkeley: University of California Press, 1978), Stanley Rosen, *Red Guard Factionalism and the Cultural Revolution in Guangzhou* (Boulder: Westview Press, 1982), Anne F. Thurston, *Enemies of the People: The Ordeal of the Intellectuals in China's Great Cultural Revolution* (New York: Knopf, 1987), Lynn White, *Policies of Chaos: The Organizational Causes of Violence in China's Cultural Revolution, op. cit.*

For firsthand accounts of witnesses to the Cultural Revolution, see Gordon Bennett and Ronald N. Montaperto, *Red Guard: The Political Biography of Dai Hsiao-ai* (Garden City, N.Y.: Doubleday, 1971), Nien Cheng, *Life and Death in Shanghai* (New York: Grove Press, 1986), B. Michael Frolic, *Mao's People: Sixteen Portraits of Life in Revolutionary China* (Cambridge: Harvard University Press, 1980), Neale Hunter, *Shanghai Journal: An Eyewitness Account of the Cultural Revolution* (New York: Praeger, 1969), Liang Heng and Judith Shapiro, *Son of the Revolution* (New York: Knopf, 1983), Ken Ling, *Revenge of Heaven* (New York: Putnam, 1972), Ruth Earnshaw Lo, *In the Eye of the Typhoon* (New York: Harcourt Brace Jovanovich, 1980), David Milton and Nancy Dall Milton, *The Wind Will Not Subside: Years in Revolutionary China, 1964-1969* (New York: Pantheon, 1976), and Yue Daiyun with Carolyn Wakeman, *To the Storm* (Berkeley: University of California Press, 1985).

Chapter Six

Page 186. Only one study has attempted to focus on the meaning of the work unit in Chinese life. See Gail Henderson and Myron Cohen, *The Chinese Hospital: A Socialist Work Unit* (New Haven: Yale University Press, 1984). See also Andrew Walder, *Communist Neo-Traditionalism: Work and Authority in Chinese Industry* (New York: Columbia University Press, 1986).

Page 188. For a description of the August 18, 1966, rally and the later Red Guard revolt, see my *Enemies of the People, op. cit.*, pp. 276-77 and pp. 92-132. See also Stanley Karnow, *Mao, op. cit.*, p. 203.

Page 192. For the conception of *luan*, see Richard Solomon, *Mao's Revolution and the Chinese Political Culture* (Berkeley: University of California Press, 1971), and White, *Policies of Chaos, op. cit.*

Page 195. Edgar Snow's *Red Star Over China* (New York: Grove Press, 1974) contains a classic account of the Long March. Harrison Salisbury retraced the route fifty years later.

Page 203. Neale Hunter, *Shanghai Journal, op. cit.*, also writes about this incident and the kidnapping of Xu Jinxian.

Page 204 Lynn White, *op. cit.*, p. 234, puts the figure at 2,500.

Page 204. For Zhang Chunqiao's rise to power in Shanghai, see Andrew G. Walder, *Chang Ch'un-ch'iao and Shanghai's January Revolution* (Ann Arbor: University of Michigan, 1977).

Chapter Seven

Page 229. For the movement to send the young to the countryside, see Thomas P. Bernstein, *Up to the Mountains and Down to the Villages: The*

Transfer of Youth from Urban to Rural China (New Haven: Yale University Press, 1977).

Page 231. Little is known in the West about the movement to ferret out the May 16 elements. See my *Enemies of the People, op. cit.*, pp. 142-43, Yang Jiang, *Six Chapters from My Life Downunder*, and Merle Goldman, *China's Intellectuals: Advise and Dissent* (Cambridge: Harvard University Press, 1981), pp. 151-53.

Page 235. See "The True Story of Ah Q," in *Selected Stories of Lu Hsun, op. cit.*, pp. 65-113.

Chapter Eight

Page 253. See again Michael Ying-mao Kao, *The Lin Piao Affair, op. cit.*

Page 253. Chen Duxiu, Qu Qiubai, Li Lisan, Wang Ming, and Liu Shaoqi were all ranking leaders of the Chinese Communist Party ultimately purged for allegedly antiparty behavior.

Page 269. For an analysis of these early Chinese reformers, see Andrew J. Nathan, *Chinese Democracy* (New York: Knopf, 1985), pp. 45-66. See also Joseph R. Levenson, *Liang Ch'i-ch'ao and the Mind of Modern China* (Berkeley: University of California Press, 1970), and Philip C. Huang, *Liang Ch'i-ch'ao and Modern Chinese Liberalism* (Seattle: University of Washington Press, 1972).

See Milovan Djilas, *The New Class: An Analysis of the Communist System* (New York: Praeger, 1957).

Page 272. See Confucius, *Analects*, translated by Arthur Waley (New York: Vintage, 1938).

Page 273. For the Li Yizhe big character poster and an analysis, see Anita Chan, Stanley Rosen, and Jonathan Unger, *On Socialist Democracy and the Chinese Legal System: The Li Yizhe Debates* (Armonk, N.Y.: M.E. Sharpe, 1985). See also Gregor Benton, ed., *Wild Lilies, Poisonous Weeds: Dissident Voices from People's China* (London: Pluto Press, 1982).

Pages 278–285. The description of the Tiananmen incident of 1976 is taken from Anne Thurston, *Enemies of the People, op. cit.*, chapter 1.

Page 281. For a description of the May Fourth Movement, see Chow Tse-tsung, *The May Fourth Movement: Intellectual Revolution in Modern China* (Cambridge: Harvard University Press, 1960).

Page 282. Many of the poems were translated in *Chinese Literature*, no. 3, 1979.

Page 282. Derk Bodde, *China's First Unifier: A Study of the Ch'in Dynasty as Seen in the Life of Li Ssu* (Leiden: E.J. Brill, 1938) is an excellent source on Qin Shi Huangdi.

Chapter Nine

Pages 287–88. This description is also taken from Anne Thurston, *Enemies of the People, op. cit.*, chapter 1.

Chapter Ten

Page 310. Only a few Chinese accounts of prison conditions after 1949 are available. See Liu Qing, "Prison Memoirs," in *Chinese Sociology and Anthropology* XV (Fall-Winter 1982-83), Gregor Benton, *Wild Lilies, op. cit.*, Nien Cheng, *Life and Death in Shanghai, op. cit.*, and Yao Yongzhan, "A Year in a Chinese Jail," in *News from AsiaWatch*, September 1, 1990, pp. 1-9. Both Nien Cheng and Yao Yongzhan describe conditions in Shanghai prisons. Yao was arrested following the June 4 massacre in Beijing, and his description of life in Shanghai No. 1 Detention Center is consistent with Ni's own testimony.

Page 317. This account is based on Ni, but Wu Zuoren has recently written about prisons in China, including those in Shanghai. His report corroborates that of Ni. See Wu Zuoren, "Tens of Millions of People Locked Up in Prisons Outside the Legal System," in *Zhengming*, Hong Kong, July 1, 1990, translated in JPRS, October 31, 1990.

Page 319. According to *ibid.*, the number of Shanghai's detention centers is now thirty.

Page 325. Nien Cheng, in *Life and Death in Shanghai, op. cit.*, also describes the handcuffing method of torture.

Page 348. For the text of the announcement to establish diplomatic relations, see Steven M. Goldstein, Kathrin Sears, and Richard C. Bush, *The People's Republic of China: A Basic Handbook*, the China Council of the Asia Society (New York: Learning Resources in International Studies, 1984), pp. 97-98.

Chapter Eleven

Page 355. For a first-hand account of the Chinese Democracy Wall movement, see John Fraser, *The Chinese: Portrait of a People* (New York: Summit Books, 1980), pp. 199-275. For an analysis, see Andrew J. Nathan, *Chinese Democracy, op. cit.*

Page 356. For a description of the Peking University elections, see Gregor Benton, *Wild Lilies, Poisonous Weeds, op. cit.*. pp. 88-99. For more on Wang Juntao, see Amnesty International, *The People's Republic of China: A New Stage in the Repression*, December 1990, p. 5.

For accounts of the Democracy Wall activists, see Gregor Benton, *Wild*

Lilies, op. cit. and *Repression in China Since June 4, 1989,* in *News from AsiaWatch,* September 17, 1990.

Page 359. Pu Yi's story was told in the Oscar-winning film "The Last Emperor," much of which was based on Pu Yi's own autobiography. See *From Emperor to Citizen: The Autobiography of Aisin-Giorro Pu Yi* (Beijing: Foreign Languages Press, 1986), vols. 1 & 2.

Page 360. A translation of Wei Jingsheng's views can be found in Benton, *Wild Lilies, op. cit.*

Page 362. Xu Wenli is still in prison and is reportedly in ill health. Ren Wanding was released in 1983 and rearrested in June 1989 and sentenced to seven years in jail. Wang Xizhe, Xu Shuiliang, and Fu Shenqi are still in jail.

Page 364. Lu Jinghua, a leader of the workers during the Tiananmen demonstrations of 1989 and on the government's most wanted list, cited the housing problem as a leading cause of worker discontent at a meeting of the Asiawatch board on December 7, 1990.

Page 374. For a smattering of Liu's translated writings, see Liu Binyan, *"People or Monsters?" and Other Stories and Reportage from China after Mao,* translated by Perry Link, *et. al.* (Bloomington: Indiana University Press, 1983). Liu has also written his autobiography, *A Higher Kind of Loyalty* (N.Y.: Random House, 1990). See also his *China's Crisis, China's Hope* (Cambridge: Harvard University Press, 1990).

Page 376. Both Ni and Liu Binyan have described to me how Liu came to write the piece about Ni and how the Maritime Academy responded, and the accounts are substantially the same.

Page 382. "A Second Kind of Loyalty" (*"Di Er Zhong Chongcheng"*) was published in Chinese in Hong Kong's *Zhengming,* October 1985 and in New York's *China Spring* (*Zhongguo zhi Chun*) in April 1986. Parts were published in English in Joint Publications Research Service in January 1986.

Page 384. See *Wo de Riji* (*My Diary*) (Hong Kong: Mingbao Publishers, 88).

Page 384. This speech was taped, and I was able to listen to it in Shanghai.

Page 390. Anyone who has ever traveled on Civil Aviation Administration of China flights knows that the airline is notorious for its delays—especially on international flights.

Epilogue

Page 393. Wang Bingzhang's announcement and the background material on him were carried in *News Roundup* (New York: Coordination Council for North American Affairs, 1982), No. 097, pp. 3-5.

Page 395. Liu Binyan and Ni both report this conversation in substantially the same way, although Liu does not mention his concern about Ni meeting with Lin Xiling.

Page 395. See Ni Yuxian, "*Wo Weisheme Likai Zhongguo?*" ("Why Did I Leave China?"), in *Zhongguo zhi Chun* (*China Spring*), April 1986.

Pages 397. These are Liu's views as presented to me in private conversation, but his public discussions are substantially the same. For instance, at a human rights meeting held at Columbia University on January 18-19, 1991, he made a similar argument.

Page 398. Liu's statement dissociating himself from Ni appeared first in newspapers on the mainland on March 1, 1986. Hong Kong's *Wenhui Bao* picked it up on March 4, 1986. Ni's response to Liu was carried in the *Shi Bao Zhoukan* in June 1986.

Page 398. The views of Ni's lawyer, Allan Lee, were made to me in February 1987.

Pages 400–404. This discussion is drawn from Anne F. Thurston, "Year of the Dragon Ends on a Note of Malaise," *Christian Science Monitor*, February 3, 1989, p. 19. See also, Andrew J. Nathan, *China's Crisis* (New York: Columbia University Press, 1990), pp. 97–116.

Page 403. I studied at Beijing Normal University in the summer and fall of 1981 and have revisited there many times. These conversations took place in early May 1989.

Page 405. Chen Jun held a press conference immediately after his return from China in February 1989, which Ni (and I) attended.

Page 406. See Committee for the Advancement of Democracy in China Press Release, "International Petitioning Movement for Democracy in China Launched by Group of Chinese Intellectuals Headed by Fang Lizhi," February 17, 1989.

Page 406. I was in attendance at the Bolinas meeting.

Page 406. For an excellent summary background on Wang Ruowang, Fang Lizhi and Liu Binyan, see Orville Schell, *Discos and Democracy: China in the Throes of Reform* (New York: Pantheon Books, 1988), pp. 119-177. For a superb analysis of Liu Xiaobo, see Geremie Barme, "Liu Xiaobo and the Protest Movement of 1989," in *The Broken Mirror: China after Tiananmen* (Chicago: St. James Press, 1990), pp. 52-100.

Page 407. Private conversation in Beijing, May 1989.

Page 408. Ni's advertisements appeared in the *Shijie Ribao*, *Zhongbao*, and *Huaqiao Ribao* on May 3, 1989.

Page 412. One of those calls was televised on CBS on May 27, 1989.

Page 413. What exactly happened within Tiananmen Square on the night of June 3-4 remains a matter of some controversy, with the Chinese government insisting that no students were killed. For the best eyewitness account by a foreigner, see Robin Munro, "Who Died in Beijing, and Why," *The Nation*, June 11, 1990, pp. 811-822. For an eyewitness account by a Chinese student leader, see Li Lu, *Moving the Mountain: My Life in China from the Cultural Revolution to Tiananmen Square* (London: Macmillan, 1990), pp. 187-203. It is generally agreed now that most of the deaths were not in the square but in the streets leading to the square.

Page 415. See Timothy Garton Ash, *The Uses of Adversity* (N.Y.: Vintage, 1990), p. 12.

Page 416. See *"Yu Yingshi deng Ershi Ren Shengming Tuichu"* ("Yu Yingshi and Twenty Others Resignation Statement"), *Shijie Ribao*, July 15, 1989.

Pages 416–417. The splits within China Spring are well known, but see Andrew Nathan, *China's Crisis, op. cit.*, pp. 93-94. For accusations against Wuer Kaixi, see Joseph F. Kahn, "Better Fed than Red," *Esquire*, September 1990, pp. 186-197. For allegations against Chai Ling, see Li Lu, *Moving the Mountain, op. cit.*, pp. 187-191.

Pages 419–420. These observations on the Liberal Democratic Party are drawn from a reading of the basic documents, loaned to me by Ni.

Page 420. For an excellent critique of the students' failure to practice democracy, see Sarah Lubman, "The Myth of Tiananmen Square: The Students Talked Democracy but They Didn't Practice It," *Washington Post*, July 30, 1889, p. C5.

Page 421. For Mao's telling of the story, see "The Foolish Old Man Who Removed the Mountains," in *Selected Readings from the Works of Mao Tse-tung* (Peking: Foreign Languages Press, 1967), pp. 260-264.

INDEX

Agriculture, 4–5, 55, 58–61, 91–92, 94, 103, 142, 268, 355, 402
Ah Mei Popo, 13
Ah Q, 235
Ah Xing, 15, 215–216
Air-raid shelters, 249
Albania, 164, 177
Anhui Province, 90–91, 99, 117, 118, 267, 318, 405
Anti-Americanism, 25–27, 45
Anti-bourgeois rights campaign, 275
Antirightist campaigns, 48–53, 67, 68, 74–75, 161, 166–258
April Five Forum (journal), 357
Arts, 166–170, 307

Baojia system, 8–9
Bathing, 262–263, 364
Belda. *See* Peking University
Beijing, 165, 167, 168, 171–174, 187–195, 204, 210, 227, 233–234, 249, 251–254, 287, 356, 362, 373–374, 384, 385, 395, 398, 401; 1976 Tiananmen incident, 280–286, 288, 289, 292–293, 302, 316, 341, 348, 355, 411; 1989 Democracy movement, xvii, xxi, 285, 356, 400, 404–415
Beijing Normal University, 403, 406, 408, 410, 411
Beijing Red Guards, 192–195
Birth control, 179, 244
Bo Yibo, 401
Buddism, 23–24, 415
Bund (Shanghai), 9, 149, 200–201, 333
Bush, George, 401

Cai Yuanpei, 405
Cambodia, 356
Canals, 4, 5

Canton, 273, 387
Cao Cao, 25
Cao family, 10, 15, 33–34
Cao Family Village, xvi, 8–71, 134, 140
Cao Xinfa, 9–10, 15
Cao Yuanming, 32–34, 36
Capitalism, 112, 137, 140, 157, 158, 205, 232, 264, 362
Charter 77, 299–300, 354
Chen Duxiu, 253, 405
Chen Jun, 405, 408, 412
Chen Qi, 180–181, 186
Chen Shizhong, x
Chen Yunghu, 114–118, 121–123
Chen Ziming, 285
Chiang Kai-shek, 23, 25, 29, 227
China News, 392
China Spring, 394–397, 412, 416
China Spring magazine, 392–393, 394, 396
Chinese Alliance for Democracy, New York, 356, 394
Chinese Charter 77, 299–300, 354
Chinese Communist Party, x, 15, 26, 45–53, 59–61, 67–69, 73, 77, 89, 93, 103, 109–115, 141, 143, 152, 166, 169–217, 251–258, 264, 269, 275, 278–286, 336, 337, 346, 356, 366, 374–375, 396, 397, 399, 400–401, 404, 418–422; Central Committee, 171, 231, 267, 291, 302; Eleventh Congress, 349; Ninth Congress, 251
Chinese *World Journal*, 392
Chinghai, 318
Chongqing, 413
Christianity, 23–24
Civil war, 15, 24, 27–30, 73, 103
Ci Xi, Empress Dowager, 17
Columbia University, 400, 406

Committee for the Promotion of Democracy in China, 405–407, 408, 412, 415–418
Communes, 55, 58, 60, 73, 91, 92, 94, 99, 168, 229
Confucius, 272
Corruption, late-1980s, 400–402
Cultural Revolution, xi, xiii, 50, 142, 166–258, 265, 267, 272, 278–279, 281–282, 318, 346, 355, 363, 371, 375, 378–384, 397, 402–403, 421, 423
Cultural Revolution Small Group, 204, 205, 210–213
Czechoslovakia, 299

Dare-to-die squads, 102–103, 202
Democracy movement(s), 207–209, 237, 263–264, 269–270, 273, 356–390, 394, 399–400, 404–422; in exile, 394–400, 405–407, 415–422; of 1979, 285, 355–360, 362; of 1986, 399; of 1989, xvii, xxi, 285, 356, 400, 404–415
Deng Pufang, 385, 401
Deng Xiaoping, xv, 184, 191, 207, 267, 276, 279, 282–289, 291, 302, 329, 355–356, 360–364, 373, 383, 385, 393, 399, 400–405, 409, 411, 418, 419
Detention centers, 307–318, 318–349
Ding Foshan, 190
Divorce, 388
Djilas, Milovan, *The New Class*, 269–270
Dong Biwu, 291
Dream of the Red Chamber, 130
Dress, 188–189, 266

Earthquake of 1976, 287–288
East China Normal University, 106, 113, 219, 223
Economy, 29, 165, 169–170, 205–206, 369, 400–402. *See also* Industrialization
Education, 28, 37–86, 107–108, 132, 134, 138, 142, 145–202, 217–224, 229–231, 273, 363–364, 402–403; study abroad, 370–374. *See also specific schools*
Elections, 356, 360–362, 366
Employment, 131–134, 186, 203, 228, 261, 358, 360–361
Executions, 30–35, 103, 234–235, 271–272, 335–338
Exile, democracy movement in, 394–400, 405–407, 415–422

Facial types, 17–18, 23
Famine (1959–1962), 60–62, 73–74, 88–94, 99, 142, 149, 203
Fang Lizhi, 399, 401, 404, 405–407, 412, 416
Federation for a Democratic China, 417
Fei Xiatong, 75
Feudalism, 189, 273
Food, 59–62, 73–74, 88–94, 179, 203, 229, 402; prison, 313–324; shortages, 60–62, 73–74, 88–94, 99, 142, 149, 203
Fortune-telling, 15–18, 296
Four Cleans Socialist Education Campaign, 142–145, 147
Four modernizations, 355–356
Four pests campaign, 53–55
Fudan University, 50, 148, 210–212, 219, 223, 366
Fujian Province, 100, 105
Funerals, 64–68, 280, 407
Fu Shenqi, 361, 362

Gang of Four, 167, 172–173, 204, 288, 297, 299, 302, 316, 335, 338, 341, 363, 380–381, 407
Gao Fei, 18, 336–337
Ge Yang, 406
Gold Mountain military base, 88–131
Gorbachev, Mikhail, 409
Grain, 47–48, 50, 59–61, 90, 100, 402
Great Britain, 29, 55, 57, 99, 149, 422
Great Leap Forward, x, 55–97, 134, 180, 363
Guan Foshan, 192
Guangdong Province, 357, 387
Guang Ming, 264, 265, 293, 296, 299, 308, 344, 354
Guangzhou, 362
Gu Jiabing, 129–131
Guomindang, 27–30, 35, 105, 115, 141, 174, 189, 192, 226, 227, 267, 325, 372, 393–394, 419
Guo Moruo, 169

Handicrafts industry, 133–134, 135, 139, 144
Havel, Vaclav, 91
Heilongjiang Province, 375
Homosexuality, 332–333
Honggehui, 210–212, 226–227
Hong Kong, 33, 67, 149, 373, 387, 405, 413–414
Housing, 363–365, 377
Hou Yi, 150
Hsia, C.T., 406
Hua Guofeng, 302, 338–339, 349

Huangpu District Detention Center, 307–349
Huangpu River, 5, 8–11, 149, 307
Huang Xixi, 264, 265, 293, 296, 297, 299, 308, 354
Hu Keshe, 193
Human Rights in China, 416
Hundred flowers campaign, 46–48, 121, 137, 395
Hu Ping, 356, 394, 405, 412, 416
Hu Qili, 193
Hu Shih, 405
Hu Yaobang, 193, 377, 399, 401, 407, 408

Individualism, 155–164
Industrialization and factories, 55–62, 91–92, 134, 140–142, 203–206, 258–266, 275–278, 318, 333–335, 353, 355–356, 358, 364, 400; hierarchy in, 258–260
Infant mortality, 20–21
Inflation, 402
Isaacs, Harold, 9

Japanese invasion (1937), 1, 2, 10, 15, 16, 24, 45, 73, 372, 423
Jiang Qing, 167, 172–173, 231, 233, 236, 276, 282, 283, 288, 363
Jiangsu Province, 88–91, 220, 221
Jiangxi Province, 195
Jiangying, 220–223
Jiang Zemin, xv
Jiaotong University, 269
Jin Ji, 164–166
Jin Renjun, 264, 265, 293, 294, 296, 300, 308, 354

Kaituo magazine, xi, 381–384
Kajia, 266–270, 272, 275, 289–290, 293–305, 308–309, 342–345, 351–354, 388
Kang Youwei, 17, 269
Khrushchev, Nikita, x, 99, 104
Korean War, 25–26, 45, 74

Labor reform camps, 34, 48, 172, 268, 273, 317–318, 327, 328, 336, 337, 348
Labor unions, 361–362
Land reform, 30, 73
Lei Feng, 108–110, 113, 114, 116–117, 122, 138, 144, 147, 155, 382
Lenin, Vladimir, 218–219; writings of, 207, 219–224, 254, 270, 381
Liang Qichao, 17, 269
Liberal Democratic Party, 419–422
Liberation Daily, 59, 203, 378

Li Buoyu, 153, 154, 174
Li Lisan, 253
Lin Biao, 144, 164, 172, 194, 218–219, 223, 227, 232–233, 236–238, 251–257, 265, 267, 273, 274, 355, 383
Lin Xiling, 395
Li Shaoqing, 162–163, 175–176
Li Shuxian, 404, 407
Liu Baifang, 406
Liu Binyan, x, xi, 75, 374–386, 394–398, 399, 406, 416, 421; "My Diary," 383–384; "People or Monsters?" 375; "A Second Kind of Loyalty," x, xi, 377, 381–384, 386, 390, 393, 394, 395, 397, 398
Liu Shaoqi, 171, 184, 191, 205, 207, 231, 253, 266, 281
Liu Xiaobo, 406, 407
Li Yizhe, 273, 357
Li Yonglin, 283
"Long Live the Victory of People's War" (speech), 164
Long March, 163, 194–195, 232
Lord, Betty Bao, 385
Lord, Winston, 385
Los Angeles, 396–398
Luan (chaos), 191–192, 228, 230
Lundeen, John, x, xii, 387
Lu Ping, 180
Lu Xun, 32, 224, 235, 236, 393

Ma Changyu, 199–201
Mai Xiande, 165
Mao Zedong, x, 23, 26, 35, 52, 55, 60, 74, 75, 89, 94–98, 100, 109, 115, 121, 122, 123, 124, 143, 151, 152, 153, 160, 165, 167, 168, 171, 172–173, 185, 188, 190–194, 206–207, 212, 218–219, 231–237, 251, 253–256, 265, 269, 274, 276, 279, 281–286, 302, 336, 337, 355, 379, 381–383, 400, 421; death of, 288–289; writings of, 87, 215, 218, 219, 223, 233, 320, 321
Marriage, 11–12, 354
Marx, Karl, 274
Marxism-Leninism, 75–76, 93, 111, 160, 218–219, 251, 272
Materialism, late-1980s, 400–402
Ma Tianshui, 209, 221, 232
May Fourth Movement (1919), 269, 281, 404, 405
May 16 Group, 230–231
Medicine, 259, 354, 393
Migration of 1968–1976, 229–230
Military, 26, 28, 31, 33, 86–132, 137, 144, 151, 172, 182, 183, 187–194, 210–212, 285, 287

Ming Dynasty, 186, 281
Monument of the Revolutionary
   Heroes (Tiananmen Square), 280,
   281, 283, 409
Moral rules, 22–24, 72–73

Nanjing, 273, 283, 357, 362
National Day, 337–339
Nationalists, 8, 15, 28, 29, 44, 73, 103,
   373, 393. *See also* Guomindang
National Tourism Administration, 401
Natural disasters, 287–288
Neighbors, Lloyd, xii–xiii
New Observer magazine, 406
New Territories, 149
New workers' villages, 140–141
New York, 356, 389–396, 398–400,
   405, 407–422
Ni, Grandmother, 63
Ni Caocao, 296, 304–305, 350, 351
Nie Yuanzi, 170–171, 175, 281
Ni family, 10, 14, 15, 30, 44, 61–63,
   87, 134, 154, 248, 249–250,
   349–350, 353
Ni Fenfen, 61–62
Ni Guansheng, xvi, xviii, 6–15, 22,
   35, 62, 63–68, 80, 134, 154, 218,
   258, 295
Ni Jizhong, xv–xviii, 1–7, 11–24, 44–
   50, 54, 56, 62–69, 74, 86, 88,
   105, 111, 136–138, 154, 226, 236–
   238, 242, 248, 251, 349, 352–
   353, 357, 371, 396, 422–423
Ni Kunkun, 13, 19–21
Ni Lingling, 304, 305, 350, 351, 388
Nineties, 406
Niupeng, 318
Nixon, Richard, 253
Ni Yuxian, ix–xxi; accused of rape,
   238–248; in the army, 86–132,
   137, 144, 151; arrests of, 224, 238–
   239, 305–310, 330; birth of, 13–
   14; book on Lenin's quotations by,
   219–224, 232, 254, 381; as a
   cadre, 366–367; childhood and
   adolescence of, 15–87; and China
   Spring, 394–397; and Cultural Revolution, 166–258; *dangan* of,
   135–139, 144, 146–147, 381–382;
   and democratic reforms in exile,
   394–422; education of, 37–86,
   138, 145–202, 217–224, 370;
   emigrates to America, 369–374,
   377–390; escapes from China,
   387–390; escapes from prison,
   224–228; expelled from Shanghai Maritime Academy, 246–248;
   factory work of, 141–148, 258–

266, 275–278, 353, 358; as a
   father, 296, 304–305, 350, 351;
   "How to Prevent People Like Lin
   Biao from Coming to Power
   Again," 274–275; "I Do Not
   Believe" big character poster of,
   292–293, 335, 353–354, 383; on
   individualism, 155–164; letter to
   Mao (1962), 94–98, 381–383, 385;
   and Liberal Democratic Party,
   419–422; and Liu Binyan, x, xi,
   374–386, 394–396, 397–398,
   421; in Los Angeles, 396–398;
   marriage to Zhao Yuefang, 238,
   244, 249–250, 271–272, 275, 296,
   306, 307, 349, 352–354, 367–368,
   385, 387, 388–390; in New York,
   390–396, 398–400, 405, 407–422;
   and 1979–1989 democratic reforms,
   344–422; ostracism of, 246–251,
   254; poetry of, 289–305, 329, 335,
   342–343, 347, 353–354, 380–
   381; political asylum of, 398, 400;
   in prison, 98–99, 224, 228, 232–
   233, 238–248, 307–350; released
   from prison, 349–355; "A Second Kind of Loyalty" article on, x,
   xi, 377, 381–384, 386, 390, 393,
   394, 395, 397, 398; and Shanghai
   Maritime Academy, 148–202,
   208, 217–224, 238–246, 266, 358–
   389, 398; and Shanghai Revolutionary Rebel Commune, 208–217,
   232, 237; threatened with execution, 337–345; and Tiananmen
   incident of 1976, 285–286, 288–
   289, 292–293, 302, 316, 341, 348;
   and women, 21, 39–44, 80–85,
   105–108, 147–148, 162, 195–198,
   222–223, 238, 243–244, 266–
   270, 289, 298–305, 342–345, 351–
   354, 358, 380, 381, 388
Ni Yuxiu, 19
Ni Yuzhang, 45–46, 50
North Korea, 177
North Vietnam, 131, 164

"On Socialist Democracy and the
   Legal System" (character poster),
   273
Opium War, 29, 422
Ostracism, 72–75, 93, 164, 249–251,
   256
Ou-fan Li, Leo, 406
Overseas relations, 371–374

Paris Commune, 207–208, 216
Passports, 370, 373, 377, 390

Pei Xingling, 114–118, 122, 125
Peking University (Beida), 148, 170,
    171, 180, 201, 202, 204, 281,
    356, 394, 403, 404, 405, 409
Peng Dehaui, 74, 92, 94, 168, 180,
    207
Peng Zhen, 184
People's Daily, x, xi, 59, 99, 171, 264,
    346, 361, 375, 376, 380, 381, 383
People's Liberation Army, ix, 26, 28,
    31, 33, 86, 196, 210–212, 221,
    222, 232, 285, 287
People's University, Beijing, 395
Pests, 53–55
Petite bourgeoisie, 140–141, 144,
    168, 189
Plays, 166–170
Poetry, 289–305, 329, 335, 342–343,
    347–348, 353–354
Pol Pot, 356
Post-Mao era, 288–422
Press, x, xi, 59, 99, 146, 169, 191,
    203, 251, 264, 274, 279, 284,
    285, 346, 361, 364, 374–387, 391–
    392, 395, 406. *See also specific
    publications*
Princeton University, 406
Prison, 98–99, 224, 228, 232–233,
    238–248, 307–350
Propaganda teams, 230–231, 236,
    237, 240–246, 250
Public Security Bureau, 77–78, 97,
    132, 241, 242, 245, 284, 300–
    304, 315, 318, 327, 329, 335, 347,
    348, 352, 357, 362–363, 371, 406
Pudong, 56, 67, 73, 149, 205, 225–
    227, 259, 296, 319, 333, 423
Punishment, systems of, 30–35, 48,
    98–99, 232–235, 238–248, 271–
    272, 307–349

Qin dynasty, 206, 282
Qing dynasty, 8, 22, 29, 269, 270,
    281, 307, 393
Qinghua University, 201, 202, 409
Qing Ming festival, 280–284
Qin Shi Huangdi, 206, 282
Qiu Linting, 301–302, 306–309, 316,
    334, 335, 339
Qu Qiubai, 253
Qu Yuan, 73

Rape, 238–248, 256, 332–333
Reagan, Ronald, 401, 409
Red Flag, 97, 274
Red Guards, 187–196, 201, 202,
    210–213, 220–221, 224, 228,
    229, 246, 265, 281, 355, 385, 401

Reference News, 251
Religion, 5–6, 22–24, 188, 415
Ren Wanding, 362
Revolutionary Committee, 185–202,
    217, 219, 220, 223, 230, 233–
    234, 246, 256–257, 267, 269
Revolutionary linkups, 199–203
Revolutionary Rebel Commune, 208–
    217, 232, 237
Revolutionary Rebel Workers, 206,
    213, 214, 216
Romance of the Three Kingdoms, 17, 24,
    25, 27, 347

Schell, Orville, 406
"A Second Kind of Loyalty" (Liu
    Binyan), x, xi, 377, 381–384,
    386, 390, 393, 394, 395, 397, 398
Shaanxi Province, 195, 318
Shanghai, 5, 9, 16, 25, 27–30, 56, 61,
    67, 88, 131, 149, 174, 180, 200–
    217, 221, 226–228, 248, 285, 289–
    306, 355–386, 398, 423
Shanghai Maritime Academy, ix, xi,
    xvii, 148–202, 208, 217–224,
    238–248, 266, 270, 358–389, 398
Shanghai People's Commune, 213, 216
Shanghai Revolutionary Committee,
    217, 233–234, 243, 256–257, 269
Shanghai Revolutionary Rebel Com-
    mune, 208–217, 232, 237
Shenzhen, 387
Si Xiongmao, 47, 50–51
Socialism, 29–30, 44, 99–100, 104,
    121, 140–147, 152, 157, 190, 199,
    207, 232, 237, 261–264, 273, 317
Socialist democracy, 356, 362
Socialist Education Campaign, 142–
    145, 147
Song Binbin, 188
Song Yaowu, 188
Soviet-Chinese relations, 99, 142,
    165–166, 249, 409
Soviet Union, x, 47, 55, 61, 98, 99–
    100, 104, 165–166, 172, 238, 253
Steel, 55–58, 59, 62, 134
Student movements, 167–202, 218–
    224, 229–231, 399, 407–415
Sun Dayu, 50–51
Sun Tzu, 285
Sun Yat-sen, 29, 393
Su Zhenhua, 330

Taiping Rebellion (1850–1864), 29
Taiwan, 45, 67, 100, 104, 165, 227,
    373, 394, 405
Tangshan, 287–288
Tan Sitong, 17, 18, 269, 270, 296

Tao Zhu, 171, 210
Taxes, 94–95, 401
Television, 284, 402
Tiananmen Square, xi, xxi, 171, 188, 192–195, 232, 280–286; 1976 incident, 280–286, 288–289, 292–293, 302, 316, 341, 348, 355, 411; 1989 Democracy movement, xvii, xxi, 285, 356, 400, 404–415
Tianjin, 192, 252, 287
Tilanqiao, 317, 341–342
Tito, President, 333
Totalitarianism, 358
Trade union elections, 360–362
Transportation, 4, 8, 251–252
Tu Weiming, 406

U.S.-Chinese relations, 25–27, 45, 100, 165–166, 253, 348, 369–370, 386
University of California, Berkeley, 397
University of Chicago, 406

Versailles Treaty, 404
Veterans' Affairs Bureau, 132, 133, 134
Vietnam War, 131, 356

Wang Bingzhang, 393–395, 396–397, 413, 416, 422
Wang Dan, 404
Wang Hongwen, 204, 206, 208, 212, 220, 221, 288
Wang Hua, 181–186, 190–191, 202
Wang Juntao, 285, 356
Wang Li, 211
Wang Liming, 183–184
Wang Meng, 75
Wang Ming, 253
Wang Ruowang, 399, 406, 407
Wang Xiuzhen, 234–235, 385
Wang Xizhe, 357, 362, 363
Water Margin, 24
Weddings, 2–4, 6–7, 11
Wei Jingsheng, 360, 362, 394, 405
Wen Hui Bao, 283
Westernism, 366
Worker-peasant-soldier propaganda teams, 230–231, 236, 237, 240–246, 250
Workers' Daily, 381
Workers' movement, 203–206, 262
Wu De, 284
Wuer Kaixi, 416–417
Wu Han, 173, 211; "Hai Rui Dismissed from Office," 168–170
Wusong, 296

Xiao Xi, 119
Xia Shengyu, 50–52, 57, 69, 77
Xidan Democracy Wall, 355
Xi Shenfa, 119, 128
Xu, Grandmother, 22–24, 30–32, 109
Xu Ahe, 19–20, 373
Xu Fengzhen, xv–xviii, 1–7, 11–24, 46–50, 56, 61–62, 87, 88, 105, 111, 238, 244, 304, 349–350, 353, 372
Xu Jian, 179–185, 190, 198–202
Xu Jinjiang, xv
Xu Jinxian, 210
Xu Shuiliang, 273, 357, 362
Xu Wenli, 357, 362
Xu Xingfa, 274–275, 293, 296, 334

Yang Guoli, 116–117, 119–120, 124–129
Yangsi, 134, 136, 271
Yangtze River, 5, 9, 25, 196–197, 220, 402
Yao Wenyuan, 167–169, 210, 211, 212, 284, 288
Ye, Mrs. , 268, 269, 285, 343, 352
Ye, Professor, 267–268, 294, 352
You Mingli, 153–154, 174
Youth League, 69–71, 72, 83–84, 111, 147–148, 157, 158, 163, 193
Yuan Shikai, 22–23, 29, 32
Yugoslavian Communist Party, 269–270, 333
Yu Heqing, 9
Yu Ying-shi, 406

Zhang Baoling, 235, 384–385
Zhang Chunqiao, 204, 206, 208, 210–217, 219, 220, 224–228, 231–237, 255, 266, 275, 282, 283, 284, 288, 383
Zhang Zhixin, 232
Zhao Yuefang, xvi–xviii, 80–85, 87, 97, 105–108, 113–114, 133, 195–198, 219, 225–226, 238; marriage to Ni Yuxian, 238, 244, 249–250, 271–272, 275, 296, 306, 307, 349, 352–354, 367–368, 385, 387, 388–390
Zhao Ziyang, 401
Zhejiang, 88
Zhen Fanrong, 152–166, 171–172
Zhengming magazine, 387, 406
Zhou Baoling, 208–210, 385
Zhou Enlai, xi, 231, 267, 276, 278–280, 283, 287, 289, 302, 383, 407
Zhou Zhian, 47, 50–51
Zhu Bing, 28
Zhu De, 26, 287, 291
Zhuge Liang, 25